BATTLE NOTES

The "Write" Stuff

"Lee Andresen brings to life the music of the 60s- The impact it had on a whole generation of vets and their families. I would recommend Lee's book to everyone with passion for music."

Rick Bartholomew, Nam Magazine

"Literally wrote the book on Vietnam era music."

Ralph Holman. Meriden Record Journal.

"Andresen's love of his subject—and his rigorous knowledge of it—come through in every chapter. The author rejects the stylistic stuffiness that characterizes many academic studies, and instead writes lucid, conversational prose, which undoubtedly replicates his classroom presentations."

Dave Driscoll. Blue Dog News.

"Lee Andresen's book discusses all aspects of popular music's role during that era...He places the mood of America square in the center of the radio dial."...Andresen's knowledge of the subject is extensive, and though he avoids singing, he can rattle off lyric after lyric of even the most obscure record.

Jeff DeRego, Hippopress. (Manchester, New Hampshire.)

"The book is a mine of useful information."

Dr. Jos W.L. Hilkhuijsen, Curator
Dutch Army Museum, Delft, Holland

Lee Andresen often regales … e Vietnam War. Andresen covers all types … r: protest songs, pro-war patriotic tunes, … calls the "music of combat," and music a…

The Veteran. (A publication … etnam Veterans Association, Washington, D.C.)

"Well researched systematic examination of U.S. pop music to come out of the Vietnam War and later. Sprightly style. Taregeted primarily at veterans. Chapters deal with music of protest, music of patriotism, African American music, etc. Useful in class as a teaching tool.

Indochina Chronology. (A quarterly publication of the Vietnam Center at Texas Tech University.)

"'Battle Notes' is more than just a recapitulation of which songs were racing to the top of the music charts in the late 1960s and early 1970s. Andresen has measured the pulse of the country and people's changing views of culture and the war through its music."

The Gusport. (Pensacola, Florida)

"Gives a real sense of the turmoil created by the controversial war and its reflection in the popular music."

Jim Lundstrom, Appleton (Wi.) Post-Crescent

"Reading the analysis of what the music meant to the soldiers, the girlfriends, moms and dads, etc. has helped me understand the impact the music of the Vietnam era had on our society (and continues to have!). The songs often had a very different meaning for those serving in Vietnam that for those at home. Lee Andresen's insightful analysis of both sides tells the whole story for the first time. I highly recommend this book to my fellow veterans looking for a musical perspective about the Vietnam experience."

Sarge Lintecum
A Vietnam vetern of three tours with the 101st Airborne
Composer and performer of "Vietnam Bules: Combat Tested."

"Vietnam had a soundtrack. Soldiers embraced the hard-edged anthems of Jimi Hendrix, The Animals and Creedence Clearwater Revival. Protestors galvanized around anti-war songs by Arlo Guthrie, Jefferson Airplane and Crosby, Stills, Nash and Young. It's all captured in "Battlenotes: The Music of the Vietnam War" by Lake Superior College history professor Lee Andresen.

Mary Thompson, Duluth News Tribune, Duluth Minnesota

"Andresen writes of high-profile songs of the era...He gave nearly equal weight to how families, friends and foes of Vietnam vets vented their feelings in song."

Debora Shaulis, The Vindicator. (Youngstown, Ohio.)

"Whatever your memories of Vietnam, historian Lee Andresen has captured them in the music of the era in *Battle Notes: Music of the Vietnam War*."

Barbara Yost. Arizona Republic

"Battlenotes" is designed, to take us all back to that era, lest we forget, via music.

Paul Skamser Jr. Superior (Wi) Daily Telegram.

"I believe the way this book has chronologically listed the music of the time along with the events taking place in Vietnam is amazing. I never realized how closely related the two were until I read what Andresen wrote. I strongly recommend this book to those who were there, but even more, to those who weren't."

Larry Yeazle, US Army Airborne (Retired)

Lee Andresen teaches a college course entitled 'Vietnam: America's Longest War.' He had integrated the music of that era into the course and has written a manuscript for publication which I was privileged to read. The detailed work involved has to be a personal labor of love.

I remember only too well the emotional confrontation engendered by the Vietnam War. Has our citizenry ever been so torn asunder - other than by our own Civil War? Some of the older Americans may not wish to relive the Vietnam era, but for those that do and for those that were not here to experience that episode in our history, this book brings it back loud and clear.

Student opinions, appropriately included, verify the efficacy of this technique. The music does for an understanding of the Vietnam Ware what our hymns do for religious understanding. Could students who didn't live during that period of our nation's history understand and truly feel the country's pain? The can now, - thank you, Lee Andresen."

Dr. Bernard Hughes, Professor Emeritus;
University of Wisconsin-Superior.Columnist on educational issues for the Superior, Wisconsin, Daily Telegram."

"I can scarcely think of him without weeping."

General Robert E. Lee of the Confederacy
upon learning of the death of his close friend
and cavalry commander J.E.B. Stuart

2nd Edition

BATTLE NOTES

...music of the Vietnam War

Savage PRESS
Box 115, Superior, WI 54880 (715) 394-9513

BATTLE NOTES *...music of the Vietnam War*

Second Edition

ISBN 1-886028-60-5

Library of Congress Catalog Card Number: 2003105958

Published by:

Savage Press
P.O. Box 115
Superior, WI 54880

715-394-9513

e-mail: mail@savpress.com

Visit us at: www.savpress.com

The author can be contacted on the Internet at Battlenotes.com

Printed in the USA.

BATTLE NOTES

...music of the Vietnam War

by Lee Andresen

"The unknown soldier who is returned to us today and whom we lay to rest is symbolic of all our missing sons... About him we may well wonder, as others have: As a child did he play on some street in a great American city? Or did he work beside his father on a farm out in America's heartland? Did he marry? Did he have children? Did he look expectantly to a bride? We'll never know the answers to these questions about his life. We do know, though, why he died. He saw the horrors of war but bravely faced them, certain his own cause and his country's cause was a noble one; that he was fighting for human dignity, for free men everywhere. Today we pause to embrace him and all who served us so well in a war whose end offered no parades, no flags, and so little thanks. We can be worthy of the values and ideals for which our sons sacrificed-worthy of their courage in the face of a fear that few of us will ever experience-by honoring their commitment and devotion to duty and country...A grateful nation opens her heart today in gratitude for their sacrifice, for their courage, and for their noble service. Let us, if we must, debate the lessons learned at some other time. Today, we simply say with pride, "Thank you, dear son. May God cradle you in His loving arms."

President Ronald Reagan, Remarks at Memorial Day Ceremonies honoring an Unknown Serviceman of the Vietnam Conflict, May 28, 1984

I dedicate this book to the Vietnam Veterans. Especially those thousands of names etched into that long black wall in Washington D.C. They are the real American heroes. It is truly sad that the American public has yet to give them the acclaim they so richly deserve and instead exalt professional athletes, rock stars, and the Hollywood gliteratti.

I also want to dedicate the book to my father Harold and my brother Jack, both of whom are deceased. They both loved to read. I only wish they were here today to read this book.

A Knock at the Door

What is the pain?
Where does it hurt?
Where is it hidden?

Is it the Purple Heart
tucked away deep in a drawer?
Or is it the letter, the memory,
the 'knock at the door,?"

You ask me: Where does it hurt?
I say: I don't know
Do I think about it?
I do.
Does it still hurt?
It always will.
Where?
I don't know.
I don't know.

So many causes-
So many battles-
So many wars-
So many...
So many...

Does anybody care? I ask.
Everybody cares, you reply.
Is it talked about?
It is talked about.
Who is talking?
I don't know, I don't know...
Loved ones, yes, they.
What do they say?
That's a secret, I'm afraid.
Me too.
Me too.

There comes a knock at the door.

Yes.
Madam, it is time.
No! He's but a boy.

Madam...
No! I won't let you.
Madam...
Who will take care of me now?
Madam...
He's married, he has a son!
Madam...
He has a son.
He has a son.

There departs 'a knock at the door'

On a quiet hill in Virginia
A flag is waving torn.
The flag will be replaced.
The old one will be buried.
A new one will be born.

It will fly high and proud
As ever it should.
Thinking it has purpose.
Fighting for what's good.

What are the answers? I ask.
Nothing we can touch, you reply.
Can we understand it?
We can only try.
We can only try.

There comes 'a knock at the door..'

I dedicate this poem to my Grandfather who is resting in a beautiful field in France, and to my father's best friend whose name is engraved in "The Wall." And all loved ones left forlorn. And to the Americans who still believe this country is worth fighting for. And especially to those who have served, no matter what the cause, the battle, the war. Thank you. I appreciate your sacrifice for our freedom. Thank you.

Sincerely,

William H. Soderlind III
Former Sergeant, USMC

Table of Contents

ACKNOWLEDGMENTS

I want to thank my mother Elsie and wife Mary Lou for their love and support and patience. In a more material way, the following persons helped me with this book, in interviews or other research and I am indebted to them: Harry Cottrell, Peter Antell, Rod McBrien, Bill Belmont, Bill Bates, Dr. Bernard Hughes, Bruce Brown, Tom Johnson, Paul Helbach, Mary Jo Berner, Rachal Jane, (a.k.a. Susan Wojnar), Tim Murphy, Larry Kusick, Roger Lambert, Gene LeRoy, Paul Kero, Larry Yeazle, Sarge Lintecum, Gerry Jaques, Michael McCann, John Seikkula, Paul Skamser Jr., Rev. Heyward Macdonald, Dr. Mike Mueller, Cindy McNaughton and Mark Berger.

Interviews:

Dennis Aho
Peter Antell
Mary Banigan
Bill Belmont
Mark Berger
Ed Bielarczyk
Tom Brewer
Mike Brimball
Bruce Brown
Billy (Jamie) Carr
Tommy Cash
Harry Cottrell
Rev. Alan Cutter
Boyd Dallos
Dick Day
Ronald Downs
Phil Ferrazano
Hershel Gober
Al Gore, Sr.
Paul Helbach
Raul Herrara
Bob Hersey
Rachal Jane
Paul Kero
Richard Keucher
Gene Leroy
John Linde
Sarge Lintecum
"Brick" Manurich
Rod McBrien
Mike McCann
Barry McGuire
Jody Miller
Dr. Mike Mittelman
Walter Mondale
Dr. Mike Mueller
Tim Murphy
Tom Neely
Dan O'Hara
Mike Pflepsen
Sal Serio
Jon Seikkulla
Bob Shelafoe
Dan Wagner
Cmdr (Ret.) David Wheat
Ron Whipp
Larry Yeazle

Chapter 1:
Introduction

I have often fantasized with my history students about taking the ultimate field trip, where we would actually ride a time machine back to a period we are studying, like the Renaissance, the American Civil War or the Roaring Twenties. We could be like latter-day Si Morley's, the hero of Jack Finney's marvelous science fiction novel, who does go back to the past.[1] Despite Einstein's theory that such an adventure may be within the realm of possibility, time travel will probably remain the stuff of science fiction for a long time to come, although I think I came close once. As I drove into Gettysburg as dawn was just breaking on a July morning several years ago, it seemed for a moment that I could see shadowy, uniformed figures materializing out of the mist-enshrouded cornfields near this bloodiest of all Civil War battlefields. Ah well. Underlying all this whimsy is the almost constant quest of the serious history teacher to make the subject become more real and meaningful to students by making them feel like they were there. One of my history professors used to thunder at students, "Were you there?" Maybe he was thinking about *You Are There*, a television show that aired during the 1950s. This program featured a television reporter interviewing participants in re-enactments of famous historical events. Completely replicating the essence of an era is probably impossible, but a recent innovation to my classes has added immeasurably to my students' appreciation of the mood of one of the most controversial and tumultuous periods in American history, the time of the Vietnam War.

The inspiration for this idea came from my love for music and the attendant awareness of how a song can trigger a flood of personal memories and virtually transport one back to long ago. I had also developed a great respect for music as the kind of powerful medium that can have an impact on the mind in a variety of ways as described by Don Campbell in *The Mozart Effect:*

"In an instant, music can uplift our soul. It awakens within us the spirit of prayer, compassion and love; it clears our minds and has been known to make us smarter. Music can dance and sing our blues away. It conjures up memories of lost lovers or deceased friends... Music is a holy place, a cathedral so majestic that we can sense the magnificence of the universe, and also a hovel so simple and private that none of us can plumb its deepest secrets. Music helps plants grow, drives our neighbors to distraction, lulls children and marches men to war. Music can... enchant leaders and nations, captivate and soothe, resurrect and transform."[2]

At the same time I was aching with nostalgia upon hearing a song from the past, I began to think that playing recorded music from the Vietnam era for my classes that study this period might add significantly to their understanding of what that time was really like. Especially Vietnam. All American wars had their music but Vietnam was a conflict in which music played an especially significant role. Beyond simply entertaining, it also shaped and articulated public opinion in unprecedented fashion. Hollywood certainly recognizes the importance of the songs, as most of the recent films about the war, good and bad, contain soundtracks loaded with the popular music of the time. This gives movies like *Apocalypse Now, The Deerhunter, Full Metal Jacket* and of course *Good Morning Vietnam,* a realism they would otherwise lack.

The Miracles "Tracks of My Tears" enjoyed renewed success in the 1980's because it was in the soundtrack for "Platoon", complete with a new title sleeve.

The popular music of the day was heard all over Vietnam during the war, and the New York Times described the conflict as "our first rock and roll war." Soldiers heard the popular music of that time all over the war zone. Musical references even became part of battlefield jargon. When a weapon was readied to fire, it went through the process of "rock and roll." The gun ships that were so devastatingly effective against the enemy were named after a popular song, "Puff the Magic Dragon" by Peter, Paul and Mary. Stephen Hunter, who has provided some of the best fiction about the war, credits his success in creating dialogue and scenes that meet the test of authenticity to listening to tapes of the music of the war. Another novel about the war that is remarkable for its realism because it uses the music frequently and effectively is Michael Herr's widely acclaimed Dispatches. Stephen King's book about Vietnam, *Hearts in Atlantis*, was inspired by a Donovan ballad from the 1960s. One of the most important protest songs of the war period, Phil Ochs' "I Ain't Marching Anymore," figures prominently in the plot as King tells the story of college students at the University of Maine who eventually come to question the propriety of the war, largely because of this song. Robert James Waller's best seller *Border Music* features two Vietnam vets, Texas Jack McGane and Bobby McGregor, who are frequently listening to and making music that is based on their experiences in the war. At least one book about the Vietnam War, Myra McPherson's *Long Time Passing,* owes its title to the lyrics from one of the best known songs about the tragedy of war, "Where Have All the Flowers Gone."[3] The most persuasive statement about the value of the music in telling the story of the Vietnam War is contained in veteran John Kertwig's memoir of his experiences there, *And A Hard Rain Fell:*

> "Julius Caesar came, and saw, and conquered. Alexander the Great subjugated the known world. We know little of the peasantry of the times, their hopes, their fears, and their emotions. The music, the social commentary of America's Vietnam era are recorded that future generations might understand them. No portrait of the period would be complete without them."[4]

Encouraged by this and other evidence that the music is vital to understanding the war, I went beyond merely theorizing and began playing recorded music from the war for my students in a class I teach at Lake Superior College, "Vietnam: America's Longest War."[5] This exercise, where students listen to, discuss and write about a cross-section of the music of the Vietnam era, is now an integral part of the course. To say I have discovered that better pedagogical "mousetrap" may be an exaggeration, but the students' written essays overwhelmingly support my thesis that music is an ideal prism through which to regard the Vietnam War. The consensus among my students was that, while they felt they had obtained at least an adequate understanding of the politics, economics, culture, military strategy, etc., of the conflict from textbooks and in the classroom, it wasn't until they heard the music that the essence of America's worst war, its "mood," was brought home to them:

> "Listening to this era of music has really given me that three-dimensional look at the period during the Vietnam War. As I sat and listened to some of these songs, I realized that I had heard many of them and didn't realize that they were from this era... some of them actually had a very strong impact on me right in class. ...I understood through the music what were the social and true gut feelings of people who were alive at this time.
>
> "For these classes, in which we listened to music of this era, the boom-box served as a type of time machine. At least, as close as we really can get to one. They did replicate the mood. The anger. The pain. The patriotism. These two days were very educational and also entertaining. Some of the music even served as a type of comic relief. Some of it was unmistakably overdone. Some of it was desperate. Some of it tried to rally people to a cause. All of the music serves as a window to a prior world. Thank you for allowing us the opportunity to listen to these samples of music."
>
> "When I took this class I wanted to learn about the Vietnam War, and up until this point, I did not completely understand

the emotional side of it. The music that was played in class portrayed the feelings of the war very well. I don't know much about the war except from what I have read and from the stories that my dad has told me about when he fought. I am not strongly for or against what took place in Vietnam because it all happened before I was born, but I do know that it had a great impact on our country and its attitude towards war. The music helped me to understand the difference in opinions on the war."

"None of my other teachers have ever used music as a method of teaching before and I am actually shocked at how much I learned. Music has a way of affecting people in different ways and I loved it. I actually felt like I was really there sometimes. I am surprised I could fight back my tears in class."

"Music, I do love music. It is one of the main things in my everyday life. I play in a punk rock band, I also used to play in a '50s and '60s rock band, and I am even thinking of pursuing music as a career in some way or other. This analysis of the lyrics of this music from the Vietnam are is a great break from studying only book material for me."

"When I think of the 1960s and early 1970s, I think of the Vietnam War... basically a nation in turmoil. ...No time machine exists to go back and really know what it was like during that era. The only way to get a true feeling...a mood of the time is to listen to the music of the time."

The music also gave essential perspective to those who couldn't be expected to remember the war years:

"I didn't grow up during the Vietnam War, hell, I wasn't even alive. I didn't experience the sorrow and political turmoil that consumed the nation during this senseless war, but I did get a taste of it from the music of that time. I heard sad laments of mothers grieving for the loss of their sons, songs of the craving for peace, and tales of brave patriotism. All of

> this music showed me a side of this nation that I had never seen. A side both of good and evil."

The songs also effected a consciousness raising for students who actually lived through the ordeal of the Vietnam War:

> "Music has always been important to me. Listening to the "oldies" takes me back in time. It helped me to recall how I felt as a concerned, caring young American. The word apathy was not in my vocabulary during the '60s and '70s. I believe you are absolutely right in your assertion that music is a reflection of its time... The music we heard in class aptly expressed the mixture of feelings that was the '60s and '70s experience."

> "This music has a lot of different meanings for me. As an old-timer, I can remember some of the feelings I had when I heard it for the first time. It's very interesting to compare those feelings to the way I feel about the music now. With my background as the wife of a disabled Vietnam veteran, I identify heavily with the pro-war movement. I always had a hard time with protestors and hippies."

The music exposed students to what is easily one of the most important facets of the critical thinking process: to assess and question, so that intellectual viewpoints can change and evolve in a natural order. As students were introduced to the recorded music of the era and increased their knowledge of history, they also enhanced "higher order" critical thinking skills like analysis, synthesis and evaluation as the essays that appear throughout this book indicate. As a lover of the English language and one who is suspicious that people "don't see with their ears anymore,"[6] I was gratified on a personal basis that what amounted to an experiment in listening to "words" worked so well and proved that the lyrical content of recorded music can be a very effective teaching tool in a history classroom. Beyond enhancing understanding and appreciation of the content of a specific subject matter, music can provide additional intellectual benefits to students:

> "We can, for a start, use rhythm as a tool to develop memory and intellect...the more stimulation a child receives through music, movement, and the arts, the more intelligent she or he will turn out... Music brings a positive and relaxing atmosphere to many classrooms as well as allowing the sensory integration necessary for long-term memory."[7]

The simple act of playing music as part of a carefully planned classroom assignment requires students to listen, think and write about what they hear in a way that imagination comes into play, resulting in some genuinely creative thoughts and ideas. That just does not happen often enough today because of television and that most obnoxious creation of modern popular culture, the music video. These silly musical skits really indoctrinate that huge segment of the population who are already far too visually oriented into what they should be thinking about the song in question. My views on this relatively recent mode of entertainment could lead to accusations that I am just another cultural conservative "crying in the wilderness" about a technological advance that is actually beneficial. However, at least one performer also seems to have some reservations about the music video. Bruce Springsteen, who does use these devices had some reservations about their value in explaining a song:

> "Either you illustrate a song, which in my case I can't do-because it's like you're gonna paint a mustache on it or something. Or you create another story to go over the song, and that's kinda silly, because there's a story already there. That's the story I wanted to tell, so to create another story to go along with, that doesn't make sense either. I've spent twenty years learning how to write so that when you hear a song you get all the information you need-you get the experience and the emotion that you need. I write with a lot of detail, and I'm proud of doing it and think I do it well. And so I'm hesitant to mess with that. You've gotta respect the integrity of the song a little bit." [8]

In any event, the ideas contained in the majority of the songs in this book were never embellished by a video, and my students were allowed to really think about what kind of message they were hearing. The music they listened to was drawn from what was indeed a prolific period in the history of recorded music. During the 1960s an almost infinite number of songs were pressed into vinyl all over the country. As a result, finding recordings of the music wasn't difficult (one can only imagine the number of songs that were written and performed about the war that didn't get beyond scribbles on scraps of paper or the sheet music stage (or onto a vinyl disc), but choosing what to play and defining what qualified as "Vietnam War music" was. It was John Steinbeck's opinion that "war songs need not be about war at all. Indeed they rarely are." He was no doubt referring to the music of World War II and how curious it was that an Australian ditty about sheepherding, "Waltzing Matilda," became one of the most celebrated war tunes of all time. He also found it remarkable how "Lili Marlene" became "immortal" after it was nearly "assassinated" by prudish Nazi elites who were offended by its theme of infidelity. It survived because it suddenly became popular with Rommel's Afrika Korps and then was embraced by British and American fighting men. How this simple song about a woman of dubious virtue who lingers by the barracks gate hoping to meet a brigadier general[9] became a wartime classic makes for an interesting story and also provides insight into songs that became part of the music of the Vietnam War. Some of the latter were never intended to make a statement about Vietnam but became closely linked to that conflict if even just a few lyrics resonated with the soldiers who were fighting in Southeast Asia. The very phrase "war songs" may conjure up images of soldiers marching to the sound of martial music like "Stars and Stripes Forever." Fewer, rather than more, of the songs that stirred patriotic passions by appealing to love of country, devotion to the flag, apple pie and all of that will be found in this book. Vietnam was different from the American wars of the past, and its music reflects this.[10] In the context of the Vietnam War, "war music" takes on a broader meaning and includes songs that are simply "about" the war, whether they protest the war, support it, or explore relatively neutral issues, or don't say anything about the war at all. In the latter case, Steinbeck can be forgiven for coming perilously close to the dreaded absolute statement, for he is at least partially correct when it comes to the music spawned by the Vietnam conflict.

The songs included in this book just scratch the surface of all the music that has to do with the war. I knew I would never find it all, but what I did find represents a very respectable cross-section of what was out there, at least that eventually was recorded. There are over seven hundred and fifty different songs in the discography attached to this book. In a concession to common sense, I decided early on to limit myself almost exclusively to the seven-inch 45-rpm records or "singles." Those little records with the big hole in the middle, which have sadly become an endangered species in the age of the high-tech compact disc.[11] Album "cuts" had begun receiving heavy air play on radio stations, but those that became highly popular were usually released as singles by the record company anyway (back in what I nostalgically regard as the "golden age" of recorded music, when a group or individual artist had to come up with at least a commercially successful single or two before the record company decided that an album was merited.) Most of the commercially successful songs, related in some way to the war, were usually easily obtainable and they are here, as well as some genuine "obscurities" of which relatively few copies were ever pressed and may never have been stocked in record stores. Some I had never heard of before I conducted a search through advertisements in various national publications that cater to those selling and seeking old records. The forgotten songs that I unearthed were usually recorded on minor labels and were probably never played on radio stations or sold in record stores. Still, they deserve inclusion here because they make a statement about the war. In a small way, the artists responsible for these songs are finally being accorded at least a modicum of the recognition to which I think they are entitled. After all, if writers and performers felt strongly enough about an issue to go to the trouble of writing a song and recording it, they deserve to be heard by someone. Some of these efforts were excellent, matching or exceeding in quality recordings that became national hits and sold millions of copies.

Most of the recordings about Vietnam can be categorized fairly easily as either "pro-war" or "anti-war" in theme. Others clearly relate to the war but are less controversial. These songs don't take a clear stand on the probity of the war but do express feelings everyone can relate to, whether it be the homesickness of a soldier on a foreign battlefield, the travails of the prisoner of war, the joy of coming home or the pain of Post Traumatic Stress Syndrome. Other discs have no obvious lyrical connection to Vietnam and are included simply because they were adopted by American troops who found the songs contained words and phrases they related to. These are songs that "struck home" with the combat troops, often for intangible and visceral reasons beyond the comprehension of the uninitiated. Those who actually fought the war in the jungles and rice paddies of Vietnam gleaned the kind of connotations from the music that people "back in the world" and even the artists and composers of these songs never intended to convey like Louis Armstrong's "What A Wonderful World." [12] The soundtrack music from the movie *Good Morning Vietnam* falls into this category, as do other records "spun" by disc jockeys at Armed Forces Radio in Saigon or listened to on tape players by the troops.

Marvelettes/Them *Good Morning Vietnam* picture sleeve

My research was conducted with the awareness that impressions about the values expressed in a song can vary from listener to listener, just as what one sees in a Rorschach ink blot test can differ enormously from what others who take this test visualize. Some of the music is very engaging and has those irresistible lyrical and melodic "hooks" that translated into enthusiastic popular acceptance. Then there are recordings that bring to mind what Mark Twain once said about the composer Richard Wagner: "His music is probably better than it sounds." Some songs are kinder to the ear because they are performed by very proficient musicians who produce melodies so seductively infectious that the superficial listener may be tempted to ignore even the most banal or offensive lyrics, thus camouflaging an argument that may have little, if any, intellectual merit. To put it more candidly, a message that is extremely and almost unbelievably offensive. There are plenty of these on both sides of the issue of whether the war was right or wrong. Not surprisingly, these controversial songs turned out to be the most memorable and, more often than not, were a "popular" topic in student essays. There are also a handful of songs in the chapter "Music About the Aftermath of the War" that may be viewed as "pathologizing" the Vietnam Veteran. However, the vast majority of veterans don't fit the stereotypes contained in "19" or "Ruby," and I want readers to be aware of this. Many of the veterans I interviewed were concerned about how they have been negatively portrayed in not only the music but also in books and movies. Everyone has a right to their views about a particular song, but I don't agree that the typical veteran is a half-crazed, drug-addicted, homicidal maniac. As one veteran told me: "We're not all crazy because we survived Vietnam."[13]

This finished product can be considered a collaborative effort by the students and me. Their essays about the music appear at the end of each chapter and are preceded by my views about the songs and how they fit into historical context. Many of the songs provided an opportunity to elaborate about a significant issue of the war as with Jefferson Airplane's "Somebody to Love" and the "credibility gap" of Victor Lundberg's "Open Letter to a Teenage Son" and how it addresses ways in which the war divided families and Creedence Clearwater Revival's "Bad Moon Rising" and the vivid way in which it captures the mood of combat soldiers in Vietnam.

All of the mistakes in this book are my responsibility. When this was still very much a work in progress, a colleague warned me to be careful with my methodology or I would falsify my results. She was giving this work far more credit than it deserves. I don't believe there is anything very scientific about what I've done. I wouldn't be surprised, though, that if someone truly gifted in statistics and research methodology had collaborated with me on this book, the numbers would support the thesis that music is an excellent tool for teaching students about history. Some interesting conclusions might have been drawn about whether students in a college classroom in Minnesota, supposedly somewhat of a "liberal" state, were creatures of their political culture in their views about the songs they heard. It is my quite unscientific impression that the awareness that Vietnam was an unpopular war, a war that the United States lost, had a bearing on how students felt about the music. This view usually resulted in essays that were quite critical of the patriotic or pro-war music and generally favorable about the music of protest, though I did read a surprisingly large number of student analyses that praised even some of the strident pro-war songs. Some of these writers were obviously influenced by the fact that they had been in the military or were related to someone who served in Vietnam. A few of the essay writers had actually fought in Vietnam, with at least one finding hearing the music too troubling an experience to tolerate:

> "The inner response to the first class of music listening was very troubling. Allow me to express my feelings and emotions after listening to several songs. I found myself experiencing some of the very same emotions it has taken years to see and understand. These feelings consisted in part of isolation, estrangement, and guilt, all the while wanting to leave that classroom as quickly as possible without having to face or speak to anyone. The feelings of thirty years ago were wanting to be dealt with the same way they were dealt with then. However, through extensive psychotherapy they are now dealt with differently. It is not beneficial for me to subject myself to a situation that jeopardizes my present health. The songs and movies and people of the '40s encour-

> aged the returning veterans. The songs and movies of the '60s and '70s tore us down and, to many, destroyed us."

That the songs stirred deep emotions in this veteran was not unexpected and perfectly understandable. He was there. Because of the huge volume of books, movies, television shows, and music about the war in the last two decades, few students, if any, began this assignment with a truly open mind. As the essays indicate, some did change their minds after hearing the music, at least in the sense that they discovered many of the songs contained a message of which they had previously been unaware. At least one student wondered if the music made him react on some subliminal level:

> "The songs I chose to write about expressed only sorrow. As I think about my selections, do they unconsciously express a view on the Vietnam War or was it just that those songs sparked my interest?"

How the majority felt about such subtle influences can't be known, but the overwhelming majority agreed that the music provided excellent social and historical context about the Vietnam War.

Aside from detailing the obvious benefits of using music as a teaching tool, I think this book will provide some other pluses. At this writing, to my knowledge, there is no book that deals exclusively with the music that was such a significant part of the Vietnam War era. Most of the books and movies that mention the songs usually accord them just a passing reference. There are plenty of lists of Vietnam songs on the Internet and other places, but they are only lists that don't reveal very much at all about how the song fit into the historical context of the war. I think this book fills a void in doing just that. In addition, by interviewing Vietnam veterans and "surfing" the Internet I have discovered that many of them are wondering about titles and artists for songs that they heard during their tour of duty. They might well have different ideas about the meaning of these songs than those presented in this book, but the attached discography[14] will, I hope, be helpful in identifying that elusive tune they heard so long ago and under such unforgettable circumstances. I clearly lack objectivity, but I think the discography I have assembled is the most complete compilation of music related to the Vietnam War in print today.

Finally, as this project progressed, it seemed to take on a life of its own, and it took me places I never thought I would go. What started out as essentially the viewpoints of me and my students about the music, evolved into a limited oral history of the Vietnam veterans and what they thought about certain songs and how they defined their own experiences in the war.[15] I am deeply indebted to them for their help and also deeply honored that they shared their memories with me.

Subsequent to publishing the 1st edition of *Battle Notes*, a website developed for the project became a great source of contacts with veterans, educators and the music industry.

Please visit our site at www.battlenotes.com.

Footnotes:

1 Jack Finney, *Time and Again.* New York, Simon and Schuster, 1970.

2 Don Campbell, *The Mozart Effect: Tapping the Power of Music to Heal the Body, Strengthen the Mind, and Unlock the Creative Spirit.* New York, Avon Books, 1997.

3 A virtual legion of folk singers recorded "Where Have All the Flowers Gone" with probably more to come. It became a staple of the repertoire at concerts and anti-war rallies during the Vietnam War but the only artist I know of who successfully recycled the song and made a chart hit out of it during the period was Johnny Rivers on Imperial records in 1965. It is interesting to note, though, that none other than the actress Marlene Dietrich released a version of the song on 45 rpm in 1964.

4 John Kertwig, *And A Hard Rain Fell.* New York, MacMillan Publishing Co., 1985 p. 23.

5 Most of the music recorded in Vietnam by many of those who served there can be found at a website compiled by Dr. Lydia Fish of the State College of New York at Buffalo. For practical reasons, I chose to confine my research to the songs that were recorded on vinyl during and immediately after the war.

6 Stephen King, *Everything's Eventual: 14 Dark Tales.* New York: Scribner, 2002. p. 13.

7 Campbell, *Mozart Effect.* p. 21.
8 Dave Marsh, *Glory Days: Bruce Springsteen in the 1980s.* New York, Pantheon Books, 1987 p. 327.
9 Susan Shillingham and Jackson J. Benson, John Steinbeck: America and Americans and Selected Nonfiction. New York: Penguin-Putnam, p.p. 291 - 292.
10 "When Johnny Comes Marching Home" made its debut during the Civil War as a "war song" or song of patriotism. However, an Irish version entitled "Jonny We Hardly Knew Ye" became a protest flavored song favored during the Civil War. Thus, it is plausible that "When Johnny Comes Marching Home" had evolved into a protest song by the time the Vietnam War rolled around. John Anthony Scott, *The Ballad of America: The History of the United States in Song-Song and Story*. New York: Bantam Books, 1985. p.p. 327 - 328.
11 I own very few compact discs. Most of the music in my collection is on vinyl, 45-rpms, 33 1/3-rpm, or even 78-rpm recordings. Initially, I was going to avoid writing about music about the war on compact discs. Most of it had originally come out on vinyl anyway. I was forced to make an exception to this policy when I discovered some of the recent and truly excellent war related music composed and sung by Vietnam veterans that is available only on compact disc. These songs and the men who perform them are discussed elsewhere in this book.
12 Most of the songs in the soundtrack had little to do with the war, but became associated it with it because they were in the soundtrack. For example, Louis Armstrong's "What A Wonderful World" was recorded in 1965 to follow up on Armstrong's mega-hit, "Hello Dolly" and turned out to be a "disaster" in terms of sales.
13 Interview with Sarge Lintecum, July 20, 2000.
14 Not all of the songs in the various discographies are discussed in this book. The decision over what to include in discussions and what to omit was not an easy one. I believe that I have made a good faith effort to include those that best address the range of issues surrounding the war. Please note that it proved impossible to find the dates when some of the recordings were released. In some cases record numbers are also missing.
15 The second edition includes a discography of over seven hundred and fifty songs, which was expanded through additional research and interviews with veterans and musicians.

Chapter 2:
The Music of Protest

All previous American wars had their music, and the vast majority of these songs were pro-war. Vietnam was unique because the protest songs outnumbered the songs that supported the war.[1] The sheer volume of antiwar music shows how unpopular the war in Vietnam had become. There were even some songs that went beyond merely opposing the involvement in Vietnam and advocated the overthrow of the American political system itself. The music with this radical view claimed that America had something evil at its core that was responsible for the debacle in Southeast Asia. Some of the most blatantly offensive tunes like "Piss on Johnson's War," "Napalm Sue," and "Hitler Ain't Dead," never were pressed into vinyl (for obvious reasons). The disenchantment with the war policy in Vietnam remained relatively subdued until the Tet Offensive in 1968. This surprise offensive which came right into American living rooms through television images of Viet Cong sappers within the confines of the U.S. Embassy compound in Saigon turned public opinion against the war. The media's interpretation that the enemy had won a huge military victory alarmed the American people and convinced them that the United States could not win in Vietnam. This steadily rising tide of opposition reached a state of critical mass with the invasion of Cambodia and bloodshed at Kent State University in the spring of 1970. These two events set off a firestorm of protest that brought the United States perilously close to a genuine revolution. The groundswell of outrage culminated with a huge anti-war march on Washington, D.C., later that spring. This development forced the already paranoid Nixon administration into a deeper siege mentality that resulted in government troops surrounding the White House and near chaos elsewhere in the capitol city where troops and protestors clashed. However the most memorable single confrontation between these elements took place at Kent State University in Ohio, where four students were killed by shots fired by national guardsmen. This tragedy spawned one of the most timely and powerfully stirring anthems of the anti-war movement, Crosby, Stills, Nash and Young's "Ohio."[2]

The song used the unfortunate deaths of the student protestors as a call to action, correctly identifying the fact that blood was shed that day as a watershed in the evolution of the anti-war movement, in that the cause now had martyrs to give it needed momentum. An undeniable sense of urgency can be detected in the ominous lyrics, which issue a rallying cry that the government has finally gone too far and that aggressive action is now needed to force an end to the war. The media helped support this view by virtually canonizing the students who died in the confrontation. Neil Young, the composer of "Ohio," said he was inspired by the *Time Magazine* cover showing a young woman looking up from the body of a dead student, an expression of agony on her face. He described the song as "music as new" but expressed reservations about having capitalized on the deaths of the students. Graham Nash, another member of the group, also had doubts about the timing of the song but for more mercenary reasons, stating that he felt "Ohio" was released too soon after the group's recording of "Teach Your Children," thereby limiting the latter's commercial success.[3] David Crosby called the recording "one of the proudest moments of my life," and spared few words in saying whom its message was intended for: "Nixon, this is you. We're pointing the finger at you, asshole."[4] "Ohio" also must have appealed to other extremists who felt it supported their viewpoint that American institutions were so thoroughly corrupted that they needed to be destroyed and reconstructed.

Another prominent group of the period, Jay and the Americans, who dominated the charts with hits like "She Cried," "Cara Mia," and "Come A Little Bit Closer," released an anti-Nixon, anti-Vietnam War song, "Tricia, Tell Your Daddy," in 1970. It suggests the unlikely possibility of Nixon's daughter imploring her father to end the war. It might be mere coincidence that the record came out during the time of Kent State, but it is possible that tragedy was the catalyst behind the group's venture into political music. "Tricia, Tell Your Daddy" is also notable because Donald Fagan and Walter Becker were involved in the arrangement. They went on to fame as "Steely Dan."

Throughout the war, a favorite theme for protestors was the inequity of the draft, and here they touched on a government policy that presented an exposed flank. Vietnam, like too many other American wars, was fought mostly by young men from poorer socioeconomic backgrounds and minorities, the "lower class," making the conflict the proverbial "rich man's war and poor man's fight." It was reminiscent of the Civil War where the wealthy paid substitutes to go and fight for them, a practice that drew a hailstorm of criticism in the music and newspapers of that time as draft riots convulsed New York City:

> "In the South, the privilege of hiring a substitute had produced the bitter slogan of 'rich man's war and poor man's fight.' In the North, commutation was even more unpopular than substitution. 'The Hundred Dollars or Your Life' blazoned headlines in Democratic newspapers. A parody of a popular recruiting song made the rounds: 'We Are Coming Father Abraham, Three Hundred Dollars More.' The price of commutation amounted to almost a year's wages for an unskilled laborer. 'The rich are exempt!' proclaimed an Iowa editor. 'Did you ever know aristocratic legislation to so directly point out the poor man as inferior to the rich?'"[5]

As the Vietnam War raged, those of privileged backgrounds didn't hire replacements but usually managed to obtain a deferment to avoid military service during the Vietnam War. Those who did wear a uniform never came close to a combat situation. Creedence Clearwater Revival's "Fortunate Son" minces few words in denouncing the badly flawed system of military conscription that sent young men without social standing and political connections off to war while those born with a "silver spoon" in their mouth were never placed in harm's way. The group's lead singer, John Fogerty, literally spits out the bitter refrain, "It ain't me, it ain't me, I ain't no senator's son. I ain't no fortunate son."[6] These words strike a nerve in reminding anyone who cared to listen that the United States is far from a classless society and that there are those who were more equal than others. While life is unfair and it is human nature to envy others who have more than you have, it is also fundamental to the human condition to fulminate when being a "have not" makes you likely to lose your life as cannon fodder on a foreign battlefield. Aside from draft dodging, "Fortunate Son" also slams the privileged class who "help themselves," but when the "taxman comes to the door, Lord, the house looks like a rummage sale." This accusation undoubtedly resonated well with latter-day Marxists who regarded the United States involvement in Vietnam as the capitalist behemoth beating down a popular communist uprising. The barrel of Creedence's shotgun also draws down on patriots, as born waving the flag but then leave the fighting of their wars to others less fortunate. Fogerty, who said the song was written in only twenty minutes while he "was screaming inside," credits Richard Nixon as his "inspiration" because he "was always saying peace with honor and my country love it or leave it, but we knew better, because the man was obviously evil."[7] It would seem that this view places the rock group on the same page with Samuel Johnson of a much earlier era, who proclaimed, "patriotism is the last refuge of scoundrels." However, unlike some of the protest music, "Fortunate Son" did not cast blame on those who fought in Vietnam, and the GI's appreciated this and even regarded the song as a morale booster.[8] In fact, "Fortunate Son" was released in 1969 and was quite topical then, but it would also have currency years later when politicians like Dan Quayle and Bill Clinton found accusations that they used political connections to avoid going to Vietnam become an embarrassing issue in their campaigns for vice-president and president, respectively. Although he did go to Vietnam as a photojournalist, a recent biography suggests that Albert Gore, Jr., who was literally a senator's son, might have been "protected" because of his father's political status when he was there for five months in 1970.[9] "Fortunate Son" also provided the title for Lewis Puller, Jr.'s memoir about serving in the Marine Corps in Vietnam and the sad story of his life afterward. That Puller chose this title for his book is ironic, for although he was the son of Marine Corps legend "Chesty Puller," and he probably could have been the embodiment of the "Fortunate Son," he chose to avoid letting his father's celebrity affect his career as a Marine.[10]

Pete Seeger's version of Phil Ochs' classic "Draftdodger Rag" is a well-deserved critique of the draft and the often absurdly unfair Selective Service rules that allowed perfectly healthy men to avoid military service while others who didn't know how to work the system were sent off to Vietnam. In his version of the song, Seeger sings about a young man who wants no part of war and recites an impressive list of physical problems and other circumstances that he is confident will make him ineligible for the draft. Although "Draftdodger Rag" is sung in a humorous and satirical vein, in reciting all the trivial ways that certain young men could avoid the draft, the song raises the issue of how unfair it was to those who couldn't qualify for an exemption. "Draftdodger Rag" represents the mind-set of millions of young men during the Vietnam War who wanted no part of the military and became remarkably inventive in dreaming up ways to "dodge" the draft. The Turtles also make this point with some emphasis in their version of a Dylan composition, "It Ain't me Babe," also recorded by Johnny Cash. David Peel's "Hey Mr. Draftboard" states emphatically that he doesn't want to go to war either. This song, which came out during the mid-1960s, bears a strong resemblance in melody and lyrics to Larry Verne's novelty hit from 1958, "Please Mr. Custer (I Don't Wanna Go)." Verne's song, which in the modern, politically correct age would have been censored, is about a soldier in General Custer's Seventh Cavalry who is also reluctant, and with good reason, to venture out to do battle with Sitting Bull and his warriors at the Battle of the Little Big Horn. The aversion to being drafted into the military became "a generational obsession"[11] as American casualties mounted and the war began to be seen as a tragic exercise in futility. One singer even suggested becoming a "criminal" in order to escape being drafted and sent to Vietnam. Arlo Guthrie, in "Alice's Restaurant," sings about how he used a conviction for littering to get the draft board to declare him unfit for military service. Michael

Nesmith, before he went on to fame with the Monkees, recorded a "bad satire" of the horribly flawed system in "New Recruit."[12] Another future rock star, Bob Seger, also took a shot at the system of conscription as part of a group known as "The Beach Bums" with "The Ballad of the Yellow Beret." Almost all of the protest music that focused on the draft came out during the mid-to late 1960s as the war escalated and hundreds of thousands of young men were inducted into the military with the likelihood of winding up in South Vietnam. An interesting exception is the Four Preps' "The Big Draft," which was released in 1962, when the Kennedy admistration's main concern in Southest Asia was Laos. The song jokingly urges the government to draft rival vocal groups so the Preps can have a monopoly on the record buying public. As the group cleverly mimics the vocal styles of their competitors, they recommend that the Platters be sent to South Vietnam! It is remarkable to see a reference to this country in a popular song in 1962, when the vast majority of Americans didn't even know where South Vietnam was and could have cared less.

Mitch Ryder's recording of "Drafted" takes a shot at the professional athletes who never had to worry about going to Vietnam because they played a game. The song's composer "Brick" Marunich said he was angered when Dave Parker became the Pittsburgh Pirates' first millionaire in 1970, and bragged that he had "paid his dues." Parker made this statement at the same time nineteen year olds were being killed in Vietnam. Marunich told me that he wrote the song to point out the injustices of the draft where kids who couldn't play centerfield for the Red Sox or quarterback for the Jets wound up in Vietnam:

> "History will show Joe went to the Super Bowl. Thousands heard it in Vietnam on American Radio. Drafted they were America's number one team. Not to play ball, but their country did call. On a faraway land, how much money should be paid to kill a fellowman and for what they call liberty."[13]

Conscientious objection became another means for men to avoid the draft, pursued by those who claimed religious or moral objections to war. Keith Everett takes a dim view of anyone who seeks to become one in "Conscientious Objectors" and disgustedly dismisses them as cowards who sit at home, content to let others die for them. He concludes with some heat that those who decide to take this route might as well be defectors. This vigorous blanket denunciation of the thousands of young men, who became CO'S during the Vietnam War, ignores the fact that many of them did go to war and were in the thick of the fight as combat medics.

Pete Seeger's other contribution to the protest music on a 45-rpm single was "Waist Deep in the Big Muddy," which was censored by the CBS television network, shocking Seeger and other adherents of free speech. They had every reason to be shocked, but those who study history know that censorship during wartime is not an uncommon governmental act. Sadly, one of the first casualties in a war is the truth. Vietnam was certainly no exception, resulting in the coining of the phrase "credibility gap" that aptly described the increasingly skeptical attitude of the public toward what they heard about the war from the Johnson administration. It is little wonder, then, that the Jefferson Airplane's "Somebody to Love," which begins with lead singer Grace Slick keening "when the truth being found to be all lies!" struck such a responsive chord with so many who were beginning to sense that the government was telling them lies about the war. Like so many other songs, "Somebody to Love" can be interpreted in different ways and may well have been written to describe the outrage of a spurned lover or as an anthem to the sexual revolution that was sweeping America during the 1960s. But it is also a song about the war because of those who identified with the way it appears to flail away at the exposed flank of the government's excessive secrecy and Orwellian double-talk about what was happening in Vietnam. Even Johnny Cash, the country legend who usually waved the flag of patriotism in his music about the war, joined ranks with those who were beginning to doubt the integrity of the government in "What is Truth?" The Lettermen, in a dramatic departure from their songs about the rapture of love, dismiss the government as men who are too old and divorced from reality to be trusted as decision makers. In "All the Gray-Haired Men," the powers that be are seen as men who do little more than mouth empty platitudes while their dangerously simplistic world view indicates that silver hair does not always mean wisdom. Their narrow-minded world view prevents these *éminence grisé* from understanding the complicated issues about the Vietnam War. This rare venture into political commentary by the Lettermen also touches on the fact that so many wars are generated by old men while the actual fighting and dying is left to the young men. Inevitably, "All the Grey-Haired Men" conjures up images of President Lyndon Johnson's "brain trust:" Robert McNamara, Dean Rusk, Walt Whitman Rostow, and General Maxwell Taylor, to name a few. Taylor advised both Kennedy and Johnson about the war and served as ambassador to Vietnam for a time. In testimony before Senator William Fulbright's Senate Foreign Relations Committee, he "dismayed" some observers with his callous disregard for the war's civilian victims: "I would doubt if we would find many B-52 strikes hitting exactly where we would like them to... but the overall effect has been very helpful." These "breezy" remarks were not an isolated incident. As recently as the 1970s, Taylor told CBS's Eric Sevareid, "Believe me, fifty thousand dead? We kill that many every year on the *highways*"[14] Fortunately, the venerable "wise men" whom Johnson summoned in early 1968 when he found himself between a rock and a hard place about what to do about the war in Vietnam, took a less cavalier view than Taylor. Although these men were in some cases old and gray, unlike "All the Gray-Haired Men" portrayed in the song, they had the wisdom to give LBJ the right advice: that the war could only be a Pyrrhic victory, if even that, and the United States needed to disengage.

As public distrust in the political leadership deepened, Dion's "Abraham, Martin and John" was released in the fall of 1968, and this wistful message about the void left by the passing of political icons like Abraham Lincoln, Martin Luther King and the Kennedy brothers struck a responsive chord with a nation that had lost faith in Lyndon Johnson and his close advisors. Any number of people who were discouraged about the war were convinced, as the song suggests, that assassin's bullets had robbed the country of the man (JFK) who would have almost certainly been able to work out a favorable resolution to the crisis caused by Vietnam or avoided the problem altogether. King and the Kennedy brothers all died relatively young, suddenly and violently. Their relative youth and the nature of their demise had a lot to do with the posthumous acclaim they have been accorded, especially JFK. That he merited inclusion in this musical tribute is yet another reminder of the huge hero role he has attained in our "national mythology." "Abraham, Martin and John" makes music yet another medium that has "transfigured" Kennedy into a figure of "almost religious longings" to the American public, as John Hellmann concludes in *The Kennedy Obsession* : "As President he became the nation's romantic lover, the object of our projected fantasies who promised to return us to the scenario of our founding in order to relive the pleasures and heal the wounds of American history." It is Vietnam that most people think about when they lament Kennedy's assassination as the turning point of the American century.[15]

Those who exhibit a syndrome known as "Camelot idealism" accept with little question the theory that had Kennedy lived, and won a second term as president, disengagement from Vietnam would have taken place cleanly and quickly. Although Dion doesn't say anything about Kennedy and Vietnam in "Abraham, Martin and John," he creates a portrait of the slain president that does little to diminish the view that he was a man who could perform such a miracle. This was a most welcome musical message in 1968, when support for the war was beginning to decline. Whether Kennedy would or could have successfully removed the United States from Vietnam or continued the war has been hotly debated by historians for about a generation now. That JFK would have removed the U.S. from Vietnam is readily and enthusiastically accepted by those who watch too much television, whose primary reading material is supermarket tabloids and who take movies like Oliver Stone's *JFK* far too seriously. Unbiased historians can point to evidence supporting a completely different conclusion: that Kennedy was a staunch cold warrior who would have continued and even expanded the American commitment to fight communism in Vietnam. "Abraham, Martin and John" also invoked the actual words of Kennedy, a technique that can't help but make those who accept highly romanticized versions of Kennedy's political prowess dewy eyed with nostalgia, reinforcing their view that his tragic death plunged America deeper into the abyss of Vietnam. How Dion, who had gained fame as a singer of rock and roll "classics" devoted to rather trivial juvenile issues like "Runaround Sue," "The Wanderer," and "Teenager in Love," came to record such a song is interesting. According to Ace Collins *Disco Duck and Other Adventures in Novelty Music,* Dion was going through a period of intense introspection and wanted to not only get back on the charts but also record a song that made a statement and made people think. It was serendipity then that Dick Holler of Laurie Records pitched a song about some of America's most prominent fallen heroes to Dion, who enthusiastically decided to record it. I was initially surprised to see this mournful and thoughtful ode included in a book devoted to "novelty songs," the kind of tunes that are known for their silliness and often bizarre and even outrageous lyrics. However, Collins describes "Abraham, Martin and John" as an "atypical" novelty song because it makes a "deep, gut wrenching point, that none of us could really answer and therefore caused our collective hearts to sigh."[16]

Whether John F. Kennedy would have withdrawn the United States from Vietnam immediately, had he lived to win a second term, is a theory hotly debated by historians today. Those historians who contend he would have continued the American commitment in Southeast Asia are probably correct. However, the song "Abraham, Martin and John," which was released during the war, owed its huge popularity to its theme of reverence for the slain president and the attendant notion that he was some kind of god. "Camelot" idealists who undoubtedly revel in music like this, regard his assassination as a watershed in the history of the twentieth century because they believe he would have extricated the country from Vietnam. Source: JFK Library

Kennedy meets with General Maxwell Taylor and Secretary of Defense Robert McNamara during the Vietnam War, some of his own "wise men." Source: JFK Library

The song was also recorded by the African American comedian Moms Mabley. The fact that "Abraham, Martin and John" pays tribute to Dr. King and his efforts in the Civil Rights movement may well have motivated her to record a version of the ballad. Her effort, however, was dwarfed by Dion's in terms of commercial success. Tommy Cash, Johnny's younger brother, also eulogized the Kennedy brothers and Dr. King in 1968, with "Six White Horses." His recording of "The Tears on Lincoln's Face" is a commentary on how agonizing the war had become for America, that the internal tumult the country was suffering was reminiscent of the travails that tormented Lincoln during the years of the Civil War. The mournful ballad brings back painful memories of the assassination of John F. Kennedy, and it also brings to mind cartoonist Bill Maudlin's drawing of the sculpted likeness of Lincoln at his memorial in Washington bent over as if convulsed with grief over yet another slain president. This poignant sketch appeared in newspapers all over the country. Cash decided to record the mournful song because he felt "a special connection with it, and it was a good song."[17] At the same time that "Abraham, Martin and John" was gaining wide acceptance, Simon and Garfunkel's "Mrs. Robinson" became one of the most popular songs of the era by linking American angst to the "disappearance" of sports icon Joe DiMaggio. Country singer Bill Anderson's "Where Have All Our Heroes Gone" also considers DiMaggio and laments the fact that there aren't more heroes like the "Yankee Clipper" around now that America's youth can look up to, rather than the unworthy contemporary icons they revere. Men like Roy Rogers and Gene Autry, Eisenhower, and General Douglas MacArthur are examples of what American role models should be like. Winston Churchill also deserves to be part of this panoply of great men, and Anderson points out that the British Prime Minister's two fingers raised in the air, "V for victory," during World War II was a more genuine sign of peace than the similar two-fingered "peace sign" that became synonymous with the anti-war movement.

Suspicions about government mendacity about the Vietnam War were confirmed when the U.S. Senate began to investigate the Gulf of Tonkin incident and the "Pentagon Papers" surfaced in 1971. It was ultimately revealed that the truth was kept not only from the public but also from highly placed government officials, a fact about which I can provide some personal testimony. In the spring of 1988, I had a chance to talk with Albert Gore Sr., who served in the United States Senate with Lyndon Johnson. He told me that President Johnson came to him in early 1964 and asked for support in the fall presidential election. When Gore said his support was contingent upon winding down the U.S. involvement in South East Asia, LBJ assured him that was just what was going to happen. Actually, unbeknownst to Gore, Johnson was already intending to do just the opposite. Sometime after the election, a chagrined Gore obtained an audience with the chief executive in the oval office and asked Johnson why he had lied to him. Gore told me that Johnson strode around the office with his hands behind his back and his head bent, and then suddenly turned around, shot his finger out and exclaimed: "I ain't gonna be the first American president that cut and run in a war!"[18]

The author's interview with Gore, Sr. provided fascinating insights into President Johnson's real reasons for fighting the Vietnam War.

The lack of faith in Johnson's integrity would become a key issue for the Nixon campaign in the 1968 presidential election, and campaign buttons were distributed stating, "Close the credibility gap, elect Nixon and Agnew." At the same time that the Johnson administration's truthfulness about the war had become a campaign issue, the president himself was placing far too much faith in a man who would also be accused of telling lies about what was going on in Vietnam. This was General William Westmoreland, who, as head of the Military Assistance Command (MAC), was responsible for American military operations in South Vietnam. He was the architect of the so-called strategy of attrition that was supposed to gradually wear the enemy down and win the war by killing enough communist soldiers while keeping American casualties at an acceptable level. The problem with this plan was that the general badly misread public opinion, and what he considered to be tolerable "kill ratios" of 10-1 and 20-1 outraged the American public. After the war, Westmoreland would be accused of inflating "body counts" as well as deliberately underestimating enemy troop strength as a ploy to convince dubious Americans that the war was being won. The scheme didn't work, and anti-war protesters tapped into public disillusionment about Americans killed in combat when they chanted, "Hey, Hey LBJ, How Many Kids Did You Kill Today." Although he was hardly an anti-war firebrand, Roy Orbison spoke for many who had begun to view Vietnam as a cause not worth a single American life in "There won't be Many Coming Home." Orbison's warning that the numbers of war dead would only increase and that no one would be spared the agony of losing a loved one turned out to be sadly prophetic.

Even the fading German Diva, Marlene Dietrich, joined the ranks of those protesting the war in song by recording "Where Have All the Flowers Gone?" She had to be persuaded to do it, but once the record was out, it became a big hit in Europe. Along with her version of "Blowin' In The Wind," it became a "pop hit" on continental jukeboxes. When she performed it on a television special at the height of the Vietnam War, she was described as having a "sorrowing grandeur."[19]

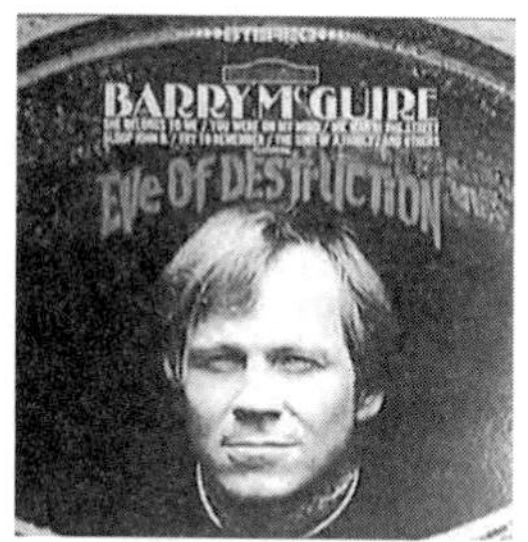

McGuire then

McGuire with fan 2001

McGuire with New Christy Minstrels-Before his venture into protest music during the Vietnam War, he co-wrote the group's big hit "Green, Green."

This was a period when there was more than enough angst for everybody and a song that is loaded with it is Barry McGuire's "Eve of Destruction,"[20] a Jerimiad set to music that not only condemns the war but also racism, politicians, hate in Red China, conflict in the Middle East, and the dangers of the Nuclear Age. McGuire sounds like a crusty Old Testament prophet as he also takes a swipe at hypocrites who don't observe the golden rule toward their fellow man but still pretend that they are religious. "Hate your next door neighbor, but don't forget to say grace." It is one of the most powerful and memorable songs of this period and had it been recorded more recently it probably would have become one of the anthems of the millennium, with its prophecy of imminent Armageddon. It also has the distinction of offering one of the most delightfully "kitschy" phrases to be found in any of the Vietnam War music, for as the singer's sense of outrage peaks, apparently even his metabolism is affected: "My blood's so mad, feels like coagulatin'!" A measure of "Eve of Destruction's" impact is that it attained the coveted number one spot on Billboard's Hot 100 charts in September of 1965 and also merited an "answer song," "Dawn of Correction" by the Spokesman. This response, as the title implies, put a more optimistic spin to the complaints contained in "Eve of Destruction" and made it to number thirty-six in Billboard's record ratings, one of the highest, if not the highest, positions registered by any "answer song" of any era. McGuire would never again make as big a splash in the popular culture of the time but would continue in the same philosophical vein with his music and recorded a reprise of Bob Dylan's "Masters of War," a song that denounces the shadowy interests that some believe are responsible for all wars. McGuire told me that his failure to capitalize on the success of "Eve of Destruction" was a blessing in disguise because had he continued the dissolute rock star lifestyle it would have killed him. I was surprised to learn that McGuire doesn't consider "Eve of Destruction" a protest song: "It wasn't a Vietnam song, it wasn't a protest song, but a societal mirror. If you went to a doctor and he diagnosed you with colon cancer, you wouldn't call him a protest doctor, would you? 'Eve of Destruction' was just a song that diagnosed the condition of the country at the time."[21] However you categorize this song, it brought McGuire from obscurity to almost overnight fame, and he was astonished at how quickly the record took off: "The writers at Dunhill Records came to me with six songs and I liked all of them and we went into the studio. We tried a couple and then I said why don't we try that "eve" song? I had the words written on a piece of paper I'd stuffed in my pocket. I pulled it out, unwrinkled it and put it on the music stand, and we cut it in three takes." Two days later it was being played on the biggest radio station in Los Angeles and a few weeks later it was the number one hit in the country. The controversial song became a "career breaker" after it was a "career maker" as McGuire and Dunhill Records were subjected to a storm of protest and even received death threats.[22] They were told to "go back to Russia" by those who regarded "Eve of Destruction" as anti-American. Right wing groups like the "Anti-Communist Christian Crusade" charged that the song was "instilling fear in our teenagers as well as a sense of hopelessness." This of course would make the entire American public easy prey for "atheistic international communism."[23]

McGuire says he found Jesus at Dennis Doherty's (of the Mamas and Papas fame) house. He picked up Good News for Modern Man (the New Testament) that Doherty had and said to himself, "I'm a modern man, and I need some good news." After a night stoned on LSD he saw the book lying on the floor and thought, "God if you get me through this night, I will give my life to you." He kept his promise and now performs in Christian concerts throughout the United States.

Today, "Eve of Destruction" still has an emotional impact, at least for me. When I heard McGuire sing it at the Duluth Gospel Tabernacle in the summer of 2001, my eyes teared up. As he looked back over his musical career before he became a Christian, he had little good to say about the commercial music business and refers to it contemptuously as a "meat market." He says that music moguls decided that any future recordings he made would not get air time because they hadn't got any "payola" the first time around: "Eve of Destruction" got played and it was an end-around touchdown as far as promotion was concerned. The record industry had already decided that my next record was not going to airtime because they didn't get their cut the first time around.[24]

Parenthetically, those who look for a lot of Dylan's music in this book may be disappointed. Although he was easily the most seminal folk/rock singer of the era and beyond, no 45-rpm singles were forthcoming that had a direct connection to Vietnam. "Subterranean Homesick Blues" does reflect the growing disenchantment with the government but doesn't directly address the war, although the radical "Weathermen" faction of the Students for a Democratic Society named itself after a phrase from this song.[25] Dylan's well-known "The Times They are A-Changin'" and "Masters of War," would be sung at anti-war demonstrations and concerts during this period, but they were actually recorded and released prior to the time that Vietnam became the kind of issue that inspired or provoked songwriters and musicians. In fact, as the war escalated and musicians began to find it a compelling topic for their music, Dylan, the ultimate protest singer, had begun receiving criticism for shying away from political and social issues in his recordings. As the country shuddered from the shock waves of the King and Kennedy assassinations and the riots at the Democratic National Convention in Chicago, Dylan was in Nashville, recording songs that "gave off no residual heat of the times."[26] In my opinion, Jimi Hendrix's version of "All Along the Watchtower" is probably the Dylan song that is most closely associated with the Vietnam War, at least in the minds of the men who actually saw combat there.

Many of the protest songs during the Vietnam era were recorded by "folk singers," artists who specialized in performing a kind of music that was notable for its bent toward social commentary. Its origins can be traced back to the earliest years of American history. During the first half of the twentieth century, when folk singers found plenty of social problems to address, the much-venerated Woody Guthrie even painted

"This machine kills fascists" on his guitar. The political role that folk singers took on was not without its risks as the popular singing group, the Weavers, found out in the early 1950s during the hysterical McCarthy era. Their outspoken views resulted in their being "black-listed" by a government pathologically paranoid about communism. Folk music enjoyed a resurgence during the 1960s when the Civil Rights movement and the Vietnam War became the kind of issues that allowed political music to flourish. Probably the most potent song of this kind in American history was "Blowin' in the Wind," by Peter, Paul and Mary, which became the anthem of the Civil Rights movement. Although the trio didn't record anything as memorable about Vietnam, their version of the "Cruel War,"[27] memorably portrays the pain of having a loved one fighting in a war. This song concerns a young woman grieving about her "Johnny" and the danger he is facing as a combatant in Vietnam. She wants to be with him so desperately that she is even prepared to disguise herself as a man and go into battle along with him. Many might regard this possibility as musical fantasy, but it is a well-documented fact that some women did don uniforms and fight along-side their men in the Civil War. The Viet Cong and North Vietnamese army also utilized females as soldiers, nurses and prostitutes. "The Cruel War" is also distinctive because of the pronounced melancholic, dirge-like quality of the musical arrangement. It is one of the most truly "sad" songs ever recorded and one of the most cloying.

The war led to adversarial relationships between war protestors and authority, especially the police, who were called "pigs" by those to the "left" of the political spectrum. One of the most vivid and enduring images of the Vietnam War is that of police in riot gear brandishing nightsticks at anti-war protestors during one of the many violent confrontations that became commonplace all over the United States in the late 1960s and early 1970s. A very well-known song that would seem to eerily capture the essence of a confrontation between the police and war protestors is Buffalo Springfield's "For What It's Worth." However, it may well be that the altercation being described is actually a typical Sunset Boulevard clash between a "bunch of cops and kids in LA," who were more worried about curfew and their right to "hang out."[28] The most famous of the battles that took place between anti-war demonstrators was in Chicago in 1968 during the Democratic National Convention and was seen by millions of people on television. An official investigation described the tumult as a "police riot." Some of the major luminaries of the left, who were involved in leading the demonstrators against the police, were prosecuted in federal court in Chicago in 1971. The trial itself degenerated into a riotous affair, as the crotchety and arbitrary old judge who presided, Julius Hoffman, didn't seem able to maintain courtroom decorum as he allowed himself to be baited by the likes of Abbie Hoffmann and Jerry Rubin. Graham Nash's "Chicago" decries what he regards as the injustice of this trial, especially Judge Hoffman's tactic of having the outspoken and demonstrative defendant Black Panther Bobby Seale physically restrained during the proceedings, which became known as the trial of the "Chicago Seven." Despite expressing outrage at the quality of justice meted out in the federal courtroom, Nash is optimistic that good things can materialize out of bad, as he predicts that the efforts of the convicted protestors and others like them will someday change the world for the better. The album cut of "Chicago" has Nash, live in concert in that very city, sarcastically dedicating the song to Chicago Mayor Richard Daley, who many believe was responsible for the rioting, when he encouraged his police to deal harshly with the war protestors. It is ironic that Nash, one of the troubadours of the anti-war movement, seems to regard Chicago as a focal point for people who want to change the world, considering the rude treatment many of their number received there. On the other hand, maybe because it was the source of such ugliness, it was the appropriate place to go and heal the wounds. Attempting to interpret the meaning of song lyrics can sometimes be as difficult as reading significance into the entrails of a chicken or tea leaves. "Chicago," at least in my opinion, contains one of the most inscrutable phrases of all the politically-oriented music of the time: "Don't ask Jack to help you, cause' he'll turn the other ear." Just who is this "Jack" and why would he turn a deaf ear?

The anti-war movement seemed to be predominately composed of the young, who often found themselves at odds with their parents who were more cautious about criticizing the government's policy in

Vietnam and were often deeply offended by their offspring's anti-war views. This led to bitter arguments and even estrangement between children and their parents in families already troubled by the well-known "generation gap." Victor Lundberg's[29] "Open Letter to My Teenage Son" describes a veritable chasm that has opened up between a dad and his male offspring, who is apparently contemplating the notion that God is dead, growing a beard and/or long hair, and burning his draft card. In a pompous, commanding tone, the father tells the errant child that his mother will always love him no matter what he does because "she is a woman," but sternly warns, in uncompromising fashion, if the draft card is burned then the birth certificate might as well be set aflame too, because he will no longer be his son. Junior is also castigated for ingratitude in daring to criticize a society that has allowed Dad to work and provide the luxuries that have made for a comfortable childhood. This soliloquy sounds vaguely like something out of the popular television series of the 1950s, "Father Knows Best," although Robert Young probably would have been more subtle with Bud. What makes this "fatherly" ultimatum even more pompous is that it is conveyed in the form of a letter. Whether or not this was one of those "absentee" fathers who traveled a lot and didn't feel he had the time to address his son directly, a face-to-face chat would have allowed for some "give and take" on both sides. Such an exchange would have been fairer and far less condescending. Based on the tone of this letter it wouldn't seem that the writer is the type of person who was at all uncomfortable about expressing his views, whatever the circumstances, but there are those prone to avoid potentially uncomfortable confrontations by "throwing messages over the fence" in this manner. "Open Letter" was one of several war-related recordings that would merit an "answer song," and Brandon Wade's "Letter From a Teenage Son" probably speaks for millions of children in a similar situation as he replies, "No Father, I won't embarrass you by burning my draft card, but I reserve the right to express what I feel in my heart." Despite the fact that Wade's record label (Phillips) promoted his response to Lundberg with a full-page ad in Cashbox, a leading record trade publication, the rebuttal went largely unheard for it never charted nationally. It is interesting to note that the young man pictured in the advertisement doesn't appear to be much of a radical. He is short-haired and rather conservatively dressed. Because it was far from a commercial success, "Letter from a Teenage Son" is in scarce supply today and is regarded as one of the truly collectible vinyl artifacts of the war. I was lucky enough to find this rarity at a local garage sale for just a few pennies. Another response to "Open Letter to a Teenage Son" that also merited an entire page in the same issue of *Cashbox,* "Letter to Dad," by a group known as Every Father's Teenage Son, fared better on the charts but its impact was still negligible. In this version, the teenager warns that if his father does want to burn his birth certificate, he will have to do it himself. The father is also advised that even if he stops calling him "son," he will still be his "dad." *Cashbox*[30] featured this record as a "newcomer pick," describing it as a "reasonable rebuttal" to the "controversial flagwaving" of "father's single." The review went on to predict that "Letter to Dad" "could pick up exposure on anti-Lundberg stations, following "the out-of-left-field" pattern of the original.

In 1962, Paul Peterson of the Donna Reed Show sang the praises of fathers and sons, as reflected in recordings like "Open Letter to My Teenage Son" and others.

Ad for Brandon Wade from Cashbox. Wade's record company gave his answer to "Open Letter to a Teenage Son" a full page ad in Cashbox, but the recording barely made a blip on the music charts.

Dick Clark felt compelled to respond to Lundberg's rebuke to American teenagers with a recording known as "Open Letter to the Older Generation."[31] Since Clark was so closely linked to the contemporary teenage scene because of his highly popular television program, "American Bandstand," I would speculate that his "letter" admonishes the parents to be a little more open-minded with their children when they question the way things are. This is just an educated guess, since I have never heard the record nor has anyone else I know of who is knowledgeable about the music of the era. Peter, Paul and Mary's "The Great Mandella" is about yet another intolerant father who sternly lectures his son who has chosen to protest the war by resisting the draft. This is more than just a philosophical disagreement based on the clash of different generations, for the family has already lost a son in the war. The father accuses the young man of thinking he is better than his deceased brother and that his anti-war views are wrong: "You're not a prophet, you're a coward." When the boy stands his ground and says that he could never go to war and kill, the father warns that he will wind up in jail where the jailer will be ordered to refuse him even bread and water. Eventually he will die, fulfilling a death wish to become a martyr in the anti-war cause. This song also makes a pessimistic statement about the futility of protesting government actions, that people have been protesting similar evils like the war for ten thousand years and all of them failed. When the youthful protestor finally does starve himself to death, the father seems to have some regrets, as he tells the "people" that they should feel secure because the bothersome advocate for change is dead. Martyrdom over the war was a rarity but it happened. The father and son enmity described in these songs destroyed families, making them yet another casualty of the war. "The Great Mandella," with its pessimism about the fate of those who fight for change, seems an odd song for Peter, Paul and Mary to sing, considering their reputation for producing some of the most forceful, powerful and successful protest songs of the era.

Many young men found themselves confronted with official intolerance by school boards, PTAs and the like when they grew long hair to express their distaste for conventional society and the war. In Jody Miller's powerful "Home of the Brave (Land of the Free)" a young man is expelled from high school because of his long tresses, and the narrow-minded parents, teachers and school administrators who collaborate to take this punitive action are condemned. The song also begs the question of how America can really be the "Home of the Brave (Land of the Free)," if this student and others like him are not granted freedom of expression. The song elevates this hirsute youth to the status of a hero because he has dared to make a statement. It is easy to visualize such punishments being meted out all over the country, especially in small, rural school districts, when students dared to be different. Administrators who reacted this way probably were too hidebound to realize that their efforts to maintain conformity were doomed to failure as the war and other powerful forces it unleashed were rapidly transforming American society. It is interesting to note that there were soldiers in Vietnam who sympathized with the students who were disciplined. When the news reached Harry Cottrell in Vietnam that the school district in his hometown had announced a similar prohibition on long hair, he and his comrades wondered if they were really fighting for freedom.[32] What makes Miller's performance of "Home of the Brave" so effective is that she connected so well with the message it was sending out: "It says it all, it sums it all up." If she had taken the advice of composers Barry Mann and Cynthia Weil she wouldn't have recorded the song. They stereotyped her as a strictly country singer because of her previous success with "Queen of the House," the "answer" song to Roger Miller's "King of the Road." Fortunately, she went with the advice of her producer at Capitol Records, Steve Miller, and waxed "Home of the Brave." Her version went head to head with one recorded by Bonnie and the Treasures who were produced by the musical genius of the 1960s, Phil Spector, who was responsible for the phenomenal success of other girl groups like the Ronnettes and the Crystals. Spector was not happy with the competition from Miller and ran full-page ads in Los Angeles newspapers as well as music trade magazines claiming "Home of the Brave" belonged to him and denouncing Miller's recording.[33] In spite of this, her effort was far more successful than the Spector backed version. She feels her success was, at least partially due to the fact that by 1965 "the girl group sound had already seen its day." Ironically, Miller's rendering of "Home of the Brave" sounds like a Spector production, but only because her producer "thought the man was God Almighty."[34]

Jody Miller won a head-to-head competition with Phil Spector with her version of "Home of the Brave." More recent Jody Miller promotional still on the left. Source: Jody Miller

Those who questioned the war and wanted to go beyond mere rhetoric about stopping it found songs like Jefferson Airplane's "Volunteers," with its call to action to join the revolution that was taking place in the streets, energizing. This record was being heard when it seemed possible that opposition to Vietnam was becoming a groundswell that might even topple the government. "Street Fighting Man" by the Rolling Stones also makes the observation that revolution is imminent in claiming that almost everywhere the sound of people marching can be heard. The impulse to mount the barricades is so infectious that the singer joins in shouting and screaming, seemingly caught up in the wave of anti-war and anti-government feeling. Considering previous songs like "Sympathy for the Devil" and the hiring of biker thugs who beat to death an innocent concert-goer at Altamont, it appears the Stones would have reveled in the violence and chaos had the country descended into the maelstrom of genuine revolution. It's also quite possible that "Their

Satanic Majesties" would have had little stomach for it had they wound up in the midst of such an upheaval. "Street Fighting Man" was released shortly after the chaos of the Democratic National Convention in Chicago in August of 1968, and the song drew criticism for what seemed to be its advocacy of revolution; some radio stations even removed it from their play lists. Political radicals who did want to overthrow the government mistakenly welcomed the Stones as "comrades" to their cause and distributed revolutionary manifestos at their concerts. Although Jagger himself said he wouldn't have been surprised to see a revolution take place in the United States, it would be an exaggeration to claim that he and his colleagues deliberately sent out a message of subversion.[35] Jagger did march in a war protest in London. Although he criticized the peace movement's lack of "battle readiness," he hurried away when the police arrived. He later recorded a song called "Everybody Pays Their Dues," lamenting the futility of trying to fight the system and end the war although he did admit it was almost impossible for artists to ignore it in their music. The Stones' song that so many people connect with Vietnam, "Paint It Black," is described as "having social echoes about recent waves of immigration to England from Pakistan and India" rather than intending to make any kind of statement about the war. Keith Richard even claimed it was cut as a "comedy track." However, the title and the dreary lyrics made it natural for those who lived through this period to identify with it.[36]

Peter Townsend of The Who recorded a recruitment commercial for the U.S. Air Force at the height of the war and freely admits that his group recorded their music to make money, not send political messages about the war. He further admits that he couldn't have cared less about what was happening in America or Vietnam at the time.[37] The British crooner Rod Stewart also recorded "Street Fighting Man" and disavowed that it was at all political. In fact, he accused those who saw his version of the song as an attempt to lead a revolution in America as mistaken and chastised Americans for reading too much into the lyrics of popular music. Stewart said he actually recorded the song because it was "funky" and he liked the lyrics.[38]

Many did think the United States was on the threshold of a political earthquake in October of 1969 when between 500,000 and 1,000,000 people participated in the Vietnam Moratorium, one of the largest anti-war rallies in American history. One Lord Brynner puts his spin on this event in "Vietnam Moratorium" that is sung to a background of what sound like Spanish horns and a calypso beat. Brynner sounds vaguely Jamaican as he intones his message in a clipped and stilted style. The Moratorium was a watershed in the anti-war movement not only for the impressive number of protestors that turned out but also for revealing how broad-based its support had become. It was no longer a movement composed primarily of radicals from the fringes of society, as demonstrated by the fact that housewives, hippies, African-Americans, financiers and disenchanted Vietnam veterans marched together to stop the war. The participants in the march that Brynner seems most fascinated with are the women, who are "dressed in black and white, holding candles, with tears streaming down their cheeks." At least one of the female marchers is a mother "whose son was killed down there by Vietnam." Seemingly incensed by relating these sad tidings, the "lordly" singer reaches a peak of outrage as he proclaims, "We have no right to be fighting in that country, destroying humanity, bring back our men, bring them back immediately!" "Moratorium" is yet another obscure vinyl artifact of the war but deserving of inclusion in this book because it is one of the few 45-rpm singles that touches specifically on one of the most impressive anti-war demonstrations. The most memorable song that became identified with the Moratorium was Phil Ochs "I Ain't Marching Anymore." Capitol Records started to promote Bob Seger's "2 + 2 = ?" when opposition to Vietnam peaked with the Mobilization in the fall of 1968. The song is a vehement denunciation of the war as a worthless cause and also a lament about a friend who died there and is now "buried in the mud of a foreign jungle land." This "average friendly guy" didn't die for freedom, but rather to "save the lies" of the politicians. There is the usual speculation that Seger did "2 + 2 = ?" to make a profit on the war, but there are those who consider the recording an act of gallantry and a rare instance where rock and roll music actually waged war against the war.[39] Although the Moratorium didn't end the war, it bothered the Nixon administration enough that it unleashed its rhetorical pit-bull, Vice President Spiro Agnew, who began a memorable verbal war on critics of the war. This would include an album of his speeches condemning anyone who opposed the Nixon administration's policies in Vietnam, called "Spiro Agnew Speaks Out On: Radicalism in our midst, Vietnam War critics, protestors, malcontents, hippies and effetism, television's responsibilities and the Republican and Democratic parties."

Even though the music performed at Woodstock was anti-war in nature the soldiers in Vietnam still regarded it as their music. One enlisted man, upon returning stateside, put together a series of slides depicting combat in Vietnam and decided to use songs from Woodstock as background, deciding this would be the most eloquent way to say what he wanted to say rather than the personal narrative he'd originally planned.[40] The mood of the huge gathering of the counter-culture in upstate New York in the summer of 1969 is best captured in Matthew Southern Comfort's "Woodstock." This euphoric rhapsody of a better world, where the sheer numbers of children of God who are coming together (and being "golden") can end the war by turning the bombers and other weapons of war into harmless butterflies, is among the most idealistic of the protest songs. Other groups, including Crosby, Stills and Nash, would record this ballad, but Matthew's Southern Comfort's version seems to convey the spirit of "Woodstock" most convincingly.

The lively musical dialogue about the war was not confined to domestic musicians: a British rock group, "The Animals" joined the fray with "Sky Pilot," a song aimed at the hypocrisy of a priest "blessing the boys" before they go off to war. There are some powerful and vivid images here, the faces of the young men "shining as they stand in line" to receive a dubious benediction prior to a mission from a "good, holy man" as the "smell of gun grease" wafts over the ceremony. "Sky Pilot" is plainly anti-war, especially a war where religion is used in such a way that the implication is that God is somehow on the side of one of the combatants. The song is also noteworthy for the inclusion of bagpipes in its instrumental background. It was heard at

"Evac" hospitals like that at the military base at Pleiku[41] as surgeons and nurses worked frantically to save the lives of horribly wounded young men just like those portrayed in the song, only minutes from one battlefield or another. It's interesting to speculate what thoughts went through the minds of those who heard "Sky Pilot" in that setting, and some probably pondered the question of where God was then. Military chaplains often had an extraordinarily difficult time convincing their flock that there was a divine design behind the war and its senseless carnage. Many enlisted men undoubtedly wondered whether it was really possible to be a Christian and a soldier at the same time. Like so many of the other songs about the Vietnam War, "Sky Pilot" has another level of meaning. The lyrics that seem to be describing a pilot maneuvering his aircraft through the heavens can also be interpreted as depicting a "drug trip."

Unlike "We Gotta Get Out Of This Place," the Animal's best-known song about the war, "Sky Pilot" was recorded with the purpose of making a statement about Vietnam. According to the group's leader, Eric Burdon, "I felt we were in a position to make it clear to the public that we were against the war." It's ironic then, that just efore the Animals launched their first American tour, the Animals were warned by their booking agents: "Don't say a f—king thing about Vietnam when you get to America."[42]

Britain's premier group, the Beatles, remained silent about the war as far as an entire song, with the possible exception of "Revolution," where they note that there is political turmoil taking place but seem to take a dim view of those who are protesting. The "Fab Four's" music had such a pervasive impact on the era that there were probably words or phrases that war protestors, as well as soldiers in combat, found illustrative of their respective experiences, especially for the Marines who found themselves marooned at Khe Sahn. Lyrical phrases like "Coming to take you away, dying to take you away" had a special meaning for them.[43] After the group disbanded, its leader, John Lennon, would form the Plastic Ono Band and contribute to the anti-war music with "Give Peace a Chance" which became something of an anthem for the peace movement and was sung by other artists at various peace rallies all over the United

States. His emergence as an outspoken opponent of the Vietnam War is considered a watershed in the politicization of rock music or the age of "political pop."[44] He went on to record "Happy X-Mas (War is Over)," a song that expresses frustration that the war is still raging during a holiday when there is supposed to be "peace on earth." Lennon was a fervent advocate for peace in other songs, too, and would literally go to bed to promote this cause, as chronicled in the autobiographical "The Ballad of John and Yoko." "Imagine," released as the war was waning in 1971, is another example of how Lennon set his pacifistic views to music. His exalted status in popular culture assured that his views about the war reached a vast audience. The fact that these views were often articulated in heavy-handed fashion drew criticism from fellow musicians, as well as the Nixon administration, which sought to have him deported. The attempt to throw Lennon out of the United States also spawned at least one memorable protest song, Neil Sedaka's beautifully plaintive "The Immigrant." In case there was any about what this song was all about, some copies of the recording bore a statement advising that it was dedicated to Lennon. His wife, Yoko Ono, went solo with "Now Or Never" in 1972. to lodge a musical complaint about the war. This record comes with a picture sleeve that has to be the most painfully graphic of any produced by record companies during the war. It depicts the corpses of Vietnamese villagers who died at the hands of American troops during the My Lai Massacre.

The picture sleeve for Yoko Ono's "Now or Never" shows the all too familiar photograph of the carnage at My Lai.

One of the most innovative and effective ways of portraying the pathos of war is found in the Simon and Garfunkel's "6 O'Clock News (America the Beautiful)" and "7 O'Clock News (Silent Night)." A newscaster drones on and on about the war and other events of the day while two of the most memorable pieces of music known to mankind provide a very moving and somber counterpoint. These songs were also recorded by a group known aptly as The Hopeful, but their effort was eclipsed by the version performed by America's most popular duo of the 1960s.

Among the recorded esoteric that is anti-war in theme is a song called "Thank God the War is Almost Over" by Shelly on the tiny Peace label of Brooklyn Park, Minnesota. The title and the name of the label leave little mystery about the sentiments expressed in this song, but one wonders when it was released. If it came out during the late 1960s, it was strictly wishful thinking; there were so many times when false hopes were raised about the war finally coming to end. Even when Henry Kissinger and Le Duc Tho were awarded the Nobel Peace Prize in 1972 for ending it, the war wasn't really over. One of the great protest singers of the time, Phil Ochs unilaterally declares the Vietnam War to be finished in his angry "The War is Over." At the same time he sardonically observes that maybe things aren't so bad after all because at least the war industry is humming along and money is being made so "we really can't complain"-a well-deserved rebuke to those who supported the Vietnam War because it was good for the economy and kept their pockets well-lined and a subject that was popular among those who sang protest music: Vietnam being yet another outrageous example of a "rich man's war and a poor man's fight."

Jim Morrison and the Doors, whose music often focused on the darker side of life, continued in the same vein with "The Unknown Soldier," who is yet another hapless victim of the ugly American war machine, who has died anonymously and without recognition, more cannon fodder, whose war is only over because he is dead. This song became a spectacular "theatre piece" for the group when it was performed live. Lead singer Morrison, who was notorious for in-concert theatrics, would pose as the "Unknown Soldier" and "die" at the hands of a firing squad and then "come alive" again and proclaim exultantly that "the war was over." To complete this act successfully it was necessary for Morrison to sing lying down,[45] which may have been a spectacular feat for some but pretty mundane for this troubled child of rock and roll, who made a kind of history by exposing his genitals during a concert in Miami. The Tombs of the Unknown Soldiers in Washington, D.C., are obviously the inspiration for this song, but ironically, because of advances in forensic pathology, there will probably never be a genuine Unknown Soldier for the Vietnam War.

Because experts about the music of the war have advised that it is one of the ultimate songs about the Vietnam War and the fact that it was featured in the soundtrack of one of the most memorable of the movies about the war, *Apocalypse Now,* I felt it necessary to include some mention of the Doors' "The End." It probably owes its prominence as a Vietnam song more to the fact it was in the movie than anything about its lyrical content. It was used in the film because those selecting music for the soundtrack liked the song and thought that it would provide effective background for the opening scene.[46] The fact that it is regarded as one of the essential songs about the Vietnam War today owes more to *Apocalypse Now* than to anything it had to say about the war at the time it was released. In 1968, it was widely regarded as a description of a drug experience, something that Jim Morrison could sing about with unquestionable veracity. Hopefully, it is the sense of futility contained in this "song" that soldiers in Vietnam related to, rather than the references to fratricide and incest that border on the obscene. During a performance at Whiskey A Go Go in Los Angeles, Morrison made "The End" even more profane, which so offended the manager of the club that he summarily fired the group.[47] The listener doesn't have to be a cultural conservative to find the words to this song offensive, and even dangerous, in the sense that it encourages murderous and unnatural behavior. The songs on the Beatles' "White Album" that allegedly triggered Charles Manson's murderous binge in Los Angeles in 1969 seem mild in comparison to "The End's" siren song of nihilism. Morrison, who was an avid student of European philosophy supposedly tapped into the ideas of Friedrich Nietzsche for this song.[48] There are those who would find black humor in the fact that Morrison said he was told by a young woman who was a patient at the UCLA Neuropsychiatric Institute that "The End" was a big favorite of the kids in her ward.[49]

Another much acclaimed group of the 1960s, Canadian The Guess Who, sang about an "American Woman," who is distasteful because her country has a "war machine" and a "ghetto scene." This repulsive female is told she is "no good" and to "stay away." Why is it a woman that symbolizes all that's wrong with America and not a man? This song is interesting not only because of its connection to Vietnam, but because it is faithful to historical myth in the sense that it blames a female for various woes. According to its ignorant viewpoint, this "American Woman" is a latter-day version of the harpies, sirens and witches who were always creating mischief for mankind. It would be justifiably criticized today as sexist.[50] At the same time that the song sends out a message of misogyny, it also reveals that the era was not a good time to be identified as an American citizen, as international public opinion was beginning to turn against the United States because of the war. The already "Ugly American" had become even uglier because of Vietnam. "American Woman" was characterized by one prominent record industry source thus: "The satirical song pictures the United States as an over-painted broad, who is 'no good for me'-sort of a 'Welfare Cadillac' in reverse."[51] Despite The Guess Who's reputation for singing anti-American music, the group was invited to sing at the White House and performed there in July of 1970 at a dinner dance for Prince Charles and Princess Anne of England.[52]

Those who opposed the war and attributed it to sinister forces that were peculiar to American political life found chapter and verse to support their position in the Pentagon Papers, which were released in the waning days of American involvement in Vietnam. These documents were revealed because of the efforts of Daniel Ellsberg, a Defense Department employee, who was on at least the periphery of many of the meetings that produced important decisions about the course of the war. Predictably, the Nixon administration attempted to suppress the documents, but the U.S. Supreme Court in a landmark decision in favor of the freedom of the press, allowed the papers to be published. Naturally, Ellsberg became a hero to those who were against the war and deplored the motives behind it. A group known as Bloodrock paid tribute to him in a forgettable song called "Thank You Daniel Ellsberg." This is one of those tunes related to the war that didn't enjoy much commercial success, and one who listens to the melody and lyrics isn't surprised because they are, at best, mediocre. It's an interesting switch in topics for Bloodrock, who previously attained rock notoriety with "D.O.A.," the dreary and quite repulsive tale of a young man and his girlfriend who are dying of injuries sustained in an automobile accident. Many musical groups were forced by the tumultuous politics of the day to record politically-oriented music, but it would be interesting to know what provided the catalyst for Bloodrock's quick transition from necrophilia to social commentary.

One of the zaniest and most memorable of the songs that objected to the war is "I-Feel-Like-I'm-Fixin'-to-Die Rag" by Country Joe MacDonald and the Fish, released at the point in the war when American casualties were increasing dramatically and almost any American family could "be the first one on your block to have your son come home in a box" as this strangely merry minuet cheerfully warns. However, young men who died in Vietnam were more likely to be shipped home in an aluminum coffin, which were beginning to arrive back in the states in alarming numbers. The happy beat and insouciance of the vocalist are in odd juxtaposition to the lyrics that reinforce the sad fact that the American public was being forced into realizing that Vietnam was no longer a remote place on the other side of the world, and the damage it was doing to the country could no longer be considered collateral, involving someone else. Country Joe and his Fish sarcastically urge college students to put down their books and go to Vietnam where they will soon find the "pearly gates" opening for them. A kind of fatal apathy is part of the message of this song, as the singer doesn't give a damn because he's going to Vietnam and this is equivalent to a death sentence. The eventuality of dying in combat had been brought about by a conspiracy of sinister and furtive economic interests: "Come on Wall Street, don't be slow... There's plenty of good money to be made by supplyin' the army with the tools of their trade." Almost every American war has had its motives questioned in the same way: that shadowy individuals motivated by greed have been a key factor in causing war in order to accommodate their own horribly selfish interests. McDonald had an enviable "pulpit" from which to gain currency for these ideas when he sang his anti-war rag to some five hundred thousand people at Woodstock. It was also sung by members of the Armed Forces who knew that they were going to Vietnam.[53] Country Joe was one of the most "political" of those who recorded message-music opposing the war, and his career probably suffered for it. Beyond his highly opinionated music, he visited military bases along with Jane Fonda, who is despised by veterans' groups for her anti-war activities, where they attempted to turn soldiers against the war. McDonald's use of the "F.U.C.K." chant as an introduction to "I-Feel-Like-I'm-Fixin'-to-Die Rag" also got him into trouble, and it cost him a spot on the Ed Sullivan Show. He kept on singing, but his songs began disappearing from radio station play lists, and his star began to fall. The Fish recorded other songs about Vietnam, including "Superbird" (which lampooned LBJ), "For No Reason," and "Maria." Although the group had little "45 presence," "Maria," which tells the story of a conversation with two returning Vietnam veterans at L.A. International Airport, was released as a single in Scandinavia. McDonald was a non-combat veteran of the Vietnam War era, as a member of the U.S. Navy Air Force. Although he was one of the most prominent anti-war critics, after the war he became an advocate for Vietnam veterans.[54] During the war, "I-Feel-Like-I'm-Fixin'-to-Die Rag" became one of the favorites of young draftees and enlisted men in Vietnam because of its "nihilistic" message. A former GI who may well be speaking for many soldiers expressed these sentiments about the song:

> "It gave me the ultimate vent to all those feelings of idiocy and lunacy about the whole war... I was forcing myself to be 'reasonable' about the war-you know, to find the middle

> course and say, 'Okay, you people didn't say you wanted the war, but we might as well do our best.' But I was really feeling that it was crazy and idiotic, and I wouldn't allow myself to express that. I guess when I heard the 'I-Feel-Like-I'm-Fixin'-to-Die Rag," I really just let it all hang out."[55]

Prior to the 1960s, to die in battle was considered a glorious and romantic end. Songs about earlier American wars, and even Vietnam, re-enforced this notion. One of the most famous expressions of this idea of "romantic killing" was Alfred Lord Tennyson's poem "The Charge of the Light Brigade," which paints with an exceedingly rosey hue a suicidal attack by British troops during the Crimean War. Because "I-Feel-Like-I'm-Fixin'-to-Die Rag " clearly rejects this notion of the romantic hero's death in combat, Country Joe has earned praise as the "unofficial musician-Poet Laureate of the rock-Vietnam generation: "If McDonald did not sound the death knell of the heroic-romantic warrior vision, we can at least say it will never be the same again."[56]

Donovan's "Universal Soldier" found a receptive audience with a key faction in the anti-war movement because of its pacifistic theme that any soldier fighting in any war is behaving immorally and that if people would simply refuse to take up arms, war would no longer be a viable instrument of national policy. If they don't, Donovan warns, then this murderous universal soldier will kill us all. This type of soldier, like the rough-hewn professional "soldiers of fortune" who had their heyday in places like the Belgian Congo and banana republics in South America, enjoys war immensely and would eagerly become part of any country's war machine. War is a business to these professional killers, and they would have few scruples about killing if the price is right. "The Universal Soldier's" plea to beat swords into plowshares and everyone will live happily ever after takes a rather superficial view of relationships between states. Many wars have come about because states had to defend themselves against invasions by their often, larger, totalitarian-oriented neighbors. The resultant call to arms was of necessity, not because all men have some bent chromosome that orders them toward the violence of war. Another less-than-cogent aspect of the song is that it doesn't take into account the fact that many men who fought in Vietnam did so with reluctance as draftees, not professional soldiers, especially toward the end of the war. It wasn't that they looked forward to combat with the enthusiasm of Donovan's prototypical "Universal Soldier," it was that they feared incurring the wrath of the United States government if they didn't go. The song also strays from accuracy by lumping all soldiers together into a composite "Universal Soldier." Steve Hassett's poem, "Christmas" also compares the troops in Vietnam with mercenaries-the Hessians, who were hired to fight in the American Revolutionary War-but like the song, this view doesn't have much evidence to support it.[57] An interview with Buffy St. Marie, who wrote this song, doesn't reveal anything about what message she intended to convey in "Universal Soldier:" she merely states that people were surprised that it was penned by a woman who was also an American Indian.[58] It could have been written about SSgt. Barry Sadler, who sang the immensely successful pro-war song, "Ballad of the Green Berets." Sadler, in addition to serving with special forces in Vietnam, hired out as a mercenary. He did more than sing about making war, he authored the popular "eternal mercenary series," "Casca." Glen Campbell, an artist who rarely recorded music with a social or political message, also came out with a version of the song titled "The Universal Soldier." The opposite of the latter is Jan Berry's "The Universal Coward," an individual who is something of a political chameleon, who doesn't have the fortitude to have a firm conviction about any of the issues of the day. Instead, he cravenly sits on the fence philosophically and doesn't belong in either the anti-war or pro-war camp. This kind of attitude may have been a rarity during the later stages of the Vietnam War when it seemed the United States had become thoroughly polarized over the issue. "The Universal Coward" was a rare venture into social commentary for Berry, who became famous along with Dean Torrance for being on the cutting edge of the surf music craze. As a duo they also recorded "Only a Boy," which is Vietnam-related and discussed in Chapter Five.

A recording titled "The Man Who Hears a Distant Drummer" includes a picture sleeve showing a soldier, with a bemused expression, regarding a daisy protruding from the barrel of the rifle he is holding. This was a familiar scene from the home front during the war as "flower children" would, if given the opportunity, decorate the weapons of troops in the same fashion. This gesture didn't always produce harmony between student war protestors and the troops. Allison Krause, one of the students who was shot to death by national guardsmen at Kent State University in May of 1970, put a flower in the rifle barrel of one of the guardsmen the day before she was killed.[59] Ironically, there is a photograph of this soldier, flashing the peace sign as Allison's flower protrudes from the end of his M-1. The latter-day Thoreau pictured on the sleeve from "The Man Who Hears a Different Drummer," a record that actually promotes Bravura cologne, is probably representative of many members of the armed forces who had begun to question the worthiness of the cause they were supposed to fight for, and with good reason. However, the song suggests that this soldier boy's consciousness-raising was brought about by using a certain brand of cologne. The other side of the picture sleeve displays a bottle of Bravura cologne along with the message, on a tag attached to the bottle, "For the Man Who Hears a Different Drummer, From the Girl Who Plays Along." Obviously, this is more of a commercial message about the virtues of Bravura and those who use it, but it is interesting to speculate why the advertising agency that came up with this idea found it worthwhile to connect their product with a man in uniform who has doubts about the war. Apparently this advertising campaign came at a point when Madison Avenue felt the time was right to co-opt some of the phraseology of the growing anti-war movement and use it in advertising the merits of various products from cars to clothing.[60] This record was released in the very late 1960s or early 1970s when more and more soldiers and returning veterans were beginning to speak out against Vietnam. Whoever recorded this song is unknown. More than likely, it was rendered by a group of anonymous "studio" musicians. The record label sheds little light on this mystery and merely states that the recording is a "Limited Edition, Arranged and Produced Exclusively for Bravura." The small print at the bottom attests to the fact that the disc was "custom pressed by Decca records."

Many companies attempted to lure customers by employing advertising campaigns that would tap into the burgeoning anti-war sentiment, as evidenced by this picture sleeve that contained a musical pitch for Bravura Cologne.

One of the more radical theories of why America was in Vietnam was offered by Steppenwolf in "Monster." According to this song almost as soon as Europeans came ashore and settled America, they began committing atrocities against innocent people and haven't stopped since. In an argument that could have been drawn from the pages of radical, revisionist histories like Howard Zinn's *A People's History of the United States,*[61] the powers that be responsible for the situation in Southeast Asia are seen as modern day versions of the self- righteous puritans who "burned the witches." The colonists not only severed ties with the British monarchy, they also gained a homeland over the dead bodies of the Indians who they brutally slaughtered as a means to this end. According to this line of reasoning, America's presence in Vietnam is easily explained by the fact that it is an evil imperialistic power that doesn't know how to mind its own business and wants to remake the world in its own image: "cuz the whole world's got to be just like us." This lengthy musical diatribe continues by stating "no matter who's the winner, we can't pay the cost" because there is a "monster on the loose...our hands are on the noose." This monster that controls America's destiny watches (with grim satisfaction, perhaps?) while the country continues to deteriorate. This malevolent creature seems to have been unleashed because "protectors and friends of a benign past" have fallen asleep and can no longer control it.

It was no surprise that it was Steppenwolf that recorded a politically powerful rant like "Monster." The group's leader John Kay had promised that their music would "centralize the thoughts and direction of our generation through music. We are a reflection of what is happening today. We could be called the thinking man's rebel with a cause."[62] By the early 1970s, many singers ceased to care about the war. Janis Ian, who showed no reluctance to take on the issue of discrimination in 1967 with her powerful "Society's Child," said it was now "boring to proselytize in her songs. The minute you preach, you are interfering with somebody else's life."[63]

There was also more benign protest music that disapproved of the war without disparaging or putting the blame on anyone, and this was written and performed by artists who were genuine pacifists. Jackie DeShannon, in songs like "What the World Needs Now is Love," gently admonished everyone to stop being angry and realize that there is just not enough love among humankind. If there were, the world would be a much better place. This message was obviously well received for the song charted well and even made it into the soundtrack of the movie "Bob and Carol and Ted and Alice." The theme of love healing all wounds was obviously popular with the "flower children" of the age who espoused the philosophy "make love not war." The anthem of this "love generation" was Scott McKenzie's beautiful "San Francisco (Be Sure To Wear Flowers In Your Hair)," which optimistically describes the power of love as sweeping the country "all across the nation, such a strange vibration, people in motion, people in motion." This sweetly sung hyperbole depicts San Francisco as the Mecca for the "flower children," who are "gentle people with flowers in their hair." Much like lemmings, these children of love find San Francisco to be a magnet that they can't resist, for once they arrive, the song promises that "there'll be a love-in there." This ballad has an infectious exuberance to it that, even a generation after its release, must make aging hippies weep with nostalgia. Tony Bennett's "I Left My Heart in San Francisco" is supposed to be the ultimate song about the world famous city, but Scott McKenzie's ode is right behind it. Groups with names like The Flower Pot Men ("Lets Go To San Francisco") and Fever Tree ("San Francisco Girls") also recorded songs glamorizing the city during the war. Some Vietnam veterans are nostalgic for San Francisco for a different reason. Many of them shipped out from there for Vietnam and Bennett's tribute to the city is the ballad that reminds them of that experience most vividly.[64] A more ambivalent view of the city is offered by the Animals' "San Franciscan Nights." Although bikers and the flower children and police are mellow and feeling "all right" and reveling in the glory of a summer night in San Francisco, the only discordant note is sounded by a malevolent cop whose face is filled with hate and unfazed by to all the love in the air.

Woodstock is another place that became celebrated because of what took place there during the war. The little hamlet in upstate New York gained its fame in 1969 when hundreds of thousands of young people gathered there hoping that their meeting could somehow change society and the course of the war. Melanie's "Candles in the Rain" and "Lay Down, Lay Down" effectively captures the mood of Woodstock. Her tribute to the event is so evocative that one can almost see the candles shimmering in the rain. In his "Old, Old Woodstock," Van Morrison gets choked up just thinking about it, speaking for those who were actually there and many who weren't. There did appear to be an unusual camaraderie there, and Melanie's description of how "close" everyone was for a few days in the summer of 1969 is not an exaggeration. Hers is obviously a very emotionally charged and highly romanticized version of what actually took place, but it does capture the essence how many people actually felt at the time. She sang the song again at a recent Woodstock reunion. On the heels of "Candles in the Rain" Melanie recorded the optimistic "Peace Will Come (According to Plan)" because of what seems to be her belief in a natural order that causes rivers to flow to the sea. According to this grand design, powerful and mystical forces beyond human control, make peace inevitable. Throughout the song, Melanie urges, "please buy one." Is she selling flowers as a symbol of peace? It may well be that the singer was still feeling some of the residual euphoria and idealism that was part of the super-charged mob psychology at Woodstock. Both of these recordings are without question related to the Vietnam War, but it is hard to see any relevance in Melanie's "What Have They Done To My Song, Ma!" At least one pundit has suggested that it is a metaphor for the body bags that were one of the most grotesque aspects of the war, an opinion that is debatable. Despite the lyrics "well they tied it up in a plastic bag and turned it upside down," this seems to be more a song about the vagaries of the music business but only Melanie would know for sure.

Ed Ames' recording of "Who Will Answer?" condemns the war for killing young men who will never meet the children they sired. The loss of these fathers also robbed America of a significant segment of its young manhood, and one can only speculate how many great scientists, physicians, and authors never had a chance to realize their potential. This song is quite distinctive because Ames conveys its message in a style that strongly resembles the Gregorian chant of the Middle Ages. This led to the misconception that "Who Will Answer?" is a religious song, which it is not. According to the lyricist Sheila Davis,[65] the words have been widely misunderstood by clergymen and laymen alike. It is really intended to be about the threat of nuclear war, apathy, religious dissension, and the angst of the younger generation. In its original form, the song (composed by L.E. Aute) was a number one hit in Spain some months before it was released in the United States in the fall of 1967. RCA introduced "Who Will Answer?" with much ballyhoo, including a performance of the song on Johnny Carson's "Tonight Show."[66] Although the high expectations were not realized, this musical social commentary remains one of the most interesting and thoughtful works of the Vietnam era. When Ames recorded "Who Will Answer?" he was in the solo stage of his musical career. During the 1950s, he had attained fame as the lead singer for the popular Ames Brothers singing group that scored hit after hit with innocent music like "You, You, You," "The Naughty Lady of Shady Lane," and "Sentimental Me." During the 1964 presidential campaign, Ames recorded "Hello Lyndon," to the tune of the famous Broadway song, "Hello Dolly." By the time Ames released his version of "Who Will Answer?" some recording artists were "serenading" Johnson in a different way.

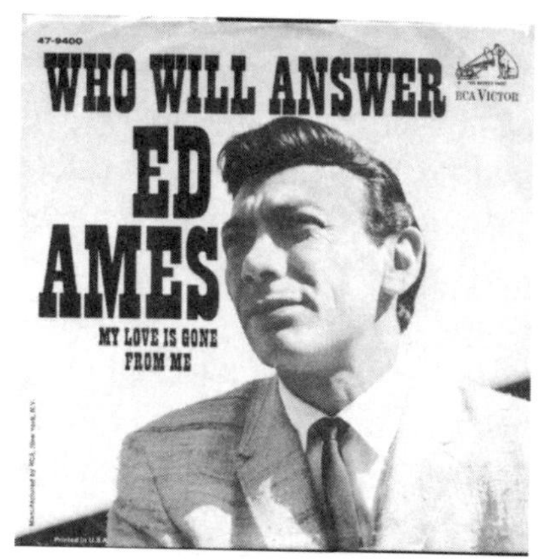

RCA Victor promoted Ames' venture into social commentary with a picture sleeve as well as an appearance on the Johnny Carson Tonight Show.

Grand Funk Railroad's "Closer to Home" seems to blame America's malaise on its leadership, as attested to by all of the references to "captains" and "ships." This particular ship and its master seem to be in extremely troubled waters, as was the captain of America's "ship of state," President Richard Nixon, during this stage of the Vietnam War. With the hindsight we have now about Nixon and Watergate, references to the captain of a ship who is obsessed by the fear that his crew will mutiny and take his ship away from him are eerily prophetic for a song released in 1970. The most famous reference to a president as "captain" is Walt Whitman's posthumous tribute, via a different kind of poetry, to the slain Abraham Lincoln, "Captain, My Captain."

Dickie Goodman poked fun at all the campus unrest caused by the war with his novelty break-in recording "On Campus" in 1969. Goodman's satire on the war era came years after he and Buchanan pioneered the break-in record with "Flying Saucers Parts I and II" in 1956. As a "reporter" delivers "live" coverage of an invasion from outer space and interviews witnesses to the event, their answers are supplied with snippets from the top hits of the day. For example, when one bystander is asked his reaction to the crisis, it is the voice of Elvis Presley that responds singing "I'm All Shook Up!" The Martians (or whatever they are supposed to be) disclaim any designs on planet Earth when they declare tunefully, "Don't want the world to have and hold," taken from Don Cherry's "Band of Gold." A brief segment of the Clatters' (Platters) "The Great Pretender" is used to describe an extraterrestrial's interviewee's earthly bewilderment: "too real is this feeling of make believe." Even though those who owned the copyrights to the songs used by Buchanan and Goodman were not amused, the "break-in" caught on with the general public because it was a genuinely innovative and humorous device to satirize issues of the time. People were also probably amused at finding the voices of their favorite singers juxtaposed into such incongruous situations. Even as the popularity of this musical fad began to fade, Goodman continued to crank out "break-ins" that fit the changing times. Vietnam was hardly a joking matter, but Goodman's parody "On Campus" was still engaging and funny. The spectacle of Mayor Richard Daley of Chicago, who is referred to as "Mr. Happiness," extolling the virtues of longhaired students' "long beautiful hair" (as sung by the Cowsills in "Hair") is delightfully absurd. When President Richard Nixon is asked at a press conference what he thinks of the campus demonstrations, his reply is the Isley Brothers "It's Your Thing." There is even a pairing of Governor Ronald Reagan and Black Power firebrand H. Rap Brown who, when asked where they met, respond with "in the ghetto," a phrase borrowed from Elvis Presley's song of the same name. Governor George Wallace uses Creedence Clearwater Revival's "Bad Moon Rising" when asked his impression of the upheaval taking place in academia. Another novelty song that caught on was "Snoopy vs. the Red Baron" by the Royal Guardsmen. The group sang about the Charles Schulz canine creation flying through the skies doing battle with the evil "bloody Red Baron of Germany." People found it to be a refreshingly escapist tune. They liked listening to the exploits of a hero fighting for an unmistakably noble cause, a welcome relief from the depressing state of affairs in Vietnam.[67]

Perhaps the most tumultuous of the "war years" was 1968, with the shock waves caused by the Tet Offensive, the assassinations of Robert Kennedy and Martin Luther King, Jr., and the decision of President Lyndon Johnson to not seek re-election. It is a well known fact that the widespread criticism of his conduct of the war had finally reached the point that the president felt it would be better for him and the country if he removed himself from the political arena. A song that directly took the president to task for Vietnam was Pete Seeger's "Waist Deep in the Big Muddy." The title proved to be a classic metaphor for the country where the United States now found itself in a quagmire, in a land that was well know, for rivers and swamps that were difficult to traverse. Unlike most of the protest music, this song was aimed specifically at LBJ. It begins as a bitter reminiscence about a "big fool" army captain who drowns in a Louisiana swamp while leading his recruits into quicksand while on maneuvers during World War II. Even as the officer moves toward his watery doom, he keeps urging his men forward until he disappears into the quagmire. The song concludes by characterizing President Johnson as a "big fool" who is leading the country into a much bigger and far more dangerous swamp in Vietnam. These were the lyrics that made censors nervous, especially when Seeger went on to make it clear that what he was singing about was as real as today's newspapers' headlines. He caused a sensation when he sang "Waist Deep in the Big Muddy" on the nationally televised "Smothers Brothers' Show" in September of 1967. At least he did when he finally was allowed to sing it. The first time he appeared on the show, nervous CBS executives, who were well aware of the controversial nature of the song, had Seeger's performance removed from the tape, much to his outrage:

> "On September 10, 1967, Tommy Smothers smiled nervously and introduced Pete Seeger to millions of American households. Pete began with "Winoweh;" then Tommy asked Pete, who was holding a twelve string guitar and fingering the strings, if he was going to sing 'that song.' The camera closed in on Seeger's face for a moment. Then it

> moved back. When it moved back, Pete was holding a banjo and "Big Muddy" had disappeared into the ether. They'd been had."[68]

"Accordingly (I Learned Some Things Today)" recited by John Linde with The Linde-Antell Body of Music begins with the voice of Johnson announcing his shocking decision and describes how this event causes at least one man to have an epiphany about his own life. Linde then proclaims joyfully, "I learned some things today," including that he is "a lucky man" because he now knows how "rewarding a smile can be and that he can walk a mile in any direction." He also exults, "When I choose to lower my head in prayer, someone will listen and someone will care." Things that were always "before his eyes" but previously invisible, are now observed with a new-found clarity. Just sitting and gazing at the sky is now cause for wonderment and the perspective of learning "that man should start to live before he learns to die" has also been gained. This virtually reborn individual can hardly wait until tomorrow to see what revelations the new day will bring. It has been suggested that there is another way to interpret this song, and that is the world as seen through the eyes of a rejuvenated Lyndon Johnson himself, feeling euphoric that the burdens of the Vietnam War will be lifted from his shoulders after the next presidential election. Another view as to what the song really means is provided by its co-author, Peter Antell:

> "Everybody remembers 1968. A sitting president decides not to seek a second term - in quite a memorable recitation to be sure - and John Linde had a great idea: 'I can't wait until - get me a tape of his speech!' And now we thought, could a 'putting together' of John and Lyndon - of Linde and Johnson - on a long suffering instrumental (with narration, whistling and chorus) we'd begun five years before, prove to be its deliverance from a basement archive in Hempstead, Long Island, Well, someone listened - someone cared and we were able to sell it to the Cadet label of Chicago."[69]

On March 31, of 1968, President Lyndon Johnson declared he would not run for another term because of the controversy caused by the Vietnam War. The announcement shocked the country and inspired Peter Antell to write and John Linde to record "Accordingly (I Learned Some Things Today.)" Source: Yoichi Okamoto. LBJ Library Collection.

Peter Antell and John Linde were a prolific songwriting duo responsible for penning hits like "Night Time" on Cameo-Parkway in 1960 and the Percell's "What Are Boys Made Of" on ABC Paramount. They also recorded together in a group known as Chants and had a modest hit on the Ecko label (1961) with "Respectable." Then they evolved into the kind of songwriters and performers who would produce one of the most profound pieces of music about the Vietnam War. Linde said that the catalyst for "Accordingly (I Learned Some Things Today)"came from watching television coverage of the war with his son, who was only two years old at the time. The boy was too young to understand what he was seeing but was sensitive enough to express consternation about the battle footage and questioned his father about it. This is what Linde had in mind when he and Antell were trying to figure out what to do to provide lyrics to fill an "instrumental track" they had created. As Antell tells it, "Accordingly" went through many incarnations before the work was finished:

"We were dissatisfied with the lyrics to a song called 'Everybody But Me.' I started tinkering with it at the Hammond organ and became inspired. These very unusual staccato figures materialized like I'd never played before, giving it a warm eeriness that was strangely compelling. The opening and closing of the record was an accidental blast created when someone bumped into the studio's echo chamber. Boy, we were having a good time. Something about it was really exciting but we had no idea what the lead part would be. For working purposes, we called it 'The Monster' referring to what we perceived in our youth and naivetÈ as the force and melodrama of this recording. The addition of my whistling added something to what we were now calling 'The Thinker' and pretty soon we had a record. This was all done in the early '60s, but it wasn't until 1968 that it was released by Cadet Records."[70] The result was the thoughtful recitation about the decision by Lyndon Johnson to leave the presidency after his term was over. It can be appreciated on two different levels: the public response as well as a very personal reaction to the president's Shermanesque announcement. "Accordingly" was intended to be read by Theodore Bikel, but it is hard to believe that he could have rendered it any better than Linde, who proves to be a most gifted narrator.

John Linde & Peter Antell as Chants also wrote songs and are shown here with members of the girl group, The Percells, who hit the charts with a Linde/Antell compositions, "What are Boys Made of?

Peter Antell (second from left, front) and John Linde (top right) scored a modest success with "Respectable" in the early 1960s, some years before they produced the profound recitation, "Accordingly (I Learned Some Things Today)."

Johnson's abdication definitely overjoyed anti-war activists, who literally danced in the streets, "whooping, laughing, and getting down." Others were more restrained, realizing that the fact the man they regarded as the "war criminal par excellence" wasn't going to run again really wouldn't bring any immediate change in the course of the war: the bombings continued and troops were still being sent to Vietnam. Some worried that the loss of a "valued enemy" might somehow actually diminish the momentum the anti-war movement had gathered. The majority of those who opposed the war worried that getting rid of Johnson would really be little more than a hollow victory. Their pathological hatred of the president even led them to believe that his peace initiative might be only a subterfuge that would lead to even more carnage in Vietnam.[71]

The Vietnam War was the great tragedy of LBJ's presidency, significantly altering what might have been a very favorable historical assessment of his time in office. I, too, have mixed feelings about him, perhaps best expressed by the remarks made by a man who, when chided about attending Johnson's funeral, said, "I'm going to pay tribute to a great man and also make sure he's dead." Whether he deserves it or not, Vietnam will always be known as "Johnson's war." The fact that he had to cope with the ordeal of America's ugliest war, as well as the avalanche of criticism for his conduct of it, aged him prematurely and led directly to his decision not to run for the presidency again. Just two days before the presidential election of 1968, I attended a rally for Hubert Humphrey at the Houston Astrodome where Lyndon Johnson turned out to be an unexpected guest. The Democratic nominee, Vice President Hubert Humphrey was locked in a tight race with Richard Nixon and the Gallup Poll released that very day showed that the race was too close to call. If Johnson was tormented by the war, he certainly didn't show it that night as he gave a very exuberant speech about Humphrey's merits, comparing him with Democratic icons of the past like Franklin Roosevelt, Harry Truman, John F. Kennedy, and even Sam Rayburn, the late Speaker of the House of Representatives, who had been a mentor and father figure to LBJ. Later that night, the president would make an angry call to Nixon, claiming that the Republicans were trying to sabotage the Paris Peace Talks for political advantage, but few knew about this at the time. It was a stunning surprise that Johnson came to show his support for Humphrey that night, because in September he had repudiated the vice president for making a speech, also in Houston, that was far too optimistic about the winding down of the Vietnam War. In fact, for almost the entire campaign, it seemed Humphrey "choked slowly on Johnson's leash."[72]

A seemingly exuberant Lyndon Johnson makes a surprise appearance at a rally for candidate Hubert Humphrey two days before the presidential election of 1968. The song "Accordingly" portrays the president as a changed man after his announcement that he would not run for a second term. Johnson's demeanor in this photograph and the speech I heard him give that night support that conclusion. He even seems untroubled by being in close proximity to an old and bitter political rival Senator Ralph Yarborough, pictured to the right of Humphrey. Source: Yoichi Okamoto. LBJ Library Collection.

In a conversation I had with Walter Mondale he told me he didn't think Johnson wanted Humphrey to win the election! I was there the night HHH made the offending remarks in the San Jacinto Room of the Rice Hotel, the same place where John F. Kennedy, in a speech to protestant clergymen in the fall of 1960, finally put the issue of his Catholicism behind him. Perhaps Humphrey chose that same room because of that symbolism, hoping that somehow it would help him escape the albatross of Vietnam, but it was not to be-the issue cost him dearly. Although Nixon was elected with a secret plan to end the war, he would actually expand it to Cambodia, and the American war would continue on for nearly five more years, and the new president would have scorn heaped upon him by the anti-war movement and its music. When Nixon drastically escalated the war in 1972 by mining Haiphong harbor, instituted a naval blockade against North Vietnam and ordered a massive air war against that country, Neil Young in "War Song" pilloried the president as "the man who says he can put an end to war" and sarcastically urged him to "blow those bridges down, burn that jungle down and kill those Vietnamese." Young also castigated the government for laying the mine fields at Haiphong by stating "our bombs are sleeping in the sea." Nixon's decisions about the war in Vietnam were done with an eye toward the fall presidential election, and the opponent he worried about most was the hawkish governor of Alabama, George Wallace. The threat was removed when Wallace was left paralyzed after an assassination attempt in May of 1972, when it appeared he would be a serious contender for the Democratic presidential nomination. Young sings about Wallace with what seems to be tasteless scorn as "shot down, and he'll never walk around."

Vice President Walter Mondale provided perspective on the relationship between President Johnson and Vice-President Hubert Humphrey during the Vietnam War.

Shown with Andresen

Both Johnson and Nixon had a strained relationship with the artistic community. These tensions were worsened when artists became highly outspoken in their criticism of the war. Singers like Bobby Darin expressed fears about a government reaction to their anti-war views that could result in an infringement of freedom of speech. In his "Simple Song of Freedom," he pleads with the government to just leave the singers alone and let them sing their songs without fear of official reprisals. At the same time that he states that American people are opposed to the war, he asks Alexander Solzhenitsyn, the Russian novelist who was banished to Siberia for his political views, to write him a letter in case the world's most famous political prisoner misses the point in the song. Was Darin sending out the warning that American protest singers might be jailed and exiled in similar fashion for their views? "Simple Song of Freedom" also criticizes "presidents, prime ministers and kings," for being the instigators of war because they enjoy it. The "Credibility Gap" is also addressed with the declaration that what "700 million" people read in the newspapers is nothing but lies. Darin also reaches out to African Americans when he assures them that all he wants is brotherhood and isn't interested in their "diamonds or your game," as when imperialistic countries exploited their continent. "Simple Song of Freedom" was also recorded in more lively fashion by the eccentric Tim Hardin. Darin felt he owed Hardin the composition after the success he had with Hardin's own "If I Were A Carpenter." Hardin was unhappy with Darin's recording of his song, claiming this version was little more than mimicry of his own singing style.[73] Darin also recorded "We Didn't Ask To Be Brought Here." Although it doesn't directly address the war, it suggests an anti-establishment bent that was a significant departure from the singer's usual fare. Both he and Hardin would die young, Darin from a heart ailment while Hardin killed himself with drugs. It would seem that the 60s and its tumult produced a number of troubled musicians like Hardin and Phil Ochs, whose music was not enough to exorcize their inner demons. Ochs, who committed suicide in 1976, may be considered a casualty of the Vietnam War.[74]

A SILENT **message to fathers and mothers of Iowa.**

We have been dying for nine, long, miserable years in Vietnam in an undeclared war . . . how many more lives do you wish to sacrifice because of your

SILENCE?

In memory of Vietnam War Dead whom our son joined on February 17, 1970 ... and to those awaiting the acceptable sacrifice in 1970

From an advertisement in the Des Moines Register April 12, sponsored by Mr. and Mrs. Gene Mullen, La Porte City, Iowa

*These 714 crosses represent the 714 Iowans who have died in Vietnam

The parents of Sgt. Michael Mullen, who died in Vietnam in March of 1970, used the gratuity pay sent them by the Army for the purpose of defraying Michael's funeral expenses, to place this ad in the Des Moines Register (April 12, 1970) calling for all mothers and fathers in Iowa to speak out against the war. The crosses represented the 714 Iowan soldiers killed in the war as of the date of the ad.[75]

Students Essays

As expected, "Letter to a Teenage Son" was one of the more controversial musical selections in provoking some vigorously stated student comments:

> "This song touches a nerve. It makes me very angry that a father would let something as artificial as a war break the special bond between a father and son. I believe that war is not something to be taken lightly, but nothing should separate family. I think it is very selfish and unfair for a father to put his son in such a situation. The father believes in what he is speaking out about, but so does his son. The son has a different perception on the war than his father, but that doesn't mean that his opinion is wrong. The father needs to respect his view and try to accept it. No one expects them to. Our diversity in our thoughts is what makes us all individually special."

The above essay writer certainly spares no words but another student was even more graphic in expressing her distaste.

> "I thought this one was literally going to make me vomit. It had me boiling mad and sick to my stomach. They had a mean feel of just being a smack in the face of the people who questioned our involvement in Vietnam. They were an unrealistic view of patriotism, at least I hope it was. I'm sure there were some radicals who felt this way, or else the song would not have been written, and that would been an American Tragedy in itself! I think the songwriters had good intentions of trying to drum up support for their side, but some of those lyrics are so off the wall and frightening, they honestly made me cringe when I heard them.

A student with a rapier- like wit found that the Lundberg recitation made him think of the '60s cartoonist Robert Crumb:

> "Thank you, Sir Victor, for stepping down from your mighty throne to bless us all with your wisdom and approval of our actions. My brain couldn't link it with the war in Vietnam at

> all, but I found it strangely intriguing. It downloaded and connected with a piece of seemingly unrelated piece of information. I'm not sure when this song was recorded (1965) but it definitely sounds like it was rooted in 1950s ideology. In the excellent documentary *Crumb,* the still dysfunctional cartoonist R. Crumb and his brothers (one a recent suicide victim) recall the memory of their bone-crushing father in the idyllic 1950s. He was a smile-at-work, eat-your-peas-and-carrots, wave-the-flag kind of guy. Victor might indeed be a fine guy, but I just couldn't get the association out of my head. Hilariously, he sounds amazingly like Ward Cleaver dressing down the Beaver. In his pompous and condescending tone, he says he wouldn't judge teens by the length of their hair and that your mother will love you no matter what you do. 'Glory, Glory, Hallelujah' plays in the background. The seemingly placid '50s sound like they would've had sort of an undefinable creepy undercurrent of repressed emotions and it sure seems present in this song. Maybe I'm all wet on this one, but it's a gut feeling."

That most students sided with the son and condemned the father's philosophy is confirmed in yet another student response:

> "It was commonplace for fathers and sons to be at odds about the war. The fathers remembered serving in WWII. The sons saw the futility of it and couldn't understand why they should die for a ridiculous and unattainable goal. This angered most fathers quite a bit. 'An Open Letter to my Teenage Son' by Victor Lundberg is a perfect example of this. In the song this father responds to his hippie son's questions. He doesn't understand why he is being cowardly and turning his back on his country. He tells him 'if you burn your draft card, burn your birth certificate. I have no son.' The father in this song was bizarrely ultra patriotic. I can understand supporting and maybe even loving your country, but this guy was a nut. His blind faith in Uncle Sam is a prime example of the mistake that was made by America

during this time. Unfortunately, I still think there were many out there that agreed with him whole heartedly at the time."

It was somewhat surprising to discover that even a former marine found Lundberg's recitation wanting:

"It started out very good, he was reading a letter he had written for his son who might be drafted. He felt that though wars are 'bloody,' they are 'necessary.' Coming from an anti-war viewpoint I would have wished to stone a man that would write such a thing to his child. I understand that you need to fight for what you believe in, but his son had his own view point on the war and he should have the right to make his own decision about it. Yes, his decision would reflect on his father. I think his father was more concerned with how people would view him if his son burned his draft card. No matter what a kid says or does, a father should never say that he no longer has a son and inform him he should burn their birth certificate. Over a war or anything else. War divides enough people. Why would you let it come between you and your family?

A minority opinion, from a student of self-professed patriotic views:

"I found the message behind 'Open Letter to A Teenage Son' good, where the father is writing a letter to his son. The father spoke of God and how one should believe in his country, which I related to. Just as I believe my father would have said, and that father did say, 'if you burn your draft card, burn your birth certificate, I no longer have a son.'"

Jefferson Airplane's "Somebody to Love" earned praise from a student with a sense of humor who felt the song was relevant to modern day political controversies:

"It is a classic and I never knew it related to the Vietnam era. I always thought it was a typical 'girl wants a boy to love' type song. After listening to the verses I realized it was not that at all. It was a very bitter and frustrated song about betrayal by the government. This rage towards Nixon makes me feel lucky to live in a time when the worst our President does is to put a cigar where it shouldn't go."

Students generally gave Creedence Clearwater Revival's "Fortunate Son" favorable reviews:

"Wow! What a harsh reality! To know that if you knew the right person, or had enough money your life would be out of danger, would be so rage producing. Is this the first American war that it has been an honor to escape, rather than to fight? Social injustice has always been present, but how can that compare with being chosen to go to Vietnam and more than possibly die? Then to realize that those you know are lucky, have connections, and are free from being drafted. It's one thing to be served the injustice of receiving lower wages for the same job, or having to work harder for opportunities; but the difference between going to war or staying home, working an office job or combat in the jungle is a matter of life and death. Although this song isn't one I'd play at home and dance to, the message is powerful and undeniably clear."

"Creedence Clearwater Revival's song 'Fortunate Son' tells me exactly how many Americans were thinking at the time. Many knew the only way they would escape the war was by being from a wealthy family, or going to college. The song painted a picture of generals giving orders to take hill after hill, never pausing to question the damage that was being done to their own troops. If I had heard this song at the time it was released, it wouldn't have changed my view on the war. I couldn't have done anything to stop my being drafted. I would have just been more pissed off at how the process of my being 'chosen' came about."[76]

"A lot of the boys had no choice except to go, and I believe this song expresses the anger soldiers felt about those who hid behind politicians as well as the whole situation of going to war. For instance, the quote about not being a senator's son makes it clear that he's not excited in going to Vietnam. This song is directed at the spineless cowards who stayed behind politics as a means of avoiding combat duties. This is a strong message being sent to anyone who will listen because they, the young soldiers being sent to Vietnam, were unwilling participants who were asked to put their lives on the line by politicians in Washington. A powerful message was being sent by the soldiers to the public. But the politicians did not care, and pretty soon the boys realized the realization of war."

"This just happens to be my favorite Creedence Clearwater Revival song. The subject of draft dodging was a large one because there were a lot of very 'privileged' young men who were 'fortunate' enough to escape the perils of the Vietnam War. The 'privileged' had many ways of avoiding the draft. They might have had a family member or a friend of the family who had the political clout to get the person rejected. Others might have gone to college, fathered children, or obtained jobs in exempted occupations. Thus the lyrics by John Fogerty; 'it ain't me, I ain't no Senator's son.' He also included in the song 'I ain't no millionaire's son,' and 'I ain't no military son.' In my opinion, these men should be branded as cowards because that's exactly what they were. While these millions of 'privileged' young men successfully dodged their military service, it shifted the burden of fighting the war to 'underprivileged.' Thousands of middle class, minority, and poor young men were shipped off to the jungles of Vietnam, and there was nothing they could do about it. The song 'Fortunate Son' had to be one of the soldier's favorites because it was a song that all of them could probably adopt as their own."

"I'll be driving home from work at night listening to the radio, when all of a sudden the disc jockey will start to play 'Fortunate Son' by Creedence Clearwater Revival. For a moment I conjure up images of a helicopter flying low over rice paddies, full of apprehensive soldiers ready to be dropped to begin a patrol, with the gunner taking an occasional shot at what may come across his sights. Then, back to reality. 'Fortunate Son' is probably one of the classic Vietnam Era songs. It conveys a strong anti-war theme about avoiding a war that you didn't want to be involved in. Possibly dying for someone else's cause, for someone else's war. But ironically, John Fogerty himself came from an upper middle class family from Berkeley, California, and joined the Army National Guard to avoid going to Vietnam. Maybe in writing this song, Fogerty was trying to justify his own actions. But regardless, he wrote a very energetic, moving piece of music that is one of the banner songs of that era. Creedence Clearwater starts off the song by describing some people who are just naturally patriotic. These Americans seem like they couldn't wait to see action, and were ready to charge into battle, guns blazing, waving the Stars and Stripes. The lyrics of this song show disdain for these kind of people and Creedence seems to be saying, hey, I'm not terribly patriotic, I'm not the son of some wealthy politician or the upper crust of American society, and I'm sure as hell not going to fight their war for them! And this was the truth at the time. People for example like George W. Bush, whose father was a United States Congressman, became a jet jockey in the Texas Air National Guard. He flew F-105's and lived the high life in a bachelor pad, while thousands of African-Americans from lower income urban families were drafted to the front lines and gave their lives. Songs like 'Fortunate Son' are a symbol of how unfair life could be to different races and social classes during the Vietnam War. The disturbing message of Vietnam is now part of history through these songs. Sadly, today there are over 50,000 names needlessly etched into a beautiful black wall in our nation's capital, to remember those who gave their lives for our freedom. Many men-white, black, rich or poor-weren't 'fortunate sons,' but still fought bravely in Vietnam."

Beyond what it had to say about the inequities inherent in the draft, students found other viewpoints in the song valuable as well:

> "It spoke of the sad reality of how this country operated. If your family had money, and you wanted to go to college, you didn't have to serve time in the Armed Forces. This situation was not fair, that poor and middle class families were the staple of the military. I never thought money could be so powerful. How naive of me. It spoke of the sad reality of how this country operated. If your family had money."

> "I had not realized that 'Fortunate Son' by Creedence Clearwater (a favorite song of mine) had any relationship to the war. I was surprised after re-evaluating the lyrics that one of its major points was that the war was not particular about the men it chose to fight. My initial interpretation was that of a young man complaining about an unfair world, which favored the rich over the poor. I see now that perhaps the young man was upset about the rich man screwing up things, helping himself to whatever and leaving the poor man to clean up the mess. I still very much enjoy the song, but it has left a more somber impression on me."

> "This song obviously related to 18 and 24 year olds at the beginning of the war. The song bleeds into the uncertainty of young men's' futures, raising questions like: Will I be chosen? Am I going to die? Should I run from it all? Portrayed is a young man who is on the other side and doesn't have to worry because of his position in society. The rhythm of the song itself caught many listeners' ears. That is when they tune out the world and feel the music. An excellent song during an era of uncertainty."

> "A lot of the boys going to Vietnam had no choice but to go, and I believe this song expresses the anger soldiers felt about those who hid behind politicians as well as the whole situation of going to war. For instance, the quote about not

> being a senator's son makes it clear that he's not going to Vietnam. This song is directed at the spineless cowards who stayed behind politics as a means of avoiding combat duties. This is a strong message being sent to anyone who will listen, because they, the young soldiers being sent to Vietnam, were unwilling participants who were asked to put their lives on the line by politicians in Washington. But the politicians did not care, and pretty soon these boys were in the rice paddies of Southeast Asia."

One Vietnam veteran had a particularly critical reaction to "Fortunate Son" and singer John Fogerty:

> "This song presupposes that only the poor were sent to Vietnam to fight. The REAL facts do not substantiate this fallacy. The percentage of minorities involved in the Vietnam conflict (blacks primarily) was very similar to the percentage existing at that time in society. John Fogerty, in my opinion, was writing about people of his own class-the wealthy. As I vet, I consider them, those who evaded the draft, as cowards and spineless jellyfish. 'Fortunate Son' somehow glorifies these folks-disgusting!"

Although this student didn't mention "Fortunate Son" specifically, hearing it must have prompted these remarks:

> "In conclusion, I would like to restate the fact that many of these songs show the extent of the atrocity forced on the poor men of this great country to go and fight a rich man's war thousands of miles from their homes and loved one's. And die for this country they believed to be so great and right. Ha!"

It was no surprise to find that a majority of students chose to write about Barry McGuire's "Eve of Destruction." This writer was virtually transported back to the past:

> "School nights at home, the evening news from the front with Mike Wallace had me glued to the TV. 'The Eastern world, it is explodin', right there on national TV. The faces

> of the boys on those broadcasts were my age, 'not even old enough to vote, but old enough to kill.' There were riots close to where I lived. Hate in Red China and in Alabama. Seemed the whole world was in a riot. That 'human respect was disintegratin,' seemed true to me. I believed we were on 'The Eve of Destruction' and I sympathized with the singer's anger at the public for not listening."

> "In 1965, Barry McGuire released a song titled 'Eve of Destruction.' In this song, his anger, rage and total disgust at the violence and war brought to us by the 'establishment' is clear. His fear of the threat of nuclear war is also expressed, as in the growing tensions this nation felt due to the lack of civil rights for its minorities."

One student who found "Eve of Destruction" too critical and deserving of criticism itself:

> "To me this radical anti-war song pretty much summed up the protestors train of thought. It sounded confused, full of hate and almost suicidal. To me it seemed mostly blind hate, most of which you couldn't make heads or tails of. Although I don't see anything wrong with having your own opinion and not agreeing with the war, this song seemed too extreme."

"I-Feel-Like-I'm-Fixin'-to-Die Rag" drew the interest of a lot of students perhaps because of the contrast between the exuberant musical background and the ominous message it conveyed.

> "It was in 1965 that LBJ, then U.S. President, began to send massive numbers of troops to Vietnam. An artist named Country Joe McDonald was compelled to respond to this by writing and releasing a comical and "happy" tune called 'I-Feel-Like-I'm-Fixin'-to-Die Rag.' This song's subject matter was anything but happy or comical. Lines such as 'whoopee we're all gonna die' and 'be the first one on your block to have your son come home in a box' seem to deny the true seriousness of the war. On the contrary, it was an

artist's attempt to reach out to his audience in the best way possible. Many of the anti-war movement's followers were also part of the 'hippy movement' as well. The hippies were by and large a comical and ridiculous bunch. Their outlandish clothes and actions made them seem to be foolish, childish, and lacking in any respect for others. This may have been the case, but they understood Country Joe's message perfectly. It was from their ranks and the ranks of their peers (men from the ages of 18 - 25 or so) that the fodder for the ever-growing war effort would come, 'what are we fighting for, I don't give a damn, next stop is Vietnam.'"

"'I-Feel-Like-I'm-Fixin'-to-Die Rag' by Country Joe and the Fish was a piece of music I had not heard before. The chorus that went 'one two three, what are we fighting for, don't ask me, I don't give a damn, next stop is Vietnam, five six seven eight, open up the pearly gates, there ain't no time to wonder why, whoopee, we're all gonna die' was reality for an eighteen year old in the year 1965 when this song came out. At that time many Americans were gung ho about war. It was during the Cold War and everyone wanted to stop Red China and the spread of communism. In 1965, men were dying in Southeast Asia and back at home the public started to realize this was going to be a long war and many deaths were yet to come. If you were so unlucky as to get drafted and go to Vietnam, you knew death was a real possibility. This nightmare was a very scary thought for a man at any age."

"'I-Feel-Like-I'm-Fixin'-to-Die Rag' was a weird song, in that without the words, it's very happy sounding. Then you add the words and it's horribly sad. One line that really caught me was, '...Whoopee, we're all gonna die...' Was some people's mentality over there that they had been there so long that they didn't care or was it sarcasm? It probably could go either way."

"I was very thrown by the 'I-Feel-Like-I'm-Fixin'-to-Die

Rag.' Country Joe and the Fish took things to a new level, with lines like 'be the first one on your block to come home in a box.' The carnival like feel to the song was not only satirical and ironic, but also very spooky. This was definitely one of the more anti-war songs and they didn't care who got angry."

Many of the students chose the songs "For What It's Worth" as a song worthy of comment:

"This song took on an ominous tone in its message with its lines such as 'What a field day for the heat, a thousand people in the street.' The fear and distrust of the authorities by many people at this time becoming evident. Also, 'There's battle lines being drawn' and 'paranoia strikes... step out of line and they'll take you away' show the ever increasing amount of frustration and fear on the part of many young people at that time."

"One of the most important components of this song is its haunting melody. It weaves in and out hypnotically as it sets the tone for the lyrics. This sets it apart from other songs of the era which tended towards bluntness while driving home their point of view. The message is different also. It's not so much a statement about the rightness or wrongness of the war as it is a call for freedom of speech and dialogue. It doesn't scream 'we're right-you're wrong.' It just quietly states the facts as seen by Stephen Stills: 'Everybody look what's goin' down.' 'Young people speakin' their mind' and the line which best summarizes the feeling of the piece: 'Nobody's right, if everybody's wrong.' It's a call for compromise—an olive branch extended to the establishment in the middle of a turbulent decade, and I believe its still valid today."

"'For What It's Worth' by Buffalo Springfield expressed the confusion felt by many of America's young. The distrust between war protestors and the police are well expressed in this song. Listening to this song reminded me of the police riots which occurred in Chicago during the 1968

Democratic Convention. Armed police sprayed tear gas and used force against peaceful protestors upon the orders of Mayor Daley. I remember coming home from freshman camp at college and turning on the television. I couldn't believe what was happening in the park and on the streets of Chicago. It was incomprehensible to me to believe that the division between Americans had become that severe. From my black and white viewpoint, the police had stopped being our protectorate. They had become the enemy."

The passionate anti-war theme in "Cruel War" was not for everyone's tastes. One student was intensely vehement in his objections:

"The song that I consider to be the worst of the list would have to be the 'Cruel War.' This song does absolutely nothing for me. If she was really in love with the guy, she would wait for him. And, if she wanted to go and fight alongside him, then so be it. Besides which, love and war are remarkably similar. Again, even if she was in love, she should have been honored that her lover would answer his nation's call. Not shocked and saddened if he decided that he should burn his draft card and refuse to go. It should be considered a privilege to be able to do something so noble for your country as risking your life. She should be a little sad but mostly joyous that he did not shirk his responsibility to his country and to his fellow countrymen. I think that Peter, Paul and Mary should have been a little more supportive of the war in general. All of us should have the right to protest things we view as not being right, but some went too far."

A young woman took a different view:

"The real weepy songs of lovers being separated by war, such as 'The Cruel War,' definitely got to me. I teared up several times, and despite having a powerful message to bleeding hearts, and I can say that because I probably am one, these songs wouldn't make people sit up and question why we were there, they make you feel sorry for the fictional characters in the song. But it's hard to equate those feelings to real people unless you had lost your brother, father, lover or husband."

Students born long after the tumult of the Vietnam War period still got a sense of it when they heard songs like "Ohio:"

"One thing I realized when I listened to this music, especially the song 'Ohio,' is that the government was sending all of these young men over there to fight for freedom, which I do not really believe was the case, but they say when we go to war, we are fighting for our country and what our country stands for. One of those things our country takes pride in is our freedom, yet people were trying to speak out for what they believe in and they are shot by their own government for doing so. This gets me in a rage. Why would anybody want to fight a war for a country where the people could not even practice their constitutional rights."

"The phrase 'four dead in Ohio' refers to the massacre of four student protestors by the troops of the Ohio National Guard. They became martyrs for the anti-war movement. Anti-war rallies occurred in many U.S. cities as student protestors demanded that the government withdraw its forces from Vietnam. These protests by students were met with resistance from police and the National Guard. The resistance only made students more angry, so they started committing random acts of violence and terrorism. It was ironic because this was a representation of the same kind of guerilla warfare that was going on in Vietnam. The students were protesting against it, yet were committing these same acts on American soil. It was a time of domestic chaos in the United States.

"Sky Pilot" was one of those songs that lent itself to interpretation, beyond the obvious message about clergymen in the theatre of war:

"'Sky Pilot' by the Animals is about a military clergyman who is giving words to have courage by, to the boys headed out to battle, even though he believes it is wrong to kill and murder.

> 'He stays behind and he meditates, but it doesn't stop the bleeding and hate.' In high school 'meditate' was a slang word for smoking pot or shooting up. This song made me feel that the clergyman had to be 'high' on drugs to be able to disregard his values. 'How high can you fly (drugging) and never reach the sky (the truth - God)?' I never felt the song had anything to do with our boys that were pilots in Vietnam. My thoughts were about the wide spread drug problem in Vietnam and America. The drugs like marijuana and heroin have the effect of a false sense of security, no caring, and warping a person's judgment. I still like this song, but I liked it more when I also had a false sense of security and warped judgment."
>
> "'Sky Pilot' by the Animals is about a priest in Vietnam and that priests in Vietnam had a big dilemma on their hands. Many of the men going into combat were looking to the priest for a reason to justify the killing. Most of the men over there were people just like any other Americans and had a problem with justifying the killing. The problem was, neither could the priests."

This student found "San Francisco" pleasant to listen to but of little consequence otherwise:

> "This song told of swaying and peace and was very beautiful and melodic, but didn't convey a very strong message other than if you objected to the war, you should go party in San Francisco. I like the feel of this song, it didn't sound angry, but again, they didn't sound very strong either. If the quiet meditative feel could have been achieved without the drug-like aura around the song, I think society as a whole would have taken the songs more seriously."

The somewhat complex and widely misunderstood "Who Will Answer?" drew this negative response:

> "One song I didn't like was 'Who Will Answer?' The singer Ed Ames starts this song out by chanting the first four vers-

es. It almost seems as if he is trying to beat a world record by chanting the words as fast as he can. I could not make out any of the words he was chanting in the first part of the song. The only part of the song that was sang clearly was 'Who Will Answer?' which appeared at the end of all four verses. About halfway through the song the whole sound of the song changes. It's almost as if it becomes an entirely different song. I found it very hard to grasp the meaning of this song. Ames sings about marriage, suicide, a man being shot and the atmosphere of a hospital. I can see how these topics relate to the Vietnam era, but I didn't fully understand what was being said about all these topics. I can't remember if you ever told us if this was a hit song or not. I don't see how it could have been. I really did not like this song."

Dion's "Abraham, Martin and John" was a source of varying interpretations to students:

"To begin, the melody is so mellow with fantastic harmony. This song could be about famous people who died and could have made a difference. For example, John F. Kennedy and the things he did for this country. It could also be about a soldier's friends that died in the Vietnam War. The song might be a soldier's point of view. It was well written. The phrase where he is wondering what happened to his 'old friend John' may refer to the soldier's friend that died and not knowing what happened to him. When Dion sings about freeing people and how the 'good die young' it could mean that John Kennedy helped many people before he was assassinated at a relatively young age. Also, many Americans believed that had Kennedy lived, he would have gotten America out of the Vietnam War. This song really gave me the feeling of what American soldiers felt in combat. I feel that all of the soldiers were good people and fought their hardest."

"A wonderful song that symbolizes the era in the worst of times...filled with emptiness: It is about a nation longing for dead heroes. It is very symbolic how the writer connects two time periods of two slain presidents who in actuality have a lot in common. Abraham Lincoln, like John Kennedy, served during a time that the nation was divided by war and racial injustice. The correlation of the two times is amazing. Upon listening to this song, I can almost envision the three standing in the mist, on a hill on a foggy spring day. They are so close they are almost attainable to reach, but yet not quite within my grasp. Maybe what they stood for was just a vision and unattainable. What price did our nation pay for our dream, our vision of freedom...dead heroes?"

Pete Seeger's "Waist Deep in the Big Muddy" led to the following comments:

"It portrayed some of the problems with the war. The leader who kept telling his troops to 'push on' almost seemed like a metaphor for our war efforts. Our leaders got themselves in a war, but didn't seem to have a real plan on how to win the war. They did not have great knowledge on the conditions in Vietnam, yet they were giving orders to the soldiers in the field, and the soldiers were expected to carry out the orders, even though they may not have agreed with those orders."

"This song expresses the ignorance of the presidential administration of Lyndon Johnson. The song is about a captain who wants his men to cross a river that he crossed weeks earlier. The men think it is too deep but the big dummy says to push on. When the captain's head disappears under the water, the men turn around and head for shore. When I listened to this song it made me think that President Johnson was the captain leading the platoon into combat like it was WWII, but times had changed and so had the river for the captain. When Johnson's head goes under the water he realized that this is not WWII but by then it was too late."

"Seeger totally disapproves of Lyndon Johnson's actions in the Vietnam War. It is the story of a captain who leads his troops into quicksand, and the soldiers can barely escape. The captain doesn't make it though. If you put this into a real life situation, LBJ leads the U.S. troops into Vietnam, and they are in a battle they can't win. LBJ, who is the captain, doesn't make it out. Johnson stated he wouldn't accept another term as president of the U.S. Seeger uses the 'Big Muddy' as an analogy for Vietnam and calls the captain, Johnson, a 'big fool.' This criticism didn't sit well with the government, especially coming from Seeger, who had been blacklisted because he was a member of the Communist Party during the 1950s. I can see why this became such a popular protest song during the war."

An interesting view from a Vietnam veteran about "Home of the Brave:"

"While I was in Vietnam 'fighting for the freedom of the Vietnamese people,' my old high school (Arcata, CA), in all the wisdom of fascist thought, expelled several boys because their hair was too long. The school board had established a policy on hair length for boys. This would have been 1966. Several boys fought the issue and took the high school to the State of California Supreme Court - three times! There I sat in Vietnam reading the local paper from back home and wondering 'what are we fighting for?' We should be back in the states protecting high school students from the arbitrary authority of school boards and school administrators. Regardless of my fellow airmen's view on hair length or the war itself (at that point nearly all of us supported the war), they were all appalled that a school would even care about hair length. Those boys won the war but lost the immediate battle. Since they were expelled from school, they started college-never finished high school to the best of my knowledge-but finished college. Eventually the school relaxed their rules on hair. This whole issue was the beginning of my transformation into questioning authority, the war, the establishment, and what is the purpose of life! Hence every cloud has a silver lining-the bastards made me think!"

Footnotes:

1 Tony Palmer, *All You Need Is Love: The Story of Popular Music.* New York. Penguin Books, 1977. p. 199.

2 This song makes evident the limitations of a two or three minute song in providing genuine insights into understanding a historical event. It very effectively captures the mood of those who were opposed to the war and regarded the deaths of the students at Kent State as just another government atrocity. However, its highly biased message should not have been taken so seriously. It wasn't an evil political system that killed the students at Kent State, but it is more likely that the fatal shots were fired by nervous young National Guardsmen who probably deeply regretted what they had done. The difficulty of avoiding bias in writing about this controversial event of the Vietnam War is obvious in James A. Michener's *Kent State: What Happened and Why.* New York, Random House, 1971.

3 David Crosby and David Bender, *Stand and Be Counted: Making Music, Making History*. San Francisco: Harper San Francisco, 2000. p. 47.

4 Tim Morse, *Classic Rock Stories.* New York, St. Martin's Press, 1998. p. 137.

5 James M. McPherson, *Battle Cry of Freedom: The Civil War Era.* New York: Random House, 1988.

6 It is ironic that John Fogerty wound up serving in the Army reserves during the Vietnam War. Craig Werner and Dave Marsh, *Up Around the Bend: The Oral History of Creedence Clearwater Revival.* New York, Avon Books, 1998. p. 49.

7 Hank Bordowitz, B*ad Moon Rising: The Unofficial History of Creedence Clearwater Revival.* New York: Schrimer Trade Books, 2001. p. 81.

8 Werner and Marsh, p.125.

9 Bill Turque, biography of Al Gore, *Inventing Al Gore: A Biography.* New York, Houghton Mifflin, 2000.

10 Lewis Puller, Jr., *Fortunate Son: An Autobiography.* New York, Grove Weidenfeld, 1991.

11 George Donelson Moss, *Vietnam: An American Ordeal.* Englewood Cliffs, Prentice-Hall Inc. 1994. p. 243.

12 Richie Unterberger, *Turn, Turn, Turn: the 60s Folk-Rock Revolution.* San Francisco: Backbeat Books, 2002. p. 222.

13 Interview Brick Marunich February 2003.

14 Tom Wells, *The War Within: America's Battle Over Vietnam.* Berkeley, University of California Press, 1994. P. 68.

15 John Hellmann, *The Kennedy Obsession: The American Myth of JFK.* New York, Columbia University Press, 1997. pp.18 - 19 .

16 Ace Collins, *Disco Duck and Other Adventures in Novelty Music.* New York: Berkeley Boulevard Books, 1996. p. 1.

17 Interview with Tommy Cash, September 12, 2002.
18 Conversation with Albert Gore Sr., 3/88.
19 Steven Bach, *Marlene Dietrich: Life and Legend.* New York: William Morrow, 1984. p. 415 and 430.
20 "Eve of Destruction" enjoys the dubious distinction of being listed as one of "The Ten Worst Dylanesque Songwriting Ripoffs" in Jimmy Guterman and Owen O'Donnell's *The Worst Rock and Roll Records of all Time.* Citadel Press, 1991.
21 Interview with Barry McGuire. July 1, 2001. Duluth, Minnesota.
22 McGuire interview.
23 Todd Gitlin. *"The Sixties: Years of Hope, Days of Rage."* New York: Bantam Books, 1987. P.196.
24 McGuire interview.
25 Nancy Zaroulis and Gerald Sullivan *Who Spoke Up?: American Protest Against the War in Vietnam 1963 -1975,* Garden City, Double and Company Inc., 1984, p. 251.
26 Bob Spitz, *Dylan: A Biography.* New York: McGraw Hill, 1989. p. 393.
27 "The Cruel War" was originally released in 1964 and re-released in 1966. This suggests that Warner Bros. executives might have been reacting to the fact that the Vietnam War had now become such an overwhelming issue that the recording was more topical. Were they also assuming that the song's anti-war theme would play better with the record buying public in 1966?
28 Interview with Bill Belmont, 8/15/99.
29 Victor Lundberg was a California advertising executive. I have also heard that he worked at a radio station in Grand Rapids, Michigan. It is no surprise that he got in the last word in the debate on vinyl also. Long after the responses to his diatribe were no longer available even by special order, record shops could still obtain "Open Letter To My Teenage Son" for customers desiring a copy. *One Spot Popular EP's LP's Singles Guide.* Mt. Prospect, One Spot Publishers, August, 1969. p. T-156.
30 "Cash Box." November 18, 1967, p. 24.
31 Interview with Tim Neely, author of *The Goldmine Standard Catalog of American Records.* 1950 - 1975. Iola (WI), Krause Publications, 1998.
32 Interview with Harry Cottrell. 10/99
33 John O'Dowd, *Jody Miller: The Little Girl With The Big Voice.* Discoveries. July, 2002. p. 42.
34 Interview with Jody Miller, 10/01.
35 Denselow, Robin, *"When the Music's Over."* London: Faber & Faber 1989. p. 99.
36 Stephen Davis, *Old Gods Almost Dead" The Forty Year Odyssey of the Rolling Stones.* New York: Broadway Books, 2001. pp.164 and 231 - 232.
37 Denselow, *When the Music's Over*, p. 108.

38 Geoffrey Giuliano, *Rod Stewart: Vagabond Heart.* New York, Carroll and Graf Publishers, 1993. p. 95.

39 Dave Marsh, *The Heart of Rock and Soul: The 1001 Greatest Singles Ever Made."* New York: New American Library, 1989. pp. 421 - 422

40 Robert Jay Lifton, *Home from the War: Vietnam Veterans: Neither Victims Nor Executioners.* New York, Simon and Schuster. p. 229.

41 Linda Van Devanter and Christopher Morgan, *Home Before Morning: The Story of an Army Nurse in Vietnam.* New York, Beaufort Books, 1983. p. 112.

42 Sean Egan, *"The Animals' Story: Unfulfilled Expectations: Eric Burdon Tells the Story"* Discoveries. September, 2001. p. 35.

43 Spencer C. Tucker (Ed.) *The Encyclopedia of the Vietnam War. Vol. I.* Santa Barbara, ABC-CLIO Inc., 1998. p. 458.

44 Denselow, *When the Music's Over.*

45 Jerry Hopkins and Danny Sugerman, *No One Gets Out of Here Alive.* New York, Warner Books, 1980. p. 151.

46 Interview with Mark Berger, who was one of the sound editors for the movie *Apocalypse Now.* 8/99. He is now with the Saul Lentz Film Center in San Francisco.

47 Hopkins and Sugerman, *No One Gets Out of Here Alive.* p. 98.

48 Hopkins and Sugerman, *No One Gets Out of Here Alive.* p. 98.

49 Morse, *Classic Rock Stories.* p. 83.

50 The Guess Who was not alone. Sexist views were not at all uncommon in music recorded by '60s artists like Led Zeppelin, The Rolling Stones and Jimi Hendrix, to name a few. The most pathetic example was recorded by a girl group, the Crystals on Phillies Records in 1962 (#105) and titled "He Hit Me (And It Felt Like A Kiss.) It is no surprise that this "warped" recording (pun intended) was finally banned. See Simon Reynolds and Joy Press, *The Sex Revolts.* Cambridge: Harvard University Press, 1995.

51 Elise K. Kirk, *Music at the White House: A History of the American Spirit.* Chicago and Urbana, University of Illinois Press, 1986. p. 327.

52 Kirk, *Music at the White House.* p. 328.

53 McPherson, *Battle Cry of Freedom.* p. 52.

54 Belmont interview.

55 McPherson, *Battle Cry of Freedom.* p. 52.

56 Lifton. *Home From The War: Vietnam Veterans: Neither Victims Nor Executioners.* p. 254.

57 Stewart O'Nan, (Ed.) *The Vietnam Reader.* New York, Anchor Books, 1998. p. 526.

58 Robbie Woliver, *Bringing it all Back Home.* New York, Pantheon Books, 1986. p. 106.

59 James A. Michener *Kent State: What Happened There and Why,* p. 256. Quote about Madison Avenue.

60 McPherson, *Battle Cry of Freedom.* p. 243.
61 Howard Zinn, *A Peoples' History of the United States.* New York, Harper and Row, 1980.
62 Erwin Stambler, *The Encyclopedia of Pop, Rock and Soul.* p. 645.
63 Gloria Emerson, *Winners and Losers: Battles, Retreats, Gains, Losses and Ruins from the Vietnam War.* New York: W.W. Norton, 1976. p. 112.
64 Interview with Tom Brewer, author of *Searching for the Good: A Young Man's Journey to War and Back.*
65 Interview with Shelia Davis, 6/99.
66 "Billboard," 12/2/67
67 Collins, *Disco Duck.* p. 194.
68 David King Dunaway, *How Can I Keep From Singing.* New York: McGraw Hill, 1983. p. 263.
69 Interview with Peter Antell, 11/02.
70 Interview with Antell.
71 Wells, *War Within.* p. 262.
72 Wells, *War Within.* p. 286. In addition to the "leash," Humphrey had to endure physical punishment from Johnson. Sometimes when Johnson sent the vice president off on a mission or errand he literally kicked him in the shins. Humphrey said these kicks were often "hard" and rolled up his pants leg to show columnist Robert Allen the scars. Larry L. King, "LBJ and Vietnam," in *A Sense of History: The Best Writing From the Pages of American Heritage.* New York, American Heritage Press, 1985. p. 791. Walter Mondale also told me that he didn't think "Lyndon wanted Hubert to win that election." Conversation with Walter Mondale, 1985.
73 Mark Brend *American Troubadours: Groundbreaking Singer Songwriters of the '60s.* San Francisco: Backbeat Books, 2001. p. 85.
74 Jeff Bleiel, *Bobby Darin: On Record, Stage and Screen.* Ann Arbor: Popular Culture Ink. 1993. p. 115.
75 C.D.B. Bryan, *Friendly Fire.* New York: G. P. Putnam's Sons 1976.
76 Written by a Marine who was in the Persian Gulf War.

HERE'S WHAT HAPPENS TO BIG

...THEY BECOME

CASH IN NOW. PLACE YOUR ORDER

The Spokesman's "Dawn of Correction," an answer to "Eve of Destruction" was probably the most successful "answer song" of the Vietnam related recordings. This full-page ad in Billboard gave the group the promotion they needed. Billboard Magazine

HIT SINGLES ON DECCA

BIG HIT ALBUMS!

WITH YOUR DECCA BRANCH IMMEDIATELY

"Hello Vietnam" hit number one on the country charts in 1965 became known to another generation because of its inclusion in the soundtrack of the movie "Full Metal Jacket." Billboard Magazine

Chapter 3:
The Music of Patriotism

Those who opposed the Vietnam War became known as "doves" while those who supported it with patriotic fervor were called "hawks," and each of these schools of thought promoted their views in the popular music of the time. The fact that there was an abundance of pro-war songs should be emphasized since there are those who are under the mistaken impression that the anti-war position was virtually the only view that was heard through the medium of recorded music. A student, whose ignorance of the existence of another side to the musical debate about the war can be excused for obvious reasons, titled his essay about the Vietnam music "The Hawks Time Forgot:"

> "Had I not taken this class, I would have never known that the hawks even existed. I would have always assumed that it was just the flower children versus the government. I always assumed that the only opposition to the doves was the government. Now it is clear to me that our entire country was divided in two. I don't understand how this fact could have eluded me, but it changed my entire outlook on the war. I'm also inclined to think that most of the MTV generation shares my ignorance. Why? One theory I have is that the flower children became the primary archetype of the 1960s. I also feel that the message of the hawks died with the realization that Vietnam was a grave mistake. This realization led to the glorification of the hippies and caused the hawks and their viewpoint to be discredited and fade from public consciousness. Thus, it benefited my grasp of history to find out that the debate was two sided about whether the Vietnam War was right or wrong. Because I was exposed

to the music of the Vietnam era, specifically the pro-war era music, I have a much more enlightened view of an important part of American history."

Craig Werner, in his book about American music, *A Change is Gonna Come,* states that the anti-war faction dominated the musical discourse about the Vietnam War. He contends that "very few" singers recorded any patriotic, pro-war music like Barry Sadler's "Ballad of the Green Berets."[1] That Werner is understating the case will be made clear during this chapter. Actually, those who supported the war were far from silent musically, and there are many recordings, both well known and obscure, that propagated the "hawkish" philosophy. Many of these patriotic tunes came from south of the Mason-Dixon line. Even as public opinion began to turn against the war after the Tet Offensive in early 1968, one region of the country remained steadfast in its support, and that was the South with its distinctive brand of music, known variously as "hillbilly," "western," "country and western," or simply "country." As the anti-war music reached a crescendo of vehement outrage, Nashville, the capitol of country music, produced songs every bit as angry in response. Anyone who knows the history of the South does not find this turn of events at all surprising. Since the Civil War and Reconstruction, "Dixie" has always been a bellwether of patriotic fervor in time of war, and even as the situation in Vietnam reached its lowest point and support for the war began to fade, the South and its distinctive music remained solidly supportive. Long before Garth Brooks and others watered it down and thus broadened its base, country and western music, with its plainly expressed views about faded love affairs ("Billy Broke My Heart at Walgreens and I Cried all the way to Sears"), getting drunk ("Tonight the Bottle Let me Down"), and the virtues of a bucolic existence ("Tumbling Tumbleweeds"), usually sung in mournful fashion by someone with a reedy, twangy voice, attracted only a parochial and, what some thought, a dim-witted audience. But by the mid-1960s, when the Vietnam War became a critical issue, country music had begun to reach a wider audience with its almost unanimous pro-war message, thus making it an important part of the musical dialogue that debated the legitimacy of the war. This was in large part a reaction to the rising tide of dissent against the war. Until "agitators and hippies started stirring things up," country performers mostly refrained from putting political views in their music, thinking that their sole business should be entertainment, and that politics and music just didn't go together very well.[2] If a country song touched on anything political, it usually contained a sanguine view, as with Lawton William's "Everything's O.K. on the LBJ," released in 1964.

Buck Owens resplendent in gold lamé in 1965. Country performers often dressed in these gaudy costumes, which seemed to delight their fans. Others may have regarded this garb as foolish, reinforcing the notion that country music was hopelessly tacky and outside the mainstream. Source: Lee Andresen

One of the most vehement of the patriotic viewpoints is found in Merle Haggard's "The Fightin' Side of Me" (1969), which makes an issue out of protesting the war. Haggard, already a country music luminary with a huge following, rages against war protestors who he characterizes as "squirrelly guys who don't believe in fightin!" With what sounds like an old fashioned "standup" country bass thrumming militantly in the background, Haggard worries that if criticism of the war continues unabated, American democracy may be doomed. As "The Fightin' Side of Me" reaches a peak of outrage, he warns that he could easily come to blows with anyone who criticizes his America. Fighting words indeed! This intolerant view about dissent is reminiscent of the well-known "my country right or wrong, but always my country," which goes back to the simpler times of Stephen Decater and the War of 1812, another unnecessary and costly American war. In case anyone misses the point, toward the conclusion of his angry denunciation of those who oppose the Vietnam War, Haggard issues yet another bellicose warning: "If you don't love it, leave it, let this song that I'm singin' be a warning!" That music like this had any kind of an audience makes it clear that the period of the Vietnam War was, to quote Voltaire, a time when it was "dangerous to be right when the country was wrong." Another flaw in the reasoning behind this song is that it never does explain how suppressing freedom of speech will preserve freedom. If a majority of people were to have embraced this view, it could have brought the "coercive elimination of dissent" and "compulsory unification of opinion" that "achieves only the unanimity of the graveyard," to quote U.S. Supreme Court Justice Robert Jackson's eloquent admonition about an attempt to suppress freedom during World War II.[3] Unfortunately, equating criticism with subversion was an all-too-frequent government reaction during the war. Even during what were supposed to be the golden days of Kennedy's "Camelot," the government took a dim view of gainsaying about American efforts in Vietnam. In the early 1960s, any American correspondent stationed in Vietnam who dared to criticize the administration's policies there was likely to be denounced as a traitor. Journalists who offered even the most objectively constructive criticism were regarded as subversive by those who occupied the corridors of power in Washington. Presidents Johnson and Nixon were even more thin-skinned about dissent, as evidenced by Nixon's calling college students who protested the war "bums" and Johnson's references to critics of the war as "nervous nellies" and worse.

Country and western star Merle Haggard recorded several hits during Vietnam with an emphatic patriotic theme. He even recycled "Soldier's Last Letter," a hit during WW II and Korea, when the Vietnam War was raging in 1970.

It would seem these presidents wanted everyone to slavishly support whatever policies they decided to pursue in Vietnam, much like the students in "Muskogee, Oklahoma, USA," the setting for one of Haggard's biggest hits, "Okie from Muskogee." This tribute to political apathy and parochialism extols the virtues of a college campus where unbelievably docile student silent "majoritarians" would never think of criticizing any government policy. The passive behavior of the student body at Muskogee, who wear "manly footwear" like "leather boots" ("beads and Roman sandals won't be seen") and would never think of using drugs and revere the college dean, was a startling contrast to other college campuses that were overwhelmed by student demonstrations because of the war. The unbelievably straight student proles at Muskogee sound like they were snatched from the 1920s and transported to the 1960s, especially when they boast about their main recreation being "holding hands and pitching woo," a practice that last had any currency on college campuses when students wore raccoon coats and drove Stutz Bearcat automobiles and Notre Dame was still trying to "win one for the Gipper." The way these pallid conformists let off steam, by drinking a dubious concoction known as "White Lighting" also dates them. Those who have decided to further their education at Muskogee appear to be a smug and condescending lot, secure in the knowledge that their political parochialism makes them perfect citizens. However, it seems that they occupy a fantasy world. If a majority of Americans had behaved like this at other junctures in American history, it is highly probable that America would not be a democracy today. Haggard says that this song was done tongue in cheek, but he sounds dead serious in other songs he recorded about similar issues. "Okie From Muskogee" has been characterized as an "anti-liberal" song, and Haggard introduced it before an audience of NCO's at Fort Bragg, North Carolina, who received the song enthusiastically. Based on this favorable reception in a military setting, he was asked to endorse the presidential candidacy of superhawk Governor George Wallace of Alabama but refused.[4] He also sang it on "The Smothers Brothers Comedy Hour" to an audience that was far different from the one he regaled at Fort Bragg. The show was later canceled by CBS, largely because of the Smothers Brothers' tendency toward airing outspoken views opposing the Vietnam War. In Merle Haggard's most recent autobiography, *House of Memories,* he states that those who watched the program probably didn't know how to take "Okie From Muskogee" with its "pro-establishment, opposition to drugs and respect for the college dean."[5] Today, Haggard is a critic of the federal policy of "zero tolerance" toward illegal drugs[6] so his views have changed, but decades ago it is obvious he had little use for those who protested the war and their life style. It is no surprise "the Hag's" distinctly patriotic music played well in Vietnam, where the troops regarded it as "their kind of music,"[7] because they agreed with the message, especially the denunciation of war protestors in "The Fightin' Side of Me."

Another country singer, with the colorful moniker "Stonewall" Jackson, also professes the view that protesting the war is foreign to American political tradition as he makes painfully clear in "The Minute Men are Turning in their Graves," a lament that the early American heroes who fought British tyranny during the Revolutionary War can't rest in peace because they are bothered by such criticism. The upshot of Jackson's diatribe is that even great American icons like Jefferson and Washington are "shedding tears of shame" because of the untoward dissent about the Vietnam War. A strange argument, since there are some very significant parallels between the British in America and the United States in Vietnam. This is one of those songs that the more you listen to it, the more farfetched it becomes, especially the statement, "I fail to understand a man who won't defend his home." With these words, Jackson is clearly implying that war protestors are wrong for failing to recognize that the war in Vietnam is actually being fought to protect the American homeland. This, of course, is the all-too-familiar "domino theory," one of the flimsiest of the pro-war arguments, a notion that arose out of the hysteria of the Cold War. Jackson took the message that he delivered quite seriously and even named his band "The Minute Men."[8] Harry Griffith's "The Battle in Vietnam" also falls prey to the historical inaccuracy that the American cause in Vietnam can be compared to the wars it fought in the past by comparing GIs to their predecessors who fought against the British during the Revolutionary War. Griffith sees a link between Concord and Vietnam that simply doesn't stand up to historical fact when he expresses the view that those who die in the Southeast Asian conflict are dying for the same reasons that their fathers died, in defense of American freedom, when they came forward "to bravely take a stand."

A common thread that ties much of the pro-war music together is the idea that the United States is fighting for the freedom of those oppressed in South Vietnam against a communist system that is being forced upon them. Defenders of the war even argued that American national security was threatened. While it is unrealistic to expect deep insights into complicated issues from a two or three minute song, the notion that defending the repressive Diem government and the tin horn dictators that followed it was going to save the country from communists, who were actually riding the popular wave of Vietnamese nationalism, was ludicrous. The governments that the United States backed in Saigon were probably even more repressive than those that ran the country under the Chinese and French. Democracy was a concept that was nearly incomprehensible to the indigenous population in South Vietnam. Communism was more attractive to the peasants, who made up the vast majority of the population in Vietnam, because it was a philosophy and way of life espoused by their own people. Still, Nashville dutifully parroted the government rationale with songs like Johnny Wright's[9] "Hello Vietnam, which warns that communism must be kept from violating America's borders, as if somehow the fate of the United States is inextricably intertwined with that of South Vietnam and the other "dominoes" in Southeast Asia. The "domino theory" was a key component of United States foreign policy during the Cold War and government policy makers worried that:

> "If one country fell to communism, its neighbors were threatened with a chain reaction of communist takeovers. The domino theory arose from fear that the withdrawal of colonial powers from Southeast Asia would lead to the fall of Vietnam, then the rest of Southeast Asia, and perhaps India, the Philippines and Indonesia. Remembering the failure of appeasement before the Second World War, policy makers believed that unchecked aggression would eventually force a larger crisis, but firmness might deter aggressors.[10]

Midway through "Hello Vietnam," Wright, in an emotional recitation, shows himself to be a firm believer in the "domino theory" when he likens Vietnam to a "fire" that, if it isn't put out, will grow larger and eventually engulf America. The best thing that can be said in defense of the anti-communist theme of this song is that it was one of the earliest views set to music about the Vietnam War (1965), when the parallel with World War II didn't seem as strained and fighting communism still had some currency. At least one other performer thought the message worth repeating. Ray Hildebrand, who along with Paula (Jill Jackson) recorded "Hey Paula," one of the biggest hits of the early 1960s, also released a version of "Hello Vietnam." By 1965, Hildebrand, like many other pop recording artists, had apparently decided that country music would be the best way to further his career, the opportunities in the "pop" field having dried up.

Wright's version of "Hello Vietnam" was probably the high water mark of his recording career as the song reached number one on the country charts. Still, the venture into the music of patriotism allowed him to come out from under the shadow of his wife, country diva Kitty Wells. Wright attempted to follow up on the success of "Hello Vietnam" with "Keep the Flag Flyin'," another emotional patriotic effort about a brother who sees his sibling die from a sniper's bullet as the two are patrolling the perimeter of their base camp. The dying brother's last words provide the title of the song. Wright's third recording about Vietnam, "American Power," is the story of a man who finds it sadly ironic that a picture of a race riot is on the front page of the hometown newspaper the same day that the funeral of his neighbor's son, another combat casualty, takes place. "American Power" suggests that this recording is another highly patriotic message, arguing that American military technology and firepower will prevail in Vietnam. Actually, the lyrics provide a very sensible view, a plea for racial harmony, raising the persuasive argument that racial conflict can only harm the war effort. It is senseless for Americans to wage a war within a war by fighting with one another because the color of their skin is different.

The naiveté about communist aggression is continued in Dave Dudley's "What We're Fighting For," where a dreadfully homesick soldier feels that keeping communism from our shores makes his time in Vietnam well spent. This GI is so troubled by the fact that his mother's letters describe protests against the war that he urges her to "tell them what we're fighting for!" He also advises that she should let everyone know that those fighting the communists don't like the war but it is a job that needs to be done, possibly to rebut charges that soldiers in Vietnam were simply murderers who enjoyed the violence and killing. As with many other songs that contain this strong patriotic theme, the faulty analogy between Vietnam and other American wars is raised when Dudley issues a warning to remember the debacles at Pearl Harbor and in Korea. It sounds as though the singer is a firm believer that the United States could be the "final domino" as he intones, "Another flag must never fly above our nation's shores," and he once again pleads with his mother to set the anti-war protestors straight on what the true and noble purpose of the fighting is. The country singer employs an even harder edge against anti-war protestors in "Vietnam Blues,"[11] the chronicle of a soldier bound for Vietnam who is so appalled by a confrontation with demonstrators who are sending a "telegram of sympathy to Ho Chi Minh," the communist leader of North Vietnam, that he can't quite believe what he is hearing and becomes "downright sick." The soldier, who has orders for Vietnam, is shocked that the telegram is not going to the surviving family members of the men who have died in Vietnam. Even a visit to a bar "to pacify" his "brain" does little to soothe the frustration caused by the encounter and the song concludes with the GI exclaiming disgustedly, "I don't like dyin' either, but I ain't gonna crawl!"

Kris Kristofferson wrote this song at a difficult period in his life: "I was really going down the tube, flyin' like a maniac and volunteerin' for Vietnam. I was really disgusted with myself for not writin' or anythin'. I was looking for anythin' with the possibility of some meaning in it."[12] Kristofferson never did make it to Vietnam and instead was assigned to West Point to teach English Literature. "Vietnam Blues," his first hit, was written in the form of a letter to the editor. This modest success was followed by "two years of futile effort."[13]

Dudley evolved into one of the strongest supporters of the Vietnam War and recorded an entire album of patriotic songs entitled "There's a Star Spangled Banner Waving Somewhere," which was one of the most memorable tunes from World War II and was also recorded by country artist Elton Britt. In Hal Willis' "The Battle of Vietnam," the fight against communism is likened to a situation where "when the surgeon needs to operate he has to use the knife, to fight the evil thing (read communism) away in Vietnam!" The song also offers the warning that the United States almost waited too long to get into World War II and we couldn't make that mistake again or this time it could be fatal: "Now is the time to back up Uncle Sam before the flag of freedom is trampled in the mud!" The badly belabored point that Americans are mired in a dangerous state of lethargy about the war is continued with the words, "While over here we're safe and sound, away from bloody strife, our soldier boys in Vietnam are fighting for their lives!"

It's a well-known fact that the men who served in Vietnam were labeled as murderers and "baby killers" and were subjected to gratuitously cruel treatment when they returned home, but Nashville was kinder and gentler to the troops in its music, often conferring on them heroic status. Unlike other artists who merely sang about it, country legend Johnny Cash actually visited Vietnam and performed there to show his gratitude to the American armed forces, which was the inspiration for his "Singing In Vietnam Talking Blues." It came as no surprise that Cash traveled to Asia to entertain "our boys." In "Man in Black," he had already expressed his concerns about the young men who were dying in Vietnam and made it known that he would use the "bully pulpit" provided by his exalted status as a country music super star to sing out about the war and other issues he felt needed addressing. In "Singing in Vietnam Talking Blues," Cash reveals that he found out what war was like firsthand when he wound up in the middle of a mortar attack by the Viet Cong at Long Binh. He also discusses the experience in one of his autobiographies, *Man in Black:*

> "June and I went to bed early and were almost asleep when we heard the first shell explode. The mortar blasts, the shelling went on all night long. The rounds came in so close to Long Binh they shook our trailer. We slept very little with the terrible din going on so nearby. At daylight the shelling stopped."[14]

He was so shaken by the experience that he expressed the hope that if he ever returned there wouldn't be any American soldiers over there to entertain, that the war would be over. "Singing in Vietnam Talking Blues" may represent an epiphany about the war for Cash because in the late 1960s, he was telling concert audiences that the war and the president had to be supported because it was simply the patriotic thing to do.[15] By the time the song was recorded in 1972, Cash had obviously had his fill of the war, at least for a time.

When Johnny Cash, shown in concert in Minneapolis in 1966, declared himself to be "The Man in Black," he charged himself with the responsibility to speak out through his music on social and political issues that he felt needed addressing. Vietnam, of course, was one such issue, and he recorded a handful of songs about the war and related issues. At his concert that I attended in Houston in November of 1969, the country star spoke out in favor of the war. Source: Lee Andresen

Johnny Cash's role as an advocate for super-patriotism would continue after the war with a tribute to the ultimate symbol of patriotic fervor in "Ragged Old Flag." This is mostly a recitation of all the battles in American history that prove the flag is worth fighting for. His enthusiasm for patriotism is particularly spirited and even bellicose in "Song of the Patriot," released in 1980. Despite his reservations about the Vietnam War, Cash now sounds pretty enthusiastic about fighting for his country. To keep America free, he will even "die harder, if I have to!" No wonder that the copy of this record I own contains an interesting inscription on the label. The previous owner of this record, who obviously disagreed with the message in "Song of the Patriot," crossed out "Cash" and scribbled in "redneck," adding, "If I get drafted for the Persian Gulf, send him instead of me." I would not be at all surprised to see similar graffiti adorning other recordings like this. Throughout his career, Cash has been sensitive to this kind of criticism, "a lot of people think of country singers as right-wing, redneck bigots, but I don't think I'm like that."[16] However, songs like "Song of the Patriot" lend a semblance of truth to this very view. Other charges about some of his other recordings, characterizing them as "bogged down with narration and self-righteousness, making Cash sound like a history teacher," seem like nit picking.[17]

At least one country record touches on the fact that many families were split by disagreements about the war. The rift was usually between father and son, but in "The Ballad of Two Brothers," Autry Inman tells the story of two siblings, Bud and Tommy, who, at least in the beginning, have vastly different views about Vietnam. The ballad starts as Bud goes off to war while Tommy goes off to the university and becomes an anti-war activist and writes home only to brag about his participation in campus peace rallies and demand another check from Dad. However, when Bud is killed in action, Tommy suddenly comes to his senses, joins the army and, apparently overwhelmed with guilt, requests to be sent to Vietnam! Returning veterans also found families divided, as related in The Charlie Daniels Band's "Still in Saigon," where a victim of Post Traumatic Stress Syndrome not only has that illness to cope with, but a younger brother who thinks he is a murderer.

A Nashville connection can be detected in one of the gloomiest perspectives on the war era, Johnny Sea's "Day for Decision," a lengthy recitation that begins with the ominous declaration, "America is in real trouble!" Sea sounds very much like the alter ego of Barry McGuire in "Eve of Destruction" as he presents yet another apocalyptic view about the Vietnam War and its impact on the United States. There is a sneer in his voice as he sternly observes that America's real troubles are not in South Vietnam but right at home, where patriotism is declining and people just don't get very pumped up at seeing "Old Glory" anymore. In fact, too many people are guilty of showing disdain for the flag by "looking at their shoe laces" rather then staring reverently at the stars and stripes when the opportunity presents itself. Americans are just too caught up in conspicuous consumption and are putting materialism ahead of patriotism. Even worse, patriotism itself has "been condemned." Who has done the condemning remains unclear, but maybe it is the mysterious "they" on whom so many of these kinds of diatribes seem to cast blame. Those who don't believe that patriotic feeling is at a dangerously low ebb are advised to "go to a party and ask someone to sing 'America' and see what happens." "Day for Decision," set to stirring patriotic music, continues on by warning that the enemy knows how lax we've become and has decided to let us decay gradually from within rather than invading. Curiously, this bleak testimony to America's terminal decadence advises that GIs in South Vietnam don't believe in the "better dead than red philosophy." This notion just doesn't fit in with the rest of the recording's almost overwhelming tone of unremitting patriotic fervor. In most cases, music that had this kind of theme made it seem that anyone who wore a uniform was automatically convinced that communism was inherently evil and needed to be fought at all costs. "Day for Decision" concludes by offering a sort of patriotic litmus test that one can take: "Lift your eyes to the American flag and if you feel a little pride, thank God, you're still an American!"

Incidentally, these final lyrics are rather difficult to hear since they are competing with a vocal group that renders a particularly powerful version of one of the most memorable of all the songs about patriotism, "America the Beautiful." Almost lost amidst all the *sturm und drang* about love of country is the more subtle message of neo-isolationism, that America should tend to its domestic problems before it gives its attention to matters overseas, a view that is not uncommon in today's political debates. "Day for Decision," also takes a swipe at the high price of getting elected to political office, a problem that still plagues the political process. With typical record company hyperbole, Warner Bros. describes the album from which "Day for Decision" was culled as "Johnny Sea's Love Letter to America." The liner notes go on to state the extravagant claim that Sea's ideas are "The New American Credo." The reader is also advised that Sea couldn't wait to get back into the studio and record even more recitations of this philosophical bent. He was quoted as saying even though "Day for Decision" "said it all" he wasn't finished yet. The voluble Sea's vinyl sermon was not exactly short and sweet. It consumed some five minutes and thirty-nine seconds. The fact that radio stations played it is something of a surprise as many singles of this length never made it onto "top forty" formatted playlists because program managers worried about the short attention span of listeners losing valuable time that could be better devoted to commercials. How Sea (a.k.a. Johnny Seay) came to be selected to deliver this sobering commentary would be interesting to know. Only two years earlier, he was just another country music wannabe, one of many Johnny Cash "sound alikes" recording forgettable tunes like "My Old Faded Rose." It is odd to find him suddenly resurfacing, delivering such powerful social commentary. In any event, "Day for Decision" would be the high water mark of Sea's career, after which he quickly faded from the public consciousness. Just before he disappeared completely, he truly returned to his country roots, charting with a vintage effort called "Three Six Packs, Two Arms and a Juke Box." One of his songs, "Willie's Drunk and Nellie's Dyin'" again brought him and his subject national attention in a feature article in *Life Magazine:*

> "Willie York had served 10 years in prison for the killing of a law officer in 1944. Johnny heard that Willie was drunk and that Nellie was in a Nashville hospital undergoing her fourth cancer operation. Johnny went home and wrote 'Willie's Drunk and Nellie's Dyin',' and it was released as a single. David Snell, a former Executive Editor of *Life Magazine,* heard the single on KIKK Houston and bought two copies of the record. He and photographer Arthur Shatz came to Tennessee and did a piece on Willie York."[18]

Johnny Sea performing in Duluth, MN, in 1964. At this time he was but a marginally successful country and western singer. His most memorable achievement as an "entertainer" would come two years later with his recording of a lengthy and outspoken social criticism called "Day for Decision."
Source: Lee Andresen

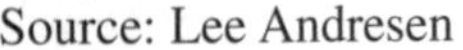

Some of the most intensely patriotic music came from Marty Robbins, one of country music's truly genius-caliber singers and songwriters who had already produced one of the greatest songs about any American war, "The Ballad of the Alamo." During the Vietnam War he released "Private Wilson White," a tribute to a soldier who dies in battle after herculean acts of heroism. To a background of bugles, Robbins announces that the nation has conferred heroic status on White, because he died while performing valorous deeds on the battlefield in South Vietnam. White is certainly deserving of accolades, for the private sustained no less than seven bullet wounds while saving the lives of eighteen or nineteen of his comrades before finally succumbing to withering enemy fire. The instrumental background, like other Nashville-generated war music, is replete with stirring bugle calls, and it is difficult to listen to without at least a twinge of emotion. A soldier who performed as valorously as White would almost certainly have been awarded America's highest battlefield decoration, the Congressional Medal of Honor. "Private Wilson White" doesn't reveal whether he was so honored. If, in fact, he did receive the medal, it would have been awarded posthumously.

Rick Robert's and Skip Ballard's "Congressional Medal of Honor" tells the story of a soldier who earned the medal by giving his own life to save those of his fellow soldiers. At the same time that the official hands the medal, in its little black box, to the hero's mother, he relates how her son came to earn it, by keeping his comrades covered with his M-16 while his comrades safely retreated. These ballads that herald exploits above and beyond the call of duty are reminiscent of similar tributes about heroic exploits in earlier wars, where it seemed no one really died in vain, as long as the cause was a noble one like God and country. It is also a perpetuation of the not-uncommon view that war is glorious and dying in battle is the most magnificent way to be wrested from the mortal coil.

As the Vietnam War wore on, though, and casualties mounted, there were even those in Nashville who took the view that maybe this war wasn't a cause worth dying for. In 1969, Tom T. Hall's lugubrious "Strawberry Farms" (1969) mentions a boy named

Bobby, whose brother died in the war but seems unable to understand why. Hall, who wrote the vigorously patriotic "Hello Vietnam" (1965), perhaps had begun to have second thoughts about the war and its objectives. Many might regard the content of this highly patriotic music with smug condescension, but for those who recorded it, the sentiments were heartfelt, if sometimes overstated. A case in point is Robbins, one of the most politically oriented of country artists and the most conservative of a very conservative Nashville country music establishment. He campaigned vigorously for archconservative Barry Goldwater against Lyndon Johnson in the presidential campaign of 1964. Two of his most strongly patriotic songs, "Ain't I Right" and "My Native Land" were considered so chauvinistic in attacking communism and war protestors that Columbia Records executives feared a backlash and refused to release them. However, Bobby Sykes, a member of Robbins' band, recorded the songs on the Sims label under the name "Johnny Freedom." He sounded so much like his mentor that those who heard the songs thought that it was Robbins singing.[19] If the rumors about the attempts to suppress anti-war music are true, then the nervousness of Columbia about Robbins' patriotic music is an interesting exception.

Legendary songwriter and performer Marty Robbins. Many of his songs were outspokenly patriotic, and his song about the Vietnam War, "Private Wilson White," is faithful to this view. Source: Lee Andresen

Another paean to patriotism that may seem hopelessly maudlin by contemporary standards is Hank Snow's "A Letter From Vietnam (to Mother)" about a soldier who is trying to cope with the death of a friend in combat, an experience that, understandably, has left the GI emotionally scarred. The sense of loss he feels is an example of how friendships forged in the heat of battle bring a closeness between men that is almost symbiotic. The song begins with the ever mournful taps as the letter writer relates the loss of his comrade in graphic fashion, describing how "his chest was blown away." The process of communicating with his mother about his grief eases the pain somewhat; as does the knowledge that the life was not lost in vain, because he died for "you (Mother), my sweetheart, and Uncle Sam." Snow also sings reverently about the flag, always an important ingredient in music of this kind.

"A Letter from Vietnam" is yet another example of a war song that, with a slight change in the words, could be applied to earlier American conflicts where old fashioned patriotism was reason enough to risk one's life on the battlefield. Ernest Tubb, who recorded songs like "Missing in Action" and "A Heartsick Soldier on Heartbreak Ridge" about World War II and Korea, expresses fundamental patriotic values in his "It's for God, and Country, and You Mom (That's Why I'm Fighting in Vietnam)." Tubb sings about a soldier whose eyes glisten with tears as he writes a letter to his mother about how much he misses the "good old U.S.A." He recounts holding the "crimson hand" of a dying comrade whose last wish is that "America" be sung again. As the tropical night descends, the soldier is forced to end his letter but looks forward to the morning when he will see Old Glory waving and know that the same flag is protecting his mother as well as his sweetheart back home. These intensely patriotic soldiers share a common bond with their brothers in arms portrayed in much of the country music about the war. They are all obedient without the slightest inclination to question or reason why they are told to do what they are doing. They suffered from being away from home and family but still had unswerving faith in what they believed were the truly noble objectives of the war. Much like Tennyson's "Light Brigade," their role was not to question or reason about their circumstances but to serve and die, if die they must. That Nashville exaggerated the patriotic fervor of soldiers in Vietnam is obvious. These songs would have been an accurate description of the mood of American fighting men in the Civil War or World War II as Stephen Ambrose writes in Citizen Soldiers:

> ".Cause and country were as critical to the GIs as to the Civil War soldiers. The differences between them were not of feeling, but of expression. Civil War soldiers were accustomed to using words like duty, honor, cause and country. The GIs didn't like to talk about country and flag and were embarrassed by patriotic bombast. They were all American boys...The GIs believed in their cause. They knew they were fighting for decency and democracy and they were proud of it and motivated by it.[20]

Such an attitude of selfless patriotism was not the consensus of soldiers in Vietnam. How the troops serving there regarded their role in the war was a much more complicated business. As Christian G. Appy points out in *Working Class War: American Combat Soldiers in Vietnam:*

> "Though many Americans arrived in Vietnam believing they were there to stop the spread of communism and to advance the cause of democracy, the actual nature of the war so fundamentally undermined these explanations that most American troops did not find in them a meaningful sense of purpose or legitimacy.... Most enlisted men found the war itself to be without point or purpose. Those who generally accepted America's right to intervene in Vietnam were most disturbed by the absence of meaningful measurements of military success, a clear definition of victory. Those who questioned the legitimacy of American involvement focused more on the senselessness and futility of even trying to fight in Vietnam. They doubted that America could ever win, or they believed the only victory likely to come from American policy would require too much destruction to justify the effort."[21]

This attitude became increasingly prevalent by the early 1970s, as less enthusiastic GIs, primarily draftees, including some who chose conscription over jail, would go to Vietnam, a situation that Bruce Springsteen sings about in "Born in the USA." According to Appy, "a useful historical division can be made between those who fought before the Tet Offensive of 1968 and those who served in the years after Tet. Most American troops would come to concur with the phrase that became the most important GI slogan about the war: "It don't mean nothin.'"[22] When these disenchanted warriors returned home they joined the ranks of the Vietnam Veterans Against the War and became a vocal part of the anti-war movement. For them, songs like Johnny Wright's "Keep the Flag Flying," ohnny Sea's "Day of Decision" and Johnny Cash's "Ira Hayes" meant little. The almost reflexive obedience to superior orders and the power of the flag to stir men to valorous deeds on the battlefield had diminished. Still, there were those involved in some of the hardest fighting in Vietnam who were true patriots and maintained reverence for the Stars and Stripes. In January of 1968, Brad Bennent, was a mortar forward observer assigned to the First Battalion of the Fourth Division Marines. He was assigned to travel up Highway One to Hue from Phu Bai where some of the most desperate fighting of the Tet Offensive was taking place. When he and his fellow leathernecks reached the city of Hue, which is surrounded by the Perfume River, the intensity of enemy resistance kept them from crossing the bridge to their objective for two days. Another six days was required to move four blocks from the Treasury Building across an open field to a facility known as the Citadel. During this time, most of it house-to-house fighting, they could see the North Vietnamese flag flying above the Citadel. The South Vietnamese banner had been removed when they were overwhelmed by the NVA. Once the marines took the building, they took down the flag and the Staff Sergeant brought out the American flag and said: "Its time." However, when headquarters was informed the American flag was flying proudly over the Citadel, the marines were ordered to replace it with the SVN colors. The response was, "Why don't you send someone up here to take it down!" The American flag flew over the Citadel until the marines finally left and handed it over to the SVN Army.[23]

The Citadel at Hue Source: Heyward Macdonald

A frequent theme of the patriotic music involves sons overseas missing their mothers and mothers, in turn, missing sons. While most mothers had to content themselves with letters and the occasional phone call, one mother took the rather unusual step of recording a birthday message to her son serving in Vietnam. Mrs. Dorothy Gorman's "Happy Birthday Son" comes complete with a picture sleeve showing Mrs. Gorman writing a letter to her boy, whose photograph (in uniform) sits beside her on a desktop. The reverse side of the sleeve conveys an interesting message:

> "Dorothy Gorman, as an American mother, sent her son to Vietnam in June. Her message, on this record, is for his birthday. He will be 21 on December 18. Vietnam is a curious place for a man to be when he becomes of voting age...or maybe it is a fitting place...Dorothy Gorman knows and says, that 'There are wars that must be fought and our sons must go to fight them.'"

This is easily one of the most interesting of the vinyl artifacts that I acquired in researching this book. One can only wonder what her expense was, for Mrs. Gorman's recording wasn't done on a tape or in a "recording booth" at a shopping center. Her message was produced on a 45-rpm disc by Tower records, which was one of the major record labels of the 1960s. One wonders how she was able to pay for the recording sessions; such studio time was not inexpensive, and one can only speculate about whether she was independently wealthy or perhaps mortgaged the farm. It is possible that Tower Records, as a public relations gesture, donated the studio time as well as the manufacturing costs of the record. I have only seen a promotional copy of "Happy Birthday Son," the kind sent strictly to radio stations, so in all probability this record never received enough airplay to justify a commercial release. Despite repeated efforts to track down the origins of "Happy Birthday Son," how it came to be remains shrouded in mystery. Whoever the professionals were that assisted Mrs. Gorman with her tribute to her son, they probably had few illusions that it would be a "hit." Unlike other recordings released during the Vietnam War, it was intended for an audience of one, and if PFC Gorman heard it in Vietnam and felt closer to home and his mother, at least momentarily, the recording served its purpose.

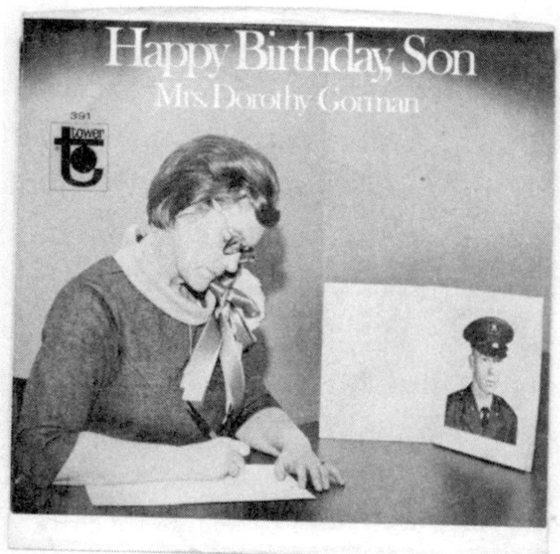

"Happy Birthday Son," Dorothy Gorman picture sleeve.

Hopefully, PFC Gorman returned safely from Vietnam[24] and Mrs. Gorman was spared the grief that was suffered by country singer Jan Howard, whose son was killed in Vietnam. She also recorded a message for her son, which was sent to him overseas. The song, "My Son," was based on a letter she had sent to her boy, Jimmy, telling him about how she was praying that he would come home safely to her. The letter was also full of reminiscences about the happy moments of his childhood, worrying about whether he would make the baseball team and get a letter jacket like the rest of the boys and fishing trips with his dad. Howard goes on to marvel about how fast Jimmy has grown up, that it seems like only yesterday that he was striding across the stage to receive his high school diploma, then the inevitable summons to serve his country, and now, he is halfway across the world. The letter ends on an optimistic note, as she expresses confidence that he will be home safely. Howard was supposed to have psychic powers, and it has been said that she dreamed of his death in Vietnam. Unfortunately, this dream came true and he was killed in combat. Howard was urged to make a song out of her letter to Jimmy and it became a hit. She went on to record an entire album dedicated to his memory. It also contains a song taken from another letter, written by her son Corky, who was serving in Vietnam at the same time his brother was killed. Despite Jimmy's death, Corky still shows unswerving love of his country and states emphatically that he is proud to be an American.[25] When Howard is asked how many children she has, she still states that she has three sons, so Jimmy lives on in his mother's heart.[26]

Another country artist, Bonnie Guitar, recorded a ballad, "The Tallest Tree," about a mother who lost a son in each of three different wars-World War II, Korea, and Vietnam. Each of them is likened to a tree, making up a kind of protective familial forest. As these "trees fall" and are killed in battle, the next son, whether it be John, Joe or Bill, then becomes her "tallest tree." This is undeniably a sad song, but the grieving mother seems to be fatalistic about her loss, accepting the fact that her sons were called to fight for their country. There is no overt sense of outrage, even when her youngest son is taken from her by the Vietnam War. The heroine of "The Tallest Tree" is remarkable for having borne three male children far enough apart in age to have fought, and sadly die, in three different wars that took place over a period of more than thirty years.

Maternal laments were a frequent theme of recordings about the war. Yet another is Carmen Carroll's "A Soldier" where a mother worries that her son will grow up to be like his father who fought in World War II and Korea. She has had to raise the son alone, what with her husband fulfilling his patriotic duty, and she senses that her boy will follow in his dad's footstep, as he will come to love his country as soldiers should. One of the most popular female performers in the history of country music, Loretta Lynn, also lent her voice to a song describing a woman's pain at losing a loved one to war in "Dear Uncle Sam." Lynn sings about a young woman who tries to reconcile her loyalty to her country with the fact that she is desperately worried that her man has been sent to Vietnam. In a dialogue with Uncle Sam, she grudgingly admits that there may be a need for the one she loves to be there but also comments that she may just need him more. All of this becomes moot when, with the ever-mournful taps being blown in the background, she receives the dreaded telegram from Uncle Sam announcing that her husband has been killed in combat. A song like this begs the question of just how many of those who lost loved ones in Vietnam remained faithful patriots, especially when it became widely known that the motives behind the war were less than noble and defeat was inevitable. Lynn actually was opposed to the Vietnam War:

> "I wasn't for Vietnam. When I told that to the hippie newspaper in Atlanta, *The Great Speckled Bird,* all my people got nervous. Both my sons were in the service in Asia, and they said there was dope and everything. It was a big waste."[27]

Those, like Mrs. Gorman, who had a loved one serving in Vietnam obviously never let them stray very far from their thoughts, although security considerations and the snafus common to the military bureaucracy made it difficult to know when they were in harm's way. This was America's first televised war, but watching the network coverage about the strategic course of the war was a very difficult way to obtain meaningful information about the unit a family member was attached to. In a way, their ignorance of the vicissitudes of a combat soldier's life in Vietnam was akin to that of those people depicted in Carl Sandburg's poem about World War I, "Buttons." These earlier Americans also yearned to know about the destiny of a family member but were limited to newspapers and sometimes a map of the battlefield erected outside the newspaper office. When news became available from the trenches of Europe, a boy would come out of the office and move buttons on the map to indicate the flow of the battle. Moving these buttons an inch or two to the right or left was an easy business, but those observing would never be able to appreciate what agonies were sustained on the battlefield in order to change the position of those buttons back home. Letters could fill this void, but only temporarily, and were received long after they were actually written. In some cases, families would get letters after they had been informed officially that their soldier had died in combat. Those who waited at home had their periods of agonizing dread but still had the pluck to continue with their day-to-day routine. "Roll Call" by Johnny Cash is insightful for describing one such person: "To Annabelle in Memphis, it was just another day, but her soldier boy and his buddies had died in a land so far away." "Annabelle," like so many others, couldn't realize that in a particular instant, far away events had changed her life forever.

Even pre-adolescent children recount their sadness at separation in war time on record as with Joey Martin in "Joey's Letter" who is unbearably sad that his big brother "Mike" needs to be in Vietnam. This little boy, of indeterminate age, recites his pride in his brother and expresses fears for his well being in a rather irritating, reedy lisping voice. There were lots of little brothers who saw older siblings they revered go off to war, but this reading does them a disservice. "Joey's Letter" is simply insipid, Joey is a caricature of himself, and the opportunity to send a serious, thoughtful message is badly bungled. It is the stuff of "Dr. Demento."

Pat Boone, whose white buck shoes and banal ballads enthralled middle America during the 1950s, is on the same page with his country counterparts in "Wish You Were Here Buddy," a fast paced effort in which he condemns war protestors as well as the then-Cassius Clay for avoiding the draft. The soldier in this song is angry that his "buddy" is back home enjoying himself while he is living in the jungle and dodging bullets. Toward the end of the song he offers the dubious invitation, "Come on over here and I'll introduce you to the Vietcong." What really incenses Boone is that not only is the man he calls sarcastically "buddy" safe at home, he is also engaging in campus anti-war rallies. Many soldiers serving in

Vietnam felt the same way, and some close friendships probably ended. Boone, who has been active in Republican politics, also recorded the patriotic "MIA/POW in 1971. When you consider this singer's political background, it is no surprise that he chose recording these kinds of patriotic viewpoints about the war. But why, then, did he release the distinctly anti-war "What If They Gave a War and Nobody Came?" in 1967?

The common man's feelings about the war are given some attention in John Wesley Ryles' "Kay," which became a hit in 1968 largely because record buyers empathized with the story of a down-and-out cab driver whose wife has abandoned him for a career in country music. Perhaps some also empathized with the cabby's nocturnal adventures that included delivering babies and punching out drunken fares that make lewd remarks about his fickle spouse. The song belongs in this book because among the people who cab around Nashville in the wee hours of the morning are soldiers from Fort Campbell, Kentucky, who tell the taxi driver how much they detest the war in Vietnam. Whether these GIs are "returnees" or on their way to Asia isn't stated, but they clearly have become opponents of the war for one reason or another. "Kay" was released in the summer of 1968, when support for the war was dwindling even within the ranks of the American military, particularly among those who had to do the scut work of fighting it.

Of the pro-war music that was non-Nashville in origin, one of the more memorable examples is Everett McKinley Dirksen's "Gallant Men," a recording that came directly from Washington, DC, intoned by a man who provided Lyndon Johnson with much-appreciated bi-partisan support for the war effort. In this highly patriotic reading, Dirksen expresses strong support for the war as well as the military conducting it. The well-known Republican U.S. Senator from Illinois intones a recitation about the bravery and heroism of "gallant men"[28] who came to America's aid throughout history, saving the country from an ugly fate at the hands of various tyrants. According to this recitation, Vietnam is the same kind of war where modern-day versions of these heroes should once again answer their country's call. Dirksen went into the recording studio because he was deeply offended at the rising tide of opposition to the war and the characterization of those who supported it as misguided patriots: "I feel it is an answer to the beatniks, draft-card burners, and those who are opposed to our efforts in Vietnam." Dirksen possessed one of the most distinctive speaking voices in the history of American politics, and his sepulchral tones give "Gallant Men" a unique dignity and enhanced its impact immeasurably. A reviewer likened the Illinois Republican's voice to "rich plum jam" and said that Dirksen's "overwhelming sincerity" atoned for the record's banal message.[29] "Gallant Men" is "musical" proselytizing of the highest order and would have gone over well as a speech on the floor of the U.S. Senate. Dirksen's recording efforts would make him the first United States Senator to win a Grammy. Particularly with the benefit of considerable hindsight, though, it is hard to see a parallel between Vietnam and other American wars where gallantry was truly needed to protect our national security. The senator's contribution to the musical dialogue during Vietnam unwittingly exposes a recurrent fallacy in the pro-war arguments: the tendency to view this war in the context of World War II, when actually they were two quite different conflicts. One of the reasons why the Vietnam War was lost is that too many key decision-makers in Washington, DC, made the same faulty comparison with disastrous results. Dirksen's unctuous vocal style invited mimicry by comedians of the day and "Senator Everett McKinley" would release a version of the Trogg's "Wild Thing" on Parkway records in 1967.[30]

Billy Carr's "What's Come Over This World" also makes the dubious case for Vietnam being like other American wars as it trots out the old argument that true patriots must rally to the cause just as they did in World War II and Korea. It also accuses those who are protesting Vietnam as "dimming liberty's light" when "they talk about freedom." Those who carry signs and burn their draft cards are behaving selfishly and would be well advised to follow the famous words of John F. Kennedy's inaugural speech, "Ask not what your country can do for you, but what you can do for your country!" The fact that they have chosen to ignore this appeal by damning what their country is doing in Vietnam and burning their draft cards is somehow tarnishing the memory of JFK who is portrayed as a martyr for freedom. This raises yet another spurious theory about what happened in Dallas in November of 1963, that Oswald's motive was anger over the Kennedy administration's policies in Vietnam. If you don't support the war in Vietnam you are against the principles the slain president "died for," and this is equivalent to desecrating the flag." Carr's "anti-war protest" harangue also takes a shot at the protest music, and Jody Miller's "Home of the Brave" in particular, when he intones, "some rock and roll singer is knockin' the home of the brave."

"What's Come Over This World" was penned by two of the premier songwriters of the day, Howard Greenfield and Jack Keller. They brought this tune to Carr, then in his late teens, and convinced him it would be a number one hit. Colpix records released the disc with a lot of patriotic hoopla including a full-page ad in *Billboard Magazine* featuring the Statue of Liberty. Although the song went to the number one position in markets like Buffalo and Boston, it failed to generate much enthusiasm anywhere else. Carr admitted that he recorded the song without a real sense of the lyrics and was surprised when concert audiences reacted with boos when he sang it. What venues he performed it in is unknown, but very possibly those who heard it and reacted with derision reflected an emerging disenchantment with the war and didn't like the fact that "What's Come Over This World" criticized those who protested the war. Carr certainly can't be faulted for failing to "sell" the song as he delivers "What's Come Over This World" with all the fervor of Barry McGuire's "Eve of Destruction." In fact, Carr sounds a lot like McGuire. Greenfield and Keller were part of the prolific songwriting stable at the Brill Building in New York City, which seemed uncannily attuned to American musical tastes. Before "What's Come Over This World," the Brill hit factory had made its mark with tunes about teenage romance and eschewed social commentary. Perhaps the fact that a pair of its best tunesmiths had crafted this message song about Vietnam meant that this modern day "Tin Pan Alley" had begun to appreciate that the war was an issue that needed to be addressed and also looked to make more money in the process.[31]

Billy (Jamie) Carr recorded "What's Come Over This World," which is best described as an anti-"war protest" song.

Probably the most well-known song of patriotism to come out of the entire Vietnam War was SSgt. Barry Sadler's "Ballad of the Green Berets." Not only did it become a number one hit on the billboard charts in 1965, it was written and recorded by an actual participant in the war, a member of the elite special forces to which his composition pays tribute. "The Ballad of the Green Berets" describes those who qualify to wear the beret as almost superhuman and how difficult it is to join their ranks: "One hundred men will test today, but only three win the Green Beret!" Sadler, whose picture can be seen on the picture sleeves and album cover as well as the cover of Robin Moore's book The Green Berets, looks like he came out of central casting just to fill this role. However, the hero portrayed in the song shows he is only human and dies in combat. Before his untimely demise, he expresses the hope that someday his son would wear "silver wings upon his chest." Shortly after its release, radio station WEBC in Duluth refused to play the record because station management thought it would remind listeners of other elite military units like the German SS. Whether such censorship was attempted elsewhere across the country is unknown, but the song was so successful that Sadler recorded an entire album of similar music and produced another hit single called "The A Team."

RCA Victor would make the grandiose claim that "Ballad of the Green Berets" was the "national theme song" for the Vietnam War. How those who fought in the war felt about the song is difficult to know for sure, but one veteran who did three tours with the 101st Airborne told me, somewhat ruefully, "I joined the army because of that damn song!"[32] Like many other idealistic young men of his generation, Boyd Dallos was moved when he first heard Sadler's tribute to the elite unit and began fantisizing about what it would actually be like to become one of these "soldiers from the skies:"

> "I imagined what it would be like to come home on leave and drive around in a red convertible, resplendent in my uniform and capture the admiration of attractive women. I remember so clearly sitting in history classes in high school where I learned about Pearl Harbor and World War II, and wishing we could have a war like that. I used to watch the television series "Combat" where Vic Morrow and Rick Jason shrugged off flesh wounds and thought I can do that! I can be a Green Beret and prove my manhood. I was even influenced by a friend of mine. When he returned home after serving as a Green Beret in Vietnam, he said I should go to Vietnam because it was a good place to buy inexpensive, state of the art stereo equipment."[33]

Listening to radio, Green Beret Boyd Dallos heard a lot of music as he worked in his darkroom at Pleiku. Source: Boyd Dallos

Dallos found the mystique of the Green Berets so compelling that he became one and volunteered to go to Vietnam. Once he had spent some time at Plei Ku in the Central Highlands attached to the Evac Hospital, his expectations of glory and romance evaporated:

> "One night we had no less than 53 casualties brought in and when my shift was over I went to the NCO club and got drunk on scotch and water. When I reported for my next shift, the physician in charge told me I was in no condition to work and dismissed me, warning that I better not do it again."[34]

Eventually, Dallos found relief from the stress of war by smoking marijuana and listening to music:

> "I was hanging around with a different crowd then who listened to the Doors, Rotary Connection, Janis Joplin, Jimmi Hendrix, Deep Purple, and Buffalo Springfield and others. They were a big deal over there. Prior to this, my musical tastes had run to Frank Sinatra and Broadway musicals like 'Man of LaMancha.' I spent a lot of time at the neighboring air base that had a building housing a library of tapes of music. I spent many hours sitting in a listening cubicle where I listened to and taped a lot of songs for my own collection. Needless to say, "The Ballad of the Green Berets" no longer had much appeal for me."[35]

The other Green Berets that I interviewed were also less than enthusiastic about Sadler's musical tribute to their exploits, feeling that it was too vainglorious a song to accurately describe the mood of a group of men who were actually quite modest about what they did.[36] One even suggested that the injury that landed Sadler in the Eighth Army Hospital at Na Trang in July of 1965 was sustained in a drunken fall from a jeep.[37] Dr. Mike Mittelman, the physician who treated Sadler, said the singer soldier was like a breath of fresh air in the usually depressing hospital setting as he kept everyone's spirits up by singing and playing his music even while he was confined to a bed and connected to medical equipment. "Ballad of the Green

Berets" had recently crested on the popular music charts but Mittelman was only vaguely aware his patient was a celebrity.[38]

Another soldier who gained celebrity while in Vietnam was Archie Bell who enjoyed the distinction of having a number one hit on the charts at the same time he was recovering from a war wound. As he lay in a military hospital in Germany his recording of "Tighten up," (along with the Drells) shot up the charts. Bell was one of the few hitmakers to see combat in Vietnam. Ironically, Vietnam inspired "Tighten Up" and also proved fatal to Archie Bell and the Drells' career. Bell had to serve out his stint in the army and by the time he was able to satisfy his military obligation, the momentum provided by the song had evaporated. Bell also recorded "A Soldier's Prayer" which is directly related to the war, but never charted.[39]

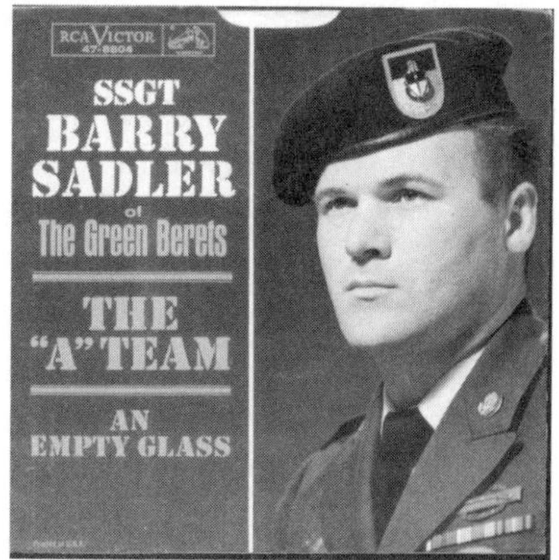

SSgt. Barry Sadler scored an international hit With "Ballad of the Green Berets" in 1965.

Sadler's third album for RCA, "Barry Sadler Back Home," was an attempt by the label to create a new image for Sadler as a singer of "love themes in a country mood." The liner notes on the record jacket take some pains to convince the record-buying public that the former Green Beret is far more than just a singer of war music. RCA's hope obviously was that the civilian side of Sadler, featuring music with "domestic themes," would capture the imagination of record buyers the way his war ballads did, but this attempt at repackaging was doomed to failure. The title of the one cut from the album that was released as a single, "One Day Nearer Home," suggests that it might be Vietnam related but it isn't. Sadler's main claim to fame as a recording artist will always be "The Ballad." Another testimony to the impact of the "Ballad of the Green Berets" was that it merited several "answer songs." "He Wore the Green Beret" by Leslie Miller is about a wife who is widowed when her Green Beret is killed in action. Even though wearing the beret has cost her husband his life, she wants her son to continue in dad's footsteps when he grows up. Then there is "The Son of a Green Beret" sung by Craig Arthur. This little boy, who sounds a lot like a clone of Joey Martin of "Joey's Prayer" fame, is full of enthusiasm about how proud he is of his father and how much he is hoping to become one of the Special Forces.

Although his musical efforts didn't attain the renown that Sadler's did, Hershel Gober, another combat veteran, recorded some patriotic songs in support of the war during the '60s. As the liner notes on his album "The Proud American read, "During a period when so many individuals are trying to sell America short and speak only of its weaknesses and what is wrong with it, Hershel sings of its strength and of the things that are right with it." Album cuts like "The Proud American," Here Am I" and "An American's Dream" fit that description admirably. His powerful voice delivers these powerful songs very effectively. Another recording by Gober, "Picture of a Man," is a particularly unique contribution to the music of the Vietnam War because it is one the few that mentions the Vietnamese people. Apparently only released as a 45-rpm recording, "Picture of a Man" is an effectively delivered lament about an American army officer grieving about the death of a young boy who happened to be in the wrong place at the wrong time in the war zone, an all too common occurrence in Vietnam. The song was ultimately translated into Vietnamese and is included in the "Vietnamese National Song Book." While in Vietnam, Gober came to know the "Vietnamese Woody Guthrie," Pham Suey, who wrote many songs about the Franco-Viet Minh War and the American War. Gober and Suey can be heard singing on "The General Edward Lansfield Tapes," which are in the Library of Congress.[40]

Gober's musical odyssey is one of the most interesting of any of the performers discussed in "Battle Notes." He began his recording career at Ace Records in New Orleans in 1959 with a record called "Get it On." The "flip side" of this disc, "The Great Tragedy," has gained more attention as a collector's item since it is probably the first tribute song recorded about the plane crash that took the lives of Buddy Holly, Ritchie Valens and the "Big Bopper," as it was waxed 24 hours after the tragic event took place. Gober toured with other Ace artists such as Frankie Ford of "Sea Cruise" fame. He went on to become closely associated with then Governor Bill Clinton of Arkansas and served as his state Director of Veterans' Affairs. When Clinton became president, Gober followed him to Washington and a high position in the country's veteran's administration. The quality of the friendship is evident in Clinton's statement that he (Gober) is "the big brother I never had." Understandably, Gober regards the charges that Clinton evaded the draft and that Gore was protected in Vietnam as "unfair."[41]

Hershel Gober singing for LBJ and Westmoreland at Cam Rahn Bay in Vietnam. Source: Hershel Gober

Hershel Gober early in his recording career. Source: Hershel Gober

Student Essays

Most students had reservations about some of the more strident patriotic music, especially Merle Haggard's:

"I think 'The Fightin' Side of Me' is down on the spectacular failure end of this musical spectrum. The combative theme to this song leaves listeners with little to think about, and probably inspired Wrangler clad good ole boys to drink Schlitz (sic) and beat the shit out of hippie protestors. If Haggard felt so passionately about the Vietnam War effort he should of grabbed one of pa's double barrels and hopped a plane to Southeast Asia. I am sure he could have afforded the plane fare."

"'Okie from Muskogee' by Merle Haggard was a song I'd heard before. I always laughed when I heard it because I though the first couple lines were funny. The rest of the song is far from funny. He is expressing severe disapproval and distaste for the 'hippie' movement...Most of the pro-war music was country. No big surprise there. The South has always been more conservative. It's just full of rednecks and hicks waiting for a war to keep them occupied. However, so much of the music wasn't so much pro-war as it was anti-hippie. The redneck despised these longhaired, dope smokin', political revolutionaries. They just wanted to run them down in their big truck, then beat them senseless with a baseball bat."

"Overall I was remarkably surprised by how much pro-war and anti-hippie music there was. Most of this bothered me and consequently I didn't like it very much. I think Merle Haggard made me angrier than any of them. The music on this side of the issue didn't seem to be looking for a solution. Rather they seemed to be looking for a fight. It almost seemed to me that they were happy about the war because it gave them a reason to fight."

Those who liked Haggard's music had good reason to:

"This song touched off some real feelings and memories in me. My husband (a Vietnam vet) to this day, hates Jane Fonda.[42] When Merle Haggard sings 'love it or leave it' I remember Bob saying we should ship Jane Fonda back to Vietnam to stay. Even now, though intellectually I believe in freedom of speech and the rights of others to do and say what they feel, I think there had to be a better way of protesting the war. The harm done to the men that fought over there has been irreparable."

A Vietnam veteran wrote the following:

"Haggard may be criticized for pushing the envelope on freedom of speech. In reality, he tells it like it is. If you don't like our country, leave it."

Another man who served in Vietnam who came to oppose the war still liked "Okie from Muskogee:"

"I always loved this song. As a Californian and an anti-war Vietnam vet, this song represented the other side - still loved it, as did most of my friends. I think the appeal of the song was that this represented, for us, a time in the past. We were raised to love 'Old Glory.' We were raised on World War II and loved our country. We were shattered by the realization that the Vietnam War was wrong, a mistake, something we never should have been involved in. My God, it would have been wonderful to still believe in 'Old Glory waving down at the courthouse.' Our innocence had been ripped from us - we were now trying to end a worthless war - to still believe in the old, to live in the old, would have been wonderful - but you cannot go back."

This student liked all of the Haggard music he heard:

"These songs show the feelings that I have toward a lot of issues. I particularly enjoyed 'Okie from Muskogee,' where

> Merle Haggard compares the country boy attitude to the hippies' attitude. I relate to these songs because it really upsets me to hear of the people of this time who showed sympathy to the Viet Cong, and hatred towards our brave soldiers. Calling them "baby killers" and other blasphemy. A soldier should not be degraded like that from a person who probably lived the easy life of traveling from party to party via the V.W. bus dreaming of change while the soldier was doing what he had to do to serve his country. I feel that a great amount of respect should be shown to our soldiers for their bravery and sufferings from a good cause turned bad."

Students generally panned the music that likened the Vietnam War to an anti-communist crusade:

> "I hate throwing stereotypes around, but it seems that country performers had major difficulties expressing their point of view in a creative manner. 'Hello Vietnam' seems more like government propaganda. It sounds like President Johnson himself could have penned the words to the song. I can totally see a C.I.A. agent waiting backstage to slip the band leader an envelope with Ben Franklins inside, congratulating him on a job well done."

> "Another song that bothered me was Kitty Well's and Johnny Wright's song. I believe the lyrics followed the main idea that the soldiers have a duty to stop communism at all cost or the United State's freedom would be lost. The woman singing the song was so calm about sending her love on his way. She only wanted a kiss goodbye and an assurance that he would write. She was certain he was doing the patriotic things and just action he needed to do. Perhaps some women felt this sense of patriotism. However, I also believe even these women must have had many fears as they watched their young men go off to fight in an unfamiliar place. The day-to-day anxieties must have been terrible for the soldiers."

While most students could only vicariously appreciate the pain caused by the family rift in "Ballad of Two Brothers" as a tragedy that happened to someone else, one student wrote about an estrangement between two brothers that had occurred in her own family:

> "Throughout history families and friends have feuded over the ethics and point of war. I, like many others, have experienced this kind of conflict within my own family...I was brought to tears when I first heard "Ballad of Two Brothers." This song brought back memories of my father and his brother disagreeing about the war. To this day they are still not on speaking terms, which is why I display dissatisfaction towards this war. My father was against the war. He expressed his views by protesting and burning his draft card. My uncle, on the other hand, served in the war. He believed in what he fought for. Neither one of them cared to listen to each other's points. They were both too stubborn and hardheaded to respect each other's opinion."

One student found the message in Autry Inman's "Ballad of Two Brothers" so offensive that he likened it to Nazi propaganda:

> "This is pro-war propaganda thinly disguised as a morality play about doing what's 'right.' The brothers are one-dimensional stereotypes. The 'good' brother does the right thing. He goes to Vietnam and dies. The 'bad' brother grows a beard, smokes pot and marches against the war and sponges off his dad. There's no mention of the fact that the 'bad' boy may find the war immoral or that he even has any moral convictions. He must not, because in the end he abandons his lifestyle to join the army and everyone lives happily ever after. At least until he, too, comes home in a body bag. The horrible thing about this song is its rigid attitude; it equates anti-war with being anti-American and anti-honor. This crap doesn't open any dialogue, it just panders to the existing prejudices of the pro-war faction. In essence, preaching to the choir. Goebbels[43] would have loved it."

"I find this song ridiculous. I do not think an anti-war brother would switch sides after his brother got killed and then sign up to go to Vietnam. If anything, I think it would make him more bitter against the war and make him protest even more."

Although the overblown "Day of Decision" earned a student's scorn, she still felt that it deserved to be heard, if for no other reason, than it did represent the viewpoint that some people held about the war:

"The worst song we heard in class, without question, was 'Day of Decision' by Johnny Sea. I felt absolutely sickened by this hateful, self-righteous piece of musical trash. The use of 'oriental' instrumentation near the end of the song was totally offensive to me. Much as I detest it though, this song does belong in this collection. No matter how ridiculous and abhorrent, this song does express a viewpoint that was held by a certain element in our country."

A student who was equally offended because he felt it attempted to indoctrinate the listener:

"The song I liked least was 'Day of Decision' by Johnny Sea. 'Day of Decision' wasn't really a song at all. In my estimation, it was an excruciatingly long propagandist poem that tried to tear into the hearts of people that knew about the love of country, honor, valor, courage...etc. For people who opposed war this poem must have meant little. I personally had a really hard time sitting through it. I thought it was very long winded, and I didn't understand having that much pride in a war that might not be a 'just war.' What kind of person really got charged up after hearing this song back during that time? I got it! Bobby Brady! From *The Brady Bunch!* Right? Maybe it was all a conspiracy. I think that Johnny Sea was a studio musician who the government paid to write a musical poem in order to boost public opinion. Compared to other mishaps that took place during the war, this conspiracy theory almost makes sense to me."

A dramatically different view, which makes one wonder if these students were listening to the same song:

> "The song 'Day of Decision,' I feel explains the war that was occurring in America. I agree with the lyrics that describe how patriotism was not being valued and it was not America that was changing, it was the people living in America that were changing. I also agree that we should be proud of who we are and what our country stands for."

A neo-isolationist view:

> "Another song that I really liked was 'Day of Decision' by Johnny Sea. I feel this song, although way over-dramatized, reflects a lot of peoples' attitudes even today about the United States' involvement in other countries' business. This song says, 'Yeah there are things going on in other countries that are not good but lets take care of business at home first. Like hunger, homelessness and our economy.'"

"Wish You Were Here Buddy" was one of many songs where students' reactions surprised me. I expected a deluge of criticism but instead:

> "I liked the song because the writer made reference to the fact that all anti-war protestors had no idea what it was like to be in a war fighting against the VC. The protestors opposed the soldiers of the war instead of the government that put them there. I never did understand why so many blamed the soldiers when many of them didn't have a choice in going to fight. This soldier's friend, Buddy, was back home in college growing his hair long and holding rallies, when this soldier was fighting for his life in a jungle somewhere thousands of miles from home. Had I heard this song back then, I think I would've decided that though I oppose the war, I am not going to take it out on the soldiers. The government sucks!"

> "One song that I did like was 'Wish You Were Here Buddy'

because it was about a soldier who is writing a letter to his buddy who is back home protesting the war while he is fighting in it and wishes to introduce his buddy to the Vietcong. I like the message of this song because I would feel the same way too if I were risking my life everyday fighting in a war while my friend had it nice and safe back home and just kept bitching about the war."

"Pat Boone's 'Wish You Were Here Buddy' is another song that I never heard until now, which I really enjoyed. He brought up a great point that I once again did not realize. While you were off fighting for your country your best friend could be off in the anti-war campaign. I'm sure this situation changed many friendships. 'Heard you been leading campus protests, while I been on a little vacation in South Vietnam.' This was something that I'm sure split many friendships up. If I was off fighting for my country and my friends were out protesting against it, I would not be too happy with them. This all just turns into the whole war and peace movement again. I just believe that no matter how close you were this was an issue that would ruin your friendship. I also really like the title of the song, 'Wish You Were Here Buddy.' That was just a great way of putting it. I love the sarcasm as the song goes on. Not ever hearing it before I did not realize it was directed to the anti-war buddy. The beat was also very catchy. I liked how Pat Boone tied it all together."

"This song is about a soldier in Vietnam who is singing to a guy back home in the U.S. He is saying sarcastically that he is having a lot of fun and that the conditions in Vietnam are great. He is telling this guy that he wishes he were there to enjoy Vietnam with him rather than a college protesting the war. I love this song because it has a nice satirical amusing twist on an otherwise somber subject. It actually proves its point better because it makes you stop and think. This song really made me understand the significance of, and respect, the soldiers who fought in Vietnam. I have always imagined that if I had been alive in the 1960s I would have been on the 'dove' side opposing the war. Until now I never really understood that the soldiers who were fighting were not necessarily making the decisions. They were not always fighting for a cause they thought was right. They were just doing their duty and fighting for their country. These soldiers deserve the utmost respect. This played a part in taking me back to the time of the war. I think that this soldier fighting in Vietnam just wants to go home and that he is singing this song to his 'buddy' in the states because he is jealous that he is comfortable and dry at home in his bed."

Interestingly, a student who obviously has a strong commitment to the First Amendment panned Stonewall Jackson's "The Minutemen are Turning in their Graves," a song that contains a similar diatribe about war protestors:

> "This song is really bad because of its misguided attempt at patriotism. Most professional soldiers and true patriots recognize that free speech is one of the reasons we fight wars. While I cannot condone some of the actions taken by some of the war protestors towards the returning vets, they did and do have the right to speak out against what they feel is wrong."

The critique that is one of my favorites, perhaps because it supports my own view, is this essay that dismisses "Joey's Prayer" in pithy and cleverly effective fashion:

> "'Joey's Prayer' is way too artificial for me. Joey's annoying 'Beaver Cleaver' voice reinforces my belief that 'Mama Look at Boo Boo'[44] may have been a better selection."

This student found "Joey's Prayer" so cloying it made him feel ill:

> "Joey's Prayer is the kind of song that would make my mother cry, but it almost makes me puke. The situation portrayed with a little brother missing his big brother was all right, but the words really sucked. They basically said, say hi to my brother, but there is no chance his brother will ever get this

> prayer. The prayer was from a young kid, but the song was written by an idiot who portrayed a young kid with some sort of mental disorder. I give this song a big two thumbs down."

A student who agreed wholeheartedly with the anti-war protest views of "What's Come Over This World's":

> "He sings about all the anti-war protestors and hippies and how their despicable actions are defiling this great country. While young men and young women are fighting for freedom in a far-off land, these malcontents back home are holding demonstrations and carrying signs when they should be focusing on supporting our troops overseas. I agree with Mr. Carr on this subject. The anti-war community was nothing but a nuisance to the America public and they accomplished nothing with their actions, actions that at times included vandalism and random terrorist acts. These demonstrators were nothing but cowards and anarchists"

The three essays quoted below convey a generally favorable opinion of the "Ballad of the Green Berets." The first, written by a man who may have a military background, is unabashedly enthusiastic. The second, written by a woman, objects to the fact that the widow is willing to sacrifice her son. A third student likens it to music from hell:

> "In my opinion, 'The Ballad of the Green Berets' was the best song of the selection we had to choose hands down. This song is both motivational and inspirational. After hearing this song, my first urge is to try to re-enlist because I know that I could walk through a ten-foot thick wall of bricks in the middle of a minefield that was covered with interlocking fields of fire from batteries of quad 50s. It really pumps a person up. In fact, I wonder if the numbers of volunteers for the Green Berets increased after this song was released? And, as for inspiration, the song says that they die. But what better way to go? You're a hero. You're part of an elite fighting force trying to stave off the spread of com-

munism in ways that would scare the hell out of mere mortal men. Besides, it appears better to die in combat with honor than to die of boredom somewhere back in the real world. Not only that, but we would get to jump out of a perfectly good airplane. Mr. Sadler really outdid himself with this song. It motivates, inspires, and it glorifies a war that was very unpopular at the time. Well done, Mr. Sadler."

"'Ballad of the Green Berets' by SSgt. Barry Sadler was also one of my favorites. It is about a man that was a Green Beret. Green Berets are America's best. About 100 men will try but only 3 will become a Green Beret. They are fearless men who fight night and day. They are willing to jump and die. I liked this song because he is so proud to be what he is, and when he died, he had only one request and that was for his son to join the Green Berets. Even though he died he was so proud to fight and die for his country. He loved it so much that he wanted his son to join it too. I just wonder how his mother would react to that. She lost her husband, would she really want to lose her son too?"

"Barry Sadler makes being part of an elite 'killing machine' awesomely redundant to say the least. I would like to rename this 'Hippy in Hell.' Why? Because hell for hippies must be something like this. You're strapped down with headphones on and the song that is played over and over again is 'The Ballad of the Green Berets.' I think that would be hell for me also."

This student's military background may have been a factor in his praise for Dave Dudley's "Vietnam Blues:"

"I loved listening to this song and in many ways feel that I would have felt the same way at the time. I was in the Marine Corps for six and a half years and at one point I had a taste of these protestors shouting hate slogans, this time directed at the troops about to go to war in the Gulf. If there ever were a lower form of pond scum in America at that time, well, these protestors would have had to dig their way above it."

For most students, the messages in the songs exercised students' intellect but sometimes, as with "Vietnam Blues," the words triggered memories of how the war brought pain on a personal level:

> In the song, 'Vietnam Blues,' I particularly hate the protestors. Today I would like to meet one of these self-righteous fools. Idiots! Years after the war, my uncle killed himself. What we know as Post-Traumatic Stress Disorder got the best of him: bouts of depression, self-medicating and flashbacks.

One student found himself so emotionally involved in the music that he put himself in the place of Dorothy Gorman's son:

> "When I was listening to the music that first week, I received an overwhelming feeling of pride and nationalism. I thought to myself, 'Wow, this is going to be great.' I get to hear some of the greatest music of this century and learn about it at the same time. However, I never expected to become so emotionally involved in the music. It all started to come together for me last week when we listened to 'Happy Birthday, Son,' by Mrs. Dorothy Gorman. This was about a mother who feared she was going to lose her son to a war that she or he could not understand. I found myself thinking of myself as one of those young men in Vietnam, fighting in a far away land and praying to survive another endless night. I could visualize my mother writing the letter to me, wishing me a happy birthday, only to have the letter arrive too late. It is people like Mrs. Gorman and her son who have made this country what it is today, and I truly respect them. I truly believe that all the young men who fought in Vietnam made this world a better place for all of us."

Footnotes:

1 Craig Werner, *A Change is Gonna Come: Music, Race and the Soul of America.* New York, Penguin Books, 1999. p. 231.
2 Barry McCloud (Ed.) *Definitive Country: The Ultimate Encyclopedia of Country Music and Its Performers.* New York, Bumper Books, 1995. p. 338.
3 West Virginia v. Barnette U.S. Supreme Court Reports. 1943.
4 McCloud, *Definitive Country: The Ultimate Encyclopedia of Country Music and Its Performers.* p. 357.
5 Merle Haggard, *My House of Memories,* New York: Harper Trade, 1999, pp. 228 - 229.
6 Steve Morse, *"Times Change but Haggard Keeps Plugging and Playing."* Minneapolis Tribune. June 11, 1999, p. 31.
7 Interview with Gene Leroy.
8 Colin Larkin, *The Virgin Encyclopedia of Country Music.* London, Virgin Books, 1998. p. 211.
9 Although only Wright's name appears on the label as the performer of this song, it is very much a duet with Kitty Wells, who was known as "The Queen of Country Music." She earned this title with hits like "It Wasn't God Who Made Honky Tonk Angels." I saw Wright and Wells sing this song together in concert in early 1965 at the Minneapolis Auditorium. Before his success with "Hello Vietnam" Wright was known as part of the duo known as "Johnny and Jack" (Angelin) who recorded "blue grass" style hits like "Poison Love" in the 1950s.
10 Spencer C. Tucker (Ed.) *Encyclopedia of the Vietnam War: A Political, Social and Military History.* Santa Barbara, ABC-CLIO, Inc. 1998. Vol. I, p. 172.
11 Written by Kris Kristofferson as "Talkin' Viet Nam Blues." 1965.
12 Kris Kristofferson interview Country Song Roundup, Charlton Publications, Derby, Connecticut Vol. 23, No. 139, February 1971.
13 Kris Kristofferson Interview, Country Song Roundup, February 1971.
14 Johnny Cash, *Man In Black: His Own Story in His Own Words.* Grand Rapids, Zondervan Publishing, 1975. p. 159.
15 Author attending a Johnny Cash concert on November 30, 1969, in Houston, Texas.
16 Larkin, *The Virgin Encyclopedia of Country Music,* p. 73.
17 Larkin, *The Virgin Encyclopedia of Country Music,* p. 364.
18 McCloud, *Definitive Country: The Ultimate Encyclopedia of Country Music and Its Performers,* pp.716 -717.
19 Larkin, *The Virgin Encyclopedia of Country Music,* p. 364.
20 Stephen Ambrose, *Citizen Soldiers.* New York, Simon and Schuster, 1997.
21 Christian G. Appy, *Working Class War: American Combat Soldiers & Vietnam.* Chapel Hill, The University of North Carolina Press, 1993. p. 208.

22 Appy, *Working Class War: American Combat Soldiers & Vietnam,* p. 208.

23 Brad Bennent (USM Retired) Memorial Day Address. Superior (WI) Elks Club, 2001.

24 Research of names on the Vietnam Memorial Wall in Washington, DC, revealed no servicemen with the last name of Gorman and a birth date of December 18th.

25 McCloud, *Definitive Country,* p. 399.

26 Jan Howard interview Country Song Roundup, Charlton Publications, Derby, Connecticut, Vol. 24, No. 161 December 1972.

27 Loretta Lynn with George Vecsey, *Coal Miner's Daughter.* New York, Warner Books, 1977. p. 219.

28 Neil MacNeil, *Dirksen: Portrait of a Public Man.* Cleveland: World Publishing Company, 1970. p. 319.

29 Ibid.

30 Actually a parody of Dirksen by *"The Hardly Worth It Players"* on Parkway Records.

31 Interview with Billy Carr, June 3, 2000. New York City.

32 Sarge Lintecum interview.

33 Interview with Boyd Dallos, December 2002.

34 Dallos Interview.

35 Dallos Interview.

36 Interviews with Larry Yeazle and Michael McCann, both of whom served with special forces in Vietnam.

37 Interview with Dan Wagner, a former Green Beret, Kearns, Utah, July, 2001.

38 Interview with Dr. Mike Mittelman, New Haven, Connecticut, July, 2002.

39 Dave Marsh *The Heart of Rock and Soul: The 1001 Greatest Singles Ever Made."* New York: New American Library, 1989. p.p. 197-98.

40 Interview with Hershel Gober, November 2001.

41 Interview with Hershel Gober, October 2001.

42 Jane Fonda visited North Vietnam during the Vietnam War and had her picture taken with North Vietnamese soldiers manning an anti-aircraft gun. This visit earned her the undying enmity of many Vietnam veterans. One of them told me that she actually helped fire the gun at American planes.

43 Joseph Goebbels was Adolf Hitler's Propaganda Minister.

44 Harry Belafonte's "Mama Look at Boo Boo" is a nonsense or novelty song that was popular during the late 1950s. It is about the trials of a father who is constantly tormented by his children who tell him he is "ugly." His wife tries to defend him by admonishing the children that this is no way to treat their father, but they respond by claiming that no one who looks so grotesque can be their daddy. Like an early version of Bart Simpson, "Boo Boo" agonizes about why nobody seems to like him. To those with an absurd sense of humor, this is a very funny song.

Chapter 4:
African American Music

I grew up in a small city in the upper Midwest during the '50s and '60s and spent most of these years in the cocoon of a sheltered white middle class existence. Although I loved music, I was denied the opportunity to hear some of the truly marvelous songs recorded by black artists that seemed to be played only on radio stations in distant urban areas. I knew this music existed by combing the Billboard charts, but by the time I finally heard some of these truly great songs, they had been "covered" by white artists and thoroughly "pasteurized" for the more lucrative all-white audience. Something was definitely lost in the process. So it was that songs like the Flamingoes' "I'll Be Home," which was originally released on the African-American-oriented Checker Records, were re-recorded in homogenized and tepid form by Pat Boone on Dot Records. This weak imitation made it into the pop top ten, while the black group's far superior version enjoyed no such success. It was much more than the lack of recognition that "devastated" the Flamingos. They also lost royalties and the proceeds from being credited as the songwriters of the tune. Another bitter pill this hapless group had to swallow was that the man who owned Checker Records, Leonard Chess, had learned how to "mine the R&B field for record gold" and encouraged Randy Wood, the owner of the much larger Dot label, to press the Boone version of "I'll Be Home."[1] Wood has been described as an "unrepentant bigot" who once warned one of his minions not to put a picture of the Mills Brothers on an album cover because "We won't sell any records in the South if they see Negroes on our albums." He and others like him felt little compunction about the business of white artists ripping off African-American performers.[2] The practice of white artists "covering" black music reached absurd proportions when the soulless Boone went so far as to attempt renditions of Fat's

Domino's "The Fat Man" and Roy Brown's "Good Rockin' Tonight" and even Little Richard's frenetic "Tutti Frutti." Another group in the Chess stable, the Moonglows were also victimized when their song "Sincerely" fell into the hands of the popular McGuire Sisters who enjoyed a fabulous commercial success with the tune, while the original languished. The lily white Crewcuts may have been the "worst" offenders of all as they came out with their own inferior versions of the Penguin's "Earth Angel," the "Nutmegs' "Story Untold" and the Chords' "Sh-Boom." In 1955, Atlantic Records earned the dubious distinction of being "the most covered label in the U.S." Ruth Brown, Atlantic Records' most popular female singer, also saw her original of "Oh What a Dream" covered by Patti Page, and Lavern Baker saw "Tweedle Dee Dee" reach number five on the black charts while Georgia Gibbs' cover went to number two on the national pop charts.[3] Brown called such covers "bare-faced duplicates, with no artistic merit whatsoever." When Gibbs "duplicated" Brown's "Mambo Baby," she wondered, "Don't they have any original ideas over there?"[4] Most white singers who were involved in this unreserved appropriation of "race music" may have had little control over what they recorded or shrugged their shoulders and said this is what happens in the record business. To her credit, Teresa Brewer, who spent months on the charts with songs like "A Tear Fell," "Empty Arms" and "You Send Me," was "always uncomfortable and guilt-stricken with this common industry practice" and felt it was "unfair and exploitive."[5] "Big bands" also bastardized songs like Chuck Berry's "Johnny B. Goode" and even white record buyers, particularly those like Troy Shondell who knew their music, began to realize that something was amiss:

> "I remember when Chuck Berry came out with 'Johnny B. Goode.' I had been listening to it over WLAC from Nashville, which played all this great R & B... all these incredible Southern records-stuff on Excello by Lazy Lester and Lightin' Slim. They'd play R & B all night and I used to lie in bed and listen.... Anyway I kept hearing "Johnny B. Goode"... so I went down to the local record store in Ft. Wayne to buy it. The

lady packages it up and I go home to play it. I take it out of the bag and it's by Ralph Materie! A Big Band version! That's what WOWO (Ft. Wayne's major radio station) was playing. They shied away from music by black artists for a long time. They went for the white cover versions, and that's what the local record stores carried as well. It sometimes took months for me to find the records I wanted."[6]

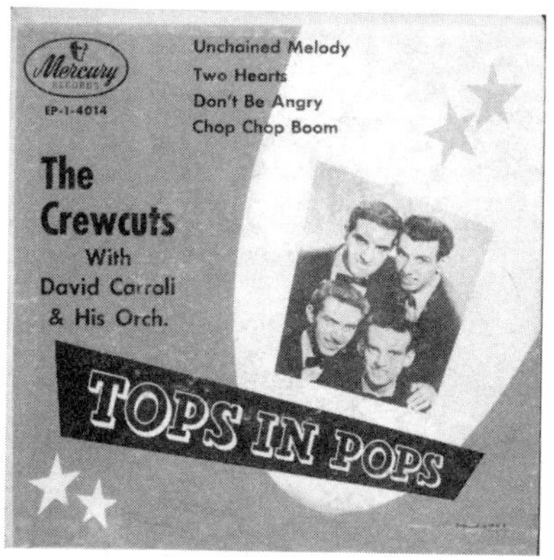

The Crewcuts frequently "covered" classic rhythm and blues songs during the '50s in less than classic fashion.

Crewcuts' recording of "A Story Untold."

Georgia Gibbs' recording of "Seven Lonely Days." Gibbs enjoyed far better chart success with songs originated by Ruth Brown and Lavern Baker than these black female artists did.

Picture of the Impressions' recording of "It's All Right" showing the sticker affixed to the label that states "Play only after 4:00 p.m."

Then there were the songs that never even made it to a cover version. I can remember poring over The Billboard Hot 100 Charts in the early 1960s and wondering what "Pushover" by Etta James or "Pain in My Heart" by Otis Redding sounded like, just knowing I was missing something. Because this music was, in a sense, verboten, they took on an enchanting air of mystery. Those titles that I scanned in this august 100 were only a fraction of the rhythm and blues and soul music that was being produced. The remainder that didn't attain "cross-over" status were relegated to "soul" or "rhythm and blues" lists that wound up in the interior of the record trade magazines, those that even bothered to rate this kind of music back then.

Outside of heavily populated urban areas that had significant concentrations of African-Americans, radio stations usually shied away from this kind of musical style because it was considered to be "race music" or "jungle music" and not appropriate fare for their white listening audience. If those who controlled programming decided a song was "too colored," it had to go or it would "contaminate the station as well as its listeners." These self- appointed guardians of morality also were concerned that advertising revenues would plunge if they played rhythm and blues and draw criticism from their snobbish cronies at the country club. Even as R & B increased in popularity and they lost listeners to stations that would play this style of music, these owners and managers' minds remained closed as they created a "quota system," whose purpose seemed to be to play as little black music as possible.[7] When radio stations received promotional copies of songs like Jackie Wilson's "Lonely Teardrops" or the Impressions' "It's All Right," disc jockeys might deign to play them, but stickers affixed to the label of the record warned program managers to wait until after 4:00 p.m. before daring to put them on a turntable. Apparently, it was considered more appropriate to send this kind of music out over the airwaves under cover of the night, lest the "respectable" daytime audience be offended. In most cases, radio stations that catered to white audiences didn't even bother playing these songs.

This censorship may have very well saved some sheltered white sensibilities from being dangerously offended. African-American music of the early 1950s, like "Work With Me Annie" by Hank Ballard and "Sixty Minute Man" by Billy Ward and the Dominoes to name a few, probably would have been too risqué for middle-class white American tastes. They were just too suggestive for mainstream tastes, with descriptions of sexual intercourse that left little to the imagination. "Work with me Annie" and its sequel "Annie Had a Baby" are loaded with double entendre. "Sixty Minute Man" features a singer bragging about his sexual prowess during a strenuous and lengthy sexual encounter. But songs like these were considered objectionable not only for their lyrics but also the fact that they were regarded as "race music"[8] and thus unfit for white consumption. Many of these songs articulated important viewpoints held by the African-American community but the vast potential white audience was denied the chance to hear them. As the country moved toward desegregation, black music finally began to be accorded the recognition it deserved. But this process didn't happen overnight and a person's taste for music was largely dictated by their race even as the black music factory at Motown began to make American popular music "color blind."

The censorship of African American music was part of a general attitude of racism in the United States that attempted to segregate blacks from whites, a practice that continued in de facto fashion well into the twentieth century and long after the war that was supposed to bring freedom to blacks had ended. As the war in Vietnam escalated in the mid-1960s, this discrimination remained in effect as the already heated battle for civil rights for African-Americans in the United States intensified. The first civil rights movement protest directed against the war took place in McComb, Mississippi, in early 1965 when a pamphlet distributed there contained statements like: "No Mississippi Negroes should be fighting in Vietnam for the White Man's freedom, until all the Negro people are free in Mississippi." When this polemic, which was released by the Mississippi Freedom Party (MFP) as part of its newsletter, drew criticism from Southern Congressmen for "lack of patriotism," the MFP issued a statement denying responsibility and blamed the remarks on local chapters of the party. However, they still insisted "it is very easy to understand why Negro citizens of McComb, themselves the victims of bombings, Klan-inspired terrorism, and harassment arrests, should resent the death of a citizen of McComb fighting in Vietnam for 'freedom' not enjoyed by the Negro community of McComb."[9] The forces of reaction, particularly in the South, began to employ violent methods to suppress blacks who demonstrated to support the cause of civil rights while legislation in Congress that promised to bring equality seemed to be moving at a snail's pace.

Many black soldiers in 'Nam wondered why they should be fighting to save a country that had treated their race so scornfully for so long and was now only grudgingly according them the rights they deserved. In spite of the fact that President Harry S. Truman had ordered the armed forces desegregated in 1946, and combat units in Vietnam were fully integrated, racial prejudice still existed in the military, and blacks serving their country encountered bigotry during basic training as well as in 'Nam. Sometimes the racism was subtle, but all too often it was blatant. Bigoted attitudes were found in every branch of the United States Armed Forces. "Appropriate entertainment" on some U.S. Navy ships included movies of World War II vintage, depicting blacks as "lazy" and "superstitious" and engaged in stealing chickens. When African Americans requested that their commanding officer substitute other films that were less offensive, he refused, saying that the movies in question didn't excite racial tensions. At least one fight that can be attributed to such stereotypical movies broke out in the chow line when a white sailor used a racial joke from a Bob Hope film toward one of the black servers. The bulkheads on the passenger lounges of two transport ships displayed artwork describing what each of the fifty states was noted for. Some of the Southern states showed blacks picking cotton, while another showed girls dancing while African-Americans provided the music. Georgia's mural showed blacks holding hoes while they munched on watermelon. Confederate flags were prominently displayed on Marine bases in Vietnam. Black complaints fell on deaf ears, even with the clergy assigned to these camps. The military justice system was also used to punish blacks well beyond the severity of their alleged crimes.[10]

Another factor that contributed to African-American angst about Vietnam was the perception that they were suffering a disproportionate number of casualties, a concern well expressed in "War" and "What's Going On?" Although final casualty statistics don't support this view, blacks still carried a heavy share of the fighting burden, especially early in the war. Between 1961 and 1966, even though they made up only 13% of the U.S. population, African Americans accounted for almost 20% of combat-related deaths in Vietnam. In 1965, they were one quarter of the Army's killed in action. They frequently contributed half the men in Army and Marine front line units. Army and Marine commanders finally yielded to pressure in 1966 and began working to decrease black combat deaths. They at least partially succeeded, as by the end of the war, African American casualties were about 12%, a figure more proportionate to their share of the general population.[11]

Racial tensions in Vietnam reached a peak during the last years of American involvement when all hope of victory was gone and the number of career black soldiers who felt duty-bound to fight the war, despite their misgivings about how their race was treated, dwindled and they were replaced by draftees, who had little motivation to fight a "white man's war." Ever adroit at manipulating public opinion to coincide with their military efforts, the enemy took aim at the American Achilles heel of race relations and began to distribute "Negro propaganda leaflets" in hopes of increasing the already festering racial enmity African-American troops felt toward whites.[12] A typical leaflet stated: "Your real war is with those who call you nigger. Your genuine struggle is in your native land. Go home now and live!" In case this message wasn't plain enough, an accompanying photograph showed a white policeman in riot gear, brandishing a nightstick as he held a handcuffed black by the arm.[13] Radicals in the "Black Power" movement had already linked racial violence in the United States to the Vietnam War. Cassius Clay's refusal to be drafted saying he "had nothin' against those Viet Congs" made tensions even worse. When Dr. Martin Luther King Jr., who had told blacks that they were doing little more than fighting the "white man's war," was assassinated in 1968, communist propagandists urged "bloods" to desert as reprisal for the death of their leader. Radio Hanoi was in the forefront of this effort, which was at least partially successful:

> "This lady by the name of Hanoi Helen came on the radio...She was saying, 'Soul brothers, go home. Whitey raping your mothers and your daughters, burning down your homes. What you over here for? This is not your war. The war is a trick of the Capitalist empire to get rid of the blacks.' I really thought - I really started believing it, because it was too many blacks than there should be in the infantry."[14]

As blacks rioted in American cities, their counterparts in Vietnam almost completely lost faith in the war as they were egged on by racist whites that resented King's opposition to the war:

> "Some white servicemen rejoiced in his death. Sailors at Cua Viet donned makeshift white robes and paraded in imitation of the Ku Klux Klan, and Confederate flags, symbols of slavery, were unfurled over Cam Rahn and Da Nang."[15]

It is little wonder that many blacks who were subjected to this kind of treatment lost respect for the military and its laws and wound up filling military prisons like the one at Long Binh, more popularly known as the "LBJ" or Long Binh Jail, in South Vietnam. Here they were sometimes confined to cells that were actually maritime shipping containers. These cruel and inhumane conditions resulted in a full-scale riot in August 1968 that pitted African-American prisoners against an all-white guard force. These racial clashes occurred wherever the American armed forces served. At Travis Air Force Base in California in May of 1971, blacks and whites rioted for four days over issues like racial discrimination in off-base housing and music, country western versus soul. When a recording of the Temptations' "My Girl" began skipping on a record player in one of the recreation rooms at Walter Reed Hospital in Washington, D.C., and white patients cheered, a racial donnybrook broke out. The brawl included men in body casts, wheelchairs, and those carrying crutches and attached to IV bags. [16]

A marine who saw combat in Vietnam in 1968 and 1969 said, "It was like there was a race riot going on over there!" However, Dan O'Hara, who served as a neuro-psychiatric technician in the Sixth Convalescent Center at Cam Rahn Bay in 1971, said the racial enmity was confined to the rear areas and that combat units in harm's way didn't worry about the color of anyone's skin since they were dependent on each other for survival:

> "There wasn't much of the racial stuff on the front line because the brothers and the whites fought as a unit. Only in the rear areas was there tension between blacks and whites. Here, things were set up for total separation. There were two armies back there, black and white. If you were standing in line for food and the server was black, ten or fifteen brothers would be allowed to cut in front of you to eat first. If you didn't go along with this, they would beat the s—t out of you. I had black guys who were friends of mine, who would stand up for me in the chow line though. But, generally it was total division between the races back there. Blacks were even embarrassed to be seen in social situations with whites."[17]

When discontented black veterans returned home, many of them enlisted in a different kind of war with far more enthusiasm. A significant number joined the Black Power Movement and the militant Black Panther's Organization in waging war against the white establishment. Maybe the ultimate insult to their pride was the knowledge that if they died for their country, they weren't even guaranteed a decent burial, that racism and segregation could follow them, even to the grave. Just such a posthumous indignity, visited upon a black soldier who died in combat in Vietnam but was denied burial in the town cemetery because of his color is chronicled in "(The Two Wars of) Old Black Joe" by Dr. William Truly, Jr. This self-described "Poet to all Mankind" recites this sordid tale of man's inhumanity to man:

(The Two Wars of) OLD BLACK JOE
from the album
"Dr. William Truly, Jr. - Poet To All Mankind"

THIS SOLDIER FOUGHT TWO WARS
ONE FROM A HILL IN VIET NAM
ONE FROM A GRAVE
WITH A LOVING MOM

HOW MANY MORE WILL BE SENT
AND BROUGHT BACK
AND FIGHT TWO WARS
BECAUSE THEY ARE BLACK

Proudly produced with humility and respect by Lelan Rogers

Dedicated to:
PFC Bill Terry – Birmingham, Alabama
Spec. 4 Poindexter Eugene Williams – Ft. Pierce, Florida

Reverend William Truly, Jr. picture sleeve.

The soldiers fought two wars
One from a hill in Viet Nam
One from a grave
With a loving mom

How many more will be sent
And brought back
And fight two wars
Because they are black

This litany of outrage is recited to the starkly simple musical background of what seems to be a "church organ." It is not great music, but this was the era when "the medium was the message," and Dr. Truly certainly had a powerful message to deliver. Whether enough people heard what he had to say is doubtful. The only copy of this recording I've seen is on a rather plain white label (House of Fox), which suggests it was pressed only for radio stations. According to information provided on the accompanying title sleeve, "(The Two Wars of) Old Black Joe" was culled from an album entitled "Dr. William Truly, Jr. - Poet to All Mankind" and was "proudly produced with humility and respect" by Lelan Rogers, a subsidiary of Lelan Rogers Enterprises in Nashville, Tennessee. The record comes with a sleeve that states that it is "dedicated to PFC Bill Terry - Birmingham, Alabama, and Spec. 4 Poindexter Eugene Williams - Ft. Pierce, Florida."

Perhaps the most vehement denunciation of the Vietnam War is Edwin Starr's raucous "War," which begins with the question, "War! What is it good for?" blurted out after an ominous drum roll. Once this question is answered emphatically with "Absolutely nothing," Starr goes on to observe sardonically that the only one who benefits from war is "the undertaker." This is likely a reference to the perception that African Americans troops in Vietnam were suffering a disproportionate number of casualties. Little is left to the listener's imagination as Starr literally screams out the lyrics.

The cover of Edwin Starr's album shows the intensity Starr has when he sings the song "War."

It is somewhat surprising that Motown Records' mogul Berry Gordy allowed this song to be released. "War" was a dramatic departure from the formula music about love and having a good time that had swelled the coffers of the Detroit label on the way to putting it on the map musically. The shrewd and profit-oriented Gordy worried whether this new and powerfully stated anti-war message might alienate record buyers as well as the government.[18] He reluctantly allowed "War" to be released but not by the extremely popular Temptations who were originally set to record it. Instead he passed it off to the then-unknown Starr, hoping this would keep the controversial song from gaining a wide audience. Of course, this subtle approach to burying the record didn't work, and it soared to the top of the record charts. In any event, "War" did not provoke the feared negative reaction and went on to carve out a niche for itself as one of the strongest anti-war messages to come from the African-American community. Starr was allowed to maintain the anti-war theme in a follow up recording that demanded "Stop the War Now!" Both "War" and its sequel came from an album entitled "Involved" where Starr is pictured on the cover looking, well, involved. His eyes are closed, his brow is furrowed with intensity and his fists are clenched. The singer is also wearing a jacket with buckskin fringes.[19]

Marvin Gaye, one of the Motown musical factory's superstars, used a phrase drawn from the lexicon of African-American culture to express his disillusionment about what was happening to his brothers in Vietnam in the achingly beautiful "What's Goin On?" Gaye is sending out the same message as Edwin Starr about the high ratio of African-American dead and wounded in Vietnam but states his case in a more subtle style that is no less effective in getting the point across. Gaye feels the fighting and the dying can be ended by love and communication. The song was released in 1971, when the Paris Peace Talks had already been dragging on for years and the United States was attempting to influence the negotiations by increasing bombings of North Vietnam. "What's Going On?" denounces this tactic with the lyrics, "We don't need to escalate!" "Escalate" became a familiar part of the nomenclature of the Vietnam War as it was used frequently by journalists to describe more troop deployments or bombing raids by the United States that increased the intensity of the conflict. Despite his exalted status at Motown, Gaye also had trouble convincing Berry Gordy that "What's Going On?" should be recorded by Motown. Gordy had little interest in politics or history and was thus remarkably oblivious of the growing dissatisfaction with the Vietnam War and the rising tide of the civil rights movement. This drove Gaye to frustration:

> "I felt myself exploding. ...Why didn't our music have anything to do with this? Wasn't music supposed to express feelings? No, according to BG, music's supposed to sell. That's his trip."[20]

Despite Gordy's attitude, "What's Going On?" became one of the company's biggest hits despite, or maybe because of, its viewpoint about the war.[21] The album was the label's first "concept album," containing cuts addressing other contemporary political and social issues like pollution in the nuclear age ("Mercy Mercy Me") and the plight of inner city blacks ("Inner City Blues"). Discoveries, a publication for record collectors, rates "What's Going On?" as one of the one hundred most important albums of the century. It compares the recording to the Beach Boys' revolutionary "Pet Sounds" as expressing the "assertion that spiritual love would solve the problems of the world." In the same article Gaye is described as Motown's "ultimate artist."[22] Even though controversial songs like "War" and "Ball of Confusion" became commercial successes despite Berry Gordy's reservations about their content, he had worried that Gaye's venture into social commentary would boomerang. The ambitious recording went on to put plenty of money into Motown's coffers. The listener must be aware of the fact that the singer was undergoing trials and tribulations in his personal life. He had a brother, Frankie, who was serving in Vietnam and although he never wrote him, it is hard to believe this didn't have some emotional impact on the delivery of the song. Most tragically, Gaye was estranged from his father, who would eventually murder him, say nothing of the other demons that made his life miserable. The fact that this famous exponent of non-violence would meet such a violent end, and at the hands of his own father, shows that truth is often stranger than fiction.

If bombs and guns and other destructive weapons that bring violence and destruction to the world aren't controlled, the future of mankind is bleak, according to Stevie Wonder in "Heaven Help Us All." Wonder proves to be yet another socially aware Motown artist as he ponders the question, "Who will help the flowers when the bombs begin to fall." He seems to feel that only some kind of divine intervention will save the lives of boys who will die before their twenty-first birthday because of the evil men who provide them with guns. This accusation could be directed at those who are responsible for the prevalence of guns in black ghettoes around the country that have resulted in high mortality rates for young African-American men. It could also be casting blame on the United States government for putting the weapons of war in the hands of young soldiers in Vietnam. The fact that the song was released in 1970 makes it probable Wonder was not only lamenting guns and violence in America but also the carnage in Vietnam. An unmistakable sense of despair pervades this song as the singer holds the pessimistic view that the cycle of violence will continue unabated, and then, as he points out in the song's refrain, "Heaven help us all!" He would also record another song with an even closer connection to Vietnam, "Front Line," which examines the plight of veterans who have been ravaged by their exposure to Agent Orange.

Many vets returned home and still felt the "pull" of their old unit. Their happiness about finally being stateside again was marred by feelings of guilt at having abandoned their buddies back in Vietnam.[23] A compelling song that addresses this issue is Change of Pace's "Bring My Buddies Back" on the obscure "Stone Lady" label. It tells the story of a soldier who has returned home but still worries about the fate of his buddies back in Vietnam. It would seem that he feels such guilt about being safe while they remain in peril that he even dreams about them, "marching all alone." Though it's evident that he is suffering from Post-Traumatic Stress Syndrome, when his girlfriend suggests this he denies it, but eventually concedes that she is right. He keeps flashing back to the dying words of a fellow soldier: "Bring my buddies back." Aside from survivor's guilt, he is also bothered by the feeling that his comrade might have survived his wounds if only there had been more doctors available. This is an interesting viewpoint, for Vietnam was a war where many badly wounded soldiers had their lives saved in almost miraculous fashion by the most modern medical technology that had ever been used in a war zone. However, rarely was a physician available on the battlefield, where a corpsman provided primary medical care to a wounded soldier until he could be lifted out by helicopter to an Evac hospital for more sophisticated medical treatment. Most of the groups that recorded soul or rhythm and blues were all black, but the foursome called Change of Pace includes one white member.

The African Americans that fought in Vietnam are honored with this memorial that is in close proximity to the Vietnam Memorial in Washington, D.C. Source: Roger Lambert

Freda Payne's "Bring the Boys Home," released in the midst of "Vietnamization" when American troops were being withdrawn from Vietnam, demands that the process move even faster: "Turn the ships around, lay the weapons on the ground." It describes the troops as tragic victims of the war, that they don't really want to be there that "they're tryin' to get home" but can't. This song and "Bring My Buddies Back" not only make the identical statement of getting the soldiers home safely, but they also seem to share the same melody, at least to the untrained ear. The fact that "Bring the Boys Home" suggests that the troops disobey orders alarmed government censors, who couldn't control soldiers in Vietnam hearing it on tape players or "pirate" radio stations. Armed Forces Radio, of course, refrained from airing such a seditious musical message. This was yet another unique aspect of Vietnam, the difficulty that the government had in insulating enlisted men from the "wrong" kind of messages.

A tour in Vietnam was a difficult experience year around but especially during the Christmas holidays. A duo called Johnny and Jon, in their recording "Christmas in Vietnam," describe in quite emphatic and soulful fashion how painful it was to be there during the Yuletide. They recognize that they won't be home for this holiday but manage to be philosophical about it: "But I can't let it bother me." Still they can't help but lament about how strange this Christmas will be in a foxhole with nothing to see but Vietcong. Homesickness prevailed the year around, as attested to in songs like William Bell's "Lonely Soldier" and Bobby Joy's "Letter from a Soldier." The latter is particularly interesting as it describes serving in Vietnam as like being on "the other side." The "Lonely Soldier" also has some unique words of comfort for his girl back in the states, telling her that she shouldn't feel so bad because there are so many others like her missing their men.

Like their white counterparts, black soldiers found that their music managed to take the edge off of being in Vietnam, at least for a while. Behind the lines, the most popular dwellings occupied by enlisted men were the ones that had plenty of music, and these were dubbed "dynamite hootches." No performer's music was played more often than that of Aretha Franklin, who was becoming a musical force to be reckoned with back in the states, where "her hits were coming like cannonballs, blowing holes in the stylized Motown sound." Blacks in Vietnam sang her praises and even compared her to the Beatles. One soldier said hearing Aretha's music brought tears to his eyes.[24] Although songs like "Chain of Fools" and "Respect" didn't directly address the war, tapes of her music became as essential a part of field kits as C-rations and morphine. She fondly recalls how Vietnam vets have expressed their gratitude for how her music helped them cope with the stress of war.[25] Like Jimi Hendrix, the appeal of Franklin's music transcended race, and Densby Fawcett, a white female war correspondent still loves songs like "I Never Loved A Man (The Way I Loved You)," "The Weight," "People Get Ready," and "Natural Woman" and plays them when she wants to write about her experiences in Vietnam.[26]

The Temptations, another of Motown's plentiful stable of recording artists, also were popular in Vietnam, regardless of race. Bob Hersey, who served with K Troop in the 11th Armored Regiment regards the Temptations' "My Girl" as his "strongest musical remembrance of the war."

> "My Girl was hot in '68 -'69 and we played it all the time. When I went on R&R to Bangkok in October of '68, all the bands in the clubs were playing it. One band substituted the words 'Thai Girl' for 'My Girl' when they sang 'talkin' 'bout, Thai girl.' I've never forgotten that."[27]

The Temptations' "Ball of Confusion" offers an apt metaphor for the war era. In a style that presages modern "rap music," the group rattles off a whole host of calamities that justify the title of the song, including increasing sales of illegal drugs, the indifference of young people, and neighborhoods struggling with tensions caused by racial transition. This chaos is compounded by "revolution" being in the air as well as "gun control, the sound of soul." There is an atmosphere of fear as people all over the world demand an end to the war in Vietnam. Curiously, the only safe place away from this pandemonium of crisis is "on an Indian reservation." An

Internet social critic wrote that he was "struck dumb" by the parallels between what the *Temptations* sang about in "Ball of Confusion" and the world today. He is certainly not alone in this observation. In his book about the group, Temptations, Otis Williams comments on the piece's timelessness as well as the fact the lyrics made it quite a mouthful for the group to sing:

> "When Norman (Whitfield) first showed us the lyrics, we were wondering how we were going to get all those damn syllables in one line. It reminded me of one of Bob Dylan's songs, 'Subterranean Homesick Blues.' Of course today, lots of people know the song by heart, but the first time...we stopped in our tracks. Fortunately, Dennis (Edwards) had a fast tongue."[28]

Despite the misgivings many blacks were beginning to have about the war, the African-American superstar James Brown, "The Godfather of Soul," recorded the patriotic "America is My Home" (1968) and received criticism from fellow African Americans who accused him of being an "Uncle Tom" and that the song was a "sell-out." Others expressed astonishment that he would dare to record such a song "after what happened to Dr. King." Brown reacted to the criticism by explaining that when he sang "America is My Home," he "didn't mean the government was my home, I meant the land and the people."[29] The fact that he campaigned for Hubert Humphrey, the Democratic presidential candidate in 1968, was seen as further proof that Brown was little more than a toady for the white man. Although Humphrey was an early champion of civil rights, some blacks blamed him for the war. Brown also drew criticism for visiting Vietnam to entertain the troops there and "carry the soul music message to the U.S. GIs." Jet Magazine, a major black-oriented magazine devoted its cover and a feature article to the tour, where Brown rebutted those who said he shouldn't go:

"I don't like the war either, but we have soul brothers over there. We are in a war which we can't get away from tomorrow. If we leave there, they (Viet Cong) may come here... Over here, we can't do anything but talk and try to keep up the morale of our black soldiers. But over there I figure that I could be right in there with them, risking our lives too, and this is what we want to do... in addition to bringing them some swinging and soulful entertainment."[30]

Other black artists like Charlie and Inez Foxx joined Brown in producing patriotic music, at least to show support for those of their race who were fighting in Vietnam (see Chapter 5).

Student Essays

Marvin Gaye's "What's Goin On?" was successful in evoking strong emotional responses from student essayists:

> "It left me sad and melancholy. I heard words in the song that I had never heard before such as, 'punish me with brutality,' 'brotherly love' and 'picket signs.' I was quite surprised. I now have a more open mind to the music I listen to and hear. Even though always knowing the words to every song might make me fall under the category of a genius, I will never again underestimate the power of the spoken word and the subliminal message that it holds."

> "The songs I liked before this class, I enjoy even more now. I also was able to hear music I had not been exposed to before this time. The song, "What's Goin On?" by Marvin Gaye has him analyzing the pain that mothers and brothers went through while their young men were off in a place unheard of by many. He didn't want to see any more tears. Women were crying for the children they had lost. When Marvin sang 'Brother, brother, brother' this song showed his emotion for all the black men who lost their lives Vietnam. 'Father, father" was a plea to the government not to escalate the war more than it had been. The year this song came out was 1971. People all over the country had picketed and Marvin Gaye wanted both sides (United States/North Vietnam) to set their weapons down, talk to each other, and come to a peaceful conclusion. This song not only made

many valid points, there was something magical about the melody. The words seemed to touch the hearts of everyone. The song also rekindled an emotion. I wanted to hear the song over and over again."

"I am most intrigued by the music from the black artists. I feel that the entire black military community should have each received a Congressional Medal of Honor just for serving a country that treated them like second-class citizens. In Marvin Gaye's song, 'What's Going On?' the tone of the music is peaceful and uplifting, but it still addressed the absurdity of the war. Gaye seemed to be addressing an unlimited audience, while some of the other artists probably did not concern themselves with the black community. In my opinion, it seemed that Marvin wanted peace for all mankind, not just for those who matched his skin color."

"This song is a good example of one where the lyrics really touch the soul of the listener. Love, not war, is the message here. Too many brothers dying, too many mothers crying. The meaning is to let the listeners realize the sadness and destruction that the war was bringing on. I can't think of a better way to send a message. This song is beautiful. The beat is danceable, and Mr. Gaye's voice is sensual. The song has appeal."

"It portrays the viewpoint of the black community about the Vietnam War. Many blacks asked the question of why they should fight for a country that denied them their civil rights. I can very much relate to the pacifistic lyrics in Gaye's eloquent song, because I feel the same way about war in general. I agree with the lyrics that state too many men are dying and believe those words of wisdom can be applied to every single one of the 58,000 soldiers killed during the war. I think even an extreme pro-war patriot could identify with Gaye's words."

Another student was more dispassionate in his appraisal of the song, finding it appealing because the message was delivered in a pleasing melodic fashion:

"It is worthy of being deemed the best of the music we heard. I like this anti-war song because it conveyed the spirit of the black community through a very ear-catching tune. It is a very soulful piece of music."

This student liked the song but disagreed with Gaye's reliance on love as a remedy:

"Personally, I do not know if I agree completely with this theme. For example, Hitler would never have understood 'love' nor would he have stopped the slaughter of Jews, gypsies, gays and other so-called social deviants kin the name of 'love.' Sadly, 'love' alone cannot always conquer and stop hate and other injustices. Sometimes war is the only way. However, the Vietnam War was an unjust war. Marvin Gaye was correct that there were far too many young men and women dying. What did they die for? When do we not blindly follow a president and NOT go to war. These are the questions that this song stirred up in my soul. These are questions that divided a nation."

Another student found Gaye's message "timeless" and one that transcended politics:

"It's a beautiful and eloquent song that, unlike a lot of the music of the era, does not feel dated. It does not deal with strictly political issues, but rather, also the problems of brutality and violence concerns of all times... In the background, which is made up to sound like a party, barely discernible words are heard asking, 'What's happening brother?' and 'What's your name?' This promotes an atmosphere of caring and connection between people, much like one would find at a party of good friends or family members."

Virtually every student found the treatment of the black soldier as described in "(The Two Wars of) Old Black Joe" to be appalling:

"I really don't like anything that reminds me of the discrimination that went on against the different races. This made me sad while listening to it. I hate to think of the fight some people fought against each other. Also, the fact that the colored men that died in combat were not allowed to be buried in "white man cemeteries" makes me angry. I can't believe that people couldn't put their race issues behind them and try to fight together."

"'(The Two Wars of) Old Black Joe' was very revealing. I live in a time and place where racism is not politically correct. I mostly run into racist jokes and snide comments about nappy hair. I was once again reminded of how far we've come and how much further we need to go. A bunch of white folk digging up their relatives because a black man was buried there does seem a little outlandish. At the same time it's not entirely out of the realm of possibility. This bizarre, ignorant behavior has always baffled me. This just shows me how much more I need to make sure I don't forget it so it doesn't happen again."

"This is a song that exposes all of the hypocrisy and ignorance of the social unrest. It tells the story of one man that represented thousands of others. Reverend William L. Truly, Jr., made me tear up thinking about such devastating injustices. Reverend Truly, like the others, sings the story as peaceful as a sunrise on a Sunday morning. I cannot believe that anyone could consider him or herself a virtuous person and simultaneously refuse to properly bury a fellow American and Christian. Sadly, half of the country at this time was living this sanctimonious existence."

Edwin Starr's "War" was distinctive because, to put it kindly, it was raucous and redundant. There were students who found it to be an amusing period piece and really didn't take it very seriously. Others had various pros and cons:

"'War' is a very good song. When I hear this song, I've always just wanted to dance to it because of the great beat. Now, after analyzing it in class, it takes on a new meaning when I hear it. I saw a movie the other day (a comedy) and they played this song. In the past, I would have just sung along. This time I found myself telling everyone that this was about the Vietnam War and I found myself more attentive to the words. I also thought how '...war...what is it good for...absolutely nothing...' is how I felt about this war. I think if I had lived during the Vietnam War, I would have been a Dove."

"While I know this was not a universal favorite with the class, I still like it for its simplicity and lyric-wise it does say a lot, you just have to get past all the noise. And it does it without saying something as inane and hopelessly unrealistic as all need to do is let love and kind words fix everything."

"This song was more colorful and vibrant than most and also had a lot of energy. Most of the anti-war songs were like this. But it was also very monotonous."

"'War' by Edwin Starr is not as eloquent as many of the other songs we heard. It certainly wasn't as cerebral and thoughtful as some of the others. However, there is something fundamentally moving about this song. It brings back the sense of outrage I felt during a time of turbulence and upset. There is something animalistic and base in the rhythm of this song, and all kidding aside, it is a lot of fun to sing."

"I am sorry, I know this is a favorite for many people out there, but I personally could never get into this song. It sounds to me like some boys/men screaming into the microphone and not explaining where they are coming from. The point of the song is a mystery to me. In a song like this I expect the writer to at least explain where he or she is coming from. I want to be able to understand their feelings. Was Edwin Starr upset about the loss of a good friend or was he seeing a possible fate that would lie ahead for him in the future. I just couldn't get into this song, it was like nothing was there. I also had a hard time understanding all that he was saying, the loud music in the background and him literally yelling. I had a hard time reaching or even receiving his message."

"This song is just an uplifting kind of song. In the song it is saying how war is wrong and a bad thing. This is something that everybody already knows, but the song has such a great beat to it that practically everyone likes it. This would have been a good song for the men over in Vietnam, because a song like this just seems to put you in a good mood."

"Edwin Starr brings a little soul to the table with his song 'War.' The meaning and purpose of this song is pretty up front, so there is no denying his message. I can feel the intensity of the rhythm pulling me up on my feet to the dance floor. Starr's enthusiasm puts me in a pew in a gospel church listening to the Reverend preaching an anti-war sermon. Edwin's message is powerful and positive, unlike the social position of black people during the war."

Some general comments about the issues raised by the African-American music about the war:

"The African-American artists we heard seemed to sense that a large percentage of 'their' nation saw them as just a bunch of colored imbeciles. I did not live through this time nor am I black. I cannot help thinking if I had been in Marvin's, Edwin's, or Reverend Truly's position, my lyrics would have been much more hostile."

"Time has moved on, and the laws and social protocols of racial equality have evolved. However, time and progress cannot change what has already happened. My peers' parents and grandparents were still sitting in the back of the bus not long ago. I think the war made everyone a bit more ego-centric, after all, who could trust anyone after the big slices of deception pie our 'fearless leaders' served the country. With just cause, I think this affected the already mistreated black community much more intensely. I think the Vietnam War has indirectly caused rap groups like Da Lench Mob to write songs like 'Guerillas in tha Mist,' where angry black men curse and preach violence upon the evil 'white devils.'

The violence in the music of today's black artists grows directly from the frustration of their past peaceful protests. Look where it got Dr. King. If only the white aristocrats of the United States government would have the courage and compassion to listen to their messages versus hiding their fear and ignorance behind fear and censorship. If only they could realize their fear of this violent music is nothing compared to the fear the black people had living in and serving a country that treated them like peons. Censorship is the enslavement of one's thoughts, and I thought we abolished slavery many years ago. Everyone is paying the price for this huge wave of paranoia. Unfortunately, this caused men and women of all colors to suffer the loss of life of a loved one. Thankfully, the music from the Vietnam War still exists as a reminder and a teacher."

Footnotes:

1 Nadine Cohoodas, *Spinning Blues Into Gold: The Chess Brothers and the Legendary Chess Records.* New York: St. Martin's Griffin, 2000. p. 129.

2 Bob Thiele, as told to Bob Golden, *What A Wonderful World: A Lifetime Of Recordings.* New York: Oxford University Recordings, 1995. p. 88.

3 Donald E. Clarke, *The Rise and Fall of Popular Music.* New York: St. Martin's Griffin, 1996. pp. 370 -371.

4 Ruth Brown with Andrew Yule, *Miss Rhythm: The Autobiography of Ruth Brown, Rhythm and Blues Legend.* New York: Donald I. Fine Books. 1996. pp. 109 - 110.

5 Thiele, p. 83.

6 Hank Davis, *"The Survival of Troy Shondell: Going Beyond One Hit Wonders."* Goldmine. p. 36. December 17, 1999.

7 Charlie Gillett, *The Sound of the City: The Rise of Rock and Roll.* New York: Outerbridge and Dienstfrey. 1970. p. 239.

8 A generation earlier, music recorded by blacks was known as 'negro sinful or secular' music, although negro "gospel" songs garnered some approval from musicologists: "the negro "sinful" or secular song is not generally as popular or well known as the spiritual among the majority of the white population." *David Hall, The Record Book.* New York: Smith and Durrell: 1940. p. 669.

9 Joanne Grant (Ed.) *Black Protest: History, Documents and Analyses: 1619 to the Present.* Fawcett: New York, 1966, pp. 415-416. The leaflet was distributed after the death of John D. Shaw, 23, a resident of McComb who was killed in Vietnam. He had participated in civil rights demonstrations in McComb in 1961

10 Gerald Astor, *The Right to Fight: African-Americans in the Military.* Novato (CA): Presidio Press, 1998. p. 68.

11 Spencer C. Tucker (Ed) *Encyclopedia of the Vietnam War: A Political, Social and Military History.* ABC-CLIO, Inc. Santa Barbara, 1998. Statements on black casualties in Vietnam. Vol. I, p. 7.

12 Blacks referred to whites as "the beast" behind their backs.

13 Appy, *Encyclopedia of the Vietnam War:* p. 224.

14 Jack Salzer (Ed.) et. al., *The Encyclopedia of African-American Culture and History.* New York, Simon and Schuste MacMillan, 1996. Vol. 5, p. 2743.

15 Salzer, *African-American Culture and History.* p. 2743.

16 Gail Byckely, *American Patriots: The Story of Blacks in the Military from the Revolution to Desert Storm.* New York: Random House, 2001. p. 419.

17 Interview with Dan O'Hara, January 2003.

18 At the same time that Gordy was wary of controversial music about Vietnam, Motown created the Black Forum spoken word label. Offerings included albums like "Free Huey" by Black Power firebrand Stokely Carmichael and a recording of Dr. Martin Luther King's speech denouncing the Vietnam War, "Why I Oppose the War in Vietnam." Then there was "Guess Who's Coming Home: Black Fighting Men Recorded Live in Vietnam," by Wallace Terry, the author of "Bloods," that was based on audio tapes compiled by Terry. There was definitely an internal struggle taking place at Motown during this time between those who wanted the label to speak out more strongly on social and political issues and those who cautioned that "message songs" would bring a slump in profits. Suzanne E. Smith, *Dancing in the Street: Motown and the Cultural Politics of Detroit."* Cambridge: Harvard University Press." pp. 230 - 231.

19 Sadly, Edwin Starr passed away in March 2003.

20 Gerald Posner, *Motown: Music. Money, Sex, and Power.* New York: Random House, 2002. pp. 172 - 173.

21 Salzer, *African-American Culture and History.* p. 1094.

22 Steve Webb, *"The Discoveries 100: Our Take on the Most Important Musicians of the Century."* Discoveries. p. 51. January 2000.

23 Roger Hayes, *On Point."* Novato (CA): Presidio Press, 2000. p. 245.

24 Stanley Goff, et. al. *Brothers: Black Soldiers in the Nam.* Novato: (CA): Presidio Press, 1982. p. 160.

25 Gerri Hirshey, *"We Gotta Get Out of This Place: The True, Tough Story of Women in Rock."* New York: Atlantic Monthly Press, 2001. p. 70.

26 Tad Bartimus, et. al. (Ed.) *War Torn: Stories of War from the Women*

Reporters Who Covered Vietnam. New York: Random House, 2002. p. 18.

27 Interview with Bob Hersey, September 2002.

28 Otis Williams with Patricia Romanowski, Temptations. New York: G.P. Putnam's Sons, 1988.

29 James Brown with Bruce Tucker, *James Brown: the Godfather of Soul.* New York: The MacMillan Publishing Company, 1986. p. 196.

30 Chester Higgins, *"JB Maps 'Soul' Tour of Vietnam For GIs."* Jet Magazine, June 6, 1968.

Chapter 5:
The Music of Combat

The technology available in the 1960s for playing recorded music allowed American troops to hear popular songs almost everywhere and anywhere they might be in the Republic of South Vietnam. Armed Forces Radio and its television service (AFTRS) in Saigon played most of the hits that were on the popular music charts in the states. However, since AFR was an arm of the military, there was a kind of subtle censorship that kept certain songs from making the "in country" radio play list.[1] Oddly, any music with a "French flavor" was also excluded.[2] Those who wanted to hear truly "hard" rock like the Doors or Jimi Hendrix and some of the more blatant protest music had to resort to tapes and tape players that could be purchased at post exchanges like "Freedom Hall" at Danang where the First Marine Division shopped.[3] Cigarettes were fourteen cents a pack and twelve packs of beer were available at bargain prices. Radios could also be purchased at most PXS and soldiers like Dennis Aho owned a Sony transistor radio as well as a Zenith Transoceanic short wave that allowed him to hear songs like the Bunkinghams' "Kind of a Drag" and other hits of the day. The music even followed Aho on R&R, and he first heard the Bee Gees' "Holiday" at Bon Di Beach in Australia.[4] Another source of the most recent hits was when a "new guy" arrived from the states, bringing the latest music with him on cassettes, eight tracks or vinyl. Sometimes those returning from R&R brought the current music with them along with elaborate sound systems, which provided a musical background for the war at places like Con Thien in northernmost South Vietnam:

> "Guys coming back from R&R had bought the most sophisticated sound systems. They were really powerful and could even compete with the noise produced by heavy artillery. I never will forget one night when we were providing artillery

> support for ground units who had been caught in a ground ambush. In between rounds, we could hear the Moody Blues 'Nights in White Satin' coming from the stereo speakers. That was really bizarre. Whenever I hear that song now, it takes me back to that night at Con Thien."[5]

Soldiers also received tapes of the music in the mail. At An Hoa, "tapes of Jimi Hendrix and the Doors almost drowned out the sound of outgoing artillery."[6] Raul Herrara who served with the "Swift Boats"[7] at Chu Lai even received a record, sent by his mother. It was a 45-rpm, an instrumental called "Soul Finger" by the Barkays. Herrara didn't ask her to send it and concluded that she heard it played at a record shop back home and figured that he'd like it and he did.[8] In these pre-Walkman days, some soldiers even attached tape players to their helmets and took the music right into the "bush" with them. However, it was easier and safer to play and enjoy the music at camps in the rear, and in these locations this was done with a vengeance:

> "When you walked down between the quonset huts at Dong Ha, from each one you could hear a different song or you might hear a Beatles' song like 'Yellow Submarine.' Walk a little farther and you might catch a country tune from the Charlie Daniel's Band. A little farther on and you could hear Barry McGuire's 'Eve of Destruction' blaring from yet another hooch."[9]

The familiar tower in Con Thien. This was about as far north in Vietnam as you could get. From this lookout post you could watch "Charlie" going through war games with the aid of a periscope. This is just across the Ben Hai River, which was the boundary for the DMZ, or the Demilitarized Zone. As long as the enemy stayed on their side of the river, all you could do was watch them train in preparation for fighting you. It was a unique place for many reasons, including the fact that you could hear songs like "Nights in White Satin" during the artillery barrages. Source: Paul Helbach

Paul Helbach stands in front of his jeep at Dong Ha, a place where the popular songs of the day could be heard virtually everywhere. Souce: Paul Helbach

Personnel at AFR took some pains to see that, no matter how distant and isolated a base camp was, troops stationed there heard their programming. If soldiers brought in a transmitter, radio engineers would see to it that the device was adjusted to the correct frequency and then provided instructions on how to set up an antenna.[10] Although there were instances where troops played radios and cassettes and even sang music in landing zones and other distinctly dangerous places in the bush, common sense usually dictated where and when they listened to music:

> "However, outside the perimeter, troops with any common sense were too concerned with their personal safety to risk their lives listening to radio entertainment. ...Though REMFs (rear-echelon mother fuckers) could listen to radio or watch television at their leisure, the radio was a luxury many people could not afford because the noise was not conducive to finding the enemy."[11]

What they heard over AFR was more than just a steady succession of Montavani and polkas[12] as stereotyped in the movie *Good Morning Vietnam.* Once an FM station was added, even jazz was a regular part of the programming. How strange it must have been to hear Dave Brubeck's jazz classic "Take Five" emanating from a patrol boat traversing the Mekong Delta or at an isolated camp in the Central Highlands. "Canned" radio shows from America were also rebroadcast, including *Hawaii Calling,* which became a regular programming feature. Unlike World War II or Korea, officers and enlisted men listened to different kinds of music, and soldiers often complained that Armed Forces Radio programming was geared toward satisfying the tastes of their superiors. One soldier, who preferred to remain anonymous, characterized Armed Forces Radio as: "the world's shittiest, small-town Midwest old-woman right-wing plastic useless propagandizing bummer unturned-on controlled low-fidelity non-stereo."[13]

Then there were the small "local" stations that operated independently of Armed Forces Radio at places like the air base at Tuy Hoa near Da Nang. There, Mike Brimball worked as an aircraft mechanic by day and spun records by night on a show called "Tom O'Neal's Spinning Wheel." According to Brimball:

> "We operated out of a little trailer at Tuy Hoa. We played 45s and albums, about 500 different songs. During the day we alternated between country and western, easy listening and pop. After midnight we played what we wanted because the officers were asleep by then. I was on the air from April of 1970 through August of that year. The guys must have appreciated what I did because when I was ready to rotate, they threw a big party for me with steaks and beer and everything."[14]

That anti-war records were played late at night by disc jockos like Brimball and others is no revelation to anyone familiar with the music scene in Vietnam. This was the first American war where a considerable amount of anti-war music was available. Troops listened to it at the same time they were fighting the war, usually on tapes or "pirate" radio stations since Armed Forces Radio eschewed songs that made anti-war statements. One of the most popular of the "pirate" stations was "Underground Saigon" where Dave Rabbitt hosted a three-hour show that was heard on a nightly basis. Rabbitt proclaimed at the beginning of one broadcast that he would say what he felt like saying and proves it by calling The Who's "See Me Feel Me," "See Me, F—k Me. Information about where the best marijuana can be found and the location of new massage parlors is also provided. The weather is given by "Captain Ivan Pansy" in a very passable impression of Teddy Kennedy. "Creighton Abrams" even is said to call in to say, "The Army sucks." That Rabbitt is anti-war isn't difficult to determine as his show is replete with comments like, "Fighting a war for someone else's freedom is like f—king for someone else's virginity." He also quotes graffiti from latrine walls that support his views: "Eighteen days until I can go home to picket and protest this f—king waste of human lives that lifers and the government call a war." Requests are phoned in (phone number is 6969) for songs like the Byrd's "Eight Miles High" to be dedicated to "my campadre' Peter and myself." "The hits just keep on comin," says Rabbitt and songs like Three Dog Nights' "Mama Told Me Not to Come," Vanilla Fudges' "You Keep Me Hanging" and Blood Rock's "DOA" are played. How the latter dirge, that describes graphically the death throes of a young couple dying of injuries sustained in an automobile accident, went over with soldiers who had already come in close proximity to death, one can only imagine. You could even buy a sweatshirt from "Underground Saigon" showing, of course, a rabbit, who displays a sign that says, "f—k it, before it f—ks you."[15]

Music that expressed reservations about the war could also be heard late at night on ships like the U.S.S. Truax when "guys with guitars would go on the mess deck and sing, including songs that were plainly anti-war." Otherwise the only music heard aboard ship was "banal Muzak."[16] Airman Ed Bielarczyk was able to hear the popular music of the day in a community building at Phu Cat Air Force Base known as the "Music Center." Here Bielarczyk and his buddies donned earphones and listened to songs on reel-to-reel tapes. Among the selections he heard was Country Joe and the Fish's "Maria" and Bob Lind's "Elusive Butterfly," which made him "think about getting back home."[17] He also identified with Jimi Hendrix's "All Along the Watchtower" because of the ubiquitous guard towers that surrounded nearly every base of any consequence in Vietnam.

Buck Sergeant Ed Bielarczyk and AFC Ballard in their office in Saigon with two reel-to-reel players (above) and close up of the players (right). The reel-to-reel players provided nearly non-stop music. Another airman named Adrian Cronauer showed a similar sense of humor in Saigon, but his exploits in Good Morning Vietnam were probably exaggerated.

Star-studded live musical entertainment was delivered to the armed forces in Vietnam by Bob Hope's USO tours. Other live entertainment of varying degrees of quality was available for the enjoyment of the military all over Vietnam. Philippine bar bands seemed to be ubiquitous and put their own "spin" on the popular song hits of the day back in the states. Although these groups were uncannily adept at musical mimicry, sometimes the singers couldn't quite manage the linguistic nuances of the English language, so the refrain of tunes like "Proud Mary" came out as "rollin, rollin' on de ribber." For some reason, "Love Potion Number Nine" was a staple of their repertoire and was played ad nauseam. However, this was a small price to pay to hear music performed in person, and the men, who were starved for any kind of entertainment as relief from the stress of war, awaited these USO shows with a keen sense of anticipation. The "Pretty Kittens," an American all-female band, composed of four eighteen- year-old women did two or three shows a day all over Vietnam during a grinding five-month tour in 1967. They performed, often from the back of a flatbed truck, at camps at Da Nang, Bien Hua, Marble Mountain, and others. An all-girl group like this was not only a unique experience for their almost exclusively male audiences, but being in Vietnam also had an impact on the girls, as singer and guitarist Bobbie Jo Pettit attests:

"We were just constantly doing shows. It was ideal because we were the same ages as most of the GIs, doing American songs from home that were very current right then. All the stuff that was just real American. Being round-eyed women was a real premium over there, and to speak English instead of Australian-type English was even more valuable. That was about a five-month tour, and it absolutely changed everything for me. I mean, I had no concept of what Vietnam was when I went over there; how I managed to agree to go, I don't know. But I'm certainly glad I did."[18]

USO shows brought the entertainment to the troops. Source: Mary Branigan

The Miss USA pageant even came to Vietnam. Source: Ed Bielarczyk

An Australian musical group, "Sweethearts on Parade," had their performance for the 1st Reconnaissance Company at a base near Da Nang ended abruptly in tragic fashion. As the group's lead singer, Miss Catherine Ann Warnes, a stunning blonde "round eye," was in the middle of a song, she "suddenly stepped back from the microphone, clutched her heart, and fell to the floor, dead." At first shouts of "sniper" went up, but an investigation revealed she had been the innocent victim of a .22 caliber bullet fired from outside the officers' club by an intoxicated soldier, who thought this was the most effective way to end a personal grudge match with another soldier. Although the soldier was later court-martialed and found guilty of "unpremeditated murder," he was later retried and exonerated of any wrongdoing.[19]

Music was also used by American forces to confuse and disorient the enemy. A former Green Beret told me that Creedence Clearwater Revival's "Run Through the Jungle" was a favorite choice for this tactic. Sometimes those on night guard duty at a base camp would turn their radios up to full volume so any Viet Cong "sappers" that might be lurking outside the wire would hear the music and know that those inside were awake and vigilant.[20] Sometimes troops would play music on the helicopter that was dropping them into a combat situation not only to distract the enemy but also to "pump themselves up" for the impending fray. The speakers were usually located on the footpads of the chopper.[21] Music was also a way for the troops to "detach" themselves from the grim business of war:

> "We were all a bunch of teenagers, and we used music to cope with the stress of war. Like when we were dropping white phosphorous rounds on the enemy. We knew that was pretty lethal stuff. Music allowed us to detach ourselves from the havoc we were wreaking."[22]

The lengthy and monotonous "In-a-Gadda-Da-Vida" by Iron Butterfly was a song that Jon Seikkulla and his comrades listened to as a way of "coming down" after a particularly difficult mission: "It gave us a connection back to the world after intense combat."[23] Line troops also loved the Beatles' version of "Act Naturally," which was played on Armed Forces Radio and even "sang along with it on their tape recorders and savored it until it belonged to them." While covering Bravo Company First Battalion 8th Cavalry on a sweep just north of the Ia Drang Valley, CBS correspondent John Laurence could hear someone toward the front of the column singing "Act Naturally" in a voice that was "pure and right on the notes, a singer's voice that rang with the rich country twang of the American South, piercing the hot jungle gloom like an arrow."[24]

Even American prisoners of war, existing under the worst possible conditions in prison camps in North Vietnam, were permitted by their captors to hear Western music; however, this was not done out of kindness but for propaganda and psychological warfare purposes. The music that blared over the camp speakers ranged from Johnny Cash and Nancy Sinatra to classical music like Brahms and Beethoven. The North Vietnamese were particularly cruel in playing Christmas carols during the holidays in order to manipulate the minds of the prisoners when they were most vulnerable. Although the POWs were aware of the reasons why they were hearing the Christmas music they enjoyed it nonetheless:

> "1966-shot-down Air Force Captain Norman McDaniel recalled hearing 'Ave Maria' over the Zoo's PA system his first Christmas in the camps and experiencing the 'greatest sadness and deepest longings that I have ever known.' Howard Rutledge granted that the carols were a ploy to manipulate the homesick Americans but welcomed the hol-

iday music nonetheless. Catching portions of an awful recording of 'Silent Night,' he found the hymn, 'scratches and all...beautiful beyond describing.'"[25]

According to David Wheat, who spent almost eight years as a prisoner of war, the North Vietnamese even encouraged their charges to form a choir one Christmas, but Wheat and his comrades were wary of the motives behind such seemingly benign overtures:

> "We had to be careful about being used in publicity photos. Sometimes we were forced into situations where it seemed we were being treated well and the North Vietnamese would exploit that for their own purposes. They wanted world public opinion to think we were having one big party and, of course, we weren't."[26]

Sometimes the prisoners of war even made their own music, using crude musical instruments provided by their jailers.[27]

Corpsmen with reel-to-reel tape player at the 71st Evac Field Hospital Pleiku. Source: Boyd Dallos

Songs could be heard even in the operating room at the 71st Evac Hospital at Pleiku, where nurses and doctors sang songs like "Pirate Jenny" and "Marat Sade." The latter tune, a lament about the oppressed masses demanding their rights, became popular among medical personnel at other bases in Vietnam.[28] The ubiquitous Hendrix and his version of the "Star Spangled Banner" was played, and loudly, at all-night parties where the exhausted and often demoralized medical staff at Plei Ku attempted to unwind. The Animals' anti-war song "Sky Pilot" also made its way to the turntable at these gatherings.[29] Music filled up "down time" for medical personnel at Camp Evans in I Corps, according to Mary Banigan, who was a nurse attached to the eighteenth surgical wing there:

> "Actually, music in Vietnam was a large part of my 'down time' during my first tour. I was very much into the music of Rod McKeun and Glen Yarborough in my quiet time. It provided a psychological retreat where I could hide my mind from whatever happened during the day or night, depending on my shift. On nights when there was in-coming, I would put on my headset, plug into my reel-to-reel and play Santana, Iron Butterfly "In-A-Gadda-Da-Vida." Heavy... I only went into a bunker once, and that was my first or second night in Camp Evans. After that, I just tuned it out and took my chances. When it came to socializing, whatever played was loud and had a beat-music that you could sing-along or dance to...When I moved to Quang Tri, I got a lot of bootleg tapes from the Philippines for my reel-to-reel and usually had music playing whenever I was in my hootch...less Santana/Iron Butterfly and more folk songs, again for the psychological release, but the songs were more of the anti-war venue...and a lot of parody songs, but I've forgotten most...like the 'Vietcong Blues' or the 'Pepsodent Song'... 'You'll wonder where the yellow went when the H-Bomb hits the Orient'.... By the time I got into my second tour, folksongs were out and I was more into Johnny Mathis and motion picture soundtracks like 'Romeo and Juliet,' but the music was less important to me, it had become background noise."[30]

Nurses and physicians let off steam by performing music in Vietnam.

Another source of music was Radio Hanoi and "Hanoi Hannah" who played the popular songs along with anti-American propaganda. Still, American soldiers listened to it anyway, because they liked the music, if not the messenger who provided it:"

> "Three nights after I got there, Hanoi Hannah gets up on the bullshit net and welcomes my unit to Vietnam. She dedicated 'Tonight's the Night' by the Shirelles to us. 'Will You Still Love Me Tomorrow?' That's the one. The little c-nt face. But I liked listening to her. She put on some good jams.[31]

Many of those serving in Vietnam were proficient musicians and put their skills to work "in country," composing and singing songs that reflected their view of what fighting the war was like. Combat troops who were out in the bush somehow managed to bring guitars with them and unwound, when they had the chance, with music. Helicopter pilots at An Khe who felt homesick when they heard Johnny Cash's mournful "Folsom Prison Blues" changed the lyrics to fit their circumstances:

> "If I had my druthers and that freedom bird was mine,
> I think I'd move my DEROS[32] a little further up the line.
> Just to piss in potable water, that'd make my day.
> And to sit on cool hard comfort and
> Shit my blues away."[33]

Many other popular songs were parodied by the troops, including "Detroit City" and "Brown-Eyed Girl," which became "Slant-eyed Girl."[34]

Of necessity, the guitar was the primary instrument for the troops in the bush. Phil Ferrazano, who served with the Ninth Infantry, used an old beat up flat-top guitar, which was given to him because he "could play some:"

Phil Ferrazano and his guitar in Vietnam.

> "The strings were old but sounded ok in the barracks at night or on the berm during guard duty. Whenever it was needed it was there. We'd drink and play old songs. It is our piece of home, to hear the songs. Songs and music was our escape from the war. We'd laugh and we'd cry at times...especially if we drank too much and a certain song would trigger a memory of home or a sweetheart. I was the 4th owner of the guitar. It had decals and signatures from different years. It was a piece of history and I would be the one to take it home. The 9th division was leaving Vietnam in 1970. The guitar was to be sent home with the last man. But as fate would have it, the guitar, as an old soldier, died. Our company area blew up and was leveled to the ground and everything was lost. A piece of all us went up in smoke. Shortly after that, a friend went off one day and found me another guitar. I left it in the tent we had set up while we were ordered into Cambodia. My buddy was killed and I was wounded, I returned to that tent alone one day after my

> hospital stay and picked up that guitar and cried like a baby. Our family of soldiers was broken up and nothing would be the same again. Last year I got an e-mail. A guy in my unit, a year before me, was searching for the last owner of the guitar. He had found all the rest except the last. The last piece in the puzzle-he had found me. Then they all knew what had happened to their treasured guitar. Like the old soldier, it had done its job and then died. It was meant to stay there with the troops. Not to go home."[35]

The official source for music in South Vietnam was Armed Forces Radio, based in Saigon, where disc jockeys "spun" records for the troops in the bush. Troops could tune in on transistor radios from even the most remote base camps deep within the country and hear essentially what was being played back in the states. Discs containing the top hits were delivered to Vietnam on a regular basis so the music that the disc jockeys played was up to date. Some of the music was of the shallow "bubblegum" variety like the 1910 Fruitgum Company's "1-2-3 Red Light" and "Simon Says," but some of it was received enthusiastically, especially if it had that "hook," lyrics that defined the war experience. The troops weren't music critics so long as what they heard came from back home. It would be hard to pick out one song that the fighting men identified with most strongly, but there is a handful that stand out, including "We Gotta Get Out of This Place" by the Animals. Gene LeRoy, a disc jockey for Armed Forces Radio in Saigon in the mid-1960s featured this as his "morning wake-up song" and played it immediately after an episode of "chicken man." Troops would hear this at about 7:20 a.m. along with LeRoy's declaration: "From the Delta to the DMZ (demilitarized zone), it's time for our early morning sing-along!"[36] It became an anthem with the average serviceman who wanted to get out of Vietnam almost as soon as he got off the plane at Tan Son Nhut Air Base in Saigon or wherever his point of origin "in country" was. Raul Herrara, who served at Chu Li in the "Seat Boats," heard it at the "Straw Elephant:"

Gene LeRoy, the host of the popular "Dawnbuster Show," spins a disc at the studios of Armed Forces Radio in Saigon.
Source: Gene LeRoy.

"The Animals' 'We've Got To Get Out of This Place' was our anthem...at least at the Straw Elephant. You would have thought it a scene from an Irish Pub. Guys would stand up and sway their arms in the air, beer cans in hand and sing along...especially at the part that mentioned those words followed by 'if it's the last thing we ever do.'"[37]

"We Gotta Get Out of this Place"[38] is really about the hopelessness of growing up in the black ghetto, but as Herrera discloses, it was the refrain that the troops really listened to as it expressed their sentiments all too perfectly. Wherever one was close to combat in South Vietnam, the lyrics "We gotta get out of this place, if it's the last thing we ever do" effectively captured the troops' mood. The lyrics, "Gonna die before your time is through," suggesting eminent doom, also hit home. One veteran summed up the collective mood, "We thought we were all gonna die."[39] For this same reason another soldier showed disdain for the song:

> "You heard this song everywhere. They really cared about playing this song. They probably had good intentions and other troops obviously enjoyed hearing it. But I didn't care for it. Because I didn't believe getting out of there was even a remote possibility for me. I just felt I would never get out of that place alive."[40]

Combat journalists like John Laurence of CBS News played "We Gotta Get Out of This Place" so frequently at a hangout known as "Frankie's House" in Saigon that the record became "worn" and "tired" and the cover "frayed from use." To Laurence it was a song about social alienation" but to those who heard it in Vietnam, it took on a special meaning by "combing their anti-social feelings with a sense of doom and morbid self pity that accompanies young men to hard places." "Frankie's" was a kind of refuge for the "crazies" who followed the war as their profession and a place where they could unwind from the stress by drinking, smoking dope, and generally "goofing off." The record cabinet contained albums by Bob Dylan, the Rolling Stones, the Beatles, the Dave Clark Five, the Byrds, Buddy Holly and Joan Baez. A collection similar to what might be found in any home back in the states. Anyone who went on R & R had strict instructions to return with newly released LPs for the "common entertainment" of those who resided at the house.[41] Similar gatherings that focused on listening to music and drinking were a way to relax and put the war on hold, at least for a while:

> "I was very much into my Mexican music from San Antonio. Prior to shipping out to Vietnam, I made certain that I took a number of my local youth bands' albums with me. Some were in Spanish while others were in English. There were times when word got around that there would be a gathering of 'vatos' (dudes) to sit, drink, and listen to and eventually sing along to our Mexican music. Perhaps some of them released their emotions in that manner. In our culture, when moved by a special song or lyric, we belt out a yell that can often linger on for a good while. The deeper the song digs into your heart and yanks out your memory of home or the 'Dear John' letter that you just received, the louder and stronger the 'grito' became. Music in the 'Nam remains a vivid part of that far away place three decades ago."[42]

Beyond speaking for countless soldiers who were unnerved by Vietnam, "We Gotta Get Out of This Place" and similar songs have been described by a sociologist as "the source of oppositional ideology" that could have "demoralized the troops." At least one source I encountered in my research states "We Gotta Get Out Of This Place" was banned by Armed Forces Radio because of pressure from the Republic of Vietnam government (RVN).[43] It is clear that LeRoy played the song on his morning show, so perhaps it was played for a time and then removed from the play list once military censors established that it was unsuitable. In what is one of the leading studies of how the music of warfare impacts on popular culture, Les Cleveland points out how relatively easy it was for soldiers to hear music that conveyed a message that denounced the war they were engaged in fighting. The military high command tried to prevent the GIs from hearing these disparaging anti-war views but was unsuccessful:

> "It was not even able to suppress the transmissions of illegal broadcasters operating from some of the major U.S. bases, making derisory comments about the war and playing hard rock. In such ways, the Vietnam warrior was exposed to contradictions about the perception of the war that could not be resolved even in the postwar period when veterans found themselves striving for recognition and acceptance."[44]

Although it couldn't have been intended to address the war, "All Along the Watchtower," the Dylan composition as rendered by Jimi Hendrix, became a favorite with most anyone who heard it in Vietnam. Phrases like "There must be some way out of here" and "There's too much confusion here" spoke for those who were bewildered and disoriented by the chaos of the war zone. On the strength of music like this, Hendrix became something of a troubadour for the troops, who felt he was playing the real "melody of the war."[45] Any historian worth his or her salt learns early on to avoid absolute statements, but if there is one song that is quintessential in describing the combat experience in Vietnam, it is Hendrix's version of "All Along the Watchtower," which he is credited with transforming "from metaphysical parable into the national anthem of America-in Vietnam and Vietnam in America."[46] As one veteran of the war attests:

> "Jimi gave us the melody of war, raw and off-key, the ragged guys who'd been shot in the field...He represented a way to

listen to your own outer limits. Being there and listening to him, no matter what the kids back home thought his music meant, they could never connect at the level we did. We were in the right zone to tune in. More intensity, more extremism. When we got back to the world, it was the soundtrack of the war; and if you tried to communicate that to people here, you couldn't make them understand, they thought you were crazy."[47]

Hendrix most famous song "Purple Haze," which is dismissed by some as drug-induced nonsense, also may have relevancy to the war. It is likely that Hendrix came up with the idea for the title from the flares used by paratroopers for "spotting" before they made their jumps. However, the song's most famous lyric phrase, "Excuse me while I kiss the sky," is open to various interpretations. Another reason that Hendrix attracted such a following in Vietnam may have been that his music could be likened to an experience with drugs. Sadly, Vietnam was the American war where drug abuse among the troops ran rampant, at the same time that a drug sub-culture was evolving in the United States. When Grace Slick urged, "Feed your head," in the Jefferson Airplane's "White Rabbit," "hippies" back home, as well as soldiers in Vietnam did just that. As troops relaxed between missions with the aid of marijuana, Simon and Garfunkel's "Sounds of Silence" put them in a reflective mood and made them think of "the absurdity of war...and the cities, neon lights and being imprisoned in the military...and the alternative possibilities of the sounds of silence." The duo's "At the Zoo" triggered images of "animals at the zoo" and an appreciation of how the song described "some kind of philosophical value for each of the animals." George Harrison's "My Sweet Lord" caused a soldier to regard "the Christ image" conveyed in the song...as well as the "Hindu image" as what he wanted to get out of religion: this essential thing, the spirit of humanity or the common bond that unites us all."[48] This thoughtful soldier, while in route to Vietnam in Hawaii, found himself torn when he heard Buffy Sainte-Marie sing her composition "Universal Soldier:"

> "It bothered me for awhile...I kept busy or pushed it out of my mind somehow and didn't really deal with it to the extent of how I was involved with it. I built up some rationalization and said, well you know, that's really nice to think about it but we've got to deal with the realities of the world. Didn't want to deal very much with fact that she was telling what I might consider the truth."[49]

Another song that cropped up in interviews I conducted with Vietnam veterans was Otis Redding's "Sittin' on the Dock of the Bay." This is yet another recording that does not have an overt connection to serving in Vietnam, but one veteran told me that when he heard the song he wished he had nothing more to do than just what Redding was singing about, sitting on a dock and just watching "the tide roll in."[50] This probably seemed like the most sublime experience imaginable compared to "humping" through the Central Highlands on seemingly interminable reconnaissance patrols. He probably speaks for many of his counterparts, because this song was one of the most frequently heard in Vietnam, whether on Armed Forces Radio or tape players carried by the troops. Many other veterans, when they hear song like this, may "feel a swift, stabbing, bittersweet nostalgia for Vietnam." One soldier called the Redding tune "pure Vietnam" because it was playing when he "stepped off the plane into Vietnam."[51]

It is worth noting that "grunts" who heard a song in the Central Highlands or at Khe Sahn attached a far different meaning to it than someone who heard the same music back in the states. An excellent example of one such song is Crosby, Stills and Nash's "Suite: Judy Blue Eyes," which is obviously the story of a particularly intense love affair. However, for Mike Mueller it will always be a song about Vietnam where he heard it under such memorable circumstances:

> "I was a district operations advisor assigned to provide support for the South Vietnamese Army (ARVN) and that meant a lot of flying around in helicopters to various locations. I remember one particular afternoon. It was just the pilot and I in a Bell helicopter doing recon. Actually, we were just

> kind of goofing off. It was just a beautiful day. We flew over rivers and jungles and the pilot performed some particularly stunning aerial acrobatics around an old shot up French mansion in the middle of nowhere. We heard "Suite: Judy Blue Eyes" out of Saigon and I will always connect that song with that day. This was not a halcyon or peaceful period in my life but for a moment it was.[52]

When Dale Day heard another popular song of the day in Vietnam, "The Eve of Destruction," it was under decidedly unpleasant circumstances. Day served in the army's 53rd General Supply Group, which hauled supplies up and down the Mekong River, sometimes as far north as Cambodia:

> "We had gunboats in front and in back of us as we went up the Mekong Delta. B-52s started dropping bombs six or seven miles away. 'Eve of Destruction' was playing on the Armed Forces Radio at the same time that those big bombs hit. I thought that if this isn't the 'eve of destruction,' I don't know what is! I heard this song recently on an oldies radio station, and it sent shivers up and down my spine as it brought back memories of that day in the Delta."[53]

As Lt. Ed Hargrove drove madly down a sniper-infested road in the Mekong Delta, desperate to reach Can Tho before dark, the strains of country singer Billy Walker's "Cross the Brazos at Waco" drifted through his mind. Hargrove easily identified with the fugitive cowpoke portrayed in the song, which is eager to reach San Antonio where he will be safe from his pursuers. Hargrove, with a M-16 beside him in a jeep that had a sandbagged floorboard, changed the lyrics to "I'll be safe when I reach old Can Tho." The Brazos became the ferry at Bassac.[54]

Peter, Paul and Mary's "Puff the Magic Dragon" also took on a new meaning within the context of the Vietnam War and became far more than a pleasant, whimsical ballad about a friendship between a dragon and a little boy or the pleasures of smoking marijuana. To combat troops, "Puff" was one of the most formidable and powerful weapons used against the enemy and provided spectacular "light shows:"

> "These old CV-47 transports and DC-3s really worked out. With all the tracer rounds and bullets spewing out of those Gatling guns, it was like those light bridges from Flash Gordon. Those guns would shoot 6,000 rounds a minute, and lit up and could put a bullet in an area the size of a football field in about a minute. The name "Puff" or "Spooky" fit these gun ships perfectly. One problem was that the Gatling guns couldn't swing 180 degrees and enemy snipers would try to take them on after they'd made their sweep."[55]

"Puff the Magic Dragon" was thought to be a song about the relationship between a little boy and a dragon, or a tune about the pleasures of smoking pot. In the context of combat, fighting men, especially those who were smoking marijuana, saw a real dragon that was actually breathing fire. Marines dubbed this gun ship "Spooky," a name derived from the Classics IV hit song from 1967, which was intended to portray a young man who is puzzled by the eccentricities of his girlfriend. I have seen this song on a number of lists of recordings that are supposed to be related to the war, and the fact that it is considered a synonym for "Puff" makes it part of the music of the Vietnam War.

"Bad Mood Rising'" by Creedence Clearwater Revival allows one to appreciate vicariously the feeling soldiers had prior to a particularly dangerous mission, as John Fogerty belts out the ominous lyrics that strongly suggest the emerging "bad moon" portends imminent doom. This message would fill even the casual, detached listener with a sense of foreboding. To say nothing of how a soldier in a combat zone surrounded by death and the almost constant realization that one's own demise may well be imminent would relate to this song. The combat experience is one that thoroughly concentrates the mind and induces a keen sense of vulnerability that can summon up all kinds of omens or portents of doom, phantasmagorical images beyond the imaginative capabilities of even the most able horror writer. Such morbid thoughts undoubtedly entered the minds of paratroopers being dropped into the Au Shau Valley for a long-range reconnaissance patrol or Marines setting up a nocturnal "listening post" around embattled Khe Shan. "Recon" patrols sent out to inspect areas recently sprayed with Agent Orange, which now resembled barren lunar landscapes, had to feel the same sensation. A veteran told me that Dak To, the scene of a particularly horrendous confrontation between the North Vietnamese army and American troops, impressed him as "the ugliest place in the world, because of all the defoliation." It reminded him of the bleak areas of "no man's land" from movies about World War I.[56] The lyrics in "Bad Moon Rising', "hope you have got your things together, hope you are quite prepared to die," could have been written about soldiers of an earlier war. Similar thoughts probably went through the minds of those Union soldiers at Cold Harbor in the Civil War, for they pinned pieces of paper listing their names and addresses of next of kin to their tunics, knowing full well that their forthcoming attack on virtually impregnable Confederate positions would be little more than suicide.

So soldiers in Vietnam shared a sense of impending doom with their predecessors in other American wars, but the battlegrounds in Vietnam had a singularly unreal cast to them, made evident in the words used by those who served there to refer to places outside the country as "the world." These soldiers of the modern era of warfare had the bleak feeling that they had been somehow separated from civilization, that they were "strangers in a strange land." Those who worried the most about the highly uncertain future were the men who had what was known as "short timer's fever," as they contemplated the possibility of dying just a few days before their tour of duty was up and they were scheduled to leave Vietnam.

Midway through their tour of duty, there were many men who simply resigned themselves to the probability that they would likely die, a view that seems to be held by those "good old boys, drinkin' whiskey and rye, singin' this'll be the day that I die," in Don McLean's musical epic "American Pie." Lincoln St. Exit's "Time Has Come, Gonna Die" leaves little to the imagination in conveying the view that anyone serving in combat in Vietnam was inevitably doomed. The singer describes a scene where thousands of planes are flying overhead and everywhere there is "flowing blood," as he repeats the refrain, "Time has come, gonna die." The most memorable phrase from this exceedingly morbid song is "If there's a hell, I know this is it." Blood Sweat and Tears jazzed up a Laura Nyro composition entitled "And When I Die," and it became a top ten hit in 1969. It caught on with troops in Vietnam, especially the marines, because it explored a topic that was never very far from their minds. Nyro intended the song to send out the message that while death was inevitable for her, there was hope for the future, because eventually she "would bring new life into the world" when her child was born.[57] The Leathernecks more than likely related to the tune because it took a cavalier attitude toward dying coupled with the fact that they had a wife back in the states who would provide a child to carry on, regardless of what happened to them. However, there were instances when the song was not well received:

> "Goodrich sang slowly, looking mournfully at Hodges...A large hand seized the neck of his guitar, killing the chords, then a massive arm wrenched the guitar from Goodrich's grasp. Goodrich looked up and found Bagger staring at him. Bagger kicked the ammo box, as if testing the strength of the wood before he kicked it out from under Goodrich. 'The song is over a Senator. Who the f—k do you think you are? That was an asshole thing to do. An asshole thing.' His former audience stared silently at him. They often sang the song among themselves, but the pointed introduction had been too much, like a gallows wish.[58]

One extremely fatalistic veteran who served two tours in Vietnam said he went over there thoroughly convinced that he was never coming back. This attitude apparently allowed him to "compartmentalize" his feelings to the degree that he was able to put the fear of dying out of his mind. However, he turned down opportunities at "R & R" because he worried he would refuse to return to Vietnam.[59]

Another Creedence song that evokes the grimness of the combat experience in Vietnam is "Run Through the Jungle," where anyone who has the misfortune to be in such a hellish place is advised to get through it as quickly as possible and "don't look back to see." The mood of terror and paranoia continues as the jungle is described as the lair of the devil, which is actively aiding the enemy-telling them where to aim "two hundred million guns." Amidst the cacophony of bombs and artillery fire, the soldier can sense that death may be near as he even hears his name being called. This eeriness becomes especially intense as the surrounding mountains produce "thunder magic," and the scene becomes something out of the deepest bowels of hell a la Dante's Inferno. A fitting description, as Vietnam veterans will attest, of the Mekong Delta, the Central Highlands, or maybe the eeriest war region of them all, the Truong Son Mountains. Even the "invincible" men who made up the crack twelve man "A-Team" that Sgt. Sadler sings about in his sequel to "Ballad of the Green Berets" may have found these areas intimidating.

"Have You Ever Seen the Rain," also by Creedence Clearwater Revival, probably makes veterans remember the seemingly unending downpours that dominated the monsoon season in Vietnam. This song, along with "Fortunate Son" are regarded as two of the best "blues" songs of the Vietnam War. More recently, Sarge Lintecum's "It Don't Mean Nothin'" is faithful to the blues genre as it realistically depicts what combat in Vietnam was like and how denial of reality was sometimes the only thing that allowed soldiers to keep their sanity:

> "It don't mean nothin', it don't mean a damn thing...
> I'm so tired of this jungle and all this monsoon rain.
> ...Sixty pound back-pack, gonna drive me insane.
> No it don't mean nothin', it don't mean a damn thing.
> That wait-a-minute bush, don't think I got enough pain.
> If you believe it don't mean nothin',
> You just might make it through the day.
> But if you have enough tomorrows,
> You know you'll have to pay."

Those musicians who specialized in "blues," music that has a lot to do with expressing pain and sadness, found the Vietnam experience to be a fertile source of material. Another blues number, "Delta Day" by Ronny and the Daytonas (supposedly to describe what an ordinary day was like for a combat soldier in Vietnam, probably slogging through the dreadful Mekong Delta), could have been a hit but didn't make it. According to John "Bucky" Wilken, who wrote and performed the song, RCA Victor in Nashville failed to promote it because it was anti-war and they didn't want to be associated with this kind of recording about the war.[60] Still, Willie Nelson's "Jimmy's Road," which makes a strong anti-war statement, came out of Nashville during roughly the same time period (1966) and was allowed to become at least a marginal success. In other parts of the country, RCA didn't seem to have any inhibitions about releasing anti-war songs recorded by groups like the Jefferson Airplane. But in Nashville, RCA executives apparently ordered patriotic songs like "The Ballad of the Green Berets" pressed and shipped without hesitation. Rumors that there were attempts made to suppress anti-war views in popular music during the Vietnam War abound, but these are difficult to prove.

Yet another area of Vietnam that found its way into a song was the so-called "Street Without Joy," an area that was actually just north of the old imperial city of Hue, in the northern part of the country. According to Tommy Finch, in "Street Without Joy-Parts I and II," this "street" or "highway" winds all the way from Hanoi to Saigon and is full of sad people whose lives have been ravaged by the war. Some of these sad cases are beggars, some are lovely and "coy" women but all share the status of victim. Finch proudly points out that there is not a "street without joy" in America where freedom is firmly entrenched because of "men who were men" that "rang the liberty bell." Although its topic makes it one of the more interesting of the songs about the war, "Street Without Joy," can only give the briefest of glimpses into what the war did to the people of Vietnam. Those wishing to know more and also fully understand why the United States went down the "primrose path" in South East Asia need to read Bernard Fall's classic Street Without Joy. This is perhaps the best book ever written about the French occupation of Indo-China during the years immediately preceding American involvement there. Fall's Hell in a Very Small Place, about the French disaster at Bien Dien Phu, is also recommended reading. Ironically, the writer/war correspondent died in the "Street without Joy," in 1967, while accompanying American troops on a combat mission.

Johnny Cash's "Roll Call" shows a keen sense of history as well as an appreciation of "mystic chords of memory" as he sings about the aftermath of battle. After the reference to "Annabelle" and the fact that her sweetheart has become another casualty of the Vietnam War, the focus of the song shifts to a disconsolate captain in Vietnam. In the strangely quiet period following what must have been a particularly hellish confrontation with the enemy, the officer walks the battlefield and muses about what has gone before. Suddenly he pulls a roster containing the names of his fallen men from his pocket and begins a roll call. At first there is no answer to this summons, but as the captain gazes up at the heavens, the soldiers begin to answer, in ghostly fashion. There are many ways to explain this strange encounter, but fundamentally, it appears that it was one officer's way of saying goodbye to his men who died in combat. This grieving officer was obviously not a "ninety day wonder" or "shake and bake," but the kind of leader who genuinely cared about those he commanded rather than his own personal advancement in the ranks of the military. It doesn't require a willful suspension of credibility to visualize scenes like that described in "Roll Call" actually taking place. This communication between the living and the dead may sound like romantic nonsense to some, but those who have walked such "hallowed ground" reveal that they have felt a strangely intense communion with soldiers who died at places like Shiloh and Gettysburg, battles of the distant past. Those who almost obsessively walk these Civil War battlefields speak convincingly of encountering "ghost spots,"[61] places where one can step into a time warp and become part of something that is long past, at least for awhile.

One of the student essayists perceived a religious aspect to the officer's strange reunion with his fallen men, suggesting that the Almighty somehow had a hand in bringing the captain together with his men again for a final roll call. Those who would scoff at such an explanation should be aware that there is at least one well-documented instance during the Vietnam War where a soldier sensed God in the midst of battle. During heavy fighting with the North Vietnamese Army at Lang Vei, Paul Longgrear was wounded in the ankle and thrown through the air, landing on his back:

> "The others saw what happened and assumed Longgrear had been killed. In fact, Longgrear had an eerie experience of speaking to God amid a sudden silence on the battlefield. After that, he got up and, using his rifle as a crutch, began to hobble to safety. He later converted to Christianity and became a minister."[62]

Another veteran, Jon Seikkulla, recounted an experience where prayer sustained him through a particularly harrowing combat experience:

> "We were surrounded by the North Vietnamese Army and badly outnumbered. All we could do was conceal ourselves and hope they didn't see us. I covered myself with some jungle foliage and hunkered down just hoping against hope to get out of this alive. I could see their shoes as they walked around looking for us. I prayed, but to my friend Petey, who had already been killed in combat. I prayed to Petey to get me through this and he did."[63]

"Roll Call" is reminiscent of Marty Robbins' "The Ballad of the Alamo," where a cowboy who rides past the ruins of the Alamo, long after the brave men there had been slaughtered by Santa Ana and his troops, hears ghostly bugles and the footfalls of marching men, as they too, seem to be answering a heavenly roll call. I gained a keen awareness of this during an interview with Green Beret Larry Yeazle as he described a clash between his unit and the North Vietnamese Army near the "Hobo Woods" just north of Saigon. The Green Berets suffered heavy casualties that day as the enemy seemed to attack out of nowhere, even firing down from the trees, catching the Americans in a deadly ambush. As Yeazle painfully related the story of this harrowing experience to me, he stated the names of his buddies who died that day, slowly and deliberately. This was his own personal "roll call." He wound up sustaining serious wounds that required treatment at an Evac hospital. When he returned stateside, those few of his comrades who survived the "Hobo Woods" were astonished that he was still alive. Perhaps he had been part of their roll call.[64] Organizations like the Ia Drang Alumni and the First Cavalry Association hold regular reunions that feature a roll call:

> "We begin by calling the roll, first reading the names of all those who fell and those who have joined them since. Then, one by one, we stand to call out our own names, ranks, military occupations, companies and battalions, and where we fought in the valley. There are no dues-those were paid in blood long ago."[65]

Stan Ridgeway's "Camouflage" has a Marine actually coming back from the dead to save the life of a buddy who is surrounded by the enemy and seemingly doomed. Bullets seem to go right through "Camouflage" or he bats them away with his hands as he rescues his friend, whose gun is empty, from certain death at the hands of the Vietcong. The man he saves from almost certain death regards his savior as "weird" when he pulls a palm tree from the ground and begins "swattin' those Charlies from here to kingdom come." "Weird" is an understatement, for the Marine is later shown the body of "Camouflage" and advised by the company medic that he was killed the night before. The last words from the ghostly hero's lips were "Semper Fi." This song has been likened to a "Vietnam Ghost Saga" and was far more popular in Europe than the United States. It is also one of the lengthiest of the Vietnam songs. The album cut runs seven and a half minutes and was abbreviated to four minutes and fifty nine seconds for release as a single. This was apparently Ridgeway's first solo effort after leaving a new wave group known as "Wall of Voodoo." "Camouflage" was culled from an album entitled "The Big Heat-Songs That Made America Great."[66] It sounds a lot like "Big Bad John," which was a huge hit for country artist Jimmy Dean in 1961, a song that also featured a big man who performed impossible heroics.

Letters from home were very important to the morale of the men serving in Vietnam, and the plight of a soldier who doesn't receive any mail at all, except from the IRS, is examined in Bill Cosby's moving recitation, "Grover Henson Feels Forgotten." Private Henson is so miserable at the lack of mail from loved ones back home that he vows he is going to write one to himself and sign it with love from his mother. Sadly, this is little more than wishful thinking, for he is estranged from her and doesn't even know who his father is, so maybe there isn't anyone out there in "the world" who cares enough to sit down and put pen to paper. Finally, in an act of desperation, Private Henson composes a letter to God. This missive requests that if he dies tomorrow, that God will write him a letter, have it read by a celestial choir, and Grover will hear it, wherever he is lying. This recording should have laid a guilt trip on anyone in the States who wasn't corresponding with a family member or friend who was serving overseas.

Those who did get mail were very grateful, especially if it was a missive like that received by the soldier depicted in the Box Tops' "The Letter," where the girl at home professes undying love and, indeed, claims she can't live without him. Naturally, this lucky man is anxious to ride the "freedom bird" that will take him back home where he can fully appreciate the outpouring of affection. This ticket would put him on the "freedom bird" back to "the world" that the vast majority of soldiers Vietnam dreamed of someday taking. Whatever a soldier's DEROS might be, letters like the one described in "The Letter" made him doubly anxious for it to arrive.

Sergeant John Peter Jorgenson sent tape recordings to his girlfriend Ruth from Vietnam in 1972, and these can be found on "Vietnam: A Sublime Homecoming," a compact disc produced by Ariele Ruth Brooke (yes, the very girl Jorgenson pours his heart out to) and the Nordic Team. At the time of the war, Ruth was a college student and wanted to write a book about her and Jorgenson's life. The tape is a wonderful chronicle of their relationship and the war, and it also provides insight into the music that was an important part of their romance. The Beatles figure very prominently as John sends in a request to a radio station to play the "Abbey Road" album for "Ruth in West Virginia from Johnny in Vietnam." He also promises to have "Here Comes the Sun" sung at their wedding and advises Ruth to listen to "I'll Get You" and "Something," which he sings into the tape recorder. Lyrics from a John Lennon song are used to describe the euphoria he feels when they become engaged, so the music speaks for him. He can't wait to get home so he can listen to the new Paul McCartney album. Sadly, the romance ends and Jorgenson changes from a rather naive, love struck young man into an embittered soldier as songs like "Cecelia" by Simon and Garfunkel and "People" by Barbara Streisand can be heard in the background as he records his bleak messages. His remarks are now laced with profanity and references to how disgusting a place Vietnam is (he is now up north near Phu Bai away from the relative calm of the barracks at Ton San Nhut) with all the alcohol and hard drugs. Three is a happy ending though: The last tape was recorded by Jorgenson, thirty-one years after they parted as he and Ruth (now Ariele and married) reunite to produce the compact disc. Their relationship was only a "temporary casuality" of the war.[67]

Not all the correspondence between soldiers and those at home were of the romantic variety. A notable exception is a story told by the Harden Trio in "Dear Brother." This song features a letter written by a brother back on the home front in response to his sibling's letter from Vietnam. The soldier has written that he has been badly wounded and has a sense of foreboding that he may not be returning home again. At the same time that he asks his brother not to reveal this bad news to their parents, he requests a detailed description of what the house looks like now. The brother responds with a detailed inventory of the family home: the new furniture that has been purchased, the high school flag still hanging on the wall of the soldier's bedroom and the fact that the picture of the two brothers in happier days still hangs above Mom and Dad's bed. Perhaps the soldier had one of those strange premonitions that he would never return home again and his brother's description was the only way he could get a sense of what things were like in that cherished place he would never see again.

Mike Pflepsen didn't go to Vietnam because his brother who was already there extended his tour so Mike went to Germany instead. However, he had an excellent vantage point from which to find out what was going on in Vietnam as he had many friends there. He also wrote and exchanged letters with buddies back home. He was the focal point for a "triangular" kind of correspondence. The topics of the letters ranged from complaints about army life in Vietnam, who was dating whom back home, and who was getting "short" on their stint in the armed forces.

Mike Pflepsen and friends before Vietnam. The war separated them, but they kept in touch by mail. Their letters offer a fascinating window into what those in the service were thinking and wondering about during that time. Their voluminous correspondence is alternately vulgar, hilarious and poignant.

Sometimes one of the guys would write from Vietnam regarding purchasing the latest Country Joe and The Fish album or the Beatles' "Sgt. Pepper's Lonely Hearts Club Band" disc. Inevitably, there are graphic passages about the "soldiers' disease", dysentery, and the travails of that all too common affliction. All of the letters are notable for the inclusion of flamboyant and sometimes vulgar nicknames from way back when. Pflepsen remarked on how he read these missives while lying on a cot in an army barracks in Germany. He has mixed feelings on not going to Vietnam:

> "I came back from the service in 1968, and now when I sit around talking with my brothers and friends who did go to Nam' and they're telling their war stories, I feel like something of an outsider. Don't get me wrong; I was lucky to avoid Vietnam. I was willing to go but just didn't get the chance."[68]

Pflepsen has had a couple of other brushes with Vietnam that are worth recounting. When he traveled to a conference on supervisory management in 1994, he met a colleague who did go there and when they relaxed over beer and snacks, there were amazing parallels in their army careers:

"We immediately started comparing notes and found out that evidently we had both been drafted and sworn in on the same date, even though he was from the Twin Cities and I was from St. Cloud. The coincidence became even more intriguing when we agreed that we had been sworn in the same room, on the same day and time, probably standing within a couple of feet of each other. We then proudly compared our Army serial numbers (given to us at that time and not the social security numbering system instituted a couple of years later) discovering that we were only a couple of digits apart! Continuing our investigation of this fascinating adventure for our youth we realized we had traveled together on the same Soo Line train to Kansas City and rode on the same bus from there to Fort Leonard Wood, Missouri (or 'Misery as we would call it later). We know we had ridden on the same bus because, even though 28 years later, we could both clearly remember the insane driver flying over the hilly two lane highways of central Missouri, passing cars pel mell and swerving around tight bends. We shared the fact that we were no longer concerned about losing our lives fighting in Vietnam, because we would never make it to Fort Leonard Wood. He ended up going to Vietnam and I to Germany, never to cross paths again until that day in Red Wing, nearly 28 years to the day later. We became and are close friends to this day. I think the bond formed on that September day in 1966 is still in place, even though we had no idea it even existed for the first 28 years."[69]

On a sadder note, Pflepsen reminisced about a buddy who was a close friend at Fort Leonard Wood, Jim Fuqua. Their bunks were next to each other and they often went out and had beers together. They went their separate ways when Fuqua was shipped out to Vietnam:

"Every time I'm in Washington, D.C., I go to The Wall. The first time I went there it was after dark, around 9 or 10 p.m. The weather was drizzling and raining. I noticed that that black granite just glistened amid all the moisture. A name sort of jumped out at me from one of the panels: Jim Fuqua. I hadn't thought of him for years and there he was, another casualty of the war."[70]

Sometimes the letters received were of the "Dear John" variety, where a girlfriend, fiancé, or wife told a soldier that their love affair was over. This event was probably as old as war itself. In the early 1950s, at the time of the Korean War, Capitol records released "A Dear John Letter" by Jean Shephard and Ferlin Husky. It begins with Shephard abruptly informing Husky, who is in Korea, that she no longer loves him and is marrying someone else that very night that she is writing the letter. A good deal of salt is rubbed into the already deep emotional wounds that have been inflicted when she demands her picture back and announces she is marrying his brother! The song never does reveal how the unlucky soldier who received this letter reacted to such news so brutally conveyed, but whatever sadness he may have felt was short-lived. In a quick follow-up to the highly successful "A Dear John Letter" called "Forgive Me John," the fickle girl has a change of heart and wants a reconciliation with the man she betrayed! For those soldiers who experienced a permanent split, the feeling of rejection was compounded by distance. A partner who was told he was no longer wanted hurt when the word came at home, but for someone thousands of miles away already existing under difficult circumstances, the blow was much heavier. Everyone had a different way of dealing with the sense of loss. Most of those jilted probably recovered and went on with the business of serving their tour of duty. Tragically, there were also some who probably took their own lives or at least seriously considered it. One depressed enlisted man went to a superior officer when his girlfriend announced that she was ending their relationship and said "Maybe I should go up north and get zapped to solve my problems."[71] Some actually did:

"I took the letter from Laura I received in the hospital as a 'Dear John.' Of the two ways to handle a 'Dear John,' I took the least final option and decided to suck it up and get on.

> On the other hand, a few guys took their DJs too hard, and something inside them snapped. They would put a .45 caliber pistol to their head and pull the trigger, or stand up in plain view during a firefight, which was almost certain death. Once I watched as a grunt stood up during a firefight and started dancing. I don't know why he didn't get shot, bullets were hitting close to me and I was flat on the ground. He was still dancing when the fight was over. Two days earlier, he'd gotten a "Dear John" letter from his wife. She'd found someone new and wanted a divorce. To him, he'd lost all reason for surviving the war. His fire team wrestled him to the ground, and when they carried him to the medivac, he was totally incoherent."[72]

How a "Dear John" letter caused a soldier to commit suicide is chronicled in B.J. Thomas' "Billy and Sue," a song that begins with the melodramatic warning that the tale to be told is so sad that the listener inevitably will shed tears. Thomas sings about a pair of American sweethearts who have dated since the "first day of school." When Billy is sent to Vietnam, Sue sends him a letter "every day," professing her love and faithfulness, which is the only ray of hope in what has become a grim existence for him. These letters seem to be the only thing that allows Billy to hold himself together. But when Sue starts "runnin' round" and sends the "Dear John" letter, Billy loses his head and his life and is consigned to a "lonely" grave. Aside from heartbreak ending in a soldier's suicide, Billy is yet another example of the obedient soldier fighting for a noble cause, in this instance fighting for country and a way of life, "a soldier's only pay." Ironically, before he receives the fatal letter, even Sue is included as part of the reason Billy is so committed to the cause of winning the war in Vietnam. At the end of the song of course, he has lost faith in just about everything. B.J. Thomas recorded "Billy and Sue" early in his career (1966) on Hickory records and the company included it as part of an album titled the "The Very Best of B.J. Thomas," which is really an exaggeration since the only real hit it contains is the sad story about Billy. Thomas' major successes would be achieved on

Scepter records in the late 1960s and early 1970s. The picture on the album shows a soldier embracing a young woman in an airport, which suggests Hickory may have been attempting to capitalize on the success of "Billy and Sue." This picture might also make the casual observer think that the long-playing record is a "theme" album about the Vietnam War, but there is only one other cut, "Vietnam," that has any connection.

Other soldiers reacted with anger when they received a "Dear John" letter and began planning how they could avenge themselves. This kind of attitude is evident in ? and the Mysterians' "96 Tears" where a man warns his girlfriend that she is going to shed tears for jilting him. Just how she will be induced to cry these "96 tears" is not specified, but it sounds like the "payback" will be a vicious one, a severe beating or worse. The promise that "we'll be together for just a little while" is an unmistakable threat. The number of instances where returning soldiers meted out punishment to "unfaithful" women is impossible to know, but it happened.

Another Billy who died in the war is sung about by Bo Donaldson and the Heywoods in "Billy, Don't Be a Hero." This time, though, the star-crossed soldier retains the love of his sweetheart, who, in fact, worries about him constantly, exhorting him to "keep your head low" and not to do anything beyond the call of simple duty so he can come home intact and marry her. But Billy can't resist his heroic tendencies, and when exhorted by his sergeant to go for reinforcements, because "we've got to hold this piece of ground," he follows orders dutifully and loses his life. When the girlfriend receives the letter notifying her of Billy's death, she throws it away in disgust. Unlike some of the heavily patriotic country music that exalts the heroic death in combat, Sue's disgusted reaction to news of Billy being killed in action makes it abundantly clear that she feels he died in vain. An ironic element in this song is that the troops are being told to hold a piece of ground. But for how long? One of the most frustrating and demoralizing things about the Vietnam War was that heavy casualties would be sustained in taking an objective, but after a relatively brief period of time, soldiers were ordered to move on to what they were told were more important objectives. The battle for "Hamburger Hill" or Hill 875 aroused widespread controversy for this reason. Like so many of these songs, "Billy, Don't Be a Hero" is excessively sentimental to some, but it still became a huge commercial success, eventually becoming the number one hit in the United States in May 1973. I was surprised to learn that this song was intended to be about the Civil War. It was the brain-child of two British writer-producers who are also American history buffs. It was originally intended to be recorded by the British group Paper Lace, but ABC Records got to it first with Bo Donaldson and the Heywoods and they had the biggest success with it. Paper Lace did record a version of "Billy, Don't be a Hero" but had waited too long and their effort barely made the charts.[73] It is my personal opinion that the song can be linked to both wars. I have seen Joan Baez' "The Night They Drove Old Dixie Down" on lists of songs that are supposed to be related to the Vietnam War. In my opinion, the only connection this song has to Vietnam is the fact that it was released in 1971, when American involvement there was dwindling dramatically. The lyrics in the Baez song, as well as The Band's version, confirm that it is a reminiscence about the Civil War. Although it is not inappropriate to associate "Billy, Don't Be A Hero" with the Vietnam War, if you listen closely to the lyrics, the connection to the Civil War is easy to detect.

Donovan, who sings about a soldier who is born to make war in "Universal Soldier," describes a different kind of fighting man in "To Susan on the West Coast Waiting for Andy in Vietnam Fighting." "Andy" writes that he resents that his career has been interrupted by the draft but is consoled by the fact that he knows Susan loves him and can "feel you here with me, just like I'm there with you." In his poetic letters, Andy separates himself from the stereotype of the hard bitten and unromantic GI when he describes "smelling the rain on the jungle greenery" and predicts that the day will come "when kings will love and love will grow." Another gentle ballad inspired by foliage is "A Ballad From Vietnam: The Rain on the Leaves" by Addiss and Crofut. The duo sings about the rain on the leaves and tears of joy when a girl's boyfriend returns safely from Vietnam as well as the bitter tears as a mother grieves when she learns her son has been killed in action. Mitch Miller and his choral group, who were the rage with televised sing-alongs during the early 1960s also recorded "A Ballad From Vietnam" and on Decca Records. Their primary success had come on Columbia where their forte was American standards like "Sidewalks of New York" and "And When You Wore a Tulip" and other sweetly sentimental ballads from the distant past.

In "Little Becky's Christmas Wish," Becky Lamb sings about a child who is so bewildered by the war that she blames the mailman for bringing a letter that makes her parents cry. She can't believe her big brother Tommy, who looked so handsome in his uniform when he was home on leave only a week before is gone. She goes up in the attic and finds his records and plays the disc that contains JFK's inaugural speech with the famous words, "Ask not what your country can do for you, but what you can do for your country." Of course in all her child-like innocence, this is all beyond her comprehension, and she promises Santa Claus if he brings Tommy home for Christmas she will accept just a few toys. "Little Becky's Christmas Wish" is a significant contribution to the music about the Vietnam War because it explores the tragic circumstances of how very young siblings dealt with the death of a much older brother in combat.

A soldier who broke up with his girl before he went overseas is the subject of the Elegants' "Letter from Vietnam (Dear Donna)." Now that he is in Vietnam, many things he took for granted stateside have taken on a new importance, including Donna, who he now wishes was waiting for him to return home. Among other insights he has gained from the perspective of serving in combat is that now he "really knows what tough is." "We thought we were tough in our black leather jackets and motorcycle boots" but that was all pretense, he realizes now. This was not an uncommon reaction for a lot of arrogant and immature young men, who were forced to grow up in order to make it through the rigors of basic training and survive in a war zone. As lead singer Vito Picone talks and sings about the contents of the "Letter from Vietnam," artillery fire and the whizzing of bullets are heard almost constantly in the background, lest there be any doubt about the setting of the song. The Elegants really didn't need a lot of sound effects to carry their music. They were one of the premier "doo-wop"[74] groups of the 1950s and had a "monster hit" with "Little Star," which became number one on the record charts in 1958. Sadly, this exceptionally talented group never came close to this pinnacle again due to inadequate promotion. "Letter from Vietnam" was among their last efforts to regain a semblance of popular success. There is conjecture that this song failed to make it because people thought that the Elegants were trying to capitalize on the Vietnam War, but recording music about the conflict didn't keep artists like Sgt. Barry Sadler and others from selling huge amounts of records that dealt with the war. There were those in the music business who wrote and/or performed music about the war simply to make money. However, Vietnam eventually became such an all-encompassing issue that it is highly unrealistic to expect the popular culture of the day to ignore it.

Another girl who was left behind is sung about in Lois Johnson's "GI Joe" where, in a voice heavy with country "twang," she professes her love for "GI Joe" who is fighting far away. In case there is any doubt about how much she loves him, she describes nightly rites of faithfulness that include "saying a prayer and kissing your picture a thousand times." Her hope is that it won't be long before he is back from "that far off country" to share happiness with her. "GI Joe" was a popular name for any soldier serving in World War II or Korea. This song is a throwback to similar music from earlier American wars not only for its title but also for its message of innocence and unselfish love. Another promise of undying love and loyalty for a boyfriend in Vietnam is found in The Fawn's "Wish You Were Here With Me," where the girl at home is proud that her man is defending his country and appreciates his sacrifice but can't help wishing that he could be with her. Despite the professions of faithfulness, she warns, "I'm a lonely girl" and "the boys won't leave me alone." This comment raises the possibility that her patience may eventually wear thin and her soldier could be receiving a "Dear John" letter. Ginger Hart's "A Girl's Prayer" portrays a more innocent young woman who is reduced to tears every time she thinks about her boyfriend who is overseas fighting for freedom. Her fidelity to her man seems unquestionable but her emotional dependency is making her life miserable. Prayer seems to be the only thing that provides her with some surcease from her sorrow and worry about how he is faring in Vietnam.

The 1960s could well be described as the golden age for "girl groups." The Crystals, The Ronettes, The Chiffons, The Shirelles and other strictly female combinations seemed to own the charts but, with the exception of the virtually-unknown The Fawns, few of these groups recorded anything about the war. However, The Chantels, who made their mark in 1958, with the powerful "Maybe," did record "The Soul of a Soldier" in 1966, about a girl whose boyfriend is in Vietnam and grudgingly accepts the fact that he needs to be there but still finds his absence emotionally painful. Although it expresses a similar angst, The Shirelles' highly popular "Soldier Boy" doesn't qualify as a Vietnam War song as it was released in 1962 when Vietnam was barely on the fringes of the public consciousness. The Shangri-las' "Remember (Walkin' in the Sand)" is a powerfully-stated lament about a boyfriend who is overseas, but it was released in 1964, very early in the war, and its difficult to confirm that it is a song about Vietnam. The group's "Long Live Our Love" is clearly related to Vietnam as they sing about a girl who will always be faithful to her boyfriend because she believes he is doing the right thing by fighting to defend his country. The fact that this couple has been separated by war only strengthens their emotional commitment to each other.

These songs of female fidelity for a man who is fighting for a noble cause are reminiscent of ballads like "You Belong to Me" and "I'll Be Seeing You" from wars of the distant past. A sharp departure is "I Should be Proud" by Martha and the Vandellas. The woman in the song is loyal to her boyfriend fighting in Vietnam but doesn't buy into the notion that he is fighting for any kind of a cause, especially when he comes home in a coffin. All the "medals and honor and glory," including a front page story in the hometown newspaper, mean nothing because her "Johnny" shouldn't have died, he wasn't fighting for her but was a "victim of the evils of society." Although people keep telling her how proud she should be, she's not. What she really wants is not "some superstar," but the "good man they took from me."

Martha and the Vandella's "Nowhere to Run" has received the greatest acclaim as a Vietnam War song because it was included in the soundtrack of Good Morning Vietnam. It was even re-released in 1988, complete with picture sleeve to promote the movie. Soldiers obviously identified with it because of the title and lyrics that described an atmosphere of inescapable doom that had become all too familiar to them. However, the song was not written about the war and was released at a time when Motown was avoiding making political statements in the music it produced. Martha and the Vandellas likely recorded the first Motown song about the Vietnam War, "Forget Me Not." However, this story of a soldier sailing off to war was not intended as a protest song even though it was released in 1968, when the war was at its height. It was only a "mild hit" but Martha Reeves said it "really hit home" with her because her brother Melvin was killed in Vietnam.[75] The group's big hit "Dancing in the Streets" is seen as one of the songs that drove home the ideal of "grand fusion between radical politics and counterculture -drugs, sex, rock 'n' roll, smash the state." For this reason "white radicals" found the "exuberant" song especially "congenial."[76] However, in my opinion, "I Should Be Proud" sends out one of the strongest and most powerful messages[77] about Vietnam and deserves to be remembered as one of the most meaningful songs about the period. Instead, it languished in obscurity because radio stations were afraid to play it and "killed it" soon after it was released. It was Motown's first war protest song, preceding "War" by several months but never earned a chance to catch on with the public because of censorship.[78]

Many of the soldiers who fought and died in Vietnam were still teenagers. Alice Cooper's teen anthem "Eighteen" is insightful not only for revealing the alienation and confusion that is a common teenage phenomenon under ordinary circumstances but how extraordinarily trying life could be for those of tender years in a combat zone. In Vietnam, a boy had to grow up very fast or very possibly perish. What should have been the halcyon days of youth were turned into a nightmare. "Eighteen" became a particularly compelling war song when it was fitted into the context of the documentary film *Letters From Vietnam,* providing the musical background to a scene showing enlisted men who are obviously in their teens. All of them seem so young as, with newly shaven heads and bewildered expressions on their faces, they are marched off to war. They seem far too young to be exposed to the horrors of combat when they should have been devoting their attention to cars, girls and their first year of college:

> "I was so damn young. I was exactly eighteen when I went to Vietnam. Suddenly I was responsible for keeping myself alive, and other men's lives too. This was a time in my life when I should have been worried about who I was going to take to the prom, cars, what kind of trousers I was going to buy, or how I was going to get into a certain girl's pants. During this time, a buddy of mine was captured by the enemy. We looked and looked for him and found him the next day. He was skinned and hanging from a tree. I just went berserk. I was no longer a teenager."[79]

Many of these boys had never been away from home before and had no idea what the war was about. John Kertwig probably speaks for many of them as he describes how callow and vulnerable he felt after arriving in Vietnam at a tender age:

> "I'm not John Wayne. I was nineteen when I arrived in Nam and scared to death. Six feet and a hundred and twenty-five pounds of skin and bones, glasses, silver fillings in my teeth. Scared to death, never a hero. I hadn't wanted to come to Vietnam. I was in the Central Highlands. If I'd been on the coast I might have tried to swim east till I drowned. The most heroic thing I'd done was reassure my family before I left. I wasn't even sure they were real anymore. Nothing existed except right now; and right now was muddy and worn and torn and desolate and hopeless. Barren. The most wretched existence I had ever known; just stumbling through it; and if you survived the day it was an occasion. If you survived the year...well, there wasn't much chance of that, and you wondered how you would die when your turn came."[80]

Kertwig lived to tell his grim story, but as you think about these young men you can't help but feel sadness for them and wonder how many of them remain forever young. Some four hundred soldiers from Minnesota who perished in Vietnam seem to stare forlornly from their photographs in Tim Ward's *The Faces Behind the Names,*[81] most of them almost strikingly youthful and innocent in appearance. Some of the books and movies about the war reinforce the notion that soldiers in Vietnam were just that: "innocent, idealistic, middle class volunteers who" were "brutalized by the war." This impression may be somewhat misleading since many recruits had already accumulated considerable street smarts. The average squad of infantrymen sent to Vietnam included young men who had already learned much about "the grimmer actualities of American life - its poverty, racism and violence." Still, the portrayal of the soldiers as youthful innocents is not entirely an exaggeration either. They did have a "political innocence," a real naivetÈ about "how American economic and military power was used in countries throughout the world or how that power was perceived in those countries. Their education about these matters came in Vietnam."[82]

Paul Hardcastle's "19" owes its title to the average age of combat soldiers in Vietnam. The cover for the 12" version of this song has the number "19" in red against a black background, taking up about a third of the space. Just above the number is the statement calling attention to the fact that the average age of combat soldiers in World War II was twenty-six, while their counterparts in Vietnam were only nineteen. Curiously, the soldiers pictured have black bands over their eyes as if it is necessary to disguise their identities. This is a device that used to be used by sensational pulp magazines of the 1950s to obscure the images of various nefarious characters. Was the cover artist attempting to send some kind of message about the war? In case there are any lingering doubts about what message this recording is attempting to convey, Hardcastle employs the rather irritating device of "sampling," whereby he keeps repeating "nininini nineteen" for emphasis. Aside from this minor flaw, which was frequently found in the popular music of the eighties, the song somewhat redeems itself by effectively including the voice of an "announcer" who describes heavy fighting near Saigon. There is also an interview with a vet who admits that he really "wasn't sure what was going on." This song laments the fact that many died so young at "nininini nineteen," the destruction of men in their prime whose average age was 19.

It is insightful in describing Vietnam as far more than just another foreign war because of the relative youth of the soldiers who waged it. Faith Willow's "There in Vietnam," also raises the issue of the youthfulness of soldiers in Vietnam as she sings about how a young man who isn't even old enough to vote can be expected to violate the Ten Commandments and "kill another man" in Vietnam. She also laments the fact that his schooling has been interrupted but adds sarcastically that you don't need much of an education to kill. Like so many others, this boy had a father who fought for freedom in World War II, whose "heart is broken" that his son if going overseas. Does the father feel this way because he knows that the war in Vietnam has little to do with preserving freedom for America? The relative youthfulness of soldiers in Vietnam was also explored in Jan and Dean's "Only a Boy," where a high school graduate finds himself fighting in the jungles of Vietnam shortly after receiving his diploma. This is yet another song that espouses the domino theory as the callow youth is described as involved in defending the borders of the United States against the "red infiltration." He does not survive this mission unscathed, as he is "shot through the shirt," which "hurts," and then "blood spurts." Jan and Dean had been hugely successful with tunes about surfing, fast cars, and teenage romance. However, of the social commentary "Only a Boy" did not score well with the record-buying public. Aside from "Universal Coward," this was Jan and Dean's only venture into protest music.

Inez and Charlie Foxx's "Fellows in Vietnam" indulges in some hyperbole about the age issue by describing the troops as "infants" who have been snatched from their mothers' arms and forced to shoot and kill. At the same time that she expresses reservations about their maturity for the ugly business of war, Inez makes an impassioned plea that they be supported, by everyone, especially those who have a friend or relative over there. The hope is that if enough people get together and show that they care, the soldiers will be motivated to leave their foxholes and kill the enemy for the cause of freedom. This song is the only English language recording I know of that appears to be something of a tribute to the many Hispanics who fought in Vietnam, as it begins with the Spanish salutation "Vaya Con Dios," or "Go with God." The "flip" side is a reworking of the old Les Paul and Mary Ford hit "Vaya Con Dios."

A "man-child" who is having a devastating emotional experience in Vietnam is the subject of Pat Farrell and the Believers' "War Boy." In the midst of combat, the young man asks if his mother can hear him calling? He goes on to tell her that he misses her "tender touch" and that he knows the war is wrong but "Mom" has to understand that her "little boy" has to stay until the war is done. His emotional distress is compounded by waves of guilt that wash over him after killing an enemy soldier. Although there have been an irreducible minimum of soldiers in every war who have actually relished killing, "War Boy's" reaction to having actually killed another human being is an experience he shares with countless other soldiers. Paul Baumer, in Erica Maria Remarque's *All Quiet on the Western Front* pours out his grief to an enemy soldier he was forced to kill with his bare hands:

> "Comrade I did not want to kill you. But you were only an idea to me before, an abstraction that lived in my mind and called forth its appropriate response. It was that abstraction I stabbed. But now, for the first time, I see you are a man like me. I thought of your hand grenades, of your bayonet, of your rifle; now I see your wife and your face and our fellowship. Why do they never tell us that you are just poor devils like us, that your mothers are just as anxious as ours, and that we have the same fear of death, and the same dying and the same agony. ...Take twenty years of my life, comrade, and stand up, take more, for I do not know what I can even attempt to do with it now."[83]

"War Boy" never charted nationally, and I had never heard of it before it was sent to me a few months ago. Initially, the title conjured up images of a young man who was resourceful at soldiering and perhaps even one of those who actually enjoyed the risks of combat, but the tormented young man in the song certainly doesn't fit this description. One of the most horrible experiences in this war, as well as others, was to witness mortally wounded young men calling out for their mothers just before they died.

A particularly touching addition to the music that focuses on soldiers' missing mothers is Connie Francis' "A Letter from a Soldier (Dear Mama)," where "Johnny, a brave soldier boy" mournfully reminisces about his childhood when his mother would hold him and chase away his fears. The song concludes in a virtual operatic aria of anguish as Francis' powerful voice gradually builds in intensity and declares: "Just how much you mean to me, now and forever more!" "A Letter from a Soldier (Dear Mama)" is significant not only for the fact that it displays the pathos of young men at war separated from their mothers, but also because Connie Francis was one of the major female luminaries of the American popular music scene in the late 1950s and early 1960s. For her to record this kind of "message" song was a sharp departure from the teenage-oriented tunes that brought her musical fame like "Lipstick on Your Collar," "Stupid Cupid," and "Where the Boys Are." On the heels of "A Letter From A Soldier (Dear Mama)," which was released in 1966, Francis would record a promotional record for the Army, "A Nurse in the U.S. Army."

Merle Haggard recycled "Soldier's Last Letter," which was originally recorded by Ernest Tubb during World War II, to tell the story of a young man serving in the Army in Vietnam. This devoted son is called away by his captain while he is in the midst of writing a letter to his mother. He is the prototype of the ever-obedient soldier as he writes that he will have to finish the note later as duty calls. Sadly, he dies in battle and the letter is never completed. Somehow this incomplete missive reaches the mother who senses that the message is strangely short and senses in that way that only mothers can that her soldier has died. In response, her hands begin trembling but she manages a prayer, asking that God protect all the sons who are in harm's way and to "keep America free." Buddy Starcher's "Sniper's Hill" features another mother who also has to go through the emotional agony of receiving a letter from a soldier son who has already lost his life in Vietnam. This tragedy is far from being just a songwriter's fantasy. There actually were families who had to endure the macabre experience of receiving letters from loved ones in Vietnam after they had already been officially notified that they'd been killed in action.

Virge Brown's "North of Saigon" is about another soldier who is writing a letter to his mother, this time from a barracks in Saigon, which he derides as a "city of heartbreak and despair." He describes whatever is north of Saigon as pretty forbidding territory, and he is right, for just on the fringes of the capital city were places like Cu Chi and Bien Hoa and the notorious Iron Triangle, place names that are forever seared into the memories of veterans who endured heavy combat with the enemy there. Cu Chi is an especially painful memory for veterans because of the frustration of dealing with the Viet Cong, who operated out of an extensive network of tunnels that extended all the way into Saigon. The soldier Brown is singing about is justifiably wary about going out into this "no-man's land," but he will do so because he believes he is fighting for freedom. The other goal that makes going into harm's way acceptable is the well-being of his mother, who he advises in his letter, "I'll think of only you as you know I always will."

Almost any song that mentioned home became a favorite with GIs in Vietnam, for it was place never very far from their thoughts. Peter, Paul and Mary's "Leaving on a Jet Plane" became one of the most popular songs ever played by Armed Forces Radio because almost everyone who heard the song looked forward with keen anticipation to doing exactly what the title stated, riding a jet plane back to "the world."[84] Tim O'Brien considered Simon and Garfunkel's "Homeward Bound" so evocative of the average soldier's yearning for home that he included it in his award-winning account of his tour of duty in South Vietnam, *If I Die in a Combat Zone, Box Me up and Ship me Home.*[85]

A soldier who is almost overwhelmingly homesick is the subject of Bobby Vinton's "Mister Lonely." He is probably even more woebegone than his comrades because he doesn't even have a girlfriend to worry about and wonders aloud why he doesn't: "How is it I failed?" This statement can also be read as a complaint that he is in the Army and overseas through no wish of his own. This is one of the teariest of the songs about soldiers missing home as Vinton literally gasps and sobs out the lyrics that center around the self-proclaimed "Mister Lonely's" wishing that he could go back home. It's a wonder that this enlisted man didn't go AWOL during basic training, as his homesickness sounds almost pathological. Vinton's "Little Barefoot Boy" ponders the question of what happened to a little boy who graduated from running about barefoot to cowboy boots and then penny loafers. He ultimately wears army boots in a foreign land where he must fight or die. He is killed in combat and now walks in Heaven wearing "sandals made of Love." Vinton had a penchant for melancholy music and his recording career didn't really take off until he recorded the mournful "Roses are Red" in the spring of 1962. His "Comin' Home Soldier" (included in Chapter 6 "Music About the Aftermath of the War) has a more upbeat message because the soldier is going home, but still comes out sounding strangely sad. Other purely romantic songs ("Blue on Blue," "My Heart Belongs to Only You," and "Rain, Rain go Away"), by this singer, who would become known as the "Polish Prince," make love out to be an experience fraught with almost constant depression.

Glen Campbell used the theme of homesickness to score one of his biggest hits with "Galveston" in 1969. A soldier remembers the "sea waves crashing" on the beach of his home town in Texas while he cleans his rifle and watches the artillery flashes in Vietnam. As is almost always the case, in this kind of musical reverie of home, a girl is remembered, and this one is visualized waiting on the beach with tears in her eyes. It sounds as though the soldier who misses her and Galveston so much is near tears himself. However, he has no choice but to continue cleaning his gun and rhapsodize about the past. Beyond its significance as Vietnam music, the ballad drew Little Richard's admiration who loved "country phrasing:" "When Glen Campbell says that one word, 'Galveston,' that shakes me up. That music is as real as the blues."[86] Marine Richard Kuecher found the song about the seaport in Texas intriguing, especially the lyrics about preparing his weapon for combat:

"Sometimes when I heard that song, we were on the eve of another patrol, and you damn well better have that M-16 ready, or sure enough it would jam on you when you really needed it."[87]

Joe South's "Don't It Make You Wanna Go Home" also struck a responsive chord with enlisted men in Vietnam, as the singer declares, "God, how I wanna go home!" The Lovin' Spoonful's "Darling Be Home Soon" speaks for countless men and women separated by the war who yearn for the day they will finally be reunited. In Stonewall Jackson's "Red Roses Blooming Back Home," a soldier who is described as being "across the wild foam" finds his homesickness becoming especially hard to deal with in spring, when he knows that his mother's red roses are growing. When Bob Shelafoe heard Donovan's "Sunshine Superman," it made him think of home but he was uncomfortable about any feelings of homesickness that the song triggered: "It made me think of home, but I didn't want to think about home. I wanted to keep my mind on what I was doing."[88]

The soldier that is the subject of Sonny Marshall's "A Soldier's Prayer" is also in the throes of an intense emotional experience but for a different reason. His epiphany is a religious one, finding God only because he is in "the hellishness" of Vietnam. In the dialogue with his newly discovered savior, the soldier ruefully admits that "I had to be in this hellish place before I could see your face. Like any soldier on a battlefield thoughts of death are never far away, I know I may come to your house tonight." But now that he has accepted God's existence, he knows "God will listen to a soldier's prayer." This song definitely lends credence to the old bromide "there are no atheists in foxholes." "A Soldier's Prayer" is part of a 45 "extended play" record and contains three other songs: "Dizzy Love," "Talk, Talk, Talk," and "My Valentine." Its deeply spiritual theme makes "A Soldier's Prayer" seem somewhat out of place with the other titles.

Virtually every element of the U.S. Armed Forces was engaged in Vietnam at one time or another. The Marines were the first large group of fighting men to be deployed there in early 1965, when they were assigned to provide security at the American air base at Da Nang. As the war grew larger, it seemed the Marines were in the forefront of nearly every major battle from Dak To to Hue and Khe Sanh, plus the almost innumerable skirmishes with the enemy that were an inevitable occurrence during "search and destroy" missions. Thus, it's fitting that Ernie Maresca's "What is a Marine" was released in 1968, when the Vietnam War was at its height. There isn't a branch of the service that enjoys the heroic status that American popular culture has conferred upon the Marine Corps, and while his recitation is undeniably a tribute, Maresca avoids making Marines seem infallible. At the same time that he describes them as "brave men" ever ready to defend America, he also recognizes their tendency as red-blooded American boys to enjoy an "occasional" drink and ogle females. These leathernecks enjoy a widely acclaimed status as United States Marines, but they are not the gods some books and movies made them out to be. Maresca marvels at the average Marine's ability to cram a huge assortment of items into his pocket, including "a comb, an autographed picture of the girlfriend, chopsticks and a church key." He humanizes the "jarhead" by describing the dreary aspects of the combat existence, the requirement to sit in a muddy foxhole in the middle of a tropical downpour holding a can of rations and a soggy pack of cigarettes without complaint. In 1961, Maresca would write and sing one of the most popular party records in rock and roll annals and now a genuine "golden oldie," "Shout, Shout (Knock Yourself Out)." Although he never again charted as high, he would continue as a highly successful writer for artists like Jimmie Rodgers, "Child of Clay," and Dion, "Donna the Prima Donna."

The experience that required the most courage to endure was that of being a prisoner of war. Merle Haggard's "I Wonder If They Ever Think of Me" hauntingly describes the ordeal of such a man who finds little to do during his incarceration than submit to the memories of home "that keep runnin'" through his mind. He thinks about his mother everyday and at night his thoughts turn to his girlfriend. The POW also remembers "Daddy sayin' you'll come back a better man" but still worries that he has been forgotten. He thinks of old friends from happier days and wonders if they even know he is alive, "still proud to be a part of Uncle Sam," and speculates that the folks back home may think he's starved to death "in this rotten prison camp in

Vietnam!" Haggard recorded a version of this song "live" during a concert in New Orleans toward the end of the war and introduced it with a moving dedication to the fighting men in Vietnam, those who had returned safely and those who are still there, and he expresses the hope they will return safely. Not surprisingly, these remarks receive thunderous applause from the audience. Some of Haggard's more outspoken music related to the Vietnam War offended some, but the message in "I Wonder If They Ever Think Of Me" should have few, if any, detractors. It stands alone as the most moving and eloquent song yet recorded about the Vietnam POWs.

Pat Boone and Captain John Cantry, USAF also sang about prisoners of war in "MIA/POW." This ballad tells the story of Captain Richard Hall, a Navy flyer who was shot down over North Vietnam in November of 1965. At first he is reported "missing in action (MIA)," and when his family finally receives word that he has been taken prisoner of war (POW), they are relieved that his status is POW and not KIA (killed in action). At least he is alive. The letter that confirms this fact is postmarked Hanoi, but Hall's wife recognizes the handwriting on the envelope. The tone of the letter her husband writes from his cell is optimistic but she now knows he is in the infamous "Hanoi Hilton" and that his words are intended to help her keep a stiff upper lip. There is little she can do but helplessly hope, as did so many other women whose husbands were imprisoned in North Vietnam. Their waiting was made more painful by suspicions that conditions in the various prison camps in North Vietnam were probably abominable, and they were right. After most of these prisoners finally came home in early 1973, it became widely known how cruelly they were treated by their captors, who flouted the Geneva Convention Rules that are supposed to assure that combatants captured by the enemy are accorded humane conditions. Long after the Vietnam War was over, the treatment of American prisoners of war and the whereabouts of those yet unaccounted for would remain a sensitive issue between the United States and the communist government in Vietnam. It wasn't until the United States government was satisfied that everything had been done to provide them with all the information about what actually happened to every POW and MIA that we established diplomatic relations with Hanoi. There may be some symbolism in the fact that the first American ambassador to Vietnam in the early 1990s, Peter Peterson, was a former prisoner of war.

Combat veteran Tim Murphy's composition "The POW-MIA" has yet to be recorded or released but has been very well-received wherever he has performed it. Although he was never a prisoner of war, he has an uncanny vicarious appreciation of that experience:

"I'm just a nameless silhouette; nobody knows my face,
Though many of you pray for me each day:
The man said you won't forget, in a dark and distant place.
I am the POW; I am the MIA.

I am a Navy pilot; I am a dead Marine;
I am the wounded grunt they couldn't find.
But I'm living still, and I'm long dead, and I'm somewhere in between,
And I can't believe that I was left behind.

They killed me in an ambush, and they captured me alive,
And I died when my Huey crashed and burned.
They over-ran my unit, but I managed to survive,
And they brought me North in chains when they returned.
They beat me and they whipped me, and they worked me 'til I dropped.
To break my will, they made their best endeavor.

When great despair had gripped me, still the torture never stopped.
And they told me: 'We can keep you here forever.'

They told me that my parents died, that my kids were grown and gone;
And my wife lost hope, and married my best friend.
But there's a prayer I hold inside, that helps me to go on:
That someone still remembers, and you'll bring me home again.

I'm just a nameless silhouette; nobody knows my face,
Though many of you pray for me every day:
The man you said you won't forget in a dark and distant place.
I am the POW; I am the MIA."

Women who were in the thick of combat as they tended to wounded men are finally given their due in a lovely and remarkably moving ballad called "'Til the White Dove Flies Alone," a song written by John Linde and Rod McBrien to commemorate the Vietnam Women's Memorial in Washington D.C. It would be difficult to find a more fitting tribute than the story of a nurse who attempts to make the last moments of a mortally wounded and delusionary soldier easier by pretending to be his girlfriend back home and they "reminisce" about the past together:

"I'll press my hand against your face and whisper, I love you too
And talk of times and things back home as if I really knew.
And for the one you wish was here, I'm crying every tear.
And tonight I'll be the one you love."

The song concludes on a keenly spiritual and uplifting note. The nurse, who more than fits the prototype of the "angel in white" reassures her charge that she will stay with him until he goes to a better place:

"But if green pastures turn to Autumn and the shepherd calls his own
I'll walk you through the valley 'til the white dove flies alone."

McBrien also played a role with Ginni Stern in composing "I Will Always Remember You," written to celebrate the completion of "The Women in Military Service for America Memorial," which was dedicated in October 1997. This tribute song was recorded by pop luminaries Kenny Rogers and Patti Austin.

Rod McBrien, the co-composer of the beautiful and moving "'Til the White Dove Flies Alone" was a member of the Valrays during the 1960s, shown above. McBrien is in the back row on the left. Source: Rod McBrien

Another heart-wrenching eulogy to the nurses is Phil Ferrazano's "Lovely Angels on the Wall," which he wrote after a trip to the Vietnam Memorial:

> "I wrote it after I learned about the eight woman army nurses on the wall. I thought back to when I was wounded and how the nurses ran back and forth taking care of us. I remember their faces and the sadness they expressed. But through it all they stood strong and tough for us. It was years later at The Wall when I saw some nurses break down and crying. It took a toll on their young lives just as it did on the ones in the field."

"Lovely Angels on the Wall' is one of the selections from Ferrazano's compact disc "Reflections: Vietnam Veterans Remembered."

Student Essays

Although some students found Haggard's other war music distasteful, "I Wonder If They Ever Think of Me," drew a favorable response:

> "Another song I really like was 'I Wonder If They Ever Think of Me,' by Merle Haggard... I liked it mainly because I read a book called *Scars and Stripes,* by Red McDaniel. The book was about a POW of six years in a VC prison camp. It gave me much more insight into how a prisoner of war feels. Does their family ever think of them? Do they know that you're still alive and proud? These were the lyrics of the songs. Once again, this would encourage my anti-war viewpoint. I can't imagine how it would be to live inside four concrete walls and have nothing to do but be tortured, to think about your last meal, and whether or not your friends and family know you're a POW. I think I would rather be dead."

A student who served in Vietnam felt that Haggard's "I Wonder If They Ever Think of Me" didn't say enough:

> "This song touches just the very tip of the true sufferings endured by the POWs. These are the true heroes of that time. It seldom is related of the torment they endured at the hands of their captors. Instead we are compelled to glorify someone like the traitor she was-Jane Fonda."

Listening to "Bad Moon Rising" and thinking about its meaning in the context of the Vietnam War was an unsettling experience for one student:

> "'Bad Moon Rising' by Creedence Clearwater starts playing on a jukebox or on the radio and I can feel the hair on the back of my neck rise. I used to own this record. This song

has always scared me; not only for what the lyrics are saying but also because of the reactions it can cause. 'Don't go round tonight its bound to take your life.' Many times I've witnessed the "thousand yard stare,"89 that far-away look in a Vietnam veteran's eyes, possibly a flash-back (a symptom of PTSD) when they hear this song. It had to be absolutely horrifying to be dropped by helicopter so deep into the jungle that you couldn't see the moon or the stars, much less your hand right in front of your face. 'Hope you got your things together, hope you are quite prepared to die.' To be scared to move or even breathe, knowing it could be your last. I can only imagine what that must have felt like, but I agree with the song because of the reactions I witnessed."

A Vietnam veteran felt "Bad Moon Rising" could have said more about the combat experience:

"This song mentions the sense of fear anyone experiences before combat. What it fails to mention is the strength and courage it takes to follow through and go ahead anyway. It fails to describe the fear that was present most every hour of every day while in Vietnam. The enemy could be the 'Mamasan' who cleaned the facilities or the barber who cut your hair. It also depicts 'the heavenly bodies' that is Mysticism, as the soldier's faith and trust. In reality, at a time before battle, peace comes only from a belief in the Almighty Creator-NOT some of His creation."

A student who had the perspective of "distance" because of his age, found "Bad Moon Rising" amply descriptive:

"This seems to be a song about soldiers thinking about their own mortality. The phrase 'anticipation of death is worse than death itself' is one that soldiers had to think about every day. A soldier surmising about his own mortality might have driven himself over the edge. What was going through a soldier's mind when he was under heavy enemy fire in the deep jungles of a country that maybe a few weeks ago he had never heard

> of? What did I do to deserve this? Will I make it through my tour in one piece and see my family again? Is today my day to die? What does it feel like to die? If I do die in this country, how will it happen? That was the important factor, because there are many ways that a soldier could perish. During combat, during non-combat, illness, accidents, being attacked by animals, or even tortured to death in a Viet Cong prison camp. Becoming a soldier during the Vietnam War must have been like stepping into your own worst nightmare."

Some of the lyrics to the Creedence music were difficult to decipher, which led to some confusion about what songs like "Bad Moon Rising" were trying to say:

> "Another song I enjoy hearing is "Bad Moon Rising." I have always liked this song, because when I was younger I thought they were singing about a bathroom on the right, not a bad moon on the rise. That was cleared up before I took this class. The song does make me think of the soldiers going out on night patrol, and being scared to death from not knowing if they were going to live 'til morning. I can understand the feeling of wanting to hide, so you wouldn't have to go out in the jungles at night and look for Viet Cong....This song does give me a sense of mystery about the time period in which young men never knew when they might get that card in the mail, and the sense of anxiety many must have had."

Because of its inclusion in the soundtrack of Good Morning, Vietnam, students were already familiar with "We Gotta Get Out of this Place" and quite prepared to write about it:

> "While listening to this music, many thoughts and emotions rushed through my head. 'We Gotta Get Out of This Place' by the Animals made me think of times when I was deployed to Saudi Arabia with the Air Force. I remember singing that song to myself and hearing other people singing it too. I know a little bit about how the soldiers in Vietnam were feeling. All that can be thought of is getting home safe-

ly. The soldiers of that era weren't that much different than the soldiers of today. Everyone just wants to get home."

"I was in the U.S. Army for eight years. While I was on active duty, I was part of the invasion force that went to Panama. I was a member of HHC 7th FSB, 7th I.D. Light. So while I was listening, I listened for the song that brought me back most to that time. ...It reminded me of sitting with my M60 machine gun at 3:30 a.m. locked and loaded waiting for the Panamanian Defense force to come. 'We Gotta Get Out of This Place' also brought to mind when I was going to leave Panama. It wasn't like I was there for a long time, but after eating MRE'S for two weeks straight, no one knew how long we were going to be there."

"'We Gotta Get Out of This Place' by the Animals has a weird meaning for me. I used to work in this buffet restaurant that served like a million people a night. Whenever this song would come on the radio, we would sing along to it and wish that we had better jobs. I can totally see how the soldiers in Vietnam would have emulated their plight with this song. A bunch of dishwashers did the first time they heard it on the radio, and dishwashing must be fun compared to combat."

The Animals' "Sky Pilot" brought back memories of a young girl's cousin, a marine, who had orders for Vietnam:

"My older cousin Bob, a Marine, got his orders in 1969. I still remember the tearful goodbyes at the airport. I knew nothing about Vietnam, only that it was a place he may not return from. Fortunately for all of us, his flight was diverted, in route, to Okinawa. We did a lot of roller skating in our basement to that song. I knew Bob wasn't in Vietnam, but it still made me wonder about those who were."

Most female students found the disgusted reaction of the young woman portrayed in "Billy, Don't Be A Hero," perfectly understandable:

> "I liked 'Billy, Don't Be A Hero,' by Bo Donaldson and the Heywoods. I think after I heard this song I wouldn't date anyone between 18 and 25 for fear they would be drafted. It touched me because she doesn't want him to be a hero because he will come home in a body bag. She wants him to come back and make her his wife. She is heartbroken and knows he won't be back so she pleads with him to stay safe and come home to her, the same thing I would've done. Billy died that day being a hero and she threw the letter away. I wouldn't have cared about being for or against the war if someone I loved was leaving to fight. I would just want to see them come home safe, the political reasons behind the war weren't worth one human life."

A young woman who chose to focus on the songs about "the women left behind" wrote this about "Billy, Don't Be A Hero:"

> "This is one of the songs that aptly reflects the sentiments of women whose men were either setting off to fight or were already fighting in Vietnam. It clearly describes the angst of a young girl whose boyfriend is going off to fight and her pleas for him to remain home with her. Perhaps the most poignant message of this song occurs when Billy's girlfriend receives a letter notifying her of his death and telling her that she should be proud because he died a hero. The only thing her mind could gasp was the fact that he was dead and was not ever returning to her."

Another analysis about another song about a "Billy" in Vietnam from a feminine perspective:

> "The song 'Billy and Sue' had a profound impact on me. The song portrayed the relationship between a soldier in Vietnam and his girlfriend back home. It was about the girlfriend waiting for the soldier to come home from war. She got anxious and started seeing other guys. She eventually sent her boyfriend in Vietnam a 'Dear John' letter. He was devastated and committed suicide on the battlefield by standing in front

of enemy fire. This song helped me to understand that there were some women who had boyfriends and husbands in Vietnam who were not faithful to them because perhaps they were lonely. It also showed me how devastating a letter like that could be to a soldier at war in a far-off country. It made me feel for the soldiers and what they went through. How lonely and frightened they must have been. Let alone that, then to receive a letter from your girlfriend that she is breaking up with you. It is unimaginable. This song gives me an idea of the overall mood of the time of the war. It helped me understand the overall dread and foreboding. It has expanded my views on war in general. That war has an overall negative affect on everyone even if we are fighting for a good cause."

Another young woman had this to say about "Billy and Sue:"

"Billy ends up going to war with the premonition of coming home to marry Sue. In the beginning Sue writes to him religiously and he felt loved, but as time wore on Sue was back with every Joe in the telephone book. When Billy finally received a letter from Sue after a long while, it turned out to be a Dear John letter. Now I had a discussion with someone whether or not people can make your mood. We came to the conclusion that no one can make your mood, they can tell you things that will affect you, but you ultimately decide how you are going to react to the news. Upon getting bad news from Sue, Billy decided to kill himself. He purposely threw himself in front of bullets and committed, in a sense, suicide."

A young man wrote the following about "Billy and Sue." This essay also made me wonder if Armed Forces Radio was prevented from playing this song:

"This song is depressing, and doesn't send a good message out to the men that were fighting. I would have been scared if I were there and started thinking about my girlfriend. If I got a letter like that I probably would have done the same thing he did."

This male student strongly identified with "Billy:"

> "I felt that 'Billy and Sue,' by B.J. Thomas was also a very moving song due to the fact that the troops were getting 'Dear John' letters back from girlfriends. The song is about a soldier who gets a letter from his girlfriend saying that she is not going to wait for him to come back. He then gets into a firefight with the enemy, stands up in a hail of gunfire and is shot dead. Now if I were getting shot at every day, and spent every moment trying to stay alive while I was humping my ass off in the jungle, the last thing I would want to see is a letter from my girlfriend saying she is leaving me for some f-ing puke in college. I think I might have to contemplate committing suicide as well; however, I would wait until I got back state side and kill her and her puke of a boyfriend."

After hearing "Eighteen," this student viewed its content in a new light:

> "The song 'Eighteen' by Alice Cooper has always been to me a sort of slow, lonesome and sad kind of song. After listening to it in the context of the war and learning that it was related to Vietnam, I have a better understanding of its content. Being eighteen and having to decide to fight or not must have been very difficult. Eighteen is really just a number and doesn't mean that a young man is really prepared for manhood and its decisions. The possibility that the young man in the song had to age before his time and might die in combat because of his immaturity left me feeling sad. Even if he survived the war, he would probably have the brain of a baby and the heart of an old man. How horrible that some of them never got the chance to experience some of life's joys. Being forced to be so independent at that age must have led to a lot of suffering. I do not think I will ever feel quite the same way about that song again."

One student claimed that Jimi Hendrix had served in Vietnam as a member of the 101st Airborne and that his experience there influenced his music and his performance of 'All Along the Watchtower:"

"His distortion and use of the 'whammy bar' were influenced by traditional Vietnamese music that he heard while he was in the service fighting in Vietnam.90 If you listen to his lyrics he has messages about how he feels about life and the war. After serving in the war he became very opposed to the war movement. He was singing about how he never thought they would ever get out of Vietnam alive in the line that said 'businessman come and drink my wine and dig my earth.' He wanted to escape from the emotional stress that was in Vietnam and his way of doing that was to smoke marijuana. He would be on night watch duty and he would talk with the other night watchers about home and about how hopeless that the Vietnam War was. He said 'there are many here among us who feel that life is a joke.' In other words they agree with his thoughts that the war was not worth fighting."

Although Hendrix was of another generation, students were quite familiar with him (because of movie soundtracks and oldies stations?). They not only enjoyed listening to his music but also found it insightful about what they felt the experience in Vietnam was like:

"This song had two parts that were extremely deep. The first part, 'there's too much confusion, I can't get no relief.' This song was about not knowing what they were fighting for and never having a goal to accomplish. Soldiers would just fight and pull back, fight and pull back. Everyday was the same grinding pace, never getting a break from killing and seeing people die all around you. Jimi Hendrix was a member of the 101st Airborne, so who better to sing about the war than him. He lived his life in Vietnam during his one year hitch. Famous or not, hero or not, he was there. The second part, 'there are many here among us, who feel life is just a joke, but you and I have been through that, and this is not our fate.' The men changed their minds while in Vietnam and didn't feel any remorse for killing. The love for country and own survival was strong. These men would do anything to make it home and leave this horrible war behind. He was telling listeners that these men were born in the United States and were not going to shed any more 'American' blood in this foreign country."

This student found "All Along the Watchtower" full of symbolism:

"It is a story of sentinels or guards, or just soldiers on watch. They are on the watchtower trying to figure out the realities of war in their conversation, and a way to get out of there (alive). The 'joker and the thief' could be characteristics each exhibits...there are those among them who think that life is just a joke, or unimportant. If life is just a joke, killing is OK and also their own lives have little meaning...the 'princes who kept the view' could be the privileged men who do not really fight in this war. The 'women come to serve them and the barefoot servants' to tell you that it is not so bad to be there as the privileged one. The war may drive men to use drugs or alcohol. ...This will make him a better fighter and more alert. 'Outside in the cold distance a wild-cat did growl' could be a comment about the danger and fighting always lurking just beyond the secure area. 'Two riders approaching' are the joker and the thief coming into the secured area from the bush. Now they can let their guard down, if only slightly."

Another student didn't find anything of value in "All Along the Watchtower:"

"This is the worst song! This song was unclear and seemed to me to be the kind of song people on drugs would 'zone out' to, especially the screaming guitar. I'll bet he never played that part the same way twice. If confusion was what he was trying to portray, he accomplished it. "

The same view about a different song "Billy, Don't Be A Hero," written by someone with a gift for satire:

"Ugh. Ever since I was about 11, my head would throb every time I heard this screeching, over dramatized, simple lump of bubble gum. I realize that every song doesn't have to contain cryptic messages or be complex to be likable, but this tune is just plain kooky music. One can only imagine the brainstorming process during the brief lyric writing session: *As he started to go, he said Billy don't stub your toooooe.* 'Scratch that - let's go with keep your head loooooow.' If Billy stubbed his toe, his head would then be low, but we'd better make sure everyone can understand the song without thinking. There isn't even a hint of lyrical innuendo-every line is laid out like a slab of musical meat. What a clever bunch of musical bards. The vocal delivery isn't only devoid of emotion, but it's full of feigned emotion-which is even worse. The instruments and melody ring of circus music or my failed fourth grade flute-e-phone lessons. I was tone deaf."

Some thoughtful remarks about "Roll Call:"

"A lot of different images went through my mind as I listened to 'Roll Call,' by Johnny Cash. This song is about an officer walking the battlefield after the battle is over. He is taking roll call as the title suggests. He learns that all of his men are dead. They aren't answering until suddenly, he hears their voices answering from the sky. When I hear this song I see an image of all these soldiers floating around above the officer like angels. The soldiers may have been killed but are alive in a sense. I think that his song possibly suggests that soldiers may be rewarded for their duty in war by God. This may be reading into it too far, but it makes sense to me. I don't think that this is necessarily an anti-war song. It could probably be viewed as pro-war or anti-war depending on who or under what circumstances it is listened to."

Although it was far from a controversial song, many students found an intense emotional connection with "Leaving on a Jet Plane:"

"As a veteran myself, the first song that I think of is 'Leaving on a Jet Plane,' written by John Denver and sung by Peter, Paul and Mary. This song always brings tears to my eyes. I can totally relate to the soldier leaving their family or loved one and going off to a foreign land. However, my departure was a time of peace in the Cold War. Even though the fear was always there for me...the possibility of going to war seemed very real and did exist. We were always on standby alerts since we were so close to the East German border...we were always combat ready. But it was just that fear of war...thank God it never became reality. For the soldiers who were sent to Vietnam, the reality was all too real. This song was very real to them...they had no idea when they would be sent back home again or if they'd ever come home alive. I feel this was one of the best songs of the era. Every time that I hear this song, it brings tears to my eyes. I envision a young man or woman clinging to their loved one, holding onto that last touch, that last kiss, that last good-bye for an eternity in their mind. Most everyone should be able to relate to this song."

"I knew this song was from the war period, but it never registered in my sometimes thick head as a war tune. But it is the perfect war song. I was unconsciously drawn to the protest songs because of their raw chaos-inducing energy. Compared to the soldiers, however, the war protestors' experiences were almost certainly just a brief phase in their lives with no real danger. Most of them likely look back on it and smile. However, I would guess that this song would have a deeper and more lasting impact with the soldiers and their families than the anti-war tunes did with the protestors. Bonds between people are usually stronger than bonds between individuals and events. 'Leaving on a Jet Plane' is a sad song and the truth is that sorrow and loss have a more profound impact on the soul than jubilation or anger. Unlike many of the narratively styled songs about exploits in battle or losing a son, this song has real soul and feeling. It seems like it would be easier for most people to identify with leaving...because of its personal tone. The minimal instrumentation only enhances the superb vocals. Less is definitely more. It is full of sadness, uncertainty, anticipation, a sense of lost time, and regret for not expressing one's true feelings until circumstances forced the issue. The impending separation reveals past indiscretions and problems for what they were, as trivial bumps in the road of life. A ton of emotions are bottlenecked in a few minutes time. I would imagine that to many couples separated by war, this was their parting song. Years later, it likely moves widows to tears of sorrow not just for the sense of loss, but regrets for perceived misdeeds towards the departed. Conversely, it could perhaps mist up couples who are still together."

"96 Tears" is about a soldier who wants to batter his girlfriend for rejecting him, but the young woman who wrote this essay sympathizes with him:

"The song '96 Tears' really bothered me. I didn't like it at all. It is about a man that is in Vietnam and he finds out that his woman left him for someone else. How cruel is this? I think it is the worst possible thing you could do to someone. Especially when a lot of the soldiers only kept on going because of their girlfriend, wife or family. He becomes very upset at the news and wants her to cry 96 tears."

A young woman reacted to "96 Tears" this way:

"Some soldiers came back from the war and had the feeling that they hadn't been loved or had been taken advantage of. This song gave me the feeling of how it felt to have your heart broken when you were far away from the one you loved. It expresses the rage these soldiers felt and leaves the distinct impression that trouble was brewing. The line 'you're going to cry 96 tears' is the singer's way of saying, 'You're going to feel the pain you put me through, and maybe then you will understand.' If you listen to the music closely, there are chords that are repeated over and over again leading to bigger and wilder notes; I believe this symbolizes dealing with the pain day after day, holding it in, and then just exploding. These soldiers had to portray a facade of being tough while fighting the war. They weren't allowed to show that they were broken hearted. Keeping all these feelings bottled up caused some to seek revenge when they returned home. To me, it seems like these soldiers were being selfish, wanting the world to stop and wait for them, but it is easy to see how it isn't fair either way. This song does a good job in relaying the message of how holding emotions in can cause only more pain, make things seem irrational, and lead to rage."

This student had a personal experience that reflects the reality of family relations during the war:

"Some of the songs like 'Billy and Sue' and 'Jimmy's Road' conveyed a message of realism about my own family's turmoil and uncertainty in their history with the Vietnam War. When I was fresh out of high school, I joined the army and my dad went berserk, especially when I told him my MOS was a 13 BRAVO-cannon crew member. He had been in Vietnam so I wondered. He shouted: 'You mean to tell me you took a combat MOS. Look in the want ads, how many f—-in cannon crewmembers are they looking for. Kid, you don't know what you got yourself into.' Once he opened up to me I understood that his older brother went for a third tour of duty in Vietnam once he found out my dad was going over there. Nobody really knows why my uncle went back for a third time. I think he went in an effort to save my dad, his little brother, from combat in Vietnam since he thought the government wouldn't put two brothers there at the same time. Anyway, it didn't work and I think my dad feels guilty to this day, because his brother eventually succumbed to Post-Traumatic Stress Syndrome. When I heard this story, I felt it was being played in unison with the lyrics of the songs I heard the past few days. As an adult now, I felt I was standing alongside them watching as they lived this era moment by moment."

FOOTNOTES:

1 Interview with Paul Kero who was a disc jockey with Armed Forces Radio in Saigon during the Vietnam War. Kero told me that it wasn't an "overt" form of censorship, because only so many songs could be included on the discs manufactured in the states for distribution to Armed Forces Radio in Saigon. "We would compare the music on the discs we received with the Billboard Hot 100 and some were missing. There may have been a pattern to it. They tended to stay away from the harder rock." February 1999.

2 This rule may have been imposed because the United States didn't want to be identified with their immediate predecessors in Vietnam, the French, who were driven out of Indo-China by Ho Chi Minh and his communist Viet-Minh. It is hard to believe that this rather silly regulation convinced very many Vietnamese that the United States were anything other than a replacement for the French or somehow had nobler motives for being there.

3 Interview with Marine platoon leader, Richard Kuecher. January 2003.

4 Interview with Dennis Aho, January 2000.

5 Interview with Paul Helbach, December 1999. Helbach was a medical corpsman, attached to the 3rd Marine Division.

6 Joseph T. Ward, *Dear Mom: A Sniper's Vietnam.* New York: The Ballantine Publishing Group. p. 55.

7 "Swift Boats" were part of the Navy's coastal surveillance force in Vietnam. They were also known as PCFs (Patrol Craft Fast) assigned to Coastal Squadron One (COSRON1) between 1965 and 1970. These vessels were initially used in Operation Market Time to prevent enemy infiltration of troops, supplies and munitions by sea. Their website is at http://www.swift boats.org/

8 Interview with Raul Herrara, November 2002.

9 Helbach Interview.

10 Interview with Paul Kero, February 1999.

11 Les Cleveland, *Dark Laughter: War in Song and Popular Culture.* Westport (CT): Praeger Publishers, 1994. p. 141.

12 The only polka song I know of that had any kind of connection to the Vietnam War was recorded by the "polka king" himself, Frankie Yankovic. It is called "Saigon Sally" and consists entirely of the title phrase repeated over and over again to the background of a generic polka beat. Men can be heard marching as military cadences are called out. "Saigon Sally" was released by Columbia Records in 1966. Whether it was among the polka music AFR was accused of over playing is unknown.

13 Tucker, Vol. I. p. 458.

14 Interview with Mike Brimball, Sandy, Utah, July 2001.

15 "Radio First Termer" by AF/Ssgt Dave Rabbit. "Vietnam's Most Notorious Unauthorized Broadcast." A Public Domain Presentation." (Four compact discs.)

16 Interview with Ron Whipp who was a 3rd class petty officer on the USS Truxta.

17 Interview with Ed Bielarczyk, November 2000.

18 Keith Walker. *A Piece of My Heart: The Story of Twenty Six Women Who Served in Vietnam.* New York: Ballantine Books, 1985. pp. 111 - 112.

19 Bruce H. Norton. *Force Recon Diary, 1969-1970.* New York: Ballantine Books, 1992. pp. 409 - 410.

20 Interview with Larry Yeazle.

21 Interview with Jon Seikkulla, who served with the 75th Rangers in Vietnam. 1/7/00.

22 Helbach Interview.

23 Seikkulla Interview.

24 John Laurence, *The Cat From Hue.* New York: Public Affairs, 2002, p. 368.

25 Rochester, Stuart I., and Frederick Kiley, *Honor Bound: The History of American Prisoners of War in Southeast Asia, 1961 - 1973.* Washington D.C. Office of the Secretary of Defense, 1998. pp. 181 - 182. Another former prisoner of war, Commander David Wheat (U.S. Navy Ret.), told me he felt a similar uplift when he heard Johnny Cash's version of "Little Drummer Boy" over a prison camp PA system on Christmas Day. Conversation with David Wheat, May 1997.

26 Interview with Commander (Ret.) David Wheat who was shot down over North Vietnam in October of 1965 and was imprisoned there until February of 1973.

27 Rochester and Kiley.

28 Lynda Van Devanter and Christopher Morgan, *Home Before Morning: An Army Nurse in Vietnam,* New York: Beaufort Books, Inc., p. 90.

29 Van De Vanter, p. 112.

30 Interview with Mary Banigan, July 2002.

31 Mark Baker, *Nam: The Vietnam War in the Words of the Soldiers Who Fought There.* New York, Berkley Books, 1983. p. 33.

32 DEROS: Date Eligible for Return from OverSeas

33 Ron Alexander and Charles W. Sasser, *Taking Fire: The True Story of a Decorated Chopper Pilot.* New York: St. Martin's Press, 2001. p. 93.

34 Lintecum Interview.

35 Interview with Phil Ferrazano, June 2002.

36 Interview with Gene LeRoy. LeRoy was a disc jockey with Armed Forces Radio in Saigon during the Vietnam War.

37 Herrara Interview, November 2002.

38 I thought it was curious that a book, that promises to provide "insights and life messages" by analyzing "classic rock songs from the sixties omits any reference to "We Gotta Get Out of this Place" and the Vietnam War. Peter Forntale and Bill Ayres, *All You Need Is Love and 99 Other Life Lessons from Classic Rock Songs.* Fireside: New York, 1998. pp. 198 - 99.

39 Interview with Bruce Brown, March 1999.
40 Interview with John Seikkula, May 2000.
41 Laurence, *The Cat From Hue,* pp. 306 - 308.
42 Herrera Interview.
43 Cleveland, *Dark Laughter*. p. 143.
44 Cleveland. *Dark Laughter.*
45 Werner, *A Change is Gonna Come*. p. 113
46 Werner, *A Change is Gonna Come*. p. 110.
47 Roger Steffens, Nine Meditations on Jimi and Nam, quoted in Werner, p. 113.
48 Robert Jay Lifton, *Home from the War Vietnam Veterans: Neither Victims nor Executioners*. New York: Simon and Schuster, 1973. p. 226.
49 Ibid.
50 Bruce Brown interview.
51 Myra McPherson, *Long Time Passing: Vietnam & the Haunted Generation.* New York, Doubleday and Company, 1984. p. 212.
52 Interview with Dr. Mike Mueller, January 2000.
53 Interview with Dale Day, August 4, 2002, Las Vegas, Nevada.
54 Thomas R. Hargrove, A Dragon Lives Forever. New York: Ivy Books, 1994. p. 151.
55 Kuecher Interview.
56 Interview with Bruce Brown.
57 Kort, Michelle, *Soul Picnic: The Music and Passion of Laura Nyro.* New York: St. Martin's Press, 2002. p. 33.
58 James Webb, *Fields of Fire.* New York: Bantam Books, 1979. pp. 316 - 317.
59 Interview with Bob Shelafoe, December 1999.
60 Michael "Doc Rock" Kelly, *"The Story Behind G.T.O."* Goldmine. July 16, 1999.
61 Tony Horwitz, *Confederates in the Attic: Dispatches from the Unfinished Civil War.* New York. Pantheon Books, 1998 p. 77.
62 Prados, John and Ray W. Stubbe, *Valley Of Decision: The Siege Of Khe Sanh.* New York, Bantam Doubleday Publishing, 1991. p. 381.
63 Seikkula Interview.
64 Yeazle Interview.
65 The Ia Drang Valley provided the setting for one of the most savage and significant battles of the Vietnam War. Lt. Gen. Harold G. Moore (Ret.) and Joseph L. Galloway, *We Were Soldiers Once and Young: Ia Drang - The Battle That Changed The War In Vietnam.* New York: Harper Collins Books, 1993. pp. 407 -408.
66 Neely Interview.
67 Ariele Brook and the Nordic Team, *"Sublime Homecoming."* (Compact Disc). 2001.
68 Interview with Mike Pflepsen, February 2003.

69 Ibid.

70 Ibid.

71 Larry Colton, *Goat Brothers.* New York: Doubleday, 1993. pp. 319 - 320.

72 Joseph T. Ward, *Dear Mom: A Sniper's Vietnam.* New York: The Ballantine Publishing Group. pp. 190 -191.

73 John Mortland, liner notes to "Sounds of the Seventies: AM Top Twenty" Warner Special Products, 1993.

74 "Doo-wop" music can be defined as a slow, sweetly romantic ballad sung by two or more vocalists who were skilled at what is known as group harmony.

75 Martha Reeves and Mark Bego, *Dancing in the Streets: The Confessions of a Motown Diva.* New York: Hyperion, 1994. p. 153.

76 Gitlin, *The Sixties.* p. 287.

77 Martha Reeves, the Vandella's lead singer, virtually shouts out these lyrics of outrage. Her intensity could be attributed to the fact her brother perished in Vietnam. Dancing in the Streets. p. 152.

78 Dancing in the Streets. p. 172.

79 Seikkula Interview.

80 Kertwig, *A Hard Rain.* p. 28

81 Tim Ward, *The Faces Behind the Names: The Vietnam War.* The Memorial Press, Bloomington, 1996.

82 Christian G. Appy, *Working Class War.* Chapel Hill & London: The University of North Carolina Press, 1993 p. 82.

83 Erich Maria Remarque, *All Quiet on the Western Front.* New York, Fawcett Crest, 1978. p. 195.

84 Kero Interview.

85 Tim O'Brien, *If I Die in a Combat Zone: Box Me Up and Ship Me Home.* New York, Dell Publishing, 1973. p. 167.

86 Peter Doggett, *Are You Ready for the Country: Elvis, Dylan, Parsons and the Roots of Country Rock.* New York: Penguin Putnam, 2000. p. 331.

87 Interview with Richard Kuecher, Platoon Seargent, U.S. Marine Corps. January 2003.

88 Shelafoe Interview.

89 This essay was written by the wife of a Vietnam veteran.

90 Hendrix was never in Vietnam. The most authoritative biography, Dave Henderson's Scuse' Me While I Kiss the Sky contains a picture of Hendrix in the uniform of the "Screaming Eagles" paratroopers in 1961, but there is nothing in the book about service in Vietnam. In fact, according to Henderson, Hendrix left the service before he could have possibly been sent overseas. He is described as showing up in Harlem in early 1963 to continue his musical career. "Purple Haze" was probably inspired by flares that paratroopers used to guide themselves into landing zones during training in the United States and this was where Hendrix obtained his inspiration, not in Vietnam.

Chapter 6:
Music About the Aftermath of the War

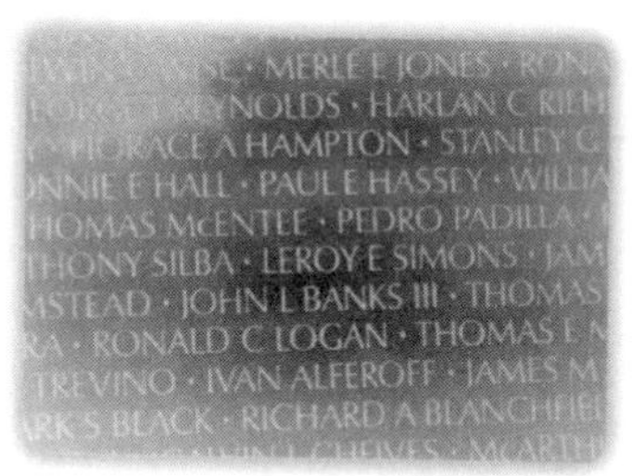

Those who fought in the Vietnam War and survived may not always display evidence of physical wounds but suffer from a less visible affliction that may be even more insidious and debilitating known as Post Traumatic Stress Syndrome (PTSS) or Post Traumatic Stress Disorder (PTSD).[1] It is sometimes called "Vietnam syndrome,"[2] a mental malady that is characterized by recurrent nightmares, inability to feel affection, acute paranoia and a variety of other symptoms. Some of these men might very well be characterized as "a generation of men who, even though they may have escaped its shells, were destroyed by the war."[3] There is no easy cure for those who are plagued by PTSS, and sometimes the mental anguish is so intense the victim becomes dysfunctional and even commits suicide. Many veterans also suffer from survivor's guilt, a chronic soul-searching as to why they were spared when their comrades in arms died. Compounding this fugue is the fact that the war was lost and victims of PTSS feel their sacrifices were in vain. Another scourge those who survived Vietnam have to endure is the disastrous consequences of exposure to Agent Orange, the chemical that was used to defoliate vast areas of jungle. One veteran, who eventually succumbed to cancer caused by the deadly herbicide, said, "I died in Vietnam, but I didn't even know it.[4]

Many Vietnam veterans remain embittered by the rude reception they received when they did come home from the war. They didn't proudly march home as "Johnny" did from other American wars but were often subjected to ridicule and worse. For them, in a sense, the Vietnam War will never be over and closure impossible to attain. Paul Hardcastle's "19" contrasts the rude reception Vietnam vets received upon returning home with the warm welcome accorded the returning veterans of World War II: "None of them received a hero's welcome, none of them, none of them!" Whoever wrote this song did some research as a Veteran's Administration study is quoted that indicates veterans of the Vietnam War were arrested at twice the rate of vets of World War II. It goes on to attribute at least part of the difficulty Vietnam vets had in readjusting to the rapidity with which they arrived home from the throes of jungle combat. Most returning World War II vets faced a relatively lengthy journey home on troop ships, allowing for a period of readjustment from the war zone. Those who'd fought in 'Nam were brought home far too quickly, as this anecdote attests:

> "The army had no debriefing or adjustment procedure. A grunt might fly to Oakland or Portland in fatigues he had worn in the bush, still caked with Vietnamese mud. In the stateside processing center he would grab a shower, a dress uniform, and a pay envelope. The army paid for a taxi to the airport. By crossing the International Date Line, it was almost possible to watch a buddy get wasted at two in the afternoon of a particular day and be in your living room at home at 2:15 of the same afternoon. There was no orientation; the army did not want to admit your head might be screwed up in Vietnam. Official army policy tried to rush a returning Vietnam warrior home as soon as possible...After a year of confusion in the Nam, the vets found themselves home, and confused again."[5]

"19" was released in 1985, one of the more recent of the Vietnam-related recordings. This gives it the advantage of enhanced perspective provided by a distance of more than a decade from the actual event. Sometimes it is difficult, if not impossible, to tell the historical tale until the smoke has thoroughly cleared. This would be especially true with regard to Post Traumatic Stress Syndrome, which has only recently received the attention it deserves in the aftermath of the war. This illness has even found its way into the courtroom, used by defense attorneys who argue that PTSS should be used as an extenuating circumstance to exonerate veterans charged with various crimes:

> "The most controversial aspect of delayed stress is the use of PTSS as an insanity defense in criminal proceedings. Many cannot comprehend or sympathize with a Vietnam veteran who holds up a 7-Eleven store or does battle with the police or holds hostages in a bank, for example. However, delayed stress experts often feel that they are acting out of two impulses. One is a risk junkie's search to recapture the thrill of combat; another is guilt. Many show little resistance or intent to pull a trigger. The theory is that they want to get caught; they are seeking a form of self-destruction, a symbolic suicide.[6]

Perhaps the best-known case of a veteran whose crime was attributed to PTSS is that of Manny Babbitt, who survived the war only to be executed by the State of California in the spring of 1999 for murder. One of the most outspoken of the musicians who opposed the Vietnam War, Country Joe McDonald called California's decision to execute Babbitt "a final verdict of disbelief in Post Traumatic Stress Disorder as an explanation for his crime." McDonald even reworked the lyrics of his famous protest song "I-Feel-Like-I'm-Fixin'-to-Die Rag" to protest Babbitt's fate.[7]

One of the most eloquent songs about the ordeal of Post Traumatic Stress Syndrome is the Charlie Daniels Band's "Still In Saigon." It is the story of a Vietnam veteran who is physically in postwar America but suffers from frequent flashbacks that transport him back to the war. To a cleverly arranged background of Oriental music, the singer laments that "every summer when it rains," he can actually "smell the jungle" and "hear the planes." Although this veteran has been away from the atmosphere of the war zone for at least a decade, all the sounds of "long ago remain forever" in his ears, including the cries of the wounded and even "the silence of the dead." The struggle with PTSS has strained relationships with his family, and his younger brother calls him a "killer" and his father proudly refers to him as a "vet." The fact that members of his family cannot agree about what he is only adds to his confused state of mind. This breeds a kind of schizophrenia and, ironically, the only place that he was sure of who he really was, was back in Saigon. Everyone this vet is close to seems baffled by his behavior and does little more than offer the less-than-helpful advice that the war has changed him irrevocably and that there is no cure for his sickness. This vet has given up all hope of ever living normally again and prays that someday he will go completely insane.

Another soldier who is suffering from postwar trauma is the subject of Arlene Harden's "Congratulations (You Sure Made a Man Out of Him)." This song details, through the eyes of a mother, how badly the war ravaged her son. At first, she is elated at his return when it seems that Pvt. James Williams will just be "Jimmy again." But it is not to be. As time passes, the mother can see where he has been in his eyes, the sadly familiar "thousand yard stare" common to many Vietnam veterans experiencing PTSS. Jimmy is still the dutiful son, taking his mother to church every day, but there is no more "singing in the shower" and it is painfully evident that he is a deeply troubled young man as he spends long periods of time simply staring out the window. The song concludes with the embittered mother sarcastically congratulating the government for "making a man out of him," the kind of man who will always be tormented by internal demons and aged far before his time. A song like this breeds skepticism about what is really meant by various military recruiting slogans that promised to make men out of boys.

The postwar period has also been difficult for Dr. Allan Cutter, who served with naval intelligence in Vietnam in 1971 - 72. These were difficult years to be there for everyone because the United States had already begun to withdraw troops with what seemed like unseemly haste. Cutter was forced to be involved in many covert missions that involved bloodshed, and he feels guilt about the role he played in these activities to this day. He metaphorizes about the impact of his experiences in eloquent and moving fashion:

> "I've looked at life as if through the lens on a tripod. The three legs supporting the tripod were family, faith and nation. In Vietnam, I lost all three legs and the lens was on the ground."

He doesn't remember much music in Vietnam because he was "too busy," but when he hears the Beach Boy's version of "The Sloop John B," especially the refrain "I wanna go home," he "flashes back" to Vietnam.

> "Sometimes when I heard that song on the car radio it affected me so much I had to pull off the road. I was very susceptible to music, particularly this song. I was trying to push away that part of me that was still over there. The memories of it were so ugly...I basically supplied a terrorist team that was part of Operation Phoenix. This part of me had been pushed away for so long, the time when I was twenty-five year old warrior. That song kind of ambushed me and brought it all back.[8]

A veteran who is coping much better with life after the war is sung about by Johnny Cash in "Drive On." Although this vet is grateful to have survived, he resents the fact that it took his country far too long to welcome him home. Dreams of men and monkeys screaming in the jungle persist, but he is consoled by the pride he feels when a fellow veteran dubs him "the walkin' talkin' miracle man from Vietnam." This is a song full of jargon that only Vietnam vets or true students of the war will be able to appreciate, as Cash sings about a "hot LZ" and "M-16s" on rock and roll. What must be a kind of Vietnam rite of passage is also described with the words, "I've seen the tiger smile and spit in a bamboo viper's eye."[9] That this soldier is no vainglorious hero is evident when he relates how scared he was and likens the combat experience as a "slow walk in a sad rain," but emphasizes that "nobody tried to do a John Wayne." Today he limps and there is a "tremolo" in his voice, but when bad memories threaten to engulf him he says, "It don't mean nothin,"[10] and he just "drives on." This recording is one of the most recent songs about the Vietnam War, and, unlike some of Cash's more bellicose patriotic tunes, it is genuinely insightful about what it was like to be in combat in Vietnam and what the aftermath has been like for a lot of veterans. It also benefits from the fact that it was released twenty years after the American war ended, for close proximity to an event does not always provide the most accurate telling of the historical tale. "Drive On" was recorded on the relatively small American label, where Cash wound up when major labels like Columbia decided to jettison "traditional" country artists in favor of the wave of "new" country, which justifiably offended country and western purists. Many radio stations have also eliminated older country artists from their play lists-a sad turn of events, as Cash and others like him recorded some of the finest country music ever heard. His recordings for the American label sound like Johnny Cash "unplugged," as it appears to be just him and an acoustic guitar providing the music. These new records are reminiscent of some of the early sides he cut at Sun Records in Memphis in the mid-1950s, where he usually had only the rather sparse backing of the Tennessee Two, Luther Perkins on guitar and Marshall Grant on bass. In 1964, long before he would sing about how Vietnam veterans fared in the aftermath of their war, Cash sang about how rudely a hero of World War II, the Native American, Ira Hayes, was treated when he returned to the United States, a song that was frequently heard at various bases in Vietnam.[11] Because of its subject matter, "The Ballad of Ira Hayes" is likely a song that Vietnam veterans relate to today. "Drive On" is something of a rarity, in that it was pressed on a vinyl 45 rpm in 1994. By this time, few, if any, of these kinds of records were being manufactured, and those that were came from companies that catered to record collectors and other aficionados of the music of the past.

In the aftermath of the war, The Vietnam Memorial, or "The Wall," has become an important part of the healing process for Vietnam veterans. At last they finally have something of substance that is a tribute to their war and the thousands who died fighting it. Millions have visited the monument to those who died in Vietnam where they make "rubbings" of the names they are all too familiar with and often leave behind personal memorials such as medals, packages of cigarettes, cans of beer and deeply moving notes, messages from the living to the dead. No matter how insignificant or trivial these offerings may seem to some, they are a way of finally saying goodbye.

Picture of the Vietnam Memorial in Washington D.C. Source: Roger Lambert

Survivors often "trace a memory" of the names like these on "The Wall."

Some of the messages left at the memorial are written by veterans racked by "survivor's guilt," who are probably destined to spend the rest of their lives blaming themselves for surviving while the men they were closest to didn't and wound up as one of 58,000 names on that long black wall. Kris Kristofferson's "Why Me" is a prayerful entreaty to God by a veteran who is trying to understand why he was spared while others he regards as far worthier than him were killed in Vietnam. His sense of self esteem is at rock bottom as he questions how God could be so kind to him when he is so plainly undeserving of even the slightest consideration from his creator. These feelings of inferiority are not an uncommon attitude for some Vietnam veterans who lost close friends in combat. Kristofferson used to dedicate this song to them when he sang it during concerts as part of a group known as "the Highwaymen." He is one of Nashville's most prolific and successful singers and songwriters and wrote "Vietnam Blues" for Dave Dudley. One veteran who feels a particularly intense connection to "Why Me" explained why the song is so meaningful to him:

> "I'm the only one left from a nine man LRRP (Long Range Reconnaissance Patrol) team. My guilt over being the only

> survivor nearly drove me to suicide. I heard Kristofferson perform this song at a concert in Phoenix and it gave me goose bumps. Whenever I hear it, it still does.[12]

Among the throngs who gather at the Wall each day are mothers who lost sons in Vietnam. "More Than a Name on a Wall" by country music's Statler Brothers describes one such mother whose trip to the Wall makes her finally realize that her son will never return. Somehow, seeing his name on the wall makes her realize that cruel fact and the reality of her boy's death is finally brought home to her. This experience brings on a flood of memories about her lost son, and she takes out a pencil and paper to make a "dusting" of his name. At the same time, she makes a prayerful entreaty to God, that her son should be regarded as more than just a "name on a wall." This grieving woman speaks for legions of mothers whose sons died in Vietnam. It is hard to listen to this song without a twinge of melancholy, for it is one of the saddest songs of all those written about America's saddest war.

Superior Vietnam Wall Memorial

Vietnam veteran Ronald Downs never forgot his best friend, Robert "Bobby" Erickson, who was killed in the war. He even named one of his sons after Erickson. Downs is pictured here with his sons at the Douglas County, Wisconsin, Vietnam Memorial. Downs was the driving force behind the establishment of this tribute to the local boys who gave their lives for the war.

In Roger Wright's "Heroes of Vietnam," the Vietnam Memorial is characterized as "the black wall," where all who died in the war "are listed one by one" and that "the years have shown you're heroes at last." The rest of the song is devoted to describing what happened to a survivor of the war named "Jim," who finished high school in 1964 and whose future was "big and bright" with the world an open door. However, this door is closed when at nineteen, Jim "marches off to Vietnam" with singularly tight-lipped determination, "without a word." In but a few weeks he is on the front lines, captured and "locked up in a cage." The song stresses that Jim is the essence of the patriotic hero, who could never be called "yellow," he was just "red, white and blue." When he returns home he is a classic case of PTSS, ruefully confessing to his wife that prior to Nam, "he had led a sheltered life" and had no awareness of the "horrors" he would experience there. Although now "sleep is hard to come by," this suffering is not in vain as Jim is comforted by the idea that he is simply paying the price for fighting "for freedom, to keep our country strong." There are Vietnam veterans, though, who may find this message less than reassuring, and while they undoubtedly appreciate other sentiments expressed in "Heroes of Vietnam," they are now painfully aware that they strived valiantly for nothing of substance.

What could be a Vietnam veteran weeping while watching televised accounts of the war in Vietnam is the subject of a song written by Mac Davis and recorded by Elvis Presley, "Don't Cry Daddy." The father becomes so distraught at seeing these films of combat that his young son becomes upset and pleads with his "daddy" not to cry and to just be an ordinary father again. The song was inspired by Davis' son telling him not to be upset about watching television coverage of the Vietnam War.[13] It is another reminder that Vietnam was the first "television war," and American families saw all its horrors right in their own homes. Aside from "If I Can Dream" and "In the Ghetto" (another Davis composition), this was one of the very few songs of social moment that "the King" of Rock and Roll ever sang.

Since I had long since stopped listening to radio stations that played contemporary music, I missed 10,000 Maniacs' song about The Wall, "The Big Parade," released in 1989. It is one of the very few songs that merited inclusion in what is supposed to be the "definitive collection of American fiction and nonfiction about the war." It tells the story of a young man who visits the Wall at his mother's behest where he joins the "slow parade" of veterans and others who search the wall for the name of someone they lost in Vietnam. In this boy's case, it appears he is searching for the name of a brother who was killed in the war. When he finally finds the name, he wonders if life would have been different had his sibling lived and whether it was the Viet Cong who killed him or his own government. "The Big Parade" has been described as depicting "the crowd at the memorial and the different connections with the dead and unsettled past."[14]

A common symptom of PTSS is an inability to feel affection and marriages ended as veterans found it extremely difficult to make the transition from war to domestic life, particularly those who came back as quadriplegics. One of these sad cases of a veteran who badly needed affection and understanding but didn't get it is depicted in Johnny Darrell's gritty "Ruby, Don't Take Your Love to Town." The paralyzed vet has the misfortune of being married to "Ruby" who proves to be an unfaithful spouse. She adds insult to injury as she slams the door in her husband's face as she goes off to yet another nocturnal tryst. This badly handicapped vet, tormented not only by his physical condition but the unfaithfulness of his wife, ruefully admits that he is far from what he used to be but wonders why he still can't at least have some vestige of spousal companionship. He reasons, to no avail, that he wasn't responsible for the war that ruined him physically and doesn't deserve to be shunned his wife. As he implores his wayward wife to stay home and stop running around on him, he warns that, if she doesn't, he will kill her.

This kind of sordid melodrama did take place in real life as too many were subjected to the same indignity by unfaithful spouses who tired of witnessing the ravages of Post Traumatic Stress Syndrome. These conflicts often led to episodes of domestic abuse and worse. At the same time, it should be stressed that those who tend to "demonize" the Vietnam veteran, whatever medium they use to do so, are often guilty of the worst kind of exaggeration. Mel Tillis, "Ruby's" composer, actually wrote the song about an injured World War II veteran, and, according to one source, he updated the lyrics by "using the current war in Vietnam." Tillis claims that he has never written a single political or protest song and that people who get that kind of message from "Ruby" are wrong. To him, it is a song about "people cut off from each other's needs and feelings, something that goes beyond any individual war or disaster.[15] Military censors didn't agree, and "Ruby" was banned from the play list of Armed Forces Radio, undoubtedly because of its content. One Vietnam vet characterized it as a song that "pathologizes" him and every other returning Vietnam veteran.[16] Although it was far from a favorite of the anti-war movement, "Ruby" is regarded as the song that finally turned the public against the war, along the way to attaining "gold record" status in 1969.[17] Gerald Stevens recorded an answer song "Billy, I've Got to Go to Town" describing her needs to get away from the pressures of living with this disabled veteran. Crooner Kenny Rogers had the biggest hit with this song, but Johnny Darrell originated it, and his reading is by far the most convincing. Darrell turned out to be one of the more unlucky artists in the country recording business, as his version of another song that became associated with Vietnam, "Green Grass of Home," was "covered" by Tom Jones, who also was far more successful with it commercially.

An intense controversy still rages about culpability in what has become known officially as "the My Lai Incident." Some believe that Lt. William Calley, who led the troops that were involved in the deaths of hundreds of South Vietnamese villagers in the small hamlet known as My Lai, was a genuine war criminal and that he was too lightly punished for his role in what some call the greatest war atrocity in American history. Others believe he was only a pawn and was just another soldier following orders, doing his job. This view is strongly stated in Terry Nelson and C Company's "Battle Hymn of Lt. Calley," which lionizes Calley to a stirring background of martial music that includes the "Battle Hymn of the Republic." Calley comes out sounding like some kind of risen Christ, who would not even contemplate the foul deeds of which he was accused. Those who find this song to their liking probably already had a preconceived notion that Calley was the victim of forces beyond his control and would agree with the many who contend there were extenuating circumstances surrounding what happened that day in that village in South Vietnam. The lyrics make the point that what happened at My Lai was at least partially due to frustration the troops felt over dealing with an unseen enemy, an enemy that inflicted pain and suffering and then disappeared. Even so, the rage born of the inability to deliver "payback" is really no excuse for the protracted carnage that took place at My Lai, which really was more of a massacre than an "incident," as it is known today. Those who regard what happened there as a war atrocity regard this song as little more than propaganda, especially the hyperbole of describing Calley as a great American hero. How the people who actually went out and bought the record feel about the controversy is impossible to tell with any certainty, but most were probably sympathetic to Calley. One of his strongest supporters was country-singing star Loretta Lynn who took her case all the way to the White House:

> "I got a letter from the then-President Nixon. I thought that was nice of him. I thought about writing back to him to ask why they put him in jail. I meant Lt. William Calley, the guy they convicted in the massacres of My Lai. I don't know much about it but it seemed strange that they should pin everything on one little lieutenant. Maybe he did wrong, but there were a lot of other people who should have known better too. Either everybody who was guilty should be put in jail or nobody should be put in jail."[18]

Calley had only been in jail for several days when disc jockeys in southern states began playing "The Battle Hymn of Lt. Calley" on a regular basis:

> "In the three days that he had been behind bars "The Battle Hymn of Lt. Calley" had sold 200,000 copies, and in South Vietnam, the Armed Forces Radio network in Saigon played it until someone high up in MACV ordered them to stop. The sentiment of many G.I.s was expressed on a wall in the city: "Kill a Gook for Calley." These events coincided with the publication of a collection of essays about social destructive-

ness in a book named *Sanctions of Evil,* which touched on My Lai and why people took part in atrocities. The title of one chapter, "It Never Happened - Besides, They Deserved It," seemed to capture the attitude of many Americans who believed Calley was truly innocent."[19]

Governor Jimmy Carter of Georgia organized an "American Fighting Men's Day," urging Georgians to drive with car headlights on and "honor the flag as Rusty had done." He was joined by other southern politicians, such as Governors George Wallace of Alabama and Ross Barnett of Mississippi, in urging support for Calley. Ironically, as president, Carter would grant a controversial amnesty to men who evaded the draft during the Vietnam War. Political pressure eventually forced President Nixon to order his release from jail pending an appeal of his sentence.[20] What kind of impact "Battle Hymn of Lt. Calley" had on bringing about this decision would be the rankest of speculation, but its viewpoint was shared by many who felt Calley had gotten a raw deal. At least one other song that addressed the martyrdom of Lt. Calley, "The Ballad of Rusty Calley," was widely played in "country bars" during this time.[21] Whether the issue spawned any other recorded music is unknown. There could have been any number of "spin-off" recordings that didn't receive significant airplay or promotion that would have brought them widespread public attention. "The Ballad of the Green Berets" spawned an almost innumerable number of songs loosely based on the philosophy of the original as sung by SSgt. Barry Sadler.

Merle Haggard, the country singer who recorded several important pro-war songs in the late 1960s, also made his views known on the war's aftermath in "Are the Good Times Really Over for Good (Wish a Buck Was Still Silver)." In this somber, almost funereal dirge, Haggard blames the war for a whole host of today's problems including worthless money, microwave ovens, drug abuse and the planned obsolescence of the automobile. Everything was fine before "the Ol' Vietnam War came along." He offers the viewpoint that America's ills in the wake of the war would be cured by a return to attitudes of the past, especially the old fashioned patriotic virtues. Only by turning the clock back can the country stop its precipitous decline, which he likens to "rollin' downhill like a snowball headed for hell." Americans need to "stand up for the flag" and "patch up the crack in the liberty bell." Haggard's nostalgia for a period when a woman's place was in the kitchen is a view that probably doesn't sit well with a lot of modern day women, who would regard it as blatantly sexist. The message of cultural despair that pervades this song is not for everyone but bringing back the "good old days" has its appeal. In another song of outrage recorded in the war's wake, "Me and Crippled Soldiers," Haggard takes the U.S. Supreme Court to task for ruling that burning the American flag is a form of expression protected by the constitution. If the same flag that was fought for in Vietnam and other wars can now be profaned, Haggard intones, veterans sacrificed in vain to save freedom. The fact that "Old Glory" can now be desecrated with impunity is the ultimate disgrace to veterans and only "me and crippled soldiers" care about the indignity to the nation's symbol of patriotism.

The Vietnam War was notable for the one-year tour of duty, and unlike some other American wars, soldiers came home while the war was still raging. One of the most popular of the songs that described this experience was the "Green, Green Grass of Home," as recorded by Tom Jones, a Las Vegas-style entertainer not widely know for recording music with deep political or social meaning. This widely recorded ballad nicely portrays the bliss of homecoming, made sweeter by the knowledge that odds were against it ever happening. The lyrics produce a setting in the mind's eye of a typical mid-American community, the "old hometown" looking "the same" as the returning soldier steps down from the train, to be met by his parents-"mama" and "papa" and his girlfriend Mary with "hair of gold and lips like cherry," who literally runs down the lane to meet him. This is one of those songs that was not intended to make a statement about the war and is actually the sad tale of a condemned man, reminiscing as his execution nears. However, the theme of the "Green, Green

Grass of Home" was one that the soldiers who made it back, and those hoping to, strongly identified with. It is entirely possible that the rather sad conclusion to "Green, Green Grass of Home," where it seems the narrator is walking the proverbial "last mile," might have had more impact on combat soldiers than the happy homecoming described at the beginning of the song. The ordeal of fighting in a war where death lurked in the next rice paddy or tree line may have made many of the G.I.s who heard this song think that coming home alive was only a remote possibility.

The theme of Bobby Vinton's mournful "Comin' Home Soldier" seems to be about a member of the Army or Marines who didn't serve in a combat zone as he makes plain that he didn't even earn a purple heart.[22] Despite the fact that he didn't earn any significant medals, he displays some pride in noting (wherever he served, perhaps somewhere in Europe?) that he fought to keep America free. Although this soldier should be happy in that he is returning home, Vinton sings it in almost mournful fashion, creating a mood of sadness and making one wonder if there aren't some mixed feelings about the tour of duty overseas ending. This could be a song for those who served during the Vietnam era at other duty stations.

"When Johnny Comes Marching Home"[23] is one of the most familiar songs of the Civil War, or any American war, for that matter. During the Vietnam War it inspired a memorable anti-war poster depicting a Veteran hobbling down some stairs on crutches. The soldier, who has obviously sustained wounds that have robbed him of the use of his legs, is in full uniform. The top of the placard displays the familiar words, "When Johnny Comes Marching Home again hurrah, hurrah." This returning soldier obviously doesn't have much to cheer about and a group known as "Help Us

Unsell the War" uses his plight to frame the message at the bottom of the poster, "Stop the Crippling. Stop the Killing. Stop the War. Write, Wire, or Call your congressman today."[24]

"When Johnny Comes Marching Home" also provides the title of a recording by Danny Wagner and The Kindred Soul (1968). It may have been a coincidence but it was released during the year that American fortunes in Vietnam were beginning to decline and American public opinion had begun to turn against the war. The original version of this song is jubilant and joyous and causes you to visualize exultant soldiers marching down the streets of their hometowns at the same time that they receive accolades from appreciative throngs of people. Wagner's song, of course, takes a much darker view of the soldiers from Vietnam coming home. Unlike their predecessors who fought in the "War Between the States," there were no parades and no adoring hordes to greet returning Vietnam veterans and express their gratitude for their sacrifices. In many cases, they were mocked and vilified. It is difficult to make out all of what Wagner has to say in this song. The music overwhelms the singer and much of the message is lost. However, I was able to distinguish enough of the lyrics to determine that the song could also be titled "If Johnny Comes Marching Home" and the concern that he might not receive the warmest of welcomes. This "Johnny" went off to Vietnam full of pride and optimism, a mood that was buttressed by scores of well wishers. However, if and when he returns it could be an entirely different story.

The Doves' "Soldiers" is another undeniably somber view of what it will be like when the fighting men return from Vietnam. The mood conveyed by this slow and lugubrious song is that of vague unease, as if the singer is actually dreading the homecoming, not knowing what to expect. It sounds as though people have gathered themselves into small groups, wondering and waiting, dreading the soldiers' return, not knowing how to behave or what to expect.

A much more buoyant returning soldier is to be found in Christie's[25] "Yellow River," where the returning vet seems ecstatic to be putting aside his weapons of war and returning to the wonderful place named in the title of the song. "Cannon fire" still lingers in his mind and he feels lucky to be returning unscathed but he is content because he will once again be in "Yellow River" where he remembers "the nights were cool" and of course the girl that he knew. It is difficult for him to contain his delight as he looks forward to soon spending his evenings "looking up at the moon in Yellow River." How many times did he and other soldiers in Vietnam look at the moon and stars and wonder what was going on at home? A puzzling line in this song is "put down my guns, the war is won." Does this mean his own personal war, the fact that he survived, is a victory? Another conclusion that might be drawn is that he thinks the United States has won or is winning the war. Since this record was released in 1970, a year during which "Vietnamization" was well underway and American troops were leaving Vietnam, this optimistic viewpoint is hopelessly unrealistic.

A sadly different kind of homecoming is the theme of Wanda Jackson's "Little Boy Soldier," where a mother and her young son await the arrival of his father at the train station. The little boy is dressed in a military uniform and is even holding a small flag as he happily waits for his dad to return from the war. The child can't understand why his mother is so sad at what should be an occasion for rejoicing. All too soon he knows, when the train pulls into the station carrying a coffin containing his father's remains. The little boy soldier's expression changes from one of joy to bewilderment as it dawns on him that his dad has become yet another casualty of the Vietnam War and will never really return home at all. "Little Boy Soldier" is a very moving musical vignette about what many families experienced, but it also leaves the listener thinking the mother is thoughtless and cold-hearted. Why didn't she prepare her son for what he was going to see at the train station? Why did she allow what is obviously a pre-adolescent child to be traumatized in this way? This song inevitably conjures up images of John F. Kennedy, Jr., saluting his father's coffin that sad weekend in November of 1963. Could composer Curly Putnam have had this picture in his mind when he wrote the song about another "little boy soldier?"

Wanda Jackson, who became the Queen of Rockabilly in the '50s, recorded many country and western hits during the 1960s including "Little Boy Soldier" in 1968, which is one of the more significant songs of the Vietnam War and the impact on families that lost a loved one in that conflict.

Photo of John F. Kennedy, Jr., saluting his father's casket on November 25, 1963. Is it likely that this picture inspired "Little Boy Soldier"? Source: Corbis

A similar homecoming, this time at an airport, is the subject of Charlotte Morgan's "He's Coming Home (From Vietnam)." A young woman sings about going to the airport where the plane is landing carrying the remains of her fiancé who is coming home in a flag-draped box. Just before he went to Vietnam, he provided her with the "happiest moment" of her life by asking for her hand in marriage, and now he has also become the reason for her saddest time. She can hardly believe that he is gone, as it seems like only a short time ago that he was "just a kid," driving her around in his car and taking her swimming.

Bruce Springsteen's "Born in the U.S.A." is about a young man who mourns the loss of a brother in the war and bitterly reminiscences how being born in "a dead man's town" doomed him to fight in Vietnam. Like many others, he was given the choice between going to jail or joining the military. Aside from the all-too-familiar story of the Hobson's Choice of jail or the military, the song is unique in suggesting that the war may have been more bitterly fought because of racial hatred. This theory is not a revelation to some historians, who feel that the war in the Pacific between the United States and Japan was especially intense because it was fought between men of different races. Whether this speculation will stand up to scrutiny is problematic, but "Born in the U.S.A." is distinctive among all the war music because it at least hints at the issue.

A related point with more evidence to support it is that America was at a disadvantage in Vietnam because too many of its fighting men let racist attitudes about the Vietnamese lull them into a fatal complacency about the enemy's fighting prowess. "Born in the U.S.A." is also noteworthy for being one of the few songs about the Vietnam War to mention an actual battle, Khe Sahn. Springsteen fiercely eulogizes a brother who died there. It was at Khe Sahn that U.S. Marines were under siege during the Tet Offensive. President Johnson and his advisors became obsessed with the fate of the garrison and considered using nuclear weapons as the only means of rescuing them. There was also a lot of conjecture, later proved to be unfounded, that Khe Sahn was a North Vietnamese trap that would become a disaster for the United States like Dien Bien Phu[26] was for the French during the Franco-Viet Minh war.[27]

Aside from being credited with a song that raises some important issues about the Vietnam War, Springsteen is a natural to provide this veteran's reminiscence. "The Boss" has been a generous supporter to the cause of Vietnam veterans. The Republican Party used "Born in the U.S.A." in President Ronald Reagan's re-election campaign in 1984, thinking that because the song was about a veteran, it fit well with Reagan's strongly patriotic views. The president even used Springsteen's name at a campaign stop in New Jersey, leading to absurd questions about which of the singer's songs he liked best. The equally absurd response, which came from campaign staffers days later, was "Born to Run."[28]

When he first heard "Born in the U.S.A." a former Green Beret who fought in Vietnam told me he felt like this:

> "It made me feel like the song was written for us. We could all stand back and give the government the finger and some of the public too for the way they treated us."[29]

The Australian group Cold Chisel uses Khe Sahn as the title for its song about a Vietnam vet who is having difficulty putting Vietnam behind him where he feels he "left" his "heart to the sappers at Khe Sahn." He wasn't able to adjust to an ordinary office job because the hours were too long for the meager pay he received. He is particularly disappointed in the women he encounters who he accuses of leading empty existences in the suburbs and whose legs are "often open" and "their minds always closed." He even goes back to Southeast Asia but finds no surcease there for his pain. As the song concludes, the disenchanted vet is preparing to fly from Sydney to Hong Kong where he will soothe his libido by finding a woman as jaded as himself and spend all night with her on a "Hong Kong mattress." Cold Chisel is renowned for its "roughhouse soul," and "Khe Sahn" is certainly faithful to this musical genre. A web page devoted to the group describes it as "Australia's most legendary rock band" and goes on to state, "Down under they are heroes, but the rest of the world hardly knows them." Since "Khe Sahn" contains some of the most tasteless lyrics of any of the Vietnam-related music, I wasn't surprised to learn that the song was banned from Australian radio for its "direct sexuality."[30]

One of the most remarkably literate of all the songs related to the war is Don William's rendering of Bob McDill's profoundly worded "Good Ole Boys Like Me." It appears to tell the moving story of a Vietnam veteran who has trouble sleeping, a symptom of Post Traumatic Stress Syndrome, and finds his mind wandering back to the halcyon days of his childhood and cultural icons like Stonewall Jackson, Uncle Remus, and Thomas Wolfe. In the midst of these nostalgic reminiscences, the vigilance that was necessary to survive Vietnam resurfaces as he is keenly aware of sounds in the night, but they don't bother him because he has already been "washed in the blood." This nocturnal reverie also includes visits from "other cultural icons like Hank and Tennessee Williams." Like many other Vietnam veterans, the narrator seems fatalistic about his future by singing, "I guess we're all gonna be what we're gonna be, but what do you do with good ole boys like me?" These words can also be read as a comment about the difficulty Vietnam veterans have had fitting into post-war society. "Good Ole Boys Like Me" is a song that could only have come from the pen of a songwriter like Bob McDill, whose scholarship in the area of American literature, and writers of the South in particular, has allowed him to embellish the lyrics of "Good Ole Boys Like Me" in such remarkably literate fashion. McDill has lectured on the writings of Robert Penn Warren at the University of South Carolina and has participated in symposia on the culture of the South.[31]

Mary Hopkin's "Those Were the Days" was recorded during the war, and although it doesn't have an obvious connection, it has appeared in many literary treatments of Vietnam and it is easy to imagine it portraying a gathering of veterans, recollecting in highly emotional fashion, perhaps induced by the consumption of alcohol, the most intense period of their lives, the war years. The "once upon a time there was a tavern" could well be alluding to the almost countless bars, saloons, and taverns that these nostalgic erstwhile warriors and their brethren frequented in Vietnam during the war. It would not be surprising either for the recounted events, horrible as they were at the time, to take on a rosy hue they don't deserve through the passage of time. The phrase "we'd fight and never lose" sounds tantalizingly like a reference to the feeling many veterans have that they weren't allowed to win because of political considerations that spawned hopelessly unrealistic "rules of engagement." In Tim O'Brien's "The Things They Carried," a soldier tells his buddy to shut up when he interrupts a tape of "Those Were The Days" and then fantasizes about going to London someday and marrying Hopkin. The fan feels that being in Vietnam has brought out these sentimental feelings in him, making him "want to hook up with girls like Mary Hopkin."[32]

Apple Records diva Mary Hopkin was a great favorite of soldiers in Vietnam shown here on her picture sleeve for "Think About Your Children."

In "Beers to You," Clint Eastwood and Ray Charles frequent taverns where they sing about having done three tours of duty in Vietnam and toast each other (with Coors beer) to "all the good times." Their war experiences don't seem to be troubling them at all as they rhapsodize about barroom brawls and numerous encounters with women while they attempt to satisfy what appears to be an almost unquenchable thirst for beer. Although this is not one of the more serious songs about how Vietnam vets fared after the war, it does show how war can "bond" men and how enduring such friendships formed in combat can be. It is a departure from most of the music about how veterans fared in the aftermath of the war, as the two ex-soldiers portrayed in "Beers to You" don't seem to have a care in the world. In fact, the nostalgia they express about the war makes it seem that they would welcome the opportunity to go back. "Beers to You" could easily be used as a beer commercial, and maybe it was. Eastwood's participation in this duet raises the question of why so many movie actors think they can sing (he can't) and why so many singers presume they can act. "Dirty Harry" can also be heard attempting to carry a tune in a duet with country singer Merle Haggard called "Bar-Room Buddies," another merry duet about the joys of beer drinking and male bonding that became a number one hit.

"Up Against the Wall Redneck Mother" was written by Ray Wylie Hubbard as an answer to Merle Haggard's "Okie From Muskogee." One observer notes that the song never achieved the acclaim of its predecessor because it attracted only an "underground audience" since radio stations wouldn't play it. The same critic offers the curious comment that the song languished in obscurity because it wasn't recorded by a "popular recording artist,"[33] although among those who waxed the song were Bobby Bare and Jerry Jeff Walker, who were far from unknowns and had their followings, especially Bare. "Redneck Mother" makes southern good old boys sound like drunken louts who do little more than get roaring drunk and wreak havoc in the taverns that are unfortunate enough to have them as patrons. It could also describe what could be a veteran who is having real difficulty adapting to life after the war. The returned soldier makes matters worse by pursuing a disastrous life style of frequenting bars where he swills boilermakers and beats up hippies. This ditty also takes a swipe at American motherhood by blaming the redneck's mother for his behavior, not the war, although plenty of veterans have found a dubious escape from the memories of the horrors of war in alcohol. Bare's song may well be satirical, but the animus against hippies and the violent behavior towards them are not really funny and are symptoms of Post Traumatic Stress Syndrome.

A more sympathetic portrait of a Vietnam vet is drawn in the Pranksters' "Don't Cry for Me: The Vietnam Vet's Song." The setting is a roadhouse in Pennsylvania where a veteran, during wasted hours of "trying to make him feel all right," tells a woman that Vietnam robbed him of his childhood. The war also took both legs, leaving him with two wooden prosthetic devices in their place. When the vet learns that his female acquaintance is only twenty four, he advises her that when he went to Vietnam he was twenty and by the time he reached her age, his "life was over." He is described as "one of those crazy Viet vets, now he just travels around" and is "a beat up looking son of a gun." He still has his pride, though, as he tells his female companion:

> "Don't cry for me lady. I don't want your sympathy.
> Don't say you understand, 'cause nobody can.
> But if you've got a little respect for me, somewhere inside,
> that's enough, believe me, for all of us who tried and died."

The picture sleeve that accompanies this record states that the song is "respectfully dedicated to the 'Nam Vets and to Pete" ("Pete" is the vet who inspired the song). Also on the sleeve is a logo showing a map of Vietnam and a helicopter. A disclaimer mentions "Chapter 40 Vietnam Vets, Columbiana Co. Ohio," with special thanks to Denny Gray, V.P. Columbiana Co. V.V.A. It does-n't take a great deal of imagination to appreciate that this record was sponsored by this branch of the Vietnam Veterans of America to set the record straight about the true feelings many veterans have about this war.

The lyrics to this song were difficult to discern and initially I was wondering what "Pennsylvania hotel night" meant. Susan Rachel (a.k.a. Susan Wojnar), the writer of the song, advised me that the phrase is actually "Pennsylvania coal town night," so the words were not as suggestive as they appeared to be. Although she advised me that the encounter did take place in a hotel, and was based, almost verbatim on an actual conversation she had with a Vietnam vet, I certainly misconstrued an important part of the song. It is some consolation to know that I am not the first, nor will I be the last, to make such an error. It brings to mind the fellow who called a record store asking for a copy of Stephen Sondheim's "Ein Kleine Nachtmuzik" ("A Little Night Music") and asked for "I'm Inclined to Knock Music." Luckily, in the case of "Don't Cry for Me," I had the opportunity to interview the writer and find out where I had botched the lyrics and also, more importantly, discover what prompted her to write the song. Many songwriters get their inspiration from abstract ideas or vicarious experience but for Wojnar the catalyst was an intensely personal experience:

> "I met this Vietnam veteran in a run-down hotel/honky-tonk on the outskirts of a once-thriving town in Western Pennsylvania, once a boom area for coal, steel and tin. The veteran in question was named "Peter." Though a self-admitted outlaw, he was not completely spiritually bereft-though this aspect of him is not presented in the song...a bit of digression then, for what its worth. Staying connected to nature was very important to him-he told how when he felt he could not go on any longer, he would find a woods or forest, walk into the thick of it alone, late at night and strip naked-and stay very still and silent for as long as he could. I know it may sound a little odd in the retelling, but he was at his most earnest and sincere when he told me to always remember this and to promise him I would try this, just once. I do remember him saying not to go through life without doing this, at least once. He, knowing I was a starry-eyed songwriter, also asked me to tell his story-'any way possible.' I have always felt it was, if you'll pardon the expression, something of a sacred honor to do so...the evening had a transcendent 'outside-of-time' quality. There was little alcohol involved. With wooden legs and all, he and I danced...it was the most awkward and beautiful of dances. I thank you for the opportunity to re-live this...I haven't really reflected on it in years."[34]

Charlie Daniels' "Uneasy Rider" describes another bar room encounter that highlights the tensions between "hippies" and "rednecks." The "Uneasy Rider" is a typically longhaired hippie who has a flat tire somewhere in rural Mississippi and is forced to go into a "redneck-looking bar" to seek assistance. Once his long-hair and peace symbol bumper sticker on his car are discovered by the patrons in the establishment, all hell breaks loose. The hippie manages to escape a beating or worse by accusing the ringleader of his assailants of being an FBI spy who is infiltrating the Ku Klux Klan and also a communist sympathizer. While the gullible slow moving and slow thinking rednecks are digesting these astonishing charges, their would-be prey makes his getaway, vowing to go through Omaha next time he travels to Los Angeles. Although the song indulges in some pretty heavy stereotyping it is an interesting period piece, not only for its reminder that there was little love lost between those in the anti-war movement and those who lived in certain parts of the South, but also references to the McGovern and Wallace presidential campaigns in 1972. A campaign where the war remained a significant issue, even though incumbent President Richard Nixon's "Vietnamization" policy had left the American military presence in South Vietnam at only a fraction of what it had been a few short years before.

One of the rock luminaries of the era, Elton John, recorded the well-known "Daniel," yet another song related to Vietnam that was inspired by a news article. "Daniel" was based on a story about a Vietnam veteran who goes home and just wants to forget about the war, but his family and friends won't let him, and instead decide that they are going to make a hero out of him. The veteran is so disillusioned by the experience that he decides to leave America and go to Spain. As his plane takes off, John sings mournfully of the departure and worries, correctly, that his "brother" still suffers from the invisible, but agonizing, wounds of Post Traumatic Stress Syndrome. Daniel is a pretty mysterious character but it is arguable that the ravages of serving in Vietnam have aged him prematurely, making him the kind of " bloody but unbowed" sympathetic figure that elevates him to a heroic status. "Daniel" might also be seen as a song about a veteran paying tribute to another veteran, a quite reasonable reaction since the combat experience in Vietnam bonded men and made them brothers in the truest sense of the word. The veteran who is the subject of John's ode also has to deal with the fact that he has lost his eyesight, probably in the war. But even though this tragic figure's eyes have "died," he still is able to "see" more than most. When Bernie Taupin, John's collaborator, gave him the words for this song, he was so enthusiastic about the topic, he sat down at the piano and worked out the musical score in about ten or fifteen minutes and recorded it by the end of the same day.[35]

Another prominent rock star who sang about remembering Vietnam through the eyes of a veteran is Billy Joel with "Goodnight Saigon," recorded in 1982. The title and the accompanying picture sleeve, which shows a number of helicopters,[36] summons up the unforgettable images of the helicopters lifting off of the roof of the United States embassy in Saigon, sometimes with people hanging desperately on the struts, in the late spring of 1975. The cliché that "a picture is worth a thousand words" applies here, for these pictures of the frantic evacuation of American personnel and Vietnamese refugees in the final days of the American presence in Southeast Asia are brutally eloquent in evoking the pain and frustration of the country's worst foreign policy blunder of the twentieth century. Joel's song is about two Marines who "became soul-mates" on Parris Island (boot camp) and left as " inmates from an asylum." Whether this is a reference to the rigorous and often demoralizing nature of Marine basic training or the combat experience in Vietnam is unclear, but at the beginning, these Marines "were gung ho to lay down our lives." Once they were "in country," these Marines' behavior didn't always conform to the Marine Code of Conduct as they "passed the hash pipe and listened to Doors' tapes" but they were still "semper fi" in the truest sense of the word, and holding "on to each other like brother to brother." When duty called, questions of right or wrong were forgotten "in the thick of the fight" knowing "we would all go down together." This song at least suggests that there was a greater *esprit de corp* in the Marines than the Army, that although these relatively "few good men" may have had doubts about the cause, they suffered in silence. The unusual camaraderie among Marines is described by Martin Russ in *Breakout: The Chosin Reservoir Campaign: Korea 1950:*

> "...Because of a tradition of loyalty which meant in practical terms that the individual Marine trusted in and relied on his comrades to an extraordinary degree, and that he himself was trustworthy and reliable...Most marines of that day believed that it was better to die than to let one's comrades die in combat. ...There was an undeniable mystique about the Marine Corps, a feeling of being vastly superior to the soldiers of the U.S. Army (Marines never refer to themselves as soldiers) alongside whom they were sometimes required to campaign. By and large, Marines were a resourceful, hardy breed, readier to go in harm's way than the Army's hapless minions."[37]

A romanticist might wish that the content of "Goodnight Saigon" justified the title, that it was somehow another "The Last Time I Saw Paris," a musical memoir about Vietnam that was more about this city and why it has such a "hold on a generation."[38] Even so, the song inevitably conjures up in veterans' minds memories of the fascinating city of Saigon and its peculiar milieu of oriental sights and sounds and aromas. For those who had been persuaded to be a Marine because they were promised they would see exotic places, Saigon certainly fulfilled that expectation. Just as the "doughboys" of World War I were electrified and titillated by Paris, their counterparts in Vietnam had to have had a similar reaction to Saigon. Joel may have indulged in poetic license in writing "Goodnight Saigon." One veteran leatherneck sergeant told me that the marines weren't permitted to go south beyond Danang and I Corps, well north of Saigon.[39] Joel's "We Didn't Start the Fire" has a much broader historical sweep than "Goodnight Saigon," as it includes a recitation of famous historical names and events ranging from Harry Truman and the Studebaker all the way to Sally Ride and "rock and roller cola wars." Ho Chi Minh and Woodstock are mentioned only in passing as well as Russia's Vietnam, Afghanistan. This ambitious song also says goodbye to George

Santayana, the imminent historian and philosopher, who is best known for warning: "Those who cannot remember the past are condemned to repeat it." This might be by far the most relevant part of the song as far as the Vietnam War is concerned, for it is abundantly clear that if presidents Eisenhower, Kennedy, Johnson and Nixon had studied history more closely, the United States might have possibly avoided the horrible ordeal it suffered in Southeast Asia.

"Jimmy's Road" by Willie Nelson is about a young man who was sent to Vietnam and had "his mind changed around" there. In the beginning of the song, Nelson sings about the grass that the young Jimmy used to "like to lay on" and "the trees he used to climb." The focus then shifts to the battleground, where he learns the business of killing and finally the grave where he is buried. Even death hasn't brought peace to Jimmy though, for when "a soldier falls, Jimmy's body dies and dies and dies." "Jimmy's Road" is among the most morbidly depressing of all the Vietnam-related music. It is not easy to listen to, even for someone who attempts to approach it with the detachment of a scholar, to say nothing of how veterans with Post Traumatic Stress Syndrome would react to hearing such a fugue. Nelson recorded this song (1966) long before he adopted the persona of "The Red Headed Stranger" and became a hirsute superstar of country music. I saw him in concert at about the time he released "Jimmy's Road," and he was clean-shaven, had short hair and was dressed in a suit.

Private Danny Blaine followed the same road as "Jimmy" and became another Vietnam casualty. Even death hasn't allowed him to escape the war and he can still hear gunfire. Danny is the ghostly narrator of Ric King's "The Return of the Soldier," which is the soliloquy of a dead man as his funeral cortege rolls through the streets of his hometown on the final journey to the grave. The deceased seems confused at first and calls out to his parents, "Hey, I'm back in Vietnam!" Then what he "sees" shifts back to the route the hearse is taking and he asks the driver to go slowly so he can see all the old familiar sights including the old movie house as well as the "Sugarbowl" where he spent so many happy, carefree hours before Vietnam interrupted and then ended his life. The people that come to "meet" him are greeted with the joy of remembrance-his football coach, the patriotic banker who promised him a job when he got back from Vietnam, and the kindly old lady who baked him cookies because he was a good paper boy. His girlfriend cries with "joy" at his grave and all the kids who grew up come for the final farewell, in which Danny participates unbeknownst to his mourners. "The Return of a Soldier" makes you think of how the troops in Vietnam must have yearned for their own version of hometown America, the way Danny did. Danny speaks, in his strange way, for all those who didn't make it back. His return, as bizarre as it was, was better than the rude welcome many veterans received from an ungrateful and insensitive public. It would be easy for some to dismiss "The Return of a Soldier" as entirely too maudlin and pretentious, but in my opinion, and I know I speak for more than just myself, I regard it as an unusually creative and compelling way of describing the painful sadness of a soldier's final journey.

All of these songs were written and performed by professionals, who, while adept at describing vicarious experiences in song, never served in Vietnam. For those who crave the authenticity of music performed by someone who was actually "in country," there are the songs of Sarge Lintecum, who did three tours in Vietnam as a member of the 101st Airborne. Lintecum, whose compact disc, "Vietnam Blues: Combat Tested for Peace," has garnered rave reviews from music critics and Vietnam veterans throughout the United States, has the advantage of singing about something he actually experienced as with "Reunion at the Wall:"

"I'm goin' to see some friends of mine I'm going to Washington
Some years ago I used to know.
Well they're all back together now
They're holdin' their heads up proud
I know I'll cry as I read their names
When I stand before the wall.
Well it was a long long time ago
But time don't heal all wounds.
So I'm goin' to see some friends of mine
Cause I got these Vietnam blues."

Lintecum's "This Shirt of Mine," also owes its powerful eloquence to the fact that it is autobiographical:

"This shirt of mine...This shirt of mine.
I put my life on the line for freedom
In this shirt of mine.
There's honor in every patch, on this shirt of mine.
Some people think I'm a Hippie.
Some think I'm insane.
Some people think I'm Halloween.
When I wear this shirt of mine."

One of the most memorable songs about the Vietnam Memorial comes from the pen of another veteran, Tim Murphy, and has been recorded by Michael McCann, who served in Special Forces in Vietnam. The fact that they were actually there gives this musical tribute, simply titled "The Wall," an eloquence and emotional intensity that makes it one of the most moving and unforgettable pieces of music I have heard about any war:

> "On a drizzly D.C. morning in the middle of July,
> My brother brought me downtown to the Mall;.
> Past the watchful eyes of Lincoln neath the weeping summer sky,
> I crossed the street to the little green and visited The Wall.
> I remember I was nervous then,
> I guess a little scared. "Cause I wasn't sure how I'd react at all,
> To see the names of the servicemen who'd been recorded there.
> Who heard the final roll call and assembled at The Wall."

The compelling refrain effectively conveys a message that there is a universality to The Wall that should touch the heart of every American:

> "And every name's a father or a son,
> or a daughter or a brother or a cousin to someone,
> Or a name might be a classmate or a friend you may recall.
> There's nearly 60,000 fallen names still waiting at The Wall."

Vietnam veterans Mike McCann and Tim Murphy perform at a Battle Notes booksigning at Anna Liffey's Pub in New Haven, Connecticutt. Both McCann and Murphy have drawn on their war experiences to produce some excellent songs about war.

It is not inconsequential that both Murphy and McCann are Irish-Americans. Someone once said that to be Irish is to know that someday the world will break your heart. In a strange way, their troubled ancestry makes these men excellent choices to portray the pathos of Vietnam. It is almost as if some kind of intangible genetic memory is at work in "The Wall" allowing Murphy and McCann to draw on all the trials that Ireland and Irishmen have encountered through history, that allows them to so effectively describe the pain of those who visit the Vietnam Memorial. The fact that both were "line troops" during the war and highly decorated is another key element that explains their virtuosity in delivering this kind of music. McCann won the Purple Heart and Bronze Star for Valor, while Murphy received the Silver Star. Murphy describes how he came to write the song about The Wall:

> "I finally saw the Vietnam Veteran's Memorial at my brother Pat's urging. He'd served several tours in 'Nam and suggested that a trip to The Wall might afford me the same solace he'd found there. I felt a vague ambivalence toward the Memorial and was uneasy about finding the names of friends and comrades I'd served with in the 4th Infantry Division, 1968 and 1969. I remember that my first visit to the VVM brought to me a deep and abiding comfort which endures to this day. I wanted others to know this peace that I'd experienced there, and so I tried to share my impressions in the lyrics of my song, "The Wall." Very few adults living in America today were not touched in some way by the experience of Vietnam. My wish is that my song will help people to come to The Wall to remember and,in their memories, find peace and comfort."[40]

By June of 1973, America had all but withdrawn its military forces from Vietnam in defeat and the country's prestige and self-esteem had dropped to perhaps its lowest point in history. International public opinion took note of this fall from grace, and various governments were less than gentle in their criticism and sometimes even gleeful that the United States had been bloodied and humiliated in Vietnam. A powerful boost to this sagging morale came on the very day that the media was alerting the world to the fact that America had pulled out of Vietnam. Gordon Sinclair, a Canadian broadcast journalist, sat down in front of the microphone for his noon newscast and told his listeners, and ultimately the world, how outraged he was at the way America was being verbally castigated by countries around the world. It caused a sensation that brought about the release of Sinclair's commentary, "The Americans (A Canadian's Opinion)," on an American record label and sold hundreds of thousands of copies. The Sinclair tribute drew a favorable reaction from every level of the American political system and became a hot topic of conversation all over the country. It is little wonder that the recording of "The Americans" was so well received in the United States, for the Canadian's eloquently stated opinion was "it is time to speak up for the Americans as the most generous and possibly the least-appreciated people in all the world." Sinclair chided the world for its ingratitude and recited an impressive list of situations where the United States had selflessly helped other nations who needed assistance in dealing with crises. The Canadian observer obviously spoke for many of his southern neighbors when in his concluding remarks when he predicted:

> "They will come out of this thing with their flag high. And when they do, they are entitled to thumb their nose at the lands that are gloating over their present troubles."

Few, if any foreigners, have received the acclaim that Sinclair did as a result of his tribute to America. It came at a time when the United States badly needed a boost. The fact that the treatise came from an outsider made it doubly convincing. The warm glow that Americans felt toward Sinclair was still present over a decade later when President Reagan visited Canada and asked to meet him. The two had a lengthy conversation, during which Reagan told Sinclair that he used to play "The Americans" in the California Governor's Mansion when he needed an uplift. The Canadian broadcaster again buoyed American spirits in 1979 with another recording entitled "The Americans (How Long Will They Take It?)."

Student Essays

Of all the sad and painful music about the post-war period, it was "More Than a Name on a Wall" that provoked the most intense emotional response from students:

> "There are so many people that look at these names on The Wall and it really doesn't have very much effect on them. However, behind every name there are people and family who care about these people. For people who have actually seen The Wall and the people there paying tribute to their lost ones, suddenly, a person realizes that there is much more than just names on a wall."

> "I feel that the best song I heard was 'More Than a Name on a Wall" by the Statler Brothers. It shows how heartbreaking it was for mothers to have their children sent to war. After the war when people in the U.S. tried to forget everything about the Vietnam War there were still people remembering the ones who didn't come back. When we see a soldier's name along with personal letters, pictures and other things left at The Wall in Washington, D.C., it reminds us that these soldiers were alive once and they still are alive in their mothers' and other loved ones' memories."

> "This was the most convincing Vietnam-related song to me out of the variety of songs we listened to in class. It really hit me hard, emotionally. The song made me visualize the mother going to The Wall with flowers and paper to rub her son's name. This caused me to think of all the rest of the people who had lost a family member in Vietnam. I guess I just can't understand why so many people had to die for no reason and this song really made me face reality and think about all the people we lost in Vietnam."

> "Songs like 'Why Me' by Kris Kristofferson and 'Still in Saigon' by the Charlie Daniels Band describe the true nature of the emotional and spiritual trauma that war generates, not

only for the soldiers fighting the war but also for their loved ones waiting for them at home. The songs 'More Than a Name on a Wall' and 'Soldier's Last Letter' touched my heart. As I listened to these songs, I could actually feel the pain of the mothers, the mother standing at The Wall remembering her son, and the other mother receiving her son's unfinished letter. I think the reason I feel so touched by these songs is because I can relate to these feelings due to being a mother myself."

"What makes the Statler Brothers' song effective is not only the vividness and almost tangible sadness we feel, but more importantly, the timelessness of 'More Than a Name on a Wall.' Many of the songs we listened to are dated. This song will be as good fifty years from now as it was the day it was written. Because of this, I will almost forgive the Statler Brothers for their idiotic song, 'Flowers On The Wall.'"

"I have been to the Vietnam Memorial in Washington, D.C. As I scanned the thousands of names, my heart went out to those who had come to say good-bye. All around me, people placed flowers and were crying; no one except them understood the pain they were going through. The song 'More Than a Name on a Wall' by the Statler Brothers expresses the hurt of family and friends who had lost loved ones in the war. The song tries to comfort those who mourn by saying they died for their country and gives the listener the idea that somehow there is virtue in that. The song also focuses on how painfully they will be missed at special times like holidays and birthdays. People in mourning felt utterly alone and I thought the harmony in the song symbolized that there were many different voices singing the same tune. In that respect, I found the song to be uplifting in knowing that you're never alone and that there is always someone out there who feels the way you do."

"Still in Saigon" made many students appreciate vicariously the torture that is PTSS:

"I like this song for a number of reasons. First, I cannot imagine what a horrible experience it must have been to fight in the jungles of Vietnam, and then to never forget it through flashbacks and nightmares. Also, it really explained the effects and tragedies of Post Traumatic Stress Syndrome. Last of all, it made me feel sad and angry at the same time. Sad because I feel for the poor people who have had to go through the grisly experience of Vietnam, and who cannot forget it. Mad because this did not have to happen, mad because we did not have to get involved in a losing battle and needlessly kill thousands of young men."

"'Still in Saigon' could very well have been the best selection that was played in class. The sense of immediacy that engulfs the lyrics of the song creates an intensity that might actually give the listener an idea of how real delusions are for some veterans. While the song was being played I thought of shell-shocked soldiers returning home to their country in search of solace but finding nothing but disdain and aloofness from the general public. How much more damage did that do?"

"The song 'Still in Saigon' by the Charlie Daniels Band, reminds me of my dad. It is a song about PTSS. This is about a man who got off a plane and got off in a whole new world. He states that he could have gone to Canada or stayed in school but instead he is there. He got home 13 months and 15 days later. He had to stay behind locked doors. Even now, ten years later, he still feels like he is in Saigon. He says the ground is covered in snow and I am covered in sweat. He can't tell anyone what is happening to him because he feels so ashamed. I think this song is so true. It is showing what people went through and what they are still going through. Many people are still in counseling because of what they were forced to see and do in the Vietnam War."

"I strongly feel that 'Still in Saigon' by the Charlie Daniels Band most honestly and truthfully depicts the feeling in

> Vietnam; it is sung as a first hand experience, which adds to its persuasiveness. The song is about a Vietnam veteran with Post Traumatic Stress Syndrome. He sings of how he's never able to leave the war, for the feelings he felt in Vietnam forever haunt him. Some call him 'killer' and some just call him 'vet' upon his return home from Vietnam, he does not know who he is anymore. Things as benign as the summertime rain even catapult him back to Vietnam in his vivid memories. Even ten years after his return home, he still cannot shake the feelings of horror that Vietnam imbedded into his memory forever. This narrator, this honest-to-goodness history book of the Vietnam War does an extraordinary job in relating feelings of trauma and sorrow that were so common to the soldiers of that horrid war. In a few words, he was convincing."

A Vietnam veteran had this plaintive response to "Still in Saigon:"

> "'Can't tell no one, I feel the shame.' WHY must we feel the shame when WE are the heroes!!?"

"Why Me" also stirred students' emotions, especially this one, who was able to relate to the song on an intensely personal level:

> "This song hits especially close to home for me. When my husband was released from Walter Reed Hospital in 1971, he no longer believed in God. He believed he had been to hell and survived by his own grit and through no help from God or anyone else. I think the spiritual lives of a lot of Vietnam vets took a real beating in that awful year they were over there. It took my husband 20 years to find God again. He no longer asks 'Why Me Lord?' He now says, 'thank you God for giving me the chance to live beyond Vietnam."

For other students, the message in "Why Me" was a more abstract, intellectual subject but it still evoked some insightful commentary:

"One of the more interesting parts of the lyrics went, 'Why me Lord, what have I ever done, to deserve even one of the pleasures I've known, tell me lord, what did I ever do, that was worth loving you or the kindness you've shown?' This, to me, meant how lucky he is to be alive and he doesn't know why. His life was spared from this tragedy. He could have easily been coming home in a box, but he made it. Many men and women in Vietnam were ashamed of the atrocities that were committed and could not deal with life in a 'regular' way when they came back home. Some men came back with a lifetime of horrific tales to entertain their buddies. Others had found their memories transformed into nightmares and nervous breakdowns. They seemed to stay by themselves and not talk about certain things they did or saw while fighting."

I wasn't surprised that young women rejected Haggard's yearnings for the past in vigorous fashion:

"I think Merle Haggard's 'Are The Good Times Really Over For Good' is the worst song! I really dislike this song, mostly for personal reasons. In this song, he describes America as once being a place of unity, now being a place of chaos. He goes on to describe how women used to cook in the home. This bothers me, and it should, I'm a woman. Only when my husband brings home a job that supports both of us comfortably will I pack up my brief case and bring down my bra-burning flag. Besides being bitter over that statement, the rest of the song just irks me. He also sings about how America wasn't unified. This is understandable, there were a lot of injustices at the time. However, because these injustices were dealt with, we have more equality and less angst. In other words, we moved on, and for the better...but don't take Merle's song for that, he still wants to go back."

Another young woman did not find the song offensive to her gender and gave it a generally favorable review, most likely because her father is a Vietnam veteran.

> "If I had to pick the song I like the most among the ones played in class, I would have to choose 'Are the Good Times Really Over for Good' by Merle Haggard. This was the only song that really gave me that 'gut feeling' of the emotional side of the war. I have heard the song many times before since I grew up around country music, but I've never really listened to the words. It gave a positive reflection to the aftermath of the war, which seemed to be uncommon compared to the reaction of the people who spit on my dad and many other vets when they returned home. Haggard described a country that had good times ahead of it. He tried to get across to his listeners that we should stand up for our flag and make the United States the 'good old country' that it was."

Yet another student found the song a simple expression of nostalgia:

> "As the title indicates, it is a reminiscence about the good time that Haggard really misses. I really related well to this song because it seems to be a very heart-broken song about when everything was better. I recall how my father and grandpa would get together and reminisce about when things in America were very peaceful and the cost of living was low."

Students unanimously empathized with the tragic figure in "Ruby:"

> "Mel Tillis' song 'Ruby Don't Take Your Love To Town' is a very emotional song that is about the after-effects of the war. Often people are naive in thinking that veterans were 'lucky' to come back from the Vietnam War alive. Yet this song addresses just how 'lucky' some of them were. It takes me from feeling sorry for the vet whose wife is cheating on him to wanting to get his gun and shoot her myself. If I had heard this song when it came out I don't believe it would have influenced my view about the war one way or the other. I would

have been more careful in my choice of a wife, though. The song really didn't take me back to that era, because many of the same things are happening to military personnel today."

"'Ruby Don't Take Your Love to Town' is an example of a neutral war song. It appeals deeply to the listener's emotions. This vet was maimed and left in a wheelchair. His inability to satisfy his wife results in her sleeping around. The profound emotional appeal of this song is conveyed not only through the despair expressed in the singer's voice but through the narration. He sings of the sound of the door slamming, he senses and anticipates her desires to leave for a night out on the town, a night spent with other men. The most painful aspect of this song is how brutally aware he is of the situation: his post-war powerlessness. Dare I say the war has left him less than a man. The story effectively transcends pro/anti-war boundaries. It is simply so human."

"In a war, you have many emotions, with love and hate being the two strongest feelings... People go to extreme measures for these two feelings. In the Vietnam War, men killed because they were trained or conditioned to hate. Face it, who wouldn't feel hate after seeing your battle buddy being killed by the enemy? Love, on the other hand, carried some of these men through the hard times. Sadly enough, in 'Ruby,' it did the opposite. It is a song about heartbreak and despair. It is about a veteran who is paralyzed from the war and cannot make love to his wife, 'Ruby.' In turn, she goes out to town and finds the things she needs. Knowing this is slowly killing her veteran husband. He is made to feel inadequate as a man and by the time the song ends he not only has fallen out of love with her, he resents her so much that he wants to kill her. Love and hate are very close emotions. Once you fall out of love, it becomes very easy to hate. This is a fact of life and one who understands this can either do damage or rise above it and learn from it."

The following essays were representative of students' feelings about the musical attempt to confer heroic status on Lt. William Calley:

> "The one song that truly galled me was 'Battle Hymn of Lt. Calley.' The rationale given for the behavior of American troops at My Lai is truly absurd. His buddies were killed left and right. Soldier against soldier or weapon against weapon is one thing; however, soldier against an unarmed villager is murder."

> "'Battle Hymn of Lt. Calley' was by far the worst song out of all of them. It was a ridiculous attempt to justify Calley's actions in being responsible for the murders of over 400 men, women, and children at My Lai."

Since Bruce Springsteen is still a very active part of the modern musical scene, most students were familiar with "Born in the U.S.A." but didn't realize its significance to the Vietnam War until they heard the song in class and really listened to the lyrics:

> "I really liked the song before we listened to it in class. It always came across to me as a song that showed patriotism. I didn't realize it was about the Vietnam War until we listened to it. This gave me another sense of what people went through during this time. When he sang, 'Got into a little home, so they put a rifle in my hand,' this made me realize that going to Vietnam was a way out of prison for some people. You were making a deal with the government. What a great way for the government to get more people over there. Another line from this song that got to me was, 'Had a brother at Khe Sahn fighting off the Viet Cong. They're still there, he's all gone.' This was an example of the bitterness that many Americans felt. They had someone very close to them blown up for no reason. Nothing came of the war except America losing too many good men while North Vietnam stayed in command. I really like how catchy the song is. It will always be one of my favorites, but now it has a different meaning to me."

> "I have listened to 'Born in the U.S.A.' many times, but I never really listened to the words. I was unaware of the meaning behind the song. I am not the only one, President Ronald Reagan praised it when it came out until a member of his staff told him the lyrics. This song deals with a man who is sent off to Vietnam to fight the 'yellow man.' He comes back to no welcome home and no job. He had a brother who didn't make it at Khe Sahn. It's ten years down the road and he really has no place to go. The song is unique to me because it came out around my generation and is powerful, and successful, and well done."

> "'Born in the U.S.A.' was another song I really liked and found fitting as a song representative of the Vietnam War. Bruce Springsteen sings about getting in a jam at home and getting sent to war as a result of his misconduct. He also sings about his brother at Khe Sahn who was killed, but how the Viet Cong he was fighting still remain. The song is very patriotic and I think it was Springsteen's intention to emphasize his patriotism. He did mention the U.S.A. nearly twenty times in the duration of his song."

Others saw it, much like the Mondale and Reagan campaigns in 1984, as being straightforwardly patriotic in the sense that those who protested the war were just as patriotic as those who supported it:

> "Of all the songs we heard this was my favorite. It has been one of my favorites for a long time, yet before this class I had never before seen it as a song from this era, only as a song that exemplifies the mood and pride of an entire country. This song has patriot written all over it. What other song than our own national anthem says more good things about this great country of ours. Bruce was able to capture my soul and heart in this piece like no one else. The song talks about how one stands up for what they believe in and in so doing realize what the consequences are. Now to me, this song is a work of art. I see the past through the eyes of the marchers and protestors

> of the war. This song brings me into Chicago for the Democratic National Convention. I can smell the tear gas coming from the police and I can also hear the pain of those being beaten for their showing of nationalism. This song does more for me than any other in the history of modern rock and roll. Now, I may be going out on a limb for this song, but it's truth and it is sung from the heart. I only wish I had been alive back then so I would have been able to march alongside of my fellow Americans, to stand up for what I believe in and to say what many others had said, 'The Whole World is Watching!'"

Although the central figure of "Up Against the Wall Red Neck Mother" was from Oklahoma, this student saw the song as yet another effort to make southerners appear backward and stupid:

> "This was by far the best song reinforcing the traditional stereotype of the South being a place populated primarily by people who are just plain stupid. 'Kickin' hippies' asses and raisin' hell' goes to show you that there were only a select minority that believed in the war and its principles. The lyrics, not to mention the music, conveyed the idea that if you have a southern accent your I.Q. drops twenty points. No wonder this song never made it to the big time."

Most students found "Up Against the Wall Red Neck Mother" to be foolish, but one student thought the "red-neck" was justified in behaving the way he did:

> "The song was very interesting....I thought it was about a guy that was in the war and came back to the United States to find hippies protesting. He is described as being in his early thirties, having little more to do for recreation than guzzling boilermakers and beating up on hippies and generally being rowdy. This shows how people that fought in the war felt about the protestors. I think that they felt lucky to have made it home after everything they had experienced, and then were faced with people who hated them for doing something they thought was right. I could really relate to

this guy. I would definitely fight with people that really opposed the war and treated me like shit because I fought for my country and risked my life."

A far different view of the same song:

"It insults the intelligence of Americans. By reducing the mentality of us down to the level of hicks who are more impressed by the killing and torturing than the fact that they are supposed to represent our country with honor and right-doing. Granted, I'm not one for war. I think it is wrong. Killing someone's family member just over a dispute with the country or their government is stupid. Acting like an immature four-year-old with a gun when you are in a different territory representing a whole country is someone who should be back in their country in the psycho ward."

A former marine was best equipped to address "Goodnight Saigon," and "What is a Marine?' (See Chapter Five):

"A couple of songs I found incredibly inspiring were, in a nostalgic sort of way, 'Good Night Saigon' by Billy Joel and 'What is a Marine' by Ernie Maresca. With the latter, I actually found myself laughing at the lyrics and at times saying, "What a crock of ..." But some of what he said was very true, and bottom line, I like it because I think there is some sort of undefined entity about 'what a Marine is.' For him to try and define it was very commendable. I don't think anyone can define it, but Billy Joel comes close to it when he sings about the Marines in Saigon. His lyrics really reminded me of the brotherhood all Marines share, not only while serving, but for the rest of their lives. 'And we will all go down together' is another line in the song that captures the *Semper Fi* of the Marine. These two songs left a warm feeling in my heart that I feel would do the same for any Marine, at some point in their lives. Note: Not all Marines feel this way, especially those young ones serving right now, but someday they too will understand, I have no doubt."

As I expected, "Jimmy's Road" by Willie Nelson made an impression with a number of students:

"It sets a very dark scene. The message was very clear about how Jimmy will never see his tree again, and how he'll never see his grass again. The words themselves are very powerful, and accompanied by the minor notes (a fugue) in the song gives the listener a spooky sense in a way."

"When you played 'Jimmy's Road' by Willie Nelson, that was the first time I had heard it, but I was immediately touched by it. The intense sadness in Willie's voice and his haunting lyrics were almost enough to move this young man to tears. I wanted to hear that song again so I went and looked for it on 8-Track or record at a local used book and record store, but they didn't have it, which was enough to move this young man to tears."

"Willie Nelson did a remarkably ideal job on 'Jimmy's Road.' This song gave me such an eerie feeling that it was scary. When he sang the lines like 'Jimmy's grave' and 'Jimmy's Road' it just sent chills up my spine. Also when he sang about where Jimmy used to play, it gave me a mental picture of 'Jimmy' and how the Vietnam War changed him when he died. The phrase about how when another soldier dies and it affects Jimmy even though he is dead, makes me think that this describes how all the soldiers stuck together. And if one dies (even if they are dead already) the other soldiers die with him. The mood of this song made me extremely grim and definitely took me back to the Vietnam era. If I had absolutely no opinion on the Vietnam War, this song would definitely turn me anti-war. For the rest of my years in this complex world, I might not remember all the words to 'Jimmy's Road,' but I will never forget the way it made me feel."

"This song is completely weird and doesn't make any sense. The rhythm is terrible and the lyrics make you wonder if Willie was on too many drugs."

"'Jimmy's Road,' I really did not like at all, it was a very depressing piece. The song talks about all the things 'Jimmy' used to do on this road and at the end he lay dead in the cemetery. It was clear from the beginning that Mr. Nelson was talking about someone who was killed in the war. I wonder if he really knew a Jimmy, or if Jimmy only existed in the song. I think the song is very anti-war, since it depicts a very sad situation. This song probably brings back very bad memories to a lot of vets. It makes me think of the families who think of their sons the same way, that's where he learned to bike, throw a football, play baseball etc. If I would have been alive during this time period, this song would have persuaded me to dodge the draft."

A student who was annoyed that songs like "Bad Moon Rising" and "MIA/POW" had a far too "happy" musical background that didn't fit with the sad lyrics was satisfied that the almost funereal instrumentation to "Jimmy's Road" fit very well with the message being conveyed:

"On the other hand, there were a lot of songs that had a much more suitable matching of words to music. I found Willie Nelson's 'Jimmy's Road' to be a good example of this. In the song, the narrator is remembering the beloved Jimmy as a young boy in the not-so-distant past. He is remembering Jimmy because he died in the war at a very young age. The music that accompanied this song was very sad and slow. I could feel the sense of loss and anger that the speaker must have been going through. I don't think I would have had the same reaction if the song had been laid out over a bubble gum tune."

A thorough and insightful analysis of Johnny Cash's "Drive On:"

"It shows the pain of the soldiers. Cash sings about the pain that a lot of soldiers felt after the war from Post Traumatic Stress Syndrome. The stress that these soldiers went through, especially for the young, was too much for anybody to bear.

> Facing death for long periods of time, and suffering with the horrific conditions of the weather, animals, insects and terrain, scarred these people permanently. Then to lose the war, and find that this was all pointless, and then to come home to find that a lot of Americans were not proud of them, but instead just the opposite. This is enough to drive anybody mad. We can all say now that the war was a mistake, and that maybe our actions were wrong, but the people that fought there were doing what they were supposed to. Many didn't have a choice and we should all respect that. Johnny Cash's voice is perfect for this song, because he has a stone cold voice that exhibits the seriousness of what he is singing about. It was so difficult for these soldiers to come home and fit back in. They left home, and came back different, almost as strangers. How could anybody understand what they went through. And imagine living with that pain, and not having anybody that understands it. 'Drive On.' I take this as this as a saying that shows how overwhelming it all was for them, and all they could do was drive on. 'It don't mean nothing,' shows how they couldn't make sense of any of the reality they faced. All they could do was 'drive on.'"

Roger Wright's "Heroes of Vietnam" evoked this intensely personal response:

> "It made me think about what a shock it must have been for the men who had to fight in Vietnam. All your dreams and aspirations put on hold. Taken from your cozy little corner of the world, away from your family and friends, and thrown into the jungles of Vietnam. Your goals quickly changing from worrying about your final exams so that you finish high school to trying to stay alive. I can now understand how so many Vietnam veterans experienced psychological problems after the war. Going from the classroom armed with books and pencils to the jungles of Vietnam armed with a machine gun. ...Listening to this music gave me a new-found understanding of my father. He fought in the war. I do not know

the experiences he had during the war, or anything about what it was like for him being in Vietnam. My parents got divorced when I was very young, and I never have had much of a relationship with my father. His life took a downward spiral when he returned from Vietnam. He was an alcoholic, and was heavily into drugs, and addicted to heroin. I was always glad that he wasn't a part of my life. I never really understood before why he decided to go down the path he chose."

"Congratulations (You Sure Made a Man out of Him)" drew a variety of responses:

"Another emotionally charged song...the psychological changes that the returning troops would endure, some of them never fully conquering it, is truly depicted in this powerful song. I have a relative who was badly injured in Vietnam. He is a Marine, and one day while partially on a bad dose of prescribed medications, took himself hostage in his own house, resulting in a stand- off with police. Luckily, the medication eventually wore off and nothing too drastic resulted from the incident. But the bottled-up emotions he must have had were set free on that day, in my opinion, and again I think of how many there are like him. These returning troops were expected to simply come home and go about a daily life like nothing had ever happened. How wrong that is. How wrong that was."

"The final category of women are those whose men returned from the war but were not the same as when they left. I think the best song to define this category is 'Congratulations' due to its straightforward message about the changes a mother sees in her son upon his return from the war two years after he left home headed for Vietnam. The song pitches sarcasm at the old belief that the armed forces would 'make a man' out of boys. In this song the mother talks about her son's loss of purpose, sense of joy, and his departure from his old beliefs. The words draw a lyrical picture of not only the physical changes that have occurred in her son, but also the psychological toll the war took on his mind."

"'Congratulations' by Arlene Harden is a song in which she is speaking to the government and telling them of the fine job they have done with their son. He used to make the children happy, feed the pigeons, and sang all of the time. Now his eyes tell of where he's been and he keeps things inside. 'Congratulations (You Sure Made a Man out of Him)' is Harden's way of telling the government how they have destroyed her son by making him into a so-called man. Her boy is now riding an emotional roller coaster that never ends. I would think that Arlene is speaking for all parents whose children came back from the war an entirely new person. I really agree with what this song says. The most humiliating thing she can do to those heartless bastards in the White House is to publicly say thanks for making my son's life a mess. I felt like I knew this kid by how well this song was performed. Kudos to Arlene Harden and shame on our government."

An unusually interesting viewpoint about "Green, Green Grass of Home:"

"This song never implies that it is about prisoners of war, though the waking up from the dream is good evidence. Prisoners focused on many things they had taken for granted before. For example, this song mentions a girlfriend's lips, the green grass, walking on the beach, and having everyday freedom. It tells the story of how the mind is fantasizing and then wakes up to the reality of being a prisoner. The voice in the song doesn't sound resentful but just thankful for the memories he has to hold onto. Having these dreams and thinking about home and of those they loved kept their hopes up. The subconscious mind is accepting, through these dreams, the fact that the prisoner can only go home through these dreams. I think this song did an excellent job of creating the dreamy image that the prisoners of war were focusing on. However, this song mainly relates to the prisoners with positive attitudes, those thinking of what they had still hoped to have. I believe there were many who felt slighted and resented soldiers that were home and with their families. It is hard for me to say how I would have felt in that situation. I'm not one to hold a grudge, but under those circumstances, you never know. I hope I would have been one to think positively and be thankful that I was at least alive."

"Green, Green Grass of Home" also triggered some personal memories:

"The reason I like this song is it is very nostalgic and brings back fond memories of my grandfather. This was his favorite song and was sung beautifully at his funeral. When I hear this song I can see him working in his garden at our family's cabin. This song doesn't really take a stand on the war, but I think it may have given soldiers a sense of hope and happiness thinking about American soil and going home to their families. This song also reminds me of my father, who passed away very unexpectedly not too long ago. During his time he had a lucky experience. He was drafted into the Navy and spent two years on a boat in the Mediterranean, and two years on a base in the Philippines. He once told me that he was approached by an officer and told if he was ever asked if he knew anything about boats, to say no, or he would be sent to Vietnam to drive patrol boats on the rivers. I admit that this does not have a lot to do with this essay, but I thought I would share the story. 'The Green, Green Grass of Home' is one of the greatest songs ever written, and I hope it stays around long after I am gone."

This young woman questioned the behavior of the mother in "Little Boy Soldier:"

"This song contains two opposing, yet equally strong emotions. The lyrics of this song are about a woman who is waiting with her young, excited son at a train station for her husband's return from the war. The young boy is dressed in a soldier suit, waving a flag, and carrying a toy gun, all of which portray some degree of patriotism and pride. While the woman waits, she weeps and it is not until the end of the song that the listener discovers that the man she and her young son have been waiting for is returning in a coffin. A major theme of this song is pride or patriotism versus the trauma of losing a loved one to the travesty of war. The song also raises many questions such as: Was the woman aware that her husband was returning in a coffin? If so, why did she choose to bring a young child along? What was her motive for dressing the young boy like a soldier? I believe that these questions directly reflect the state of mind the woman was in and her own way of dealing with her husband's death."

A similar view:

"The saddest song is definitely 'Little Boy Soldier' by Wanda Jackson. The story of a mother and her young son waiting for the train to bring the little boy's daddy home; however, the mother didn't tell her son his daddy was dead and lying in a coffin. The song touches the heart, because that poor child is going to be confused and devastated. After listening to this song, I was upset that the mother didn't tell the little boy that his daddy was dead, instead the little boy had his hopes up waiting to give his dad a big hug."

Footnotes:

1 According to Dr. Mike Mueller, the psychologist who is the director of the Vietnam Veteran's Center in Duluth, Minnesota, Post Traumatic Stress Syndrome (PTSS) is a condition that has affected veterans of other wars. It is not peculiar to Vietnam. Sometimes it was called "shell shock" or "battle fatigue." The diagnostic phrase, Post- Traumatic Stress Syndrome

originated relatively recently, about 1980. PTSS is not strictly a disease caused by being in a war. Civilians who have been through a particularly harrowing experience can suffer from it as well. Interview with Dr. Mike Mueller, January 5, 2000.

2 Although it has similar symptoms, "Vietnam Syndrome" is different from Post Traumatic Stress Syndrome in a sense because it is a product of distinctive socio-cultural influences, including "where the country was at during that time and how the war was conducted." et. al. Mueller Interview.

3 Remarque, *All's Quiet.* p. 3.

4 Fred A. Wilson, *Waiting for an Army to Die: The Tragedy of Agent Orange.* New York: Vintage Books, p. ix.

5 Kertwig, *A Hard Rain.* p. 111.

6 Myra MacPherson, *Long Time Passing: Vietnam and the Haunted Generation.* New York: Doubleday and Company, 1984. p. 75.

7 Country Joe MacDonald website-www.countryjoe.com.

8 Cutter interview.

9 "Seeing the tiger smile" and "spit in a bamboo viper's eye" likely refer to encounters American soldiers had with what appeared to be friendly Vietnamese during the day, knowing that at night, they could turn into dangerous Viet Cong adversaries. The Bamboo Viper is one of the most poisonous snakes in the world. The fact that they abounded in Vietnam added to the tension level of fighting the most difficult of American wars. Interview with Sarge Lintecum, August 1, 1999.

10 "It don't mean nothin'" was a very common phrase used by combat soldiers as they philosophically shrugged off extreme adversity. According to Lintecum, who did three tours of duty in Vietnam as a member of the 101st Airborne: "We said this hundreds of times a day when the going was rough. It meant just shut up and ascend."

11 Interview with Ronald Downs, November 1999.

12 John Siekkula Interview.

13 Larkin, *The Virgin Encyclopedia of Country Music.* p. 113.

14 Stewart O'Nan, *The Vietnam Reader.* New York, Doubleday, 1998. p. 296.

15 Mel Tillis, with Walter Wager, Stutterin' Boy. New York: Rawson Associates, 1984. pp. 166 - 167.

16 Paul Helbach Interview.

17 Peter Goldman and Tony Fuller, et. al,. *Charlie Company: What Vietnam Did To Us.* New York, William Morrow and Company, 1983 p. 10. "Ruby" was first released on United Artists Records by Johnny Darrell in April of 1967. Apparently it wasn't until Kenny Rogers, who was working his way toward mega-stardom by then, recorded and released the song in August of 1969 that it had the alleged impact that it did on public opinion about the war. This was another song that was not allowed on the play list of Armed Forces Radio for obvious reasons. In morbidly detailing the woes of a badly

injured veteran, it is clearly an anti-war song.

18 Lynn, Loretta *Coal Miner's Daughter,* New York, Warner Books, 1976, p. 199.

19 Michael Bilton and Kevin Sim, *Four Hours in My Lai.* New York, Penguin Books, 1992. p. 340.

20 Arthur Everett, et. al., *Calley.* New York: Dell Books, 1971. p. 21.

21 McPherson, *Long Time Passing.* p. 587.

22 Toward the end of the Vietnam War purple hearts were doled out so promiscuously (as an attempt to boost morale?) that that soldiers referred to them derisively as "gongs." Rick Atkinson, *The Long Gray Line: The American Journey of West Point's Class of 1966.* Boston, Houghton Mifflin Company, 1989.

23 Kim Weston reprised "When Johnny Comes Marching Home" on MGM Records in 1968. It seems an odd choice since it is simply a straightforward re-telling of the Civil War story. The lyrics are identical to the original version, and no anti-war or pro-war spin can be detected.

24 Marilyn B. Young and John J. Fitzgerald and A. Tom Grunfeld, (Editors), *The Vietnam War: A History in Documents.* New York: Oxford University Press, 2002. p. 151.

25 It seems odd that the record label states "Yellow River" was recorded by Christie when the song was recorded by Jeff Christie.

26 The worry by the United States that Khe Sahn would become another Dien Bien Phu was labeled as "preposterous" by Stanley Karnow in his *Vietnam: A History.* New York, Penguin Books, 1984. p. 540.

27 In August of 1954, France suffered one of the worst military defeats in history at Dien Bien Phu. The debacle probably did more to shape the fate of the world than Agincourt, Waterloo, or Stalingrad. Bernard B. Fall, Hell in a *Very Small Place: The Siege of Dien Bien Phu.* New York, Harper & Row Publishers, 1967. p. 448.

28 Dave Marsh, *Glory Days: Bruce Springsteen in the 1980s.* New York, Pantheon Books, 1987. pp. 259 - 260.

29 Larry Yeazle interview.

30 Cold Chisel Official Webpage. http//www.coldchisel.com.au/

31 Barry McCloud, *Definitive Country: The Ultimate Encyclopedia of Country Music and Its Performers.* Berkley Publishing Group, New York, 1995. p. 529.

32 Tim O'Brien, *The Things They Carried New York: Penguin Books,* 1990. p. 235.

33 Jimmie N. Rogers, *The Country Music Message Revisited.* Fayetteville: The University of Arkansas Press. 1989. p. 173.

34 Interview with Rachel Jane. (a.k.a. Susan Wojnar.). July 1999.

35 Morse, *Classic Rock.* p. 80

36 The helicopter is one of the most identifiable symbols of the Vietnam War.

Sometimes called "hueys," "choppers" or "gun ships," this vehicle played a very important role for the United States in its conduct of the war. They were used in the operations of the Air Cavalry to insert and extract contingents of army, marines and special forces all over the country. Many badly wounded fighting men owe their lives to the efficiency and speed with which helicopters conveyed them to emergency medical facilities or to air craft carriers in the South China Sea.

37 Martin Russ, *Breakout: The Chosin Reservoir Campaign, Korea 1950.* New York, Fromm International, 1999. p. 81.

38 Safer, Morley, *Flashbacks: On Returning to Vietnam.* New York, Random House, 1990.

39 Kuecher Interview.

40 Tim Murphy, *"Still Waiting at the Wall: The Story Behind the Song."* Newspaper article. Source unknown.

Chapter 7:
"The Music Now"

One of my students titled his essay "The Music That Will Last Forever" and I think it will. At least I hope it does. I suppose I could be accused of being a cultural dinosaur, but anytime I hear the popular music that is being cranked out today I feel an acute sense of cultural despair. I wholeheartedly agree with music historian Donald Clarke who wrote that today's music industry "cranks out a higher percentage of inferior product than ever before." I also concur with his judgment "that most of it could disappear overnight and nobody would miss it."[1] When I think of the money that is spent buying contemporary music I am reminded of what H.L. Mencken said a long time ago: "No one has ever gone broke underestimating the taste of the American public."

There are those who would consider my favorite songs to be relics of the past. However, a generation later, much of the music spawned by the Vietnam War has stood the test of time quite well. Many of the commercially successful songs that were released during the war can be heard regularly on various "oldies" stations all over the United States and not necessarily because they are war related. "For What It's Worth," "Fortunate Son," and "Ohio" are enjoyed today because they are considered "classics" from an important period in the evolution of rock music. A student who is keenly aware of this wrote the following:

> "A lot of people still listen to the music from that time frame. Our parents who grew up during the war still have the records lying around the house somewhere. We listen to these records and hear the music that spurred a revolution and it fires up our mind to ask questions. We ask our parents why did such and such write this song? Their response is,

> 'Because he was protesting a war in a place called Vietnam.' Many individuals still listen to that music and wonder what went on. Was the music from that time meant to be so revolutionary? I can't honestly answer that question. Anyone who even listens to the radio can hear songs played from that time. On KQDS you hear many of the songs played during the Vietnam War. Songs by The Who, The Rolling Stones, Jefferson Airplane and so on. Tune in to KOOL 101 and you can hear songs from some of the other artists who wrote and starred in this musical revolution. The music that started it all is still with us today and showing us the events that happened so long ago."

A lot of people like hearing these songs again because of the pleasant memories they evoke, without really paying serious attention to the lyrics. Many of my students were too young to have heard this music but heard them on "oldies" stations. When they studied the music in class they realized that what they thought were just listenable tunes actually were vehicles for profound social commentary. To the combat veterans of the Vietnam War, of course, the memories provided by these songs can be quite painful and may even exacerbate Post Traumatic Stress Syndrome. As one veteran puts it:

> "Nam was Rock and Roll. Our World War II dads grew up on Swing, Jitterbug, Race Music, Crooner's, Country. Some went back to serve in the Korean Conflict. I was born in '48 in Welch, West Virginia, a true baby boomer. Dad, the World War II Vet, moved to Philly, South Philly that is, where I grew up on Fabian Cards, Bandstand, Southstreet, Chubby Checker, the Twist, plus the Stroll, Steel Pier, and all the rest. Rock and Roll was forming and changing while I was growing old enough from the street at 19 to be drafted into the Rock and Roll Vietnam War. The songs from that time that I listen to today bring back memories and emotions of my first day in the boonies with my feet hanging out of a chopper going into a firebase (out in the bush). Building bunkers, how thick the jungle with wait a minute vines, waiting for a pack-

age from home. Malaria cutting point, 3 days without water, pulling OP by day and LP by night. Fatigues made for two! Carrying the dead and the wounded: what the Hell was objective, being wounded and our welcome home? I served as an infantryman for CCO1-12 4th INF."[2]

Some of the songs of the tumultuous years of the Vietnam War are now included in the play lists of "easy listening" format stations that refer to what they play as the "music of your life." In a way it is, although most of the songs played on these stations are far blander in content. Some of the "war music" will pop up as "muzak" that can be heard in elevators, supermarkets, and other places. We seem to live in a society where it is impossible to find a public place without music blaring in the background. It seems strange somehow that some of the truly controversial and powerful music that defined such a painful period in American history has been reduced to such a banal context. A case in point is one of the most memorable songs spawned by the Vietnam War, Barry Sadler's "Ballad of the Green Berets." It is now available on compact disc through various music catalogues, one of which hawks it like this:

> "Depending on your political persuasion, this 1966 album could be viewed as a courageous, patriotic rejoinder to the anti-war fervor that was sweeping the country at the time, or as an unintentionally hilarious camp classic. Either way, it's a genuine '60s artifact. LONG requested by our customers! We've included the entire album with artwork intact, plus Barry's other charting single the "The A Team."

Curiously enough, the Sadler disc appears on the same page as advertisements for "50 Elvis Hits for under $20," "Christmas Eve with Burl Ives," and "20 Carpenter Classics." Another company attempts to woo buyers by crediting the tribute to Special Forces with a more serious message:

> "In 1966, Staff Sergeant Barry Sadler of the U.S. Army Special Forces wrote and recorded "The Ballad of the Green

Berets," a #1 hit based on his experiences in Vietnam. The immense popularity of this song inspired him to record many other great songs of wartime bravery, danger, and hardship including "The A Team," and "A Trooper's Lament" They're all here in this special edition of his #1 album from 1966."

Again, its interesting to note that occupying the same page in this catalogue are "Arthur Fiedler and the Boston Pops," "The Best of Barbershop Quartets," and "Olde Piano Rolls." Perhaps this is only fitting but "Ballad of the Green Berets" has come a long way from stirring controversy and being banned in Duluth to being hyped as music that will make you nostalgic. All of the music in "Battlenotes" has traveled a considerable distance to provide an excellent source of insight into what the Vietnam War did to America. As we enter another century, recording artists still occasionally refer to the war, and this will doubtless continue. "Vietnam (Isn't Over)," by a "metal thrush punk band" known as "Moral Disgust" is a good example.

Moral Disgust picture sleeve.
Source Sal Serio of Moral Disgust

Recorded in 1992, long after the Vietnam War was over, "Vietnam (Isn't Over)" portrays a crazed Vietnam vet who murders his family with "heavy artillery from the surplus store." The weapons "feel so right in his hands" because "he thinks he's back in Vietnam." This "Johnny" is "never coming home," and the "death wish won't leave him alone." Sal Serio, the lyricist, told me that this ghastly portrayal of a vet in the throes of the worst kind of Post Traumatic Stress Syndrome was inspired by the "Reagan years of military invasions" and movies like "Platoon" and "Born On the 4th of July" that "brought out some of the more unsavory aspects of the Vietnam war into the public's consciousness. Almost as if enough time had finally passed since the end of the war to discuss things previously unmentionable." ...Also popular at that time were like the 'Friday The 13th' series. My song is a twisted dichotomy of both the anti-Vietnam war movies, and gory slasher movies of that era."[3] Serio said that this kind of music went over well with audiences. His older brother, who was with the airborne in Vietnam, doesn't like it though. More than likely, his distaste for "Vietnam (Isn't Over)," springs from its anti-war or unpatriotic theme as well as how the Vietnam vet is so thoroughly demonized.

The cover of an album by "Deadspot," another punk rock group, shows perhaps the most famous (infamous?) photograph taken during the Vietnam War: Brigadier General Nguyen Ngoc Loan, the commander of the Vietnamese National Police, blowing the brains out of a Viet Cong suspect with a snub-nosed pistol. The scene is described as "Adios Dude." None of the songs on this album are related to Vietnam, and the picture was undoubtedly used for its shock value, a favorite tactic of groups like "Deadspot."

Deadspot's "Adios Dude" album cover

The Vietnam veterans themselves have provided some of the best recent music about the war. Although they are not as well known as the professional musicians who sang about the war, these men have the advantage of knowing their subject matter thoroughly, having lived it. Among the veterans-turned-recording artists is Michael McCann, a former paratrooper and Green Beret wounded in Vietnam, who has issued a CD composed of powerful battlefield ballads know as "Soldier's Songs." Sarge Lintecum, who served three tours in Vietnam as a member of the 101st Airborne, has received awards from Bill Board Magazine for his "Vietnam Blues\Combat Tested Blues For Peace." Another is Phil Ferrazano, whose musical reminiscences are a welcome addition to this book.

The American Civil War still finds its way into the contemporary musician's song bag, as with Dwight Yoakam's "I Sang Dixie when He Died" and one popular country group, "Confederate Railroad," obviously has some roots in the "War Between the States." A thorough analysis of the music pertaining to this war would probably be as historically insightful as the songs of Vietnam have been about that more modern conflict. A book about the music of the Civil War would also be much easier to write as most of the music about that conflict is well within the realm of "public domain" and free to use as the author chooses without undue expense or encountering the vagaries of dealing with music publishers.

I'm convinced that what the popular music of the day had to say about certain significant issues would be valuable in other academic disciplines like literature and sociology. There are other writers who have already demonstrated that the music provides clues to why and how things happened the way they did. Michael McCann, for example, has created a classroom exercise called "Hooked on History through Music." Perhaps the most important result of studying these songs that tell us so much about the dynamic of the tumultuous Vietnam era may well be to keep history from repeating itself. As one student suggested:

> "Nobody deserves to go through the suffering that the people went through because of Vietnam. I hope people can take the music and get the meanings out of it. I hope we can also use it as a tool so we never have to let a tragedy like this happen again."

As this book is going to print, the televised "Iraqi Freedom" conflict reaches a peak with the demolition of the Bagdad Sadaam statute after only twenty days. I believe that it is highly unlikely that this conflict will have a distinctive soundtrack simply because of the short duration of the conflict. Where Vietnam was our first "rock and roll" war, "Iraqi Freedom" seems to be the world's first televised war. The music of this recent conflict, highly patriotic in the first days of the war, has no enduring melody or lyrics but instead is the fade in and out of cable-TV 24 hours-a-day news alerts. Scrolling messages across the bottom of the screen, split screen and maps touched by retired general who tell Americans of the strategies. DA!-DA!-DAA! plays while moving bold lettering ALERT comes into focus on the screen. But this tune we have become all too familiar with because of the Clinton Impeachment, the Presidential Election controversy, the Beltway Sniper and the Elizabeth Smart return to her family.

Other issues of note will follow this conflict. Embedded reporters with the troops and embedded retired military on the cable stations criticizing and then being criticized will be more remembered. "Bagdad Bob," the Iraqi Minister of Mis-Information will be recalled as a cartoon character as he declares the Iraq victory while a U. S. tank is almost within camera shot over his shoulder. Arab country television showing horrific scenes of injured Iraqi citizens. All the while the Democrats trying to run for President in the midst of this will be remembered for inept statements like John Kerry's calling for a "regime change in America" even with President Bush's actions in the war approval ratings in the 70s. Protesters in the strong holds of liberalism like San Francisco and Berkeley blocking roads and bridges and attempting to deter humanitarian supplies movement.

Great triumphs like the rescue of POW PFC Jessica Lynch, the first POW rescued since World War II. The Iraqi attorney who risked his and his family's lives to lead the coalition to PFC Lynch's location in a hospital being used for Iraqi military operations. The unfortunate find at that location of nine American military buried at that site. American troops used their hands to uncover the bodies.

American troops and the Country took great pride in this operation supporting the creed that no colleague will be left behind. The victory of finding the seven POWs who had been displayed on Arab television while under interrogation, against the Geneva Convention rules. The seven were found walking alongside the roadway because another Iraqi citizen lead troops to their location.

The unending search for weapons of mass destruction having mixed successes with finds of converted trucks, larges caches of hollow-head missiles and underground storage bunkers. Suicide bombers at check-points including the Iraqis using a pregnant woman to lure the American troops for destruction. Lt. Col. Chris Hughes showing leadership by having his troops kneel, point their guns at the ground and smile to quiet an angry mob who thought the Americans would take over a mosque. These will all be remembered. Most importantly, the American troops in Iraq will be honored and appreciated in a different way than the troops in Vietnam. Wounded and killed non-citizen troops were granted citizenship by President Bush. Where the United States was changed so dramatically by 9/11 with a swell of patriotism throughout the country. Perhaps because of this event along with the terrible treatment the veterans endured when they came home from Vietnam, Americans will not make that same mistake again.

Footnotes:

1 Clarke, *The Rise and Fall of Popular Music.* p. ix-x.

2 Letter from "Brick" Manurich. January 2003.

3 Interview with Sal Serio, February 2003.

Chapter 8:
Travels With Battle Notes

Battle Notes turned out to be far more of a success than I had anticipated. The theme of the music of the Vietnam war as an aid to understanding the tumult the war caused and as a teaching tool has attracted a respectable readership. Since November of 2000, when the book was first published, it has taken me all over the country for various promotional activities such as book signings and presentations to service clubs. I've signed books and talked to groups as far east as Augusta, Maine, and as far west as Salt Lake City, Utah, and many points in between. The travel, which is an absolute necessity for any author who wants to properly promote his or her book, has been a very pleasurable experience for me, as I've always had a bit of the wanderlust and enjoy meeting people. I've met Vietnam veterans, fellow academics, and people simply interested in the results of my research. These meetings also paid the dividend of supplying interviews for this edition of Battle Notes which is a better book than the first in many ways especially because so many people shared their reminiscences so generously.

The first really successful "signing" took place at the Changing Hands bookstore in Tempe, Arizona, several months after *Battle Notes* was published. Thanks to Barbara Yost and her generous praise for the book in the *Arizona Republic,* more people that I ever expected came and listened to my remarks and bought books, which I was happy to sign at their request. One attendee in particular, a young woman who sat in the front row and scribbled furiously while I was talking, piqued my interest and I found out later that she is a professor of theater at the Arizona State University and intended to use my book as a reference for a play she was writing about the Vietnam War.

My appearance at Jabberwocky's in Eagle River, Wisconsin, on Memorial Day was also exciting as I signed copies of *Battle Notes* destined for the library at Northern Pines High School. I am grateful to Mary Jo Werner, the owner of radio station WJOR for vital publicity for the event. Another special day was in New Haven, Connecticut, where former Green Beret Mike McCann hosted a signing for me at Anna Liffey's Irish Pub complete with music provided by McCann and Tim Murphy, another Vietnam veteran. The staff at Barnes and Noble in New Haven were very accommodating and brought the books to the pub and made sure that anyone who wanted to purchase *Battle Notes* did so. Because of McCann's dogged "advance work," another signing, at the Barnes and Noble in Farmington, Connecticut, the next evening turned out very well. He is an excellent promoter and saw to it I was interviewed on some of the leading radio stations in the area and received vital "ink" in many newspapers. Another high point of the trip was my appearance on Joey Reynolds's highly popular national radio talk show from the studios of WOR in New York City. Meeting rockabilly artist Ersel Hickey in the "green room" while I waited to "go on" was a thrill for me, and he provided me with many fascinating anecdotes about his career in the music business.

Then it was on to Salt Lake City where I addressed the downtown Kiwanis Club at the posh Inn on Temple Square. *The Salt Lake City Tribune* said I was doing the "Wasatch Mountain tour" and I lived up to that description with a signing at the Barnes and Noble in Sandy, Utah, as well as a presentation at the library in Kearns. The trip was concluded with an appearance on Utah Public Radio at the studios at KUER on the University of Utah at Salt Lake campus. I spent an hour with the producer of the program "Radio West," Doug Fabrizio, where we discussed "What is the Quintessential Vietnam Song?"

I traveled to the deep South in the middle of another horrid Wisconsin winter to Barnes and Noble stores in Mount Pleasant, South Carolina, and Savannah, Georgia. It was my privilege to speak before the Savannah Kiwanis club at the historic Pirate's House Restaurant located in the city's beautiful Waterfront District. I will be eternally grateful to Bill Edwards who said such nice things about me and *Battle Notes* on during the morning show on WTKS. This free publicity, the lifeblood of any successful book tour, was undoubtedly the reason why the local Barnes and Noble sold so many books.

Just this past summer I ventured into New England and signed at Barnes and Noble stores in Saratoga Springs, New York, Holyoke, Massachusetts, Manchester, New Hampshire, and Augusta, Maine. New Hampshire seems to be a rather insular state if the well-known Manchester Union Leader and New Hampshire Public Radio in Manchester are any indication. Neither will spare ink or broadcast time on anything that isn't some way related to the state. At least that's what they told me. However, an excellent counterbalance to this provincialism is provided by Manchester's weekly newspaper of the arts scene, the *Hippo Press,* which reviewed my book and even sent a reporter out to the local Barnes and Noble to interview me the night of my appearance there. An interview on Maine Public Radio's "Maine Things Considered" with Matthew Alegro helped make for an excellent turnout at the Augusta Barnes and Noble the next day. This signing also provided me with a moving experience I will never forget, signing a copy of *Battle Notes* to the "memory of Leon Poland," who died in Vietnam with only one month left in his tour of duty. Of all the books I have inscribed, this is likely the most noteworthy. On a much lighter note, serendipity brought me to Johnny Rocket's '50s style diner in Providence, Rhode Island, where diners are given coins and encouraged to play the jukebox, which is loaded with song favorites from the past. When someone played the Vietnam era's "Respect" by Aretha Franklin, the jukebox was turned up and several of the waitresses and waiters came out from behind the counter and danced and sang!

"Respect," one of the most memorable songs of the Vietnam era, is still on the jukebox at Johnny Rocket's retro diner in Providence, Rhode Island. When it plays, employees sing and dance to the music.

Battle Notes itself has gone many places I wasn't able to go, at least not yet. It is in the library at the University of Hong Kong, Australia, Switzerland, and England and is being used as a reference at the Dutch Army Museum for an exhibit on Vietnam "protest music." I suspect it has made it to other venues I probably don't know about. It has also turned up at a number of websites operated by booksellers, naturally these include Amazon and Barnes and Noble, but a number of smaller ones also, some that tout the fact they have a copy "signed by the author." Albris sells one such copy for $29.95, a substantial mark up over the 1st edition's usual retail price of $14.95. Does that mean my "autograph" is worth $15.00? For those who are more frugal about buying books, *Battle Notes* has even shown up on Ebay and can be obtained there for just $10.00. This leads me to a less than scientific conclusion about the book's success: it has moved beyond the plateau of being bought by friends and has now entered a different realm where persons unknown have decided it is worth reading and spending their hard earned money on.

I think the major reason why Battle Notes has covered the territory it has is because of the wondrous Internet through which my website, constructed and tended by my wife Mary Lou, has received thousands and thousands of "hits" in a little over a year. In just a few days after the terrible events of September 11th, there were over 15,000 visitors to www.battlenotes.com looking for patriotic music and calls from all over the world looking for more of the same. The Internet has become the perfect medium for promoting a book, compact disc, or movie, created by people who don't otherwise have the connections or resources to reach a wide audience. I have received e-mails from all over the world commenting on the book and the vast majority of these communications have been favorable. I've also had many, many inquiries about songs and have managed to provide the title, sometimes with just a few lyrics as a hint. A lot of those who contact me want to know if I also can provide a compact disc of the songs and I have to respond that regretfully, I can't. The cost and logistics involved in such an effort would be well beyond my capabilities. Such a disc is badly needed. What is available at present just scratches the surface of the music of the period.

Afterword

The system I used to decide whether a song should be included in the chapter on "Music of Protest" or "African-American Music" may seem arbitrary to some readers. An example is the controversial "Open Letter to a Teenage Son" by Victor Lundberg. This diatribe against war protestors wound up in the chapter devoted to "The Music of Protest" along with some of the songs it spawned rather than in "The Music of Patriotism," where Lundberg's rantings would have been in better company. Other songs like "Eve of Destruction" wound up in more than one chapter. Another challenging task was trying to decide what recordings of the day contained music about the Vietnam War and therefore deserved inclusion in this book. I discovered that this was an almost impossible goal that I failed to reach in the first book. It was extremely helpful that readers of the first edition of *"Battle Notes"* offered suggestions as to what I missed the first time around. The fact that there are many "new" songs in this second edition is testimony to some pretty glaring omissions the first time around and that I listened to people who wondered why such and such a song wasn't included originally. There were also a handful of songs that will forever remain a mystery as to whether they were inspired by the Vietnam War. One that was a real puzzle was James Taylor's "Fire and Rain." The lyric about "flying machines in pieces on the ground" would appear to be a definite reference to Vietnam for obvious reasons, but then again, before Taylor achieved solo stardom he was a member of a moderately successful group known as "The Flying Machine." It is plausible that he is actually singing about the breakup of this group. The very title "Fire and Rain" certainly describes two very frequent events in Vietnam. The woman in the song, "Suzanne," is also shrouded in mystery. Where did she go? Who were the people whose "plans put an end to" her? Did she go crazy with worry over her boyfriend in Vietnam? Did her parents decide that he wasn't right for her because being in an unpopular war made him a villain? What about the fact that she is gone? Usually it was the other way around and the sweetheart who was fighting the war didn't return. At least I had the advantage of being able to hear "Fire and Rain" since it was a highly popular song that is still played frequently on various radio stations. In spite of these suggestive lyrics, I've since learned that the tune was not intended to make a statement about Vietnam.

The fact that I am a record collector as well as a historian made my research easier. Some of the songs needed for this book were already in my collection. Most of those that I had to buy, some at outrageous collector's prices, were already familiar to me so I was usually able to avoid wasting money on songs whose titles sounded like a good fit but actually weren't even remotely related to Vietnam. There were exceptions, most notably Sandy Posey's "Bring Him Home Safely to Me." I had never heard this song before but the title and the year (1970) seemed right so I met the extravagant price of the record dealer only to discover I was wrong. The song is actually about a housewife, who worries, in highly melodramatic fashion, about her husband when he leaves her side to go off to work for the day. It is the kind of message that would make feminists blanch, and I was chagrined that I paid so much for a record I couldn't even use except to describe the pitfalls of accumulating recorded music for a book of this kind. Barry Sadler's "One Day Nearer Home" was another expensive miscue on my part. I felt sure, as the title suggested, that this would be about a homesick soldier counting the days until he could leave Vietnam and return to the United States but, again, I was proven wrong. By the time Sadler went into the studio to record this song, RCA had begun to groom him as a singer of a different kind of music and he just wasn't going to sing about war anymore. Unfortunately, he was unable to make the transition to a broader based audience. I fared better with Roy Orbison's "There Won't Be Many Coming Home." While this recording was not a rarity, I had never heard it before and the title was intriguing. I discovered that it had been released by MGM as the flip side to a relatively obscure song titled "You'll Never be Sixteen Again." I found out via the Internet that the song was part of an album titled "The Fastest Guitar in the West," which was the soundtrack for a movie about Confederate sympathizers who attempt to rob the federal mint in San Francisco during the Civil War for all the obvious reasons. Orbison and his guitar played a major role in the film. I had all but decided to exclude "There Won't be Many Coming Home," thinking that it would be related to what those rebel desperadoes tried to do so many years ago. However, when I was finally able to hear the song it was obvious that it belonged to the Vietnam era.

Among the songs that were clearly related to Vietnam but contained messages about more than one issue relating to the war is Paul Hardcastle's "19." While the title refers to the youthfulness of combat soldiers in Vietnam it also has something to say about the ravages of Post Traumatic Stress Syndrome. Accordingly, it is analyzed in the chapter dealing with "The Music of Combat" as well as the chapter that deals with "Music About the Aftermath of the War." Most of Merle Haggard's songs are to be found among the "Pro-War Music" but there are two selections by him in other chapters also. Marvin Gaye's "What's Going On, and Edwin Starr's "War" could fit in the chapter about the "Music of Protest," but it seemed more appropriate that they be placed with those songs that expressed the views of African-Americans about the war. Victor Lundberg's "Open Letter to My Teenage Son" would not be out of place in the chapter on "Music of Patriotism" but was a better fit in the chapter devoted to "The Music of Protest." "Ruby" (Don't Take Your Love to Town) could qualify for inclusion in that chapter too because it is clearly an anti-war song, but since it describes how a veteran fared after the war, it belongs in "Music About the Aftermath of the War."

I had intended to include a chapter in this book about the music that was inspired by the heavy usage of drugs during the Vietnam War but decided against it because I discovered the topic was well beyond the scope of this book. There are so many songs that came out of the "drug culture" that it would be impossible to do justice to them all in a single chapter. The cost of obtaining more music permissions would have been prohibitive.

Finally, I apologize again for the songs that I missed. Most of these were of limited popularity and reached only a very local or strictly regional audience. There are also numerous album cuts that I had to eschew because this book had to be written with a realistic page limit in mind. It almost goes without saying that there are also many songs that don't say anything about Vietnam but do, inevitably, bring back memories of the war to soldiers, protestors and anyone else who heard them during that time. For very special reasons, they are very much a Vietnam War song, at least to them.

Discography

This discography is sourced to the original 45 or album when possible. Not all songs in this listing are discussed in the text of Battle Notes. This list has been compiled to present the range of music released during the Vietnam conflict.

Artist	Song Title, Recording Label, Number and Year
Addiss & Crofut.	"A Ballad from Vietnam: The Rain on the Leaves." Columbia 43744.
Spiro Agnew.	"Spiro Agnew Speaks Out On: Radicalism in our Midst, Vietnam War critics, Protesters, Malcontents, Hippies and Effetism, Television's Responsibilities and the Republican and Democratic Parties."
All of the Above.	"The War is Over." Paramount 0196 1973.
Ed Ames.	"Changing, Changing." RCA 479726 1969.
Ed Ames.	"Hello Lyndon." 1964.
Ed Ames.	"Who Will Answer?" RCA Victor 47-9400 1967.
Bill Anderson.	"Where Have All the Heroes Gone." DECCA 32744 1970.
Eric Burdon and the Animals.	"San Franciscan Nights." MGM K 13769 1967.
Eric Burdon and the Animals.	"Sky Pilot." MGM K 13939-SS 1968.
Eric Burdon and the Animals.	"We Gotta Get Out Of This Place." MGM 13382 1965.
Louis Armstrong.	"What a Wonderful World." ABC 10982 1967.
Craig Arthur.	"The Son of a Green Beret (A Childs Ballad of the Green Beret)" Holton Records H-619666-A & B 1966.
The Auditions.	"Returning Home from Vietnam." Freckles Records AO1OT-A 1973.
Hoyt Axton.	"Soldier's Last Letter." Colpix 802.
- B -	
Joan Baez.	"The Night They Drove Ol' Dixie Down." Vanguard 35138 1971.

Joan Baez. "Carry It On." Vanguard VSD 79313 1971.
Jackie Wilson & Lavern Baker. "Think Twice." Brunswick 55287 1965.
The Band. "The Night They Drove Ol' Dixie Down." Capitol 2635 1969.
Susan Benting "Thirty Years (Nam's Not Over Yet)." 2003
Moe Bandy. "Chiseled in the Wall." 1995.
John Barbour. "Viet Nam." World Pacific RW8492.
Bobby Bare. "Christian Soldier." Rice 5057 1973.
Bobby Bare. "Detroit City." RCA 47-8183 1963.
Bobby Bare. "500 Miles Away From Home." RCA 47-8238 1963.
Bobby Bare. "GI Joe." 1995.
Bobby Bare. "God Bless America Again." RCA 74-0264 1969.
Bobby Bare. "Talk Me Some Sense." RCA Victor 47-8699 1965.
Bobby Bare. "Up Against the Wall Redneck Mother." RCA Victor PB-10556-B 1976.
The Bar-Kays. "Soul Finger." Volt 148 1967.
Ortheia Barnes. "Waiting for Joey." Coral 62529.
Beach Boys. "Pet Sounds." Brother/Reprise MS 2197 1974.
Beach Boys. "Sloop John B." Capitol 5602 1966. 1969.
Beach Bums (Early Bob Seger). "The Ballad of the Yellow Beret." Are You Kidding Me? 1010 1966.
Beatles. "Act Naturally." Apple 5498 1971.
Beatles. "The Ballad of John and Yoko." Apple 2531 1969.
Beatles. "Get Back." Apple 2490 1969.
Beatles. "Here Comes the Sun." Apple SO383 1969.
Beatles. "Hey Jude." Apple 2276 1968.
Beatles. "I'll Get You." Swan S-4152-1 1964.
Beatles. "Sgt. Pepper's Lonely Heart Club Band." Capitol 2653 1967.
Beatles. "Something." Apple 2654 1969.
Beatles. "Yellow Submarine." Capitol 5715 1966.
Beatles. "Yesterday." Capitol 5498 1965.
The Bee Gees. "Holiday." Atco 6521 1967.
Archie Bell and the Drells. "A Soldier's Prayer." Atlantic Promo
Archie Bell and the Drells. "Tighten Up." Atlantic 2478 1968.
William Bell. "Lonely Soldier." STAX STA-0070/SM-00409-PL 1970.
William Bell. "Marchin Off to War." STAX 191 1966.
William Bell. "Soldier's Goodbye." STAX 199 1966.
Bellamy Bros. "Old Hippie." MCA Curb 52579 1985.

Toby Ben.	"Draft Call." Venture 613.
Toby Ben.	"Peace Wake Up to the Sunshine." Venture 613.
Tony Bennett.	"I Left My Heart In San Franciso." Columbia 4-42332
Susan Benting & Roland Caire, Jr.	"Thirty Years (Nam's Not Over Yet)." Soaring Eagle Enterprise Music, 2003
Jan Berry.	"The Universal Coward." Liberty F-55845 1965.
Big Three.	"Come Away Melinda." FM FM-9001 1962.
Black Fighting Men Recorded Live in Vietnam.	"Guess Who's Coming Home" Black Forum HS1924.
John R. Black.	"God Help Us Lyndon." & other collections Vietnam Farewell & Vietnam Farewell II 1991.
Blood, Sweat & Tears.	"And When I Die." Columbia 4-45008. 1969.
Bloodrock.	"D.O.A." Capitol 3009 1971.
Bloodrock.	"Thank You Daniel Ellsberg." Capitol 3451 1971.
Tiffany Bolling.	"Thank God the War is Over." Canyon 19. 1969.
Bonnie and the Treasures.	"Home of the Brave. (Land of the Free)." PhiDan 1965.
Pat Boone & the Mike Curb Congregation.	"MIA/POW (Prisoner of War Song)." MGM K14242 1971.
Pat Boone. Came."	"What if they Gave a War and Nobody Dot 16998 1967.
Pat Boone.	"Wish You Were Here Buddy." Dot. 45-16933/MB21546 1966.
Private Charles Bowens & the Gentlemen from Tigerland.	"Christmas in Vietnam." Rojac RA-111 1967.
The Box Tops.	"The Letter." Mala 565 1967.
Bravura Limited Edition.	"The Man Who Hears a Different Drummer." Decca Custom Pressing #202. 239 1971.
Elton Britt.	"There's a Star Spangled Banner Waving Somewhere." 1944.
Michael James Brody, Jr.	"The War is Over." RCA 0309 1971.
Brothers of Soul.	"Wait for Me." BOO 1970.
James Brown.	"America's My Home Parts I and II." King Records 6112 1968.
Virge Brown.	"North of Saigon." Big Country BC-214-2 1969.
Jackson Browne.	"For America." Elektra/Asylum 7-69566 1986.

Dave Brubeck.	"Take Five." Columbia 41479 1960.
Don Bryant.	"The Lonely Soldier." Hi Records 2114 1969.
The Buckinghams.	"Kind of a Drag." U.S.A. 860 1966.
The Buffalo Springfield.	"For What It's Worth (Stop, Hey What's That Sound)." Atco 6459 1967.
Eric Burdon and War.	"Spill the Wine." MGM K14118 1970.
The Byrds.	"Draft Morning." Columbia CL-2775 1968.
The Byrds.	"Eight Miles High." Columbia 43578 1966.
The Byrds.	"My Back Pages." Columbia 44054 1967.
The Byrds.	"Turn, Turn, Turn." Columbia 43424 1965.

- C -

C Company featuring Terry Nelson.	"The Ballad of Rusty Calley." 1971.
C Company featuring Terry Nelson.	"Battle Hymn of Lt. Calley." Plantation 1971.
C Company featuring Terry Nelson.	"Routine Patrol." Plantation PL-73 1971.
Roy C.	"Open Letter to the President." Alaga 1006 1971.
Cactus.	"You Can't Judge a Book By Its Cover." ATCO. 6782. 1971.
Glen Campbell.	"Galveston." Capitol 2428 1969.
Glen Campbell.	"Private John Q." Capitol 5545 1965.
Glen Campbell.	"The Universal Soldier." Capitol 5504 1965.
Candy and the Kisses.	"Soldier Baby (of Mine.)" Cameo 355 1965.
Canned Heat.	"Going Up the Country." Liberty 56077 1968.
Captain John Canty U.S.A.F.	"M.I.A./P.O.W. (Prisoner of War Song)." MGM K14192 1972.
Billy Carr.	"What's Come Over This World." Colpix Records CP-791 1965.
James Carr.	"Let's Face Facts." Goldwax 3002S 1968.
Carmen Carroll.	"A Soldier." Mira 8003 1967.
Maybelle Carter (Mother Carter).	"I Told Them What You're Fighting For." Columbia CS 9275 1970s.
Wilf Carter (Montana Slim).	"A Mother's Son in Vietnam."
Johnny Cash.	"The Ballad of Ira Hayes." Columbia 43058 1964.
Johnny Cash.	"Drive On." American 18091 1994.
Johnny Cash.	"Folsom Prison Blues." Columbia 44513 1968.
Johnny Cash.	"It Ain't Me Babe." Columbia 43145 1964.
Johnny Cash.	"Man in Black." Columbia 45339 1971.
Johnny Cash.	"The One on the Right is on the Left." Columbia 44-43496 1965.
Johnny Cash.	"Ragged Old Flag." Columbia 46028. Re-released in 1989 as Columbia 69067 1984.

Johnny Cash.	"Roll Call" Columbia 4-44373 1967.
Johnny Cash.	"Singing In Vietnam Talking Blues." Columbia 4-45393 1971.
Johnny Cash and Marty Robbins.	"Song of the Patriot." Columbia 1-11283 1980.
Johnny Cash.	"What Is Truth?" Columbia 45-45134 1970.
Tommy Cash.	"Six White Horses." EPIC 5-10540 1968.
Tommy Cash.	"The Tears on Lincoln's Face." EPIC 5-10673.
The Central Nervous System.	"It Takes All Kinds." Laurie LR-3421 DJ Promo 1968.
The Chambers Bros.	"Love, Peace and Happiness." Columbia 45088 1970.
The Chambers Bros.	"People Get Ready." Columbia 43816 1966.
The Chambers Bros.	"Time Has Come Today." Columbia 43816 1966.
Change of Pace.	"Bring My Buddies Back." Stone Lady SL-006-A 1968.
The Chantels.	"Soul of a Soldier." Verve VK-10387 1966.
Ray Charles & Clint Eastwood.	"Beers to You." Warner Bros. WBS49608 1980.
The Cheetahs.	"Soldier Boy." Philips 1964.
Chicago.	"Dialogue (Parts 1 and 2)." Columbia 45717 1972.
Chi-lites.	"Have You Seen Her?" Brunswick. 55462 1971.
Chi-lites.	"Oh Girl." Brunswick. 55471 1972.
Chi-lites.	"There Will Never Be Any Peace (Until God is Seated at the Conference Table." Brunswick 55512 1974.
Chiffons.	"Sailor Boy." Laurie 3262 1964.
(Jeff) Christie.	"Yellow River." EPIC 5-10626 1970.
Chylds.	"Show Me the Peace Sign." Bold 3337 1969.
Dee Clark.	"I'm A Soldier Boy." VeeJay 62-2622 1962.
Dick Clark.	"Open Letter to the Older Generation." 1967.
Classics IV.	"Spooky." Imperial 66259 1967.
Jimmy Cliff.	"Vietnam." Island Records 6014 003. A & M 1167. 1970. Reprise 1383 1977.
The Clovers.	"Love Potion #9." United Artists 0133 1973.
Joe Cocker.	"Give Peace a Chance." A & M 1200 1970.
Joe Cocker.	"With a Little Help From My Friends." A & M 991 1968.
Leonard Cohen.	"The Song of Isaac." Columbia KC 31724 1973.
Cold Chisel.	"Khe Sahn" Unknown Australian Label 1978.
The Committee.	"Wide Wide World of War." Promotion E.P PR-197 1973.

Sam Cooke.	"A Change is Gonna Come." RCA 447-0820 1964.
Alice Cooper.	"Eighteen." Warner Bros 7449 1971.
Bill Cosby.	"Grover Henson Feels Forgotten." Uni 55223 1970.
Country Joe and the Fish.	"F.U.C.K. Chant."
Country Joe and the Fish.	"For No Reason." Vanguard VSD 79299 1969.
Country Joe and the Fish.	"I-Feel-Like-I'm-Fixin'-To-Die Rag." Vanguard. 1967.
Country Joe and the Fish.	"Johnny's Gone to War." 1965.
Country Joe and the Fish.	"Maria." Vanguard VSD 79299 1969.
Country Joe and the Fish.	"Superbird." 1965.
Country Joe and the Fish.	"Thank the Nurse."
Country Joe and the Fish.	"The Girl Next Door (The Combat Nurse)."
Country Joe and the Fish.	"War, War, War." Vanguard 79315 1973.
Country Joe and the Fish.	"Welcome Home."
Cream.	"White Room." ATCO 6617 1968.
Creedence Clearwater Revival.	"Bad Moon Rising." Fantasy 622 1969.
Creedence Clearwater Revival.	"Fortunate Son." Fantasy 634 1969.
Creedence Clearwater Revival.	"Have You Ever Seen the Rain." Fantasy 655 1970.
Creedence Clearwater Revival.	"Run Through the Jungle." Fantasy 641 1970.
Creedence Clearwater Revival.	"Proud Mary." Fantasy 619 1969.
Creedence Clearwater Revival.	"Who'll Stop the Rain." Fantasy 637 1970.
Crosby, Stills and Nash.	"Find the Cost of Freedom." Atlantic 2740 1970.
Crosby, Stills and Nash.	"Suite: Judy Blue Eyes." Atlantic 2676 1969.
Crosby, Stills, Nash and Young.	"Ohio." Atlantic 45-2740 Atlantic 1970.
Crosby, Stills, Nash and Young.	"Teach Your Children." Atlantic 2735 1970.
Crosby, Stills, Nash and Young.	"Woodstock." Atlantic 45-2723 1970.
Mike Curb Congregation.	"Burning Bridges." MGM 14151 1970

- D -

Da Lench Mob.	"Guerillas in tha Mist." CD produced by Ice Cube
The Charlie Daniels Band.	"Still in Saigon." EPIC 14-02828 1982.
The Charlie Daniels Band.	"Uneasy Rider." Kama Sutra 576 1972.
Bobby Darin.	"Simple Song of Freedom," Motown 1193 1971.
Bobby Darin.	"We Didn't Ask To Be Brought Here." Atlantic 2305 1965.
Johnny Darrell.	"Green, Green Grass of Home." United Artists 3594 1966.

Johnny Darrell.	"Ruby, Don't Take Your Love to Town." United Artists 50126 1967.
Spencer Davis Group.	"Gimme Some Lovin." United Artists. 0115 1973.
Spencer Davis Group.	"I'm a Man." United Artists. 0116 1973.
Jimmy Dean.	"Big Bad John." Columbia 42175 1961.
John Deer.	"The Battle Hymn of Lt. Calley."" Royal American RA-34A 1971.
Delfonics.	"Didn't I (Blow Your Mind This Time)." Philly Grove 161 1970.
Delfonics.	"La La Means I Love You." Philly Grove 150 1968.
Delfonics.	"Ready or Not Here I Come (Can't Hide from Love)." Philly Grove 154 1968.
Delfonics.	"Somebody Loves You." Philly Grove 154 1968.
The Dells.	"Does Anybody Know I'm Here?" Cadet 5631 1968.
The Dells.	"On the Dock of the Bay." Cadet 5658 1969.
Patricia Denson & The Soul Expressions.	"Home from Vietnam" Achillian 502
John Denver.	"Leaving on a Jet Plane." RCA 45-217 1969.
John Denver.	"Readjustment Blues." Aerie RCA Victor 4607 1971.
Jackie DeShannon.	"What the World Needs Now is Love." Imperial Records 66110 1965.
Marlena Dietrich.	"Where Have All the Flowers Gone." Liberty 1964.
Marlena Dietrich.	"Blowin' in the Wind." Liberty 1964.
Dion.	"Abraham, Martin and John." Laurie 3464 1968.
Senator Everett McKinley Dirksen.	"The Gallant Men." Capitol 5805. 1966.
Disillusioned Younger Generation.	"Who Do You Think Your'e Foolin.'" DYG 748 1968.
The Dixie Drifters.	"Dear John Letter." Platinum 2300.
Bo Donaldson and the Heywoods.	"Billy Don't Be a Hero." ABC Records ABC-11435 1974.
Donovan.	"Mellow Yellow." Epic 10098 1966.
Donovan.	"Sunshine Superman." Epic 10045 1966.
Donovan.	"To Susan on the West Coast Waiting." EPIC 15-2296 1969.
Donovan.	"Universal Soldier." Hickory 1338 1965.
Donovan.	"The War Drags On." Hickory 45-P-1417 1966.

The Doors.	"The End." Elektra EKL 4007 1967.
The Doors.	"Riders on the Storm." Electra EKS-45738-A 1971.
The Doors.	"The Unknown Soldier."" Elektra 45628 1968.
Leon Douglas.	"Damn Nam (Ain't Goin to Vietnam)." Flying Dutchman 1967.
The Doves.	"Soldiers." Vanguard 35140 1971.
Dave Dudley.	"Soldier's Last Letter." Mercury SR 61057 1966.
Dave Dudley.	"There's a Star Spangled Banner Waving Somewhere." Mercury SR 61057 1966.
Dave Dudley.	"Vietnam Blues. (Talkin' Viet Nam Blues, Kristofferson)." Mercury. 72550 1966.
Dave Dudley.	"What We're Fighting For." Mercury 72500 1965.
Bob Dylan.	"Blowin in the Wind." Columbia 42856 1963.
Bob Dylan.	"It Aint' Me Babe." Asylum 45212 1974.
Bob Dylan.	"Masters of War." Columbia CL1986 1963.
Bob Dylan.	"Subterranean Homesick Blues." Columbia 43242 1965.
Bob Dylan.	"The Times They Are a Changin." Columbia CL2105(M) 1964.

- E -

Ronnie Earl.	"Welcome Home(Dedicated to the Vietnam Veterans)."
Earls.	"I Believe." Barry and Old Town Label 1149 1963.
Earth Opera.	"American Eagle Tragedy." Elektra EK-45636A 1968.
The Elegants and Vito Picone.	"A Letter From Vietnam (Dear Donna)." Laurie Records LR-3283 1965.
Keith Everett.	"Conscientious Objector." Tmp-ting. TMP-118 B
Every Father's Teenage Son.	"Letter to Dad." Buddah 25 1967.
Everybody's Children.	"The Time is Now." Date 2-1673

- F -

Donna Fargo.	"Soldier Boy." Cleveland International 10 1991.
Pat Farrell and the Believers.	"War Boy." Diamond Records Inc. D-236 1967.
Happy Fats.	"Birthday Thank You Tommy, From Viet Nam." Rebel Records 513

Happy Fats.	"Dear Mr. President." Rebel Records 501
Happy Fats.	"Veteran's Plea." Rebel Records 501
Happy Fats.	"A Victim of the Big Mess (Called the Great Society)." Rebel 510
Ed Faucett.	"Hippy Stomp." Oil Capitol 1230.
Ed Faucett.	"Letter from Vietnam, Dear Mother." Oil Capitol 1230.
The Fawns.	"Wish You Were Here With Me." CapCity CC-105 1966.
Phil Ferrazano.	"Joe Plays His Guitar."
Phil Ferrazano.	"Lovely Angels on a Wall."
Phil Ferrazano.	"Mekong River, I'm Going Home."
Phil Ferrazano.	"Son's & Daughter's Song."
Phil Ferrazano.	"Touching Your Name."
Fever Tree.	"San Francisco Girls (Return of the Native)." Uni 55060 1968.
Tommy Finch.	"Street Without Joy. Parts I and II." Cobra Z-10000 1969.
Five Man Electrical Band.	"Signs." Lionel 3213 1971.
Five Stairsteps.	"America Standing." Buddah 188 1970.
Five Stairsteps.	"Peace is Gonna Come." Buddah 213 1971.
The Flying Burrito Brothers.	"My Uncle." A&M Records 4175 1969.
The Flowerpot Men.	"Let's Go To San Francisco." Deram 7513 1967.
Capt. Jesse Fountain.	"I'm Marchin'." Cameo 457.
The Four Preps.	"The Big Draft." Capitol 4716 1962.
Inez and Charlie Foxx.	"Fellows in Vietnam." Dynamo D-119 1968.
Garland Frady.	"Ballad of the Unknown Soldier." Filmways FW 102.
Connie Francis.	"Letter From a Soldier (Dear Mama)." MGM K13545 1966.
Connie Francis.	"A Nurse in the U.S. Army." MGM 13550 1966.
Aretha Franklin.	"Chain of Fools." Atlantic 45-2464 1968.
Aretha Franklin.	"I Never Loved a Man (The Way I Love You)." Atlantic 2386 1967.
Aretha Franklin.	"(You Make Me Feel Like) A Natural Woman." Atlantic 2441 1967.
Aretha Franklin.	"RESPECT." Atlantic 45-2403 1967.
Aretha Franklin.	"People Get Ready." Atlantic 8176 1968.
Aretha Franklin.	"The Weight." Atlantic 2603 1969.
Freddy.	"Hundert Mann un ein Befehl." Polydor 52681L

Johnny Freedom (Bobby Sykes).	"Ain't I Right."
Johnny Freedom (Bobby Sykes).	"My Own Native Land."
Johnny Frigo Singers.	"This is America-Part I." Heartbeat.
Johnny Frigo Singers.	"This is America-Part II." Heartbeat.

- G -

Crystal Gale.	"'Til The White Dove Flies Alone." 1993
Stan Garland.	"Like an Eagle." 1995.
Delia Gartrell.	"See What You've Done, Done (Hymn#9)." Right On
Gary and the Knight Lites.	"Lonely Soldier's Pledge." Bell Records 643 1966.
Gary and the Knight Lites.	"So Far Away From Home." Bell Records 643 1966.
Marvin Gaye.	"Mercy Mercy Me (The Ecology)." Tamla 54207 1970.
Marvin Gaye and the Love Tones.	"Soldier's Plea." Tamla 54063 1962.
Marvin Gaye.	"What's Going On." Tamla 54201 1971.
Bobby Gentry.	"Ode to Billie Jo." Capital 5950. 1967.
Georgia Gibbs.	"Dance with me Henry." Mercury 70572x45.
Major Hershel Gober.	"An American's Dream." ABC Paramount Records 1964.
Major Hershel Gober.	"The Great Tragedy." Ace Records 1959.
Major Hershel Gober.	"Here I Am." ABC Paramount Records 1964.
Major Hershel Gober.	"Picture of a Man." Buddah Records BDA152
Major Hershel Gober.	"The Proud American." ABC Paramount Records 1964.
Bobby Goldsboro.	"Broomstick Cowboy." United Artist 952 1965.
Dickie Goodman.	"On Campus." Cotique 158. 1969.
Dorothy Gorman.	"Happy Birthday Son." Tower 391 1967.
Grand Funk Railroad.	"Closer to Home." Capitol 2877 1970.
Grand Funk Railroad.	"People, Let's Stop the War." Capitol P-3217 1972.
The Green Berets.	"Give Me A Try." UNI 55230 1970.
Cal Green.	"Johnny's Gone to Vietnam." Mutt and Jeff.
Lee Greenwood.	"God Bless the USA." MCA 52386 1984.
Harry "Griff" Griffith.	"The Battle in Vietnam." Copeland CSS-636
The Guess Who.	"American Woman." RCA 0325 1970.
The Guess Who.	"No Time." RCA 74-0300 1969.
The Guess Who.	"These Eyes." RCA 74-0102 1969.
Bonnie Guitar.	"The Tallest Tree." Dot 45-16919 1966.

Arlo Guthrie.	"Alice's Restaurant." Reprise 0877 1969.
- H -	
Merle Haggard.	"Are the Good Times Really Over for Good?" Epic. 02894 1982.
Merle Haggard and Clint Eastwood.	"Bar Room Buddies." Elektra E-46634 1980.
Merle Haggard and The Strangers.	"The Fightin' Side of Me." Capitol 2719 1970.
Merle Haggard.	"Me and Crippled Soldiers." Curb Records NR-76832 1980.
Merle Haggard.	"Okie From Muskogee." Capitol. 2626 1969.
Merle Haggard and the Strangers.	"Soldier's Last Letter." Capitol 3024 1971.
Merle Haggard.	"I Wonder If They Ever Think of Me." Capitol 3488 1972.
Daryl Hall with the Cellar Door.	"The Princess and the Soldier." AMY Records. A-T1.049
Dora Hall.	"Let There Be Peace." Cozy Records 1971.
Tom T. Hall.	"Strawberry Farms." Mercury 72913 1969.
Claire Hamill.	"We Gotta Get Outta This Place." Konk Promo 1974.
Paul Hardcastle.	"19" Chrysalis VS4-42860 1985.
Arlene Harden.	"Coming Home Soldier." Columbia 4-45365.
Arlene Harden.	"Congratulations (You Sure Made a Man out of Him)." Columbia 4-45420 1971.
The Harden Trio.	"Dear Brother." Columbia 4-43710 1966.
Tim Hardin.	"Simple Song of Freedom." Columbia 44920 1969.
Capt. Ty Harrington.	"When the Green Berets Come Home." Monument 45-1115
Capt. Ty Harrington.	"A Gun Don't Make A Man." Monument 45-1115
Craig Harris.	"Field of Stone." 1995.
George Harrison.	"Give Me Love (Give Me Peace on Earth)." Apple 1862 1973.
George Harrison.	"My Sweet Lord." Apple 2995 1970.
Freddie Hart.	"Purple Heart." 1995
Don Hart and the Fyve.	"Soldier Comin Home." Cool School 2002.
Ginger Hart.	"A Girl's Prayer." Kef Records P-2680 1968.
John Hartford.	"I Didn't Know the World Would Last This Long." RCA 47-9753 1969.
John Hartford.	"Orphan of World War Two." RCA 47-9753 1969.
Richie Havens.	"Here Comes the Sun." Stormy Forest. 686 1971.

Edwin Hawkin.	"Blowin in the Wind." Buddah 145 1970.
Edwin Hawkin.	"Pray for Peace." Buddah 145 1970.
Lee Hazelwood.	"In the Army." Mercury MEP 87 1964.
Hedgehoppers Anonymous.	"It's Good News Week." Parrot 9800 1965.
Jimi Hendrix.	"All Along the Watchtower." Reprise Records 0767 1968.
Jimi Hendrix.	"Purple Haze." Reprise Records 0597 1967.
Jimi Hendrix.	"Star Spangled Banner." Reprise Records 1044 1971.
Zerben Hicks & the Dynamics.	"Lights Out." RCA 9278
Ray Hildebrand.	"Hello Vietnam." Philips 40339 1965.
Don Hinson.	"The Protest Singer." Star-Burst 123 1960s
Chico Holiday.	"God, Country and My Baby." Phoenix 6190.
Chico Holiday.	"Show Us the Way." Karate 518
Johnny Holiday.	"Show the Peace Sign." Bold 3410 1969.
Don Holiman and the Sky Pilot Choir.	"Letter to Hanoi." IPI Records IPI1.
Hollies.	"He Ain't Heavy, He's My Brother." Epic 10532 1969.
The Hopeful.	"7 O'Clock News (Silent Night)." Mercury 72637 1966.
The Hopeful.	"6 O'Clock News (America the Beautiful)." Mercury 72637 1966.
Mary Hopkin.	"Think About Your Children." Apple 1825 1969.
Mary Hopkin.	"Those Were The Days." Apple 1801 1968.
Lightnin Hopkins.	"Vietnam War."
Lightnin Hopkins.	"War is Starting Again."
Jan Howard.	"My Son." Decca 32407 1968.
Freddie Hubbard.	"Black Soldier." Atlantic SD 1576.
Freddie Hubbard.	"This is Combat I Know." Atlantic SD 1576.
Freddie Hubbard.	"What a Good Time for Kent State." Atlantic SD 1576.

- I -

The Impressions.	"Amen (1970)." Curtom CR1948 1970.
The Impressions.	"Choice of Colors." Curtom 1943 1969.
The Impressions.	"This is My Country." Curtom CR1934 1969.
Autry Inman.	"Ballad of Two Brothers." Epic 5-10389 1968.
Iron Butterfly.	"In-A-Gadda-Da-Vida." Atco 6606 1968.
Iron Butterfly.	"Soldier in Our Town." Atco 6782 1969.
Iron Butterfly.	"Soul Experience." Atco 6647 1969.
Burle Ives.	"The Sixties." Decca 31918 1966.

- J -

Jim Jackson.	"Welcome Me Home." Sandbag 102.
Wanda Jackson.	"Little Boy Soldier." Capitol 2245 1968.
The James Gang.	"Gunk #40." ABC 11272 1970.
Tommy James and the Shondells.	"Chrystal Blue Persuasion." Roulette 7050 1969.
Jan and Dean.	"Only a Boy." Warner Bros 7151 1967.
Jay and the Americans.	"Tricia (Tell Your Daddy)." United Artist 50683.
Jefferson Airplane.	"Hymn to an Older Generation."
Jefferson Airplane.	"Somebody to Love." RCA 9140 1966.
Jefferson Airplane.	"Volunteers." RCA 9248 1969.
Jefferson Airplane.	"We Can Be Together." RCA 9248 1969.
Jefferson Airplane.	"White Rabbit." RCA 9140 1966.
Billy Joel.	"Goodnight Saigon." Columbia 38-03780 1983
Billy Joel.	"We Didn't Start the Fire." Columbia.73021 1989.
Elton John.	"Daniel." MCA Records 40046 1973.
Johnny and Jon.	"Christmas in Vietnam." Jewel 776 1968.
Lois Johnson.	"GI Joe." Epic 5-9898.1967.
John Paul Jones.	"Baja/A Foggy Day in Vietnam." Parkway 915M. 1970.
Tom Jones.	"Green, Green Grass of Home." Parrot 45-40009 1966.
Bobby Joy.	"Letter from a Soldier." Tangerine 981 1971.
Fate, Fed & Harvie June.	"The Love of a Soldier." Royal American RA-8

- K -

Debbie Lori Kaye.	"Soldier Boy." Columbia 4-43454.
Rodd Keith.	"Vietnam Sweetheart." Preview 1241 1974.
The Kendalls.	"It's Raining on my Hero." 1995
Marvin Moran.	"The Ballad of John Kennedy." Raynard RS-10023 1963.
Dave Kennedy.	"J.F.K. Rest in Peace." Raynard RS-10023 1963.
Joe (Wild Thing) King.	"Hold On. (the testifyin' side: in Vietnam writing to his woman.)" Columbia 5806 1967.
Joe (Wild Thing) King.	"On My Way Home." Columbia 5806 1967.
Dr. Martin Luther King, Jr.	"Why I Oppose the War in Vietnam." Black Forum Records 451.
Ric King.	"The Return of a Soldier." Capitol P5845. 1966.

Ric King.	"Hymn To A Returning Soldier." Capitol P5845. 1966.
Kingston Trio.	"Last Night I had the Strangest Dream." Capitol 5132 1964.
Kingston Trio.	"Where Have All the Flowers Gone." Capitol 4671 1961.
Johnny Konchal.	"John-John." KB 6-7063A 1964.
Kris Kristofferson.	"Why Me." Monument 8571 1973.

- L -

La'Shell & Shelletts.	"My Soldier Boy Over There." Eagle Records E-102A
Frankie Laine.	"I Believe." Columbia 4-39938 1954.
Becky Lamb.	"Little Becky's Christmas Wish." Warner Bros. 7154.
Emanual Laskey.	"A Letter from Vietnam." Westbound W-1458
The Laurendeu Sisters & The Laurel Westerers.	"Wars Like Vietnam." Marquis 1124.
Calvin Lee.	"I'll Be Home (Wait and See)." Minit Records 655.
Jim Lea.	"Mystery in Hanoi." RCI Records 3003-A 1971.
Tom Lehrer.	"MLF (Multi-Lateral Force) Lullaby." Reprise RS-6179. 1965.
Tom Lehrer.	"Send the Marines." Reprise RS-6179 1965.
John Lennon & KYA's Tom Campbell & Bill Holley.	"1969 PeaceTalk Part 1 and Part 2." KYA 4616 1969.
John Lennon. (As the Plastic Ono Band).	"Give Peace a Chance." Apple 1809 1969.
John Lennon and Yoko Ono.	"Happy Xmas (War is Over)." Apple 1842 1971.
John Lennon Plastic Ono Band.	"Imagine." Apple 1840 1971.
J. B. Lenoir.	"Vietnam Blues." Polydor/Crusade 24-4011 1970.
The Lettermen.	"All the Gray Haired Men." Capitol 2196 1968.
Lincoln St. Exit.	"Time Has Come Gonna Die." Mainstream 722 1971.
Bob Lind.	"Elusive Butterfly." United Artists 0032 1973.
The Linde-Antell Body of Music.	"Accordingly (I Learned Some Things Today)." Cadet 5611 1968.
Lance Lindsey.	"How Do You Tell a Small Boy." Voices in Vital America

Lance Lindsey.	"Wake Up America." Voices in Vital America
Sarge Lintecum.	"It Don't Mean Nothin."
Sarge Lintecum.	"Reunion at the Wall."
Sarge Lintecum.	"This Shirt of Mine."
Sarge Lintecum.	"Vietnam Blues - Combat Tested for Peace."
London Phogg	"The Times to Come." A & M promo 1968.
Lord Brynner.	"Vietnam Moratorium." Hilary LB-406-B 1965.
The Love Generation.	"Meet Me At the Love-in." Audition 66254
Lovin Spoonfull.	"Darlin Be Home Soon." Kama Sutra. 1967.
Victor Lundberg.	"An Open Letter to My Teenage Son." Liberty 55996 1967.
Loretta Lynn.	"Dear Uncle Sam." Decca 31893 1966.
Loretta Lynn and Conway Twitty.	"God Bless America Again." MCA Records 40572 1976

- M -

Moms Mabley.	"Abraham. Martin and John." Mercury 72935 1968.
Mary Macgregor & Hal Atkinson The Good Life Singers.	"America Again." Willow 4601
Ernie Maresca.	"Shout, Shout." Seville 117 1962.
Ernie Maresca.	"What is a Marine?" Laurie 3447 1968.
Mark Five.	"Search Your Mind." NVVI 141.
Sonny Marshall.	"A Soldier's Prayer." Air 5064 1964.
Martha and the Vandellas.	"Dancing in the Streets." Gordy 7033 1964.
Martha and the Vandellas.	"Forget Me Not." Gordy 7070 1968.
Martha and the Vandellas.	"I Should Be Proud." Gordy 7098 1970.
Martha and the Vandellas.	"Nowhere to Run." Gordy 7039 1965.
Martha & the Muffins.	"Saigon." Dindisc Records.
Joey Martin.	"Joey's Letter." Imperial 66273
Joey Martin.	"Joey's Prayer." Imperial 66273
Michael Martin, Tim Holiday.	"Who Are the Names on the Wall?" Windmill Productions UR 4324
Lane Martine.	"The Recruit." Decca 32621.
Marvelettes.	"Danger Heartbreak Dead Ahead." Tamla 54120 1965.
Richard Marx.	"Don't Mean Nothin."
Masqueraders.	"Let's Face Facts."
Sammy Masters.	"The Letter (from South Viet Nam)." Galahad G-538.
Sammy Masters.	"Little Ben." Galahad 538.

Matthew's Southern Comfort.	"Woodstock." Decca 32774 1970.
Paul Mauriat.	"Love is Blue (L'amour est bleu)." Philips 1967.
Curtis Mayfield.	"Back to the World." Curtom CRS-8015 1973.
Rev. Orvis Mays.	"Tribute in Prayer (From a Soldier in Vietnam)." Songbird Records SBLP202
Michael McCann.	"Soldiers Song."
Michael McCann.	"The Wall."
Les McCann & Eddie Harris.	"Compared to What." Atlantic OS-13133 1969.
Bobby McDowell.	"I'm Coming Home." Amy 955.
Barry McGuire.	"Eve of Destruction." Dunhill 4009 1965.
Barry McGuire.	"Masters of War." Dunhill 4098 1965.
Scott McKenzie.	"San Francisco (Be Sure to Wear Flowers in Your Hair)." Ode ZS7-103 1967.
Senator Everett McKinley. (The Hardly Worth It Players)	"Wild Thing." Parkway Records P-127-B 1962.
Don McLean.	"American Pie." United Artist 50856 1971.
Bill Medley.	"Peace Brother Peace." MGM 14000 1968.
Mel and Tim.	"Mail Call Time." Bamboo 114 1970.
Melanie.	"Candles in the Rain." Buddah 167 1970.
Melanie.	"Laydown." Buddah 167 1970.
Melanie.	"Peace Will Come(According to Plan)." Buddah 186 1970.
Melanie.	"What Have They Done to My Song Ma." Buddah 268 1971.
Metallica	"One." S&M Metallica Album
The Mighty Hannibal.	"Hymn #5." Josie 964 1966.
Jody Miller.	"Home of the Brave (Land of the Free)." Capitol 5483 1965.
Leslie Miller.	"He Wore a Green Beret." RCA Victor 45-8786 1965.
Mitch Miller and the Gang.	"A Ballad From Vietnam." Decca 31843 1965.
Minutemen.	"Vietnam."
Miracles.	"The Tracks of My Tears." Tamla 54118 1965.
Joni Mitchell.	"The Beat of Black Wings." Geffen Records 1988.
The Mitchell Trio (w/John Denver).	"The Sound of Protest (Has Begun to Pay)." Mercury MG 21067 1966.
Flora Molton.	"The Sun Will Shine in Vietnam." Moltons 0002
The Monitors.	"Greetings (From Uncle Sam)." V.I.P. 25032 1965.
The Monkees.	"Zor and Zam." The Birds, the Bees & the
Monkees	Colgem 109 1968.
The Moody Blues.	"Nights in White Satin." Deram 85023 1968.

The Moody Blues.	"Tuesday Afternoon (Forever Afternoon)." Deram 85028 1968.
Jeff Moore.	"Unknown Soldier." 1995.
Moral Disgust.	"Vietnam (Isn't Over)." 1992.
Charlotte Morgan.	"He's Coming Home (from Vietnam)." Upland 7457 1969.
Van Morrison.	"Brown Eyed Girl." Bang Records W-10127
Van Morrison.	"Old, Old, Woodstock." Warner Bros. WB7573 1972.
Mountain.	"Flowers of Evil." Windfall 5501 1971.
Tim Murphy.	"The POW/MIA."
Ron Murry	"What If They Gave a War." Genna 1001.
The Music Explosion.	"We Gotta Go Home." Laurie 3414 1967.
Myriad.	"Cruel War." AT 815N-5001 1966.

- N -

Graham Nash.	"Chicago." Atlantic 45-2804 1970.
Graham Nash.	"Oh Camile (The Winter Soldier)."
Graham Nash	"The Wall." 1999.
Graham Nash and David Crosby.	"The Wall Song." Atlantic 7220 1972.
Fred Neil.	"Four Chaplains." Epic 5-9435.
Willie Nelson.	"Jimmy's Road." RCA 74-0162 1969.
Jim Nesbitt.	"Clean the Slate in '68." 59-1039 1968.
Jim Nesbitt.	"Heck of a Fix In '66" Chart 1350.
Michael Nesmith.	"The New Recruit." Colpix 787 1965.
1910 Fruitgum Company.	"1-2-3 Red Light." Buddah 54 1968.
1910 Fruitgum Company.	"Simon Says." Buddah 24 1968.
9th Street Exit.	"Never Be the Man My Brother Was." Solid Foundation 107 1974.
Noah's Ark.	"Purple Heart." Liberty 12345 1970.

- O -

O'Jays.	"There's Someone (Waiting Back Home)." Neptune 12 1969.
Oak Ridge Boys.	"Come On In." ABC 12434 1978.
Phil Ochs.	"Day of Decision." Elektra EKS 7287 1965.
Phil Ochs.	"Draftdodger Rag." Electra EKS 7287 1965.
Phil Ochs.	"I Ain't Marchin Anymore." Elektra EKS 7287 1965.
Phil Ochs.	"The War Is Over." A&M 132 1968.
Octopus.	"The Unbluesy U. S. Blues." ESP 2000 1969.
Yoko Ono.	"Now or Never." Yoko Ono Plastic Ono Band 1853 1972.

Roy Orbison.	"There Won't be Many Coming Home." MGM 13760 1967.
Vernon Oxford.	"Redneck! (The Redneck National Anthem)." RCA Victor PAB10693 1976.

- P -

Beulah Palmer and 3rd Avenue.	"My Man in Vietnam." BEM 1005.
Paper Lace.	"Billy Don't Be a Hero." Mercury 73479 1974.
Billy Parker.	"American, You're Beautiful to Me." 1995.
Alan Parsons.	"Brother Up in Heaven." CNR 530 00 98 1998.
Tom Paxton.	"Jimmy Newman." Electra 45674 1970.
Tom Paxton.	"Lyndon Johnson Told the Nation." EKS-7298 1965.
Tom Paxton.	"My Son John." Elektra 7317 1966.
Tom Paxton.	"Peace Will Come (According to Plan)." Reprise 1110 1972.
Tom Paxton.	"Talking Vietnam Pot Luck Blues." Elektra 74019 1968.
Johnny Paycheck.	"Prisoner of War."
Freda Payne.	"Bring the Boys Home." Invictus 9092 1971.
David Peel and the Lower East Side.	"The American Revolution." EKS-74069 1970.
David Peel and the Lower East Side.	"Hey Mr. Draftboard" 1968." EKS-74069 1970.
David Peel and the Lower East Side.	"The Hippie from New York." Apple Promo SRO 6546 1972.
Peter, Paul and Mary.	"500 Miles." Warner Bros. 5334 1963.
Peter, Paul and Mary.	"Blowin in the Wind." Warner Bros 5368 1963.
Peter, Paul and Mary.	"The Cruel War." Warner Bros 5809 1964, 1966.
Peter, Paul and Mary.	"The Great Mandella (The Wheel of Life)." Warner Bros. 7067 1967.
Peter, Paul and Mary (Excerpts Eugene McCarthy).	"If You Love Your Country." Pepaman Music Corp 140677 1968.
Peter, Paul and Mary.	"Leaving On a Jet Plane." Warner Bros 7340 1969.
Peter, Paul and Mary.	"Puff." Warner Bros 5348 1963.
Peter, Paul and Mary.	"Where Have All the Flowers Gone?" 1963.
Paul Petersen.	"My Dad." Colpix Records CP-663 1962.
The Players. (Herb Butler & the Dells)	"He'll Be Back." Minit 32001 1966.
The Players.	"Glad You Waited." Minit 1966.

The Pranksters.	"Don't Cry for Me: the Vietnam Veteran's Song." Jerger 1986.
Elvis Presley.	"Don't Cry Daddy." RCA 47-9768 1969.
Elvis Presley.	"If I Can Dream." RCA 47-9670 1968.
Elvis Presley.	"In the Ghetto." RCA 47-9741 1969.
Chuck Price.	"Welcome Home 96."
Charley Pride.	"Beyond the Wall." 1995.
John Prine.	"Sam Stone." Atlantic 2815 1971.
Pucho.	"Vietnam Mambo." Prestige. A3-428 1966.
- Q -	
? (Question Mark) & the Mysterians.	"96 Tears." Cameo 428 1966.
- R -	
Rainbow Press.	"There's a War On." Mr G Records G 817B
The Raindrops.	"God Bless Our Soldier Boys in Vietnam." Preview 1029.
The Raindrops.	"To the Sons of America." Preview 1029.
The Ramparts.	"The Death of Emmett Till Part 1 & Part 2." Dootone Records 382.
Frankie Randall.	"Let's Go to San Franscio." RCA Victor 47-9426.
Dave Ranno.	"Part of Me is Still in Vietnam." Ranno Records RR 8601 1986.
Rascals.	"People Got to Be Free." Atlantic 2537 1968.
Razzy & the Neighborhood Kids.	"I Hate Hate." Aquariad AQ601
Otis Redding.	"I'm Coming Home." Volt 45-152 1967.
Otis Redding.	"(Sittin On) The Dock of the Bay." Volt 45-157 1968.
Redgum.	"I Was Only 19 (A Walk in the Light Green)." Epic ES844 1983.
Jerry Reed.	"Fighting for the USA." RCA 8730 1965.
Jerry Reed.	"Navy Blues." RCA 8730 1965.
Diane Renay.	"Kiss Me Sailor." 20th Century Fox 477 1964.
Diane Renay.	"Navy Blue." 20th Century Fox 456 1964.
Don Reno & Benny Martini.	"A Soldier's Prayer in Vietnam." Monument 912.
Lil Richard.	"Jade Do Viet Nam Polka." Chicago 387.
Riders of the Sky.	"Letter Home." 1995
Stan Ridgeway.	"Camouflage." IRS 52875 1986.
Tex Ritter.	"God Bless America Again." Capitol 2815
Tex Ritter.	"Lonely Soldier Boy." Capitol 4644.

Johnny Rivers.	"The Tracks of My Tears." Imperial 66244 1967.
Johnny Rivers.	"Where Have All the Flowers Gone." Imperial 66133 1965.
Marty Robbins.	"Ain't I Right." Columbia 43651 1966.
Marty Robbins.	"The Ballad of the Alamo." Columbia 41809 1960.
Marty Robbins.	"My Own Native Land." Columbia 43651 1966.
Marty Robbins.	"Private Wilson White." Columbia 43500 1966.
Rick Roberts and Skip Ballard.	"Congressional Medal of Honor." Twin 2898 1969.
Derrik Roberts.	"There Won't be any Snow (Christmas in the Jungle)." Roulette R-4656
Roscoe Robinson.	"Don't Forget the Soldiers (Fighting in Viet Nam)." Gerri Records 002
Tom Robinson.	"War Baby." Sector 27.
Jimmie Rodgers.	"The Wreck of the John B." Roulette 4260 1960.
Johnny Rodriguez.	"You're a Hero to Me." 1995.
Kenny Rogers & Patti Austin.	"I Will Always Remember You." 1997.
Kenny Rogers.	"Ruby. Don't Take Your Love to Town." Reprise 0829 1969.
The Rolling Stones.	"Everybody Pays Their Dues." 1968
The Rolling Stones.	"Paint It Black." London 901 1966.
The Rolling Stones.	"Platoon B in Vietnam Theme."
The Rolling Stones.	"Street Fighting Man." London 909 1968.
The Rolling Stones.	"Sympathy for the Devil." Get Yer Ya-Ya's Out! London NPS5 1970.
Ronny and the Daytonas.	"Delta Day." "The Last Letter." RCA 1967.
Rouzan Sisters.	"Men of War." Frisco Records Inc. 113.
The Royal Guardsmen.	"Snoopy vs. The Red Baron." Laurie 3366 1966.
Leon Russell.	"Everybody's Talkin Bout the Young." Dot 16771 1965.
Mitch Ryder.	"Drafted." Obscure 2 Track CD.
John Wesley Ryles.	"Kay." Columbia 4-44682 1968.

- S -

SSgt. Barry Sadler.	"The A Team." RCA. 47-8804 1966.
SSgt. Barry Sadler.	"The Ballad of the Green Berets." RCA. 47-8739 1966.
SSgt. Barry Sadler.	"Letter From Vietnam." RCA. 47-8739 1966.

SSgt. Barry Sadler.	"Little Bird of Vietnam."
SSgt. Barry Sadler.	"One Day Nearer Home." RCA 47-8966 1966.
SSgt. Barry Sadler.	"Salute to the Nurse." RCA 47-8739 1966.
Buffy Sainte-Marie.	"Universal Soldier." Vanguard VSA 3/4 1970.
Sam the Sham and the Pharoahs.	"Wooly Bully." MGM I13322.
The Sand Pebbles.	"Flower Power." Calla C-148.
Jack Sanders.	"The Viet Nam Blues."
Tommy Sands.	"Old Oaken Bucken-Air Force Promo." United States Airforce-Music in the Air No 127. Early 60's
Santana.	"Evil Ways." Columbia. 45069 1970.
Johnny Sea.	"Day for Decision." Warner Bros 5820 1966.
Troy Seals.	"Mama Hold My Hand." Rising Sons 7155.
The Searchers.	"Love Potion Number Nine." Kapp KJB-27 1964.
Neil Sedaka.	"The Immigrant." Rocket 40370 1975.
The Seeds.	"March of the Flower Children." GNP Crescendo 394 1967.
Pete Seeger.	"Bring 'Em Home." 1966.
Pete Seeger.	"Draftdodger Rag." Columbia 43699 1966.
Pete Seeger.	"Last Train to Nuremberg." Columbia 30729 1971.
Pete Seeger.	"Waist Deep in The Big Muddy." Columbia. 4-44273 1967.
Pete Seeger.	"Where Have All the Flowers Gone." Columbia CS 9416 1967.
Bob Seger.	"2 + 2 = ?." Capitol 2143 1968.
Johnny Selph.	"All I Want for Christmas is My Baby." Bion 1968.
The Shangri-las.	"Long Live Our Love." Red Bird 10-048 1966.
The Shangri-las.	"Remember (Walkin' in the Sand)." Red Bird 10-008 1964.
Shelly.	"Thank God the War Is Almost Over." Peace. 101-a. 1971.
Jean Shepard and Ferlin Husky.	"A Dear John Letter." Capitol 2502 1953.
Jean Shephard and Ferlin Husky.	"Forgive Me John." Capitol 2586 1953.
The Johnny Shines Band.	"So Cold in Vietnam." Testament 2212 1966.
Shirelles.	"Hippie Walk Part 1 & Part 2." Scepter 12217 1968.
Shirelles.	"Tonight's the Night." Scepter 1208 1960.
Shirelles.	"Soldier Boy." Scepter 1228 1962.
Paul Simon.	"Mother and Child Reunion." Columbia 4-45547 1972.

Simon and Garfunkel.	"At the Zoo." Columbia 44046 1967.
Simon and Garfunkel.	"Bridge Over Troubled Water." Columbia 45079 1970.
Simon and Garfunkel.	"Cecelia." Columbia 45133 1970.
Simon and Garfunkel.	"Homeward Bound." Columbia 43511 1966.
Simon and Garfunkel.	"I'm A Rock." Columbia 43617 1966.
Simon and Garfunkel.	"7 O'Clock News (Silent Night)." Columbia JZSP 11649 1966.
Simon and Garfunkel.	"6 O'Clock News (America the Beautiful)." Columbia JZSP 11649 1966.
Simon and Garfunkel.	"The Sounds of Silence." Columbia 43396 1965.
Frank Sinatra.	"High Hopes." kb-2077.
Nancy Sinatra.	"The Cruel War." Reprise 20188 1963.
Nancy Sinatra.	"These Boots Are Made For Walkin." Reprise 0432 1965.
Gordon Sinclair.	"The Americans (A Canadian's Opinion.)" Avco 4628 1973.
Gordon Sinclair.	"The Americans. (How Long Will It Take?) "
Clayton Sinclair.	"In Saigon." CA-Song Records.
Red Skelton.	"The Pledge of Allegiance." Columbia 4-44798 1969
Patrick Sky.	"Luang Prabang." Adelphi Records 4101 1973.
Sly and the Family Stone.	"Hot Fun in the Summertime." EPIC 10497 1969.
Sly and the Family Stone.	"I Want to Take You Higher." EPIC 10450 1969.
Cal Smith.	"MacArthur's Hand." MCA Record's 40563.
Lonnie Leston Smith.	"Give Peace a Chance." Sunburst CBS 8660 Promo 1970.
O. C. Smith.	"La La Peace Song." Columbia 10034 1974.
Patti Smith.	"Gung Ho." Arista 2000.
Suzie Smith.	"Teenage Soldier." Preview 1247.
The Smubbs.	"Rosary Anne." 1968
Hank Snow.	"Letter From Vietnam (To Mother)." RCA 9012 1966.
Jimmy Snyder.	"Our Boys in Viet Nam Are Coming Home." Charity CH4392.
Soul Searchers.	"Christmas in Viet Nam." Song Bird 1187
Joe South.	"Don't It Make You Wanna Go Home." Capitol 2592 1969.
Joe South.	"The Games People Play." Capitol 2248 1968.
Wayne Spence & Smiling Faces.	"Love's Stronger Than Hate." Peace WFS Exclusive

Wayne Spence & Smiling Faces.	"Thank God for Peace." Peace WFS Exclusive
Richard Spencer and the Winstons.	"Say Goodbye to Daddy." Metromedia.
Spinners.	"Could It Be I'm Falling in Love." Atlantic 2927 1972.
Spirit of US.	"He Ain't Heavy - He's My Brother." Viva V-641
Spirit of US.	"Simple Song of Freedom." Viva V-641
Spokesman.	"Dawn of Correction." Decca 31844 1965.
Bruce Springsteen.	"Born in the USA." Columbia 38-04680 1984.
Bruce Springsteen.	"Galveston Bay." Columbia 67454 1995.
Bruce Springsteen.	"War." Columbia 06342 1986.
The Staple Singers.	"I'm Just Another Soldier." STAX 0125 1972.
Buddy Starcher.	"The Fall of a Nation." Decca 32012. 1966.
Buddy Starcher.	"Sniper's Hill." Sparton P1443
The Starfires.	"Cry for Freedom." 1965.
Brenda Starr.	"Soldier Boy (My Soldier Boy)." Polydor 2-14032.
Edwin Starr.	"Ball of Confusion (That's What the World is Today)."
Edwin Starr.	"Stop the War Now." Gordy 7104 1971.
Edwin Starr.	"War." Gordy 7101 1970.
Statler Brothers.	"More Than a Name on a Wall." Mercury 874196 1989.
Steppenwolf.	"Magic Carpet Ride." ABC Dunhill 4161 1968.
Steppenwolf.	"Monster." ABC Dunhill 4221 1969.
Cat Stevens.	"Peace Train." A&M 1291 1971.
Geraldine Stevens.	"Billy, I've Got to Go to Town." World Pacific. 77927.
Ray Stevens.	"America, Communicate with Me." Barnaby Records ZS7 2016
The Stewart Family.	"The Soldier's Prayer Book." 4 Star 45-1652.
Rod Stewart.	"Street Figntin' Man." Mercury 61264 1970.
Stephen Stills.	"Soldier." CBS BA 222226 1970.
Stone Poneys.	"Different Drum." Capitol 2004 1968.
Stonewall Jackson.	"The Minute Men are Turning in Their Graves." Columbia 4-43552. 1966.
Stonewall Jackson.	"Red Roses Blooming Back Home." Columbia. 4-44625 1968.
Stories.	"I'm Coming Home." Kama Sutra 545 1972.
Barbara Streisand.	"People." Columbia CS2215 1964.
Sugar and Spice.	"Cruel War." White Whale 295.
Sugarloaf.	"Green Eyed Lady." Liberty 56183. 1970.

The Superbs.	"So Glad You're Home." Symbol 8 1969.
The Superbs.	"The Dawning of Love." Symbol 8 1969.
The Supremes.	"Some Day We'll Be Together." Motown 1969.
Suzie and the Raindrops.	"Good-bye My Soldier, Good-bye My Love." Preview 1280.
Swamp Dogg.	"Sam Stone."

- T -

James Taylor.	"Fire and Rain." Warner Bros. 7423 1971.
Johnny Taylor.	"Jody's Got Your Girl and Gone." Stax 0085 1970.
The Temptations.	"Ball of Confusion (That's What The World Is Today)." G7099 1970.
The Temptations.	"My Girl." Gordy G-7038. 1965.
10,000 Maniacs.	"The Big Parade." Blind Man's Zoo Delektra/Asylum 960815-1
Joe Tex.	"I Believe I'm Going to Make It." Checker 4033 1966.
Joe Tex.	"I Can't See You No More (When Johnny Comes Marching Home Again)." Dial 4095 1969.
Them.	"Baby Please Don't Go." Parrot. 9727 1965.
Them.	"Gloria." Parrot. 9727 1965.
B.J. Thomas.	"Billy and Sue." Warner Bros 5491 1964. Hickory 1395 1966.
B.J. Thomas.	"These Colors Won't Run." 1995
B.J. Thomas.	"Vietnam." Joed TR-119 1965.
Leon Thomas.	"Damn Nam" (Ain't Goin' to Vietnam) Parts I and II." Flying Dutchman 26009 1971.
Mike Thomas.	"Prayer for Today." Tin Pan Alley 71-665
Three Dog Night.	"Momma Told Me Not to Come." Dunhill. 4239 (PS). 1970.
Dr. William Truly Jr.	"(The Two Wars of) Old Black Joe." House of the Fox 2 PS 1971.
Ernest Tubb.	"A Heartsick Soldier on Heartbreak Ridge." Decca 46389 1953.
Ernest Tubb.	"It's for God, and Country, and You Mom (That's Why I'm Fighting in Vietnam)." Decca 3186. 1966.
Ernest Tubb.	"Missing in Action." Decca 46389 1953.
Glenn W. Turner.	"America and What it Means to Me." Souncot 1134.
Glenn W. Turner.	"The Unstoppable Americans." Souncot 1134.

The Turtles.	"It Ain't Me Babe." White Whale 222 1965.
The Turtles.	"Let Me Be." White Whale 224 1965.
- U -	
Uglys.	"Wake Up My Mind." Astor AP1458 1968.
- V -	
Valli.	"Hurry Home to Me (Soldier Boy)." Scepter 1233 1962.
Vanilla Fudge.	"You Keep Me Hanging On." Atco 6495 1967.
Larry Verne.	"Please Mr. Custer." ERA 3024 1960.
Vietnam Veterans Organization.	"Angel in Green."
Bobby Vinton.	"Comin Home Soldier." EPIC 5-10090 1966.
Bobby Vinton.	"Little Barefoot Boy." EPIC 5-10397 1968.
Bobby Vinton.	"Mister Lonely." Epic 9730 1964.
- W -	
Brandon Wade.	"Letter From a Teenage Son." Phillips 40503 1967.
Danny Wagner and Kindred Soul.	"When Johnny Comes Marching Home." Imperial 66327 1968.
Billy Walker.	"Cross the Brazos at Waco." Columbia 43120 1964.
Billy Walker.	"Forgotten Angels." 1995.
Edie Walker.	"Don't Cry Soldier." Mew 102.
Jerry Jeff Walker.	"Up Against the Wall Redneck Mother." MCA 382 1973.
Jerry Jeff Walker.	"Dear John Letter Lounge." MCA 40570 1976.
Jerry Wallace.	"The Son of a Green Beret." Mercury. 72589 1966.
Dick Wannebo.	"Goodbye Saigon." Copper State CSR 2023 A.
War.	"Get Down." United Artists 50815 1971.
The War Babies.	"War Baby." UNI 55164 1969.
Dionne Warwick.	"Say a Little Prayer." Scepter Records SCE 12203X 1967.
Kim Weston.	"When Johnny Comes Marching Home." MGM K13928 SS 1968.
The Whispers.	"P.O.W.-M.I.A." Janus Records J212 1973.
The Who.	"Pinball Wizard." Decca 32519 1969.
The Who.	"See Me, Feel Me." Decca 32729 1970.
The Who.	"Won't Get Fooled Again." Decca 32846 1971.
John Bucky Wilken.	"Delta Day (No Time to Cry)." RCA 9492 1967.

Don Williams.	"Good Ole Boys Like Me." MCA 41205 1980.
Lawton Williams.	"Everything's OK on the LBJ." RCA Victor 47-8407 1964.
Mike Williams.	"Lonely Soldier." Atlantic 2339 1966.
Hal Willis.	"The Battle of Vietnam." Sims 288 1966.
Faith Willow.	"There in Vietnam." Bubble 1968.
Al Wilson.	"La La Peace Song." Columbia 10031 1974.
Susan Wojnar.	"Don't Cry for Me - The Veteran's Song."
Howlin Wolf.	"Vietnam."
Stevie Wonder.	"Front Line." Original Musiquarium 1 Tamla 6002 1982.
Stevie Wonder.	"Heaven Help Us All." Tamla 54200 1970.
Stevie Wonder	"Think of Me As Your Soldier." Tamla 54208 1971.
Johnny Wright.	"A Dear John Letter." Decca EP 7-34345.
Johnny Wright.	"Hello Vietnam." Decca 31821 1965. EP 7-34345.
Johnny Wright.	"I'm Doing This for Daddy." Decca 32002. 1966.
Johnny Wright.	"Keep the Flag Flying." Decca 31875. 1966.
Johnny Wright.	"American Power." Decca 32152 1966.
Johnny Wright.	"Solidier's Last Letter." Decca EP 7-34345.
Roger Wright.	"Heroes of Vietnam." 615 S1003A 1985.
Ruby Wright.	"Billy Broke My Heart At Walgreens (I Cried All The Way To Sears)." Recording Industries Corp. S 145-64 1965.

- X -

None

- Y -

Frankie Yankovic and his Yanks.	"Saigon Sally." Columbia 4-43596 1966.
Glenn Yarbrough & the Limeliters.	"I See America." Stax STA-0185.
Neil Young.	"War Song." Reprise. 106 1972.

- Z -

Frank Zappa.	"I Don't Wanna Get Drafted." Zappa WS7-73000 1980.

Bibliography

Appy, Christian G., *Working Class War: American Combat Soldiers in Vietnam.* Chapel Hill: The University of North Carolina Press, 1993.

Alexander, Ron and Sasser, Charles, W. *Taking Fire: The True Story of a Decorated Chopper Pilot.* New York: St. Martin's Press, 2001.

Ambrose, Steve, *Citizen Soldiers.* New York: Simon and Schuster, 1997.

Astor, Gerald, *The Right to Fight: A History of African Americans in the Military Novato (CA)*: Presidio Press, 1998.

Atkinson, Rick, *The Long Gray Line: The American Journey of West Point's Class of 1966.* Boston: Houghton Mifflin Company, 1989.

Bach, Steven, *Marlene Dietrich: Life and Legend.* New York: William M. Morrow and Company, Inc., 1992.

Bartimus, Tad, et. al., (Ed.) *War Torn: Stories of War from the Women Reporters who Covered Vietnam.* New York: Random House, 2002.

Baker, Mark, *Nam: The Vietnam War In The Words Of the Men Who Fought There.* New York: Berkley Books, 1983.

Bilton, Michael and Sim, Kevin, *Four Hours in My Lai.* New York: Penguin Books, 1992.

Bleiel, Jeff, *Bobby Darin: On Record, Stage and Screen. Ann Arbor:* Popular Culture Ink. 1993.

Bordowitz, Hank, *Bad Moon Rising: The Unofficial History of Creedence Clearwater Revival.* New York: Schirmer Trade Books, 2001.

Brend, Mark, *American Troubadours: Groundbreaking Singer Songwriters of the 60s.* San Francisco: Backbeat Books, 2001.

Brown, James with Bruce Tucker, James Brown: *The Godfather of Soul.* New York: The MacMillan Publishing Company 1988.

Brown, Ruth with Andrew Yule, *Miss Rhythm: The Autobiography of Ruth Brown, Rhythm and Blues Legend.* New York: Donald I. Fine Books, 1996.

Byckley, Gail, *American Patriots: The Story of Blacks in the Military from the Revolution to Desert Storm.* New York: Random House, 2001.

Campbell, Don, *The Mozart Effect: Tapping the Power of Music to Heal the Body, Strengthen the Mind and Unlock the Creative Spirit.* New York: Avon Books, 1997.

Cash, Johnny, *Man In Black: His Own Story in His Own Words.* Grand Rapids: Zondervan Publishing, 1975.

Clarke, Donald, *The Rise and Fall of Popular Music.* New York: St. Martin's Griffin. 1996.

Clark, Charlie, *"Our Tears." VVA Veteran.* February, 1986

Cleveland, Les, *Dark Laughter: War in Song and Popular Culture.* Westport (CT): Praeger Publishers, 1994.

Cohodas, Nadine, *Spinning Blues Into Gold: The Chess Brothers and the Legendary Chess Records.* New York: St. Martin's Griffin, 2000.

Collins, Ace, *Disco Duck and Other Adventures in Novelty Music.* New York: Berkeley Boulevard Books, 1996.

Colton, Larry, *Goat Brothers.* New York: The Ballantine Publishing Group, 1993.

Country Song Roundup *Jan Howard interview,* Charlton Publications, Derby, Connecticut, Vol. 24, No. 161 December 1972.

Country Song Roundup *Kris Kristofferson Interview,* Charlton Publications, Derby, Connecticut Vol. 23, No. 139, February 1971.

Crosby, David and Bender, David, *Stand and be Counted: Making Music, Making History.* San Francisco: Harper, 2000.

Davis, Hank, *"The Survival of Troy Shondell: Going Beyond One Hit Wonders."* Goldmine. December 17, 1999.

Davis, Sheila, *The Craft of Lyric Writing.* Writer's Digest Books, Cincinnati, 1985.

Davis, Stephen, *Old Gods Almost Dead: The Forty Year Odyssey of the Rolling Stones.* New York: Broadway Books, 2001.

Denselow, Robin, *When the Music's Over: The Story of Political Pop.* London and Boston: Faber and Faber, 1989.

Doggett, Peter, *Are You Ready for the Country: Elvis, Dylan, Parsons and the Roots of Country Rock.* New York: Penguin Putnam, 2000.

Dunaway, David King, *How Can I Keep From Singing.* New York: McGraw Hill, 1983.

Egan, Sean, *"The Animals' Story: Unfullfilled Expectations: Eric Burdon Tells the Story."* Discoveries. September, 2001.

Emerson, Gloria, *Winners and Losers: Battles, Retreats, Gains, Losses and Ruins from the Vietnam War.* New York: W.W. Norton, 1976.

Fish, Lydia, *The Vietnam Folklore and Music Project.* (Internet Web Site) 1993.

Fall, Bernard B., *Hell in a Very Small Place: The Siege of Dien Bien Phu.* New York, Harper & Row Publishers, 1967.

Finney, Jack, *Time and Again.* New York: Simon and Schuster, 1970.

Forntale, Peter and Ayres, *Bill All You, Need Is Love and 99 Other Life Lessons from Classic Rock Songs.* Fireside: New York, 1998.

Gillett, Charlie, *The Sound of the City: The Rise of Rock and Roll.* New York, Outerbridge and Dienstfrey, 1970.

Garr, Gillian, *She's a Rebel: The History of Women in Rock & Roll.* Seattle: Seal Press, 1992.

Gitlin, Todd, *The Sixties: Years of Hope, Days of Rage.* New York: Bantam Books, 1987.

Giuliano, Geoffrey, *Rod Stewart: Vagabond Heart* New York: Carroll and Graf Publishers, 1993.

Golden, Bob, *What A Wonderful World: A Lifetime Of Recordings.* New York: Oxford University Recordings, 1995.

Goldman Peter, and Tony Fuller, *Charlie Company: What Vietnam Did to Us.* New York, William Morrow and Company, 1983.

Goff, Stanley, with Sanders, Robert and Smith, Clark, *Brothers: Black Soldiers in the Nam.* Novato (CA): Presidio Press, 1982.

Grant, Joan, *Black Protest: History, Documents and Analyses.* 1619 To the Present. New York: Fawcett, 1966.

Hall, David. *The Record Book.* New York: Smith and Durell, 1940.

Haggard, Merle and Russell, Peggy, *Sing Me Back Home: My Story.* New York: Pocket Books, 1981.

Hargrove, Thomas R., *A Dragon Lives Forever.* New York: Ivy Books, 1994.

Hayes, Roger, *On Point.* Novato (CA): Presidio Press, 2000.

Hellmann, *The Kennedy Obsession: The American Myth of JFK* New York: Columbia University Press, 1997.

Henderson, David, *'Scuse Me While I Kiss the Sky: The Life of Jimmy Hendrix* New York, Bantam Trade Edition, 1965.

Herr, Michael, *Dispatches.* New York, Vintage Books. 1991.

Higgins, Chester *"JB Maps 'Soul' Tour of Vietnam For GIs."* Jet Magazine, June 6, 1968.

Hirsey, Gerry, *We Gotta Get Out Of This Place: The True, Tough Story Of Women In Rock.* New York: Atlantic Monthly Press.

Hopkins, Jerry and Sugerman, *Danny, No One Here Gets Out Alive.* New York: Warner Books, 1980.

Horwitz, Tony, *Confederates in the Attic: Dispatches from the Unfinished Civil War.* New York: Pantheon Books, 1998

Karnow, Stanley, *Vietnam: A History.* New York: Penguin Books, 1984.

Kelly, Michael *"Doc Rock - The Story Behind G.T.O."* Goldmine. 7/16/99.

Kertwig, John, *And A Hard Rain Fell.* New York: MacMillan Publishing Co., 1985.

Kirk, Elise K., *Music at the White House: A History of the American Spirit.* Chicago and Urbana: University of Illinois Press, 1986.

King, Stephen, *Everything's Eventual: 14 Dark Tales.* New York: Scribner, 2002.

Kort, Michelle, *The Music and Passion of Laura Nyro: Soul Picnic.* New York: St. Martin's Press, 2002.

Laurence, John, *The Cat From Hue.* New York: Public Affairs, 2002.

Larkin, Colin, *The Virgin Encyclopedia of Country Music.* London: Virgin Books, 1998.

Lifton, Robert Jay, *Home From The War: Vietnam Veterans: Neither Victims Nor Executioners.* New York: Simon and Schuster.

Lynn, Loretta, *Coal Miner's Daughter*, New York, Warner Books, 1976

Marsh, Dave, *Glory Days: Bruce Springsteen in the 1980s.* New York: Pantheon Books, 1987.

Marsh, Dave, *The Heart of Rock and Soul: The 1001 Greatest Singles Ever Made.* New York: New American Library, 1989.

McCloud, Barry, and contributing writers, Definitive Country: *The Ultimate Encyclopedia of Country Music and its Performers.* Berkley Publishing Group, New York, 1995.

MacNeil, Neil, *Dirksen: Portrait of a Public Man.* Cleveland: World Publishing, 1970.

McPherson, James M., *Battle Cry of Freedom: The Civil War Era.* New York: Random House, 1988.

McPherson Myra, *Long Time Passing: Vietnam & the Haunted Generation.* New York: New American Library, 1984.

Michener, James A., *Kent State: What Happened and Why.* New York: Random House, 1971.

Moore, Lt. Gen. Harold G., and Joseph L. Galloway, *We Were Soldiers Once...And Young: Ia Drang—The Battle That Changed The War In Vietnam.* New York, Harper Collins Books, 1993.

Morse, Steve, *"Times Change but Haggard Keeps Plugging and Playing."* Minneapolis Tribune. 6/11/99

Morse, Tim, *Classic Rock Stories.* New York, St. Martin's Press, 1998.

Mortland, John Liner notes to *"Sounds of the Seventies: AM Top Twenty"* Warner Special Products, 1993.

Moss, George Donelson, *Vietnam: An American Ordeal.* Englewood Cliffs: Prentice-Hall Inc. 1994.

Norton, Bruce H., *Force Recon Diary, 1969, 1970.* New York: Ballantine Books, 1992.

O'Brien, Tim, *If I Die in a Combat Zone: Box Me Up and Ship Me Home.* New York, Dell Publishing, 1973.

O'Brien, Tim, *The Things They Carried* New York: Penguin Books, 1990.

O'Dowd, Jim, *"Jody Miller: The Little Girl With The Big Voice."* Discoveries (July, 2002)

O'Nan, Stewart, *The Vietnam Reader.* New York, Doubleday, 1998.

Palmer, Tony. *All You Need is Love: The Story of Popular Music.* New York: Penguin Books, 1979.

Prados, John and Stubbe, Ray W., *Valley of Decision: The Siege of Khe Sahn.* New York: Bantam Doubleday Publishing, 1991.

Posner, Gerald. *Motown: Music, Money, Sex, and Power.* New York: Random House, 2000.

Puller, Jr., Lewis, *Fortunate Son: An Autobiography.* New York: Grove Weidenfeld, 1991.

Reich, Dale E. *"Rockets Like Rain: A Year In Vietnam."* Central Point, (Oregon): Hellgate Press, 1987-2001.

Reeves, Martha and Bego, Mark, *Dancing in the Streets: The Confessions of a Motown Diva.* New York: Hyperion Publishing, 1994.

Remarque, Erich Maria, *All Quiet on the Western Front.* New York: Fawcett Crest, 1978.

Reynolds, Simon and Press, *Joy, The Sex Revolts.* Cambridge: Harvard University Press, 1995.

Rochester Stuart I., and Kiley, Fredrick, *Honor Bound: The History of American Prisoners of War in Southeast Asia, 1961-1973.* Washington D.C. Office of the Secretary of Defense, 1998.

Rogers, Jimmy N., *The Country Music Message: Revisited.* Fayettville: The University of Arkansas Press, 1989.

Romanowski, Patricia, *Temptations.* New York: G.P. Putnam's Sons, 1988.

Russ, Martin, *Breakout: The Chosin Reservoir Campaign, Korea 1950.* New York: Fromm International, 1999.

Salzer Jack (Ed.) et. al. *The Encyclopedia of African-American Culture and History. Vols 1-5.* New York: Simon and Schuster MacMillan, 1996.

Safer, Morley, *Flashbacks: On Returning To Vietnam.* New York: Random House, 1990.

Scott, John Anthony, *The Ballad of America: The History of the United States in Song and Story.* New York: Bantam Books, 1985.

Slick, Grace, with Cagan, Andrea, *Somebody to Love?* New York: Warner Books, 1998.

Shillingham Susan, and Benson, Jackson J., *John Steinbeck: America and American s and Selected Nonfiction.* New York: Penguin-Putnam.

Smith, Susan, *Dancing in the Street: Motown and the Cultural Politics of Detroit.* Cambridge: Harvard University Press, 1999.

Spitz, Bob, *Dylan: A Biography.* New York: McGraw Hill, 1989.

Steffens, Roger, *Nine Meditations on Jimi and Nam*

Steinbeck, John IV, *In Touch.* New York, Dell 1968, 1969.

Stambler, Irwin, *The Encyclopedia of Rock, Pop, and Soul.*

Terry, Wallace, *Bloods: An Oral History of the Vietnam War by Black Veterans.* New York, Ballantine Books, 1984.

Thiele, Bob, as told to Bob Golden, *What a Wonderful World: A Lifetime of Recordings.* New York: Oxford University Press, 1995.

Tillis, Mel, with Walter Wager, *Stutterin' Boy: The Autobiography of Mel Tillis.* New York: Rawson Associates, 1984.

Tucker, Spencer C. (Ed), *Encyclopedia of the Vietnam War: A Political, Social and Military History.* ABC-CLIO, Inc. Santa Barbara: 1998. *"Statements on black casualties in Vietnam."* Vol. I, p. 7.

Turque, Bill, *Inventing Al Gore: A Biography.* New York, Houghton Mifflin, 2000.

Unterberger, Richie, *Turn, Turn, Turn.* San Franciscio: Backbeat Books, 2002.

Walker, Keith, *A Piece of My Heart: The Story of Twenty Six Women Who Served in Vietnam.* New York: Ballantine Books, 1985.

Webb, Steve, *"The Discoveries 100: Our Take on the Most Important Musicians of the Century."* Discoveries. January, 2000.

Wells, Tom, *The War Within: America's Battle Over Vietnam.* Berkeley: University of California Press, 1994.

Werner, Craig, *A Change is Gonna Come: Music, Race and the Soul of America.* New York, Penguin Books, 1999.

Woliver, Robbie, *Bringing it all Back Home.* New York, Pantheon Books, 1986.

Young, Marilyn, and Fitzgerald, John J. and Grunfeld, A. *Tom, The Vietnam War: A History in Documents.* New York: Oxford University Press, 2002.

Van Devanter, Linda, with Morgan, Christopher, *Home before Morning: The Story of an Army Nurse in Vietnam.* New York: Beaufort Books, Inc. 1983

Ward, Don, *The Faces Behind the Names: The Vietnam War.* Bloomington (IL): Memorial Press, 1996.

Ward, Joseph T., *Dear Mom: A Sniper's Vietnam.* New York: The Ballantine Publishing Group, 1991.

Webb, James. *Fields of Fire.* New York: Bantam Books, 1979.

Wilcox, Fred A, *Waiting for an Army to Die: The Tragedy of Agent Orange.* New York: Vintage Books, 1983.

Zaroulis, Nancy and Sullivan, Gerald , *Who Spoke Up?: American Protest against the War in Vietnam 1963-1975.* Garden City: Doubleday and Company, 1984.

Zinn, Howard, *A Peoples' History of the United States.* New York: Harper and Row, 1980.

Other Sources:

Morthland, John, *Liner Notes Sounds of the 70's AM Top 20*, New York, Warner Special Products. 1993.

Neely, Tim. *The Goldmine Standard Catalog of American Records.* Iola (WI) 1998.

One Spot Popular Guide EP's LP's Singles. Mt. Prospect, One Spot Publishers. Various issues. Published on a monthly basis.

Whitburn, Joel. *Billboard Hot 100 Charts: The Sixties.* Record Research, Menomonie Falls, 1990.

Whitburn, Joel. *Billboard Hot 100 Charts: The Seventies Record Research,* Menomonie Falls, 1990

Whitburn, Joel. *Billboard Book of Top 40 Country Hits. Billboard Books,* New York, 1996

Whitcomb, Ian. *After the Ball: From Pop Music to Rock.* Proscenium Press, New York, 1972.

About the Author

Lee Andresen

© Derek Neas, used by permission of Duluth News Tribune

Lee Andresen teaches history and political science at Lake Superior College in Duluth, Minnesota. One of his most popular classes is about the music of the Vietnam War.

He resides in Superior, Wisconsin with his wife Mary Lou and their pets Gizmo, Kit Kat and Jonah. Aside from teaching he spends his time attempting to organize his huge record collection as well as reading and traveling to book signings and personal appearances all over the country.

The author would enjoy hearing from readers. He may be contacted through his website: www.batlenotes.com <http://www.batlenotes.com> .

2nd Edition

To order additional copies of...

BATTLE NOTES

...music of the Vietnam War

or receive a copy of the complete Savage Press Catalog

contact us at:

Phone Orders: 1-800-732-3867

Voice and Fax: (715) 394-9513

email: mail@savpress.com

Visit On Line at: www.savpress.com

Visa or MasterCard accepted

Savage PRESS

Box 115, Superior, WI 54880 (715) 394-9513